THE PHILOSOPHY OF CHARLIE KAUFMAN

THE PHILOSOPHY OF POPULAR CULTURE

The books published in the Philosophy of Popular Culture series will illuminate and explore philosophical themes and ideas that occur in popular culture. The goal of this series is to demonstrate how philosophical inquiry has been reinvigorated by increased scholarly interest in the intersection of popular culture and philosophy, as well as to explore through philosophical analysis beloved modes of entertainment, such as movies, TV shows, and music. Philosophical concepts will be made accessible to the general reader through examples in popular culture. This series seeks to publish both established and emerging scholars who will engage a major area of popular culture for philosophical interpretation and examine the philosophical underpinnings of its themes. Eschewing ephemeral trends of philosophical and cultural theory, authors will establish and elaborate on connections between traditional philosophical ideas from important thinkers and the ever-expanding world of popular culture.

Series Editor

Mark T. Conard, Marymount Manhattan College, NY

Books in the Series

The Philosophy of Stanley Kubrick, edited by Jerold J. Abrams
Football and Philosophy, edited by Michael W. Austin
Tennis and Philosophy, edited by David Baggett
The Philosophy of the Coen Brothers, edited by Mark T. Conard
The Philosophy of Film Noir, edited by Mark T. Conard
The Philosophy of Martin Scorsese, edited by Mark T. Conard
The Philosophy of Neo-Noir, edited by Mark T. Conard
The Philosophy of Horror, edited by Thomas Fahy
The Philosophy of The X-Files, edited by Dean A. Kowalski
Steven Spielberg and Philosophy, edited by Dean A. Kowalski
The Philosophy of the Western, edited by Jennifer L. McMahon and B. Steve Csaki
The Philosophy of Science Fiction Film, edited by Steven M. Sanders
The Philosophy of TV Noir, edited by Steven M. Sanders and Aeon J. Skoble
Basketball and Philosophy, edited by Jerry L. Walls and Gregory Bassham
Golf and Philosophy, edited by Andy Wible

THE PHILOSOPHY OF
CHARLIE KAUFMAN

EDITED BY
DAVID LaRocca

THE UNIVERSITY PRESS OF KENTUCKY

Scholarly publisher for the Commonwealth,
serving Bellarmine University, Berea College, Centre College of Kentucky,
Eastern Kentucky University, The Filson Historical Society, Georgetown College,
Kentucky Historical Society, Kentucky State University, Morehead State
University, Murray State University, Northern Kentucky University, Transylvania
University, University of Kentucky, University of Louisville, and Western
Kentucky University.
All rights reserved.

Editorial and Sales Offices: The University Press of Kentucky
663 South Limestone Street, Lexington, Kentucky 40508-4008
www.kentuckypress.com

15 14 13 12 11   5 4 3 2 1

Library of Congress Cataloging-in-Publication Data

The philosophy of Charlie Kaufman / edited by David LaRocca.
    p. cm. — (The philosophy of popular culture)
  Includes bibliographical references and index.
  Includes filmography.
  ISBN 978-0-8131-3391-1 (hardcover : alk. paper)
  ISBN 978-0-8131-3392-8 (ebook)
  1. Kaufman, Charlie, 1958—Criticism and interpretation. I. LaRocca, David,
1975-
  PS3561.A842Z75 2011
  812'.6—dc22   2011008529

This book is printed on acid-free paper meeting
the requirements of the American National Standard
for Permanence in Paper for Printed Library Materials.

Manufactured in the United States of America.

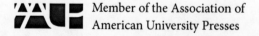 Member of the Association of
American University Presses

Contents

ACKNOWLEDGMENTS

I offer sincere thanks to the contributors of this volume for writing essays that both celebrate and enact the best qualities of their subject. It is a testament to the contributors' dedication to intellectual rigor and inventiveness that, in the midst of busy lives, they produced these remarkable essays. That they were generous with their time and their artful practice compounds the debt.

At the University Press of Kentucky, Stephen M. Wrinn gave me a warm welcome to the press and has shared thoughtful guidance ever since; Anne Dean Watkins provided vital editorial support through the production process; and Mark T. Conard, who envisioned this book as part of his series, continuously encouraged its development from the first proposal.

I thank two anonymous readers for the press whose positive assessment of the book proposal was the impetus to commence writing; two anonymous readers, also solicited by the press, for constructive comments on and enthusiastic endorsement of an earlier version of the manuscript; and Donna Bouvier, a freelance editor for the press, whose assistance vastly increased the clarity and consistency of the final text.

I benefited from the privilege of working in the Frederick Lewis Allen Room at the New York Public Library, which provided the conditions for concentrated study at the corner of Fifth Avenue and Forty-Second Street.

Many thanks to Lorna K. Hershinow for copyediting that enhanced the flow and logic of many sentences.

Lastly, with pleasure, I offer gratitude to Dr. K. L. E. LaRocca, to whom I owe the greatest debt. In her graceful and inspiring intellectual companionship and rigorous critical insight she has helped me improve the structure of my arguments and the coherence of my work.

INTRODUCTION

Charlie Kaufman and Philosophy's Questions

DAVID LAROCCA

When I asked a leading philosopher—one of the most influential and celebrated of the last half-century—if he would contribute to this volume on the work of Charlie Kaufman he politely replied: "Dear David, I have to be honest—I don't know who Charlie Kaufman is, or what he has done, or why I should have views about him. I'm really sorry." It's easy enough to chalk up the scholar's kind rebuke and gentle rejection to his own lapse: perhaps he is not a moviegoer; perhaps he has seen Kaufman's films but did not recall the name; and so on. But the philosopher's "who-what-why" remains apt for any fan of Kaufman's work: Who is Charlie Kaufman, what has he done, and why should we have views about him? The present volume is an effort to provide clear, emphatic, and convincing replies to these questions. The thirteen contributors address the philosophical richness of Charlie Kaufman's work—how it helps us understand better the enduring questions of human existence. Neither the individual essays nor the volume as a whole propose to offer a theory of Charlie Kaufman's philosophy; rather, we present a series of elegant, cogent, and lively engagements with the philosophical and literary multiplicities of meaning and significance in his many celebrated films. As Kaufman says, "My movies don't offer lessons." He also says, "I try to be truthful in writing."[1] Our aim is no different.

The Philosophy of Charlie Kaufman marks the first collection of essays devoted exclusively to a rigorous philosophical exploration of Kaufman's work by a team of capable and critical scholars from a wide range of disciplines.[2] In fact, the contributors themselves give strong evidence for the diversity of interest in Kaufman—they include political theorists and philosophers, classicists and theologians, professors of literature and filmmakers, literary critics and poets. Some of the existing secondary literature on Kaufman's screenplays and films has been written by contributors to the present volume, and many of them are returning here to Kaufman having spent the past decade watching, teaching, and writing on his work. These fourteen new essays—all commissioned and written expressly for this volume—reflect the depth and maturity of these scholars' ongoing research on Kaufman's films. As the authors draw from and reappraise the extant secondary literature they inevitably develop new and appealing ways to further the conversation about the meaning of Kaufman's work. In addition, the Kaufman films that have appeared in recent years offer the chance for these seasoned Kaufman scholars to look again at his earlier work and to see what new insights emerge from his development as a screenwriter and director. Part of what is explored in this book is the nature of adaptation—from page to screen, from screenwriter to director—and how these transformations are understood.

Other titles in the Philosophy of Popular Culture series have thus far focused on established directors and perennial genres. In the present book, by contrast, we're looking at a first-time director who has written several celebrated and influential screenplays. And yet, for having written the screenplays for six feature films, one might say that Kaufman's influence is somewhat disproportionate to his output. Because of the critical and cultural impact of his screenplays, the films are often referred to as "Kaufman films"—thereby eliding the usual influence attributed to the directors who made them. Furthermore, one who refers to "Kaufman films" is seldom corrected for committing a solecism. Kaufman's success as a screenwriter challenges the long-established notion of the director as auteur, since it is highly unconventional to speak of a screenwriter as the prime creative force of a motion picture.[3] Instead of the usual practice of emphasizing—detractors might say overemphasizing—the influence of the director (the hallmark of auteur theory), with Kaufman we seem to have swung to the opposite extreme, thereby attenuating the crucial contribution directors make—for good or ill. Consider a case in which a Kaufman screenplay is not faithfully adapted to the screen: Would we still wish to call it a Kaufman film? Does speaking of a "Kaufman film" become more complicated (albeit more familiar) when Kaufman is also its director? Replies to these questions may begin to suggest how Kaufman's prominence as a screenwriter forms a still-nascent critique of auteur theory and prompts us to consider alternatives to the customary theories of film authorship. A sure sign of the deep, pervasive cultural resonance of his work is found in the neologism

"Kaufmanesque"—which suggests that Kaufman's work and approach to filmmaking has been transformed into its own genre. It is now both informative and complimentary to speak of work by people other than Kaufman as Kaufmanesque.[4]

Other outward signs of Kaufman's success and influence can be seen in the profusion and pedigree of his industry awards—both nominations and wins—along with frequent inclusion in various laudatory top ten lists. Kaufman's awards include an Academy Award for Best Original Screenplay (*Eternal Sunshine of the Spotless Mind*) and Academy Award nominations for Best Adapted Screenplay (*Adaptation*) and Best Original Screenplay (*Being John Malkovich*). From the British Academy of Film and Television Arts (BAFTA) he won best screenplay for these films, and was nominated for Golden Globes for the same films. At Cannes, for his directorial debut, *Synecdoche, New York,* he was nominated for a Palme d'Or, the festival's most prestigious prize.

In the abundance of critics' "best of" lists where Kaufman's work is featured, we find Roger Ebert declaring *Synecdoche, New York* the best film of its decade: "Kaufman has made the most perceptive film I can recall about how we live in the world."[5] David Edelstein of *New York* magazine agrees that Kaufman made the best film of the decade, but that it was *Eternal Sunshine of the Spotless Mind*—"the most marvelous, the most resonant, the best movie of the aughts"—and noted that *Adaptation* is among the five films "we'll still be talking about in 2020."[6] Matt Zoller Seitz of *Salon* magazine named Kaufman one of the two best directors of the decade, perhaps especially noteworthy since Kaufman has only one feature-film-directing credit: "Taken together, his scripts are more distinctive, creatively unified, and relevant to modern life than the collected works of almost any contemporary filmmaker, domestic or foreign."[7] Walter Chaw declares, "There may be no more vital an American voice at this moment."[8] And John Patterson, film critic for the *Guardian,* notes, "Originality is a much sought-after property in Hollywood these days, and you can tell how rarely it's achieved by the fact that the only time you ever hear the word uttered is when a new Charlie Kaufman script gets filmed."[9]

Who Is Charlie Kaufman?

Charlie Kaufman was born Charles Stewart Kaufman in New York City in 1958 to Myron and Helen Kaufman. He grew up in Massapequa, New York, and graduated from high school in West Hartford, Connecticut, in 1976, where he participated in clubs dedicated to TV production and drama. While there, he acted in a theater production of *Dr. Jekyll and Mr. Hyde*.[10] He briefly attended Boston University and studied filmmaking at New York University without graduating. He married a woman named Denise and had two children with her. He lived in Minnesota for a while in the late 1980s, where he worked for the Minneapolis *Star Tribune* and at the Minneapolis Institute of Arts; while in Minnesota, he published a couple of articles in *National Lampoon*. In 1991 he moved to Los Angeles and became a writer for television shows, including *Get a Life,* a sitcom about an adult paperboy living in St. Paul (1990–1992); *The Trouble with Larry* (1993); *The Dana Carvey Show* (1996); and *Ned and Stacey* (1996–1997), for which he wrote three episodes and produced twenty-two. While working with Chris Elliott on *Get a Life* he made some short films that aired on *Late Night with David Letterman.* During this time Kaufman wrote a screenplay adaptation of Philip K. Dick's *A Scanner Darkly,* which remains unproduced.[11] Kaufman produced many episodes of *Ned and Stacey,* co-produced episodes of the short-lived *Misery Loves Company* (1995), and during the five years he was pitching his screenplay about a puppeteer who enters a portal into John Malkovich's brain, he always insisted on being that project's executive producer.[12] Kaufman's tenacious demand for creative control won out: his first feature film, *Being John Malkovich*, was a critical success and set the standard for his ongoing stipulation to have exacting and far-reaching control over his creative work.

In addition to television and feature film, Kaufman has also created a work for the theater. Cartel Burwell, the composer who scored *Being John Malkovich* and *Adaptation*, thought to rekindle the format of the radio play and brought in collaborators Joel and Ethan Coen to join Kaufman in his theater debut, a project entitled Theater of the New Ear. The Coen brothers wrote *Sawbones*, and Kaufman wrote *Hope Leaves the Theater* (2005), which starred Hope Davis and Meryl Streep. In it, Davis watches a play (starring Streep, playing herself) along with the audience, then leaves the theater, or rather the play, thus creating another layer of a play-within-a-play scenario. "Charlie Kaufman" is referred to.[13] Kaufman's contribution to the Theater of the New Ear was described as "a Pirandellian triumph."[14]

During the Los Angeles production, the Coens' play was replaced by *Anomalisa*, written by Francis Fregoli, a pseudonym for Charlie Kaufman. The name is drawn from the Fregoli delusion (or delusion of doubles), a disorder in which a person believes that several people are in fact a single person using various disguises. The delusion is named for Leopoldo Fregoli, an Italian actor who was known for his ability to change appearance during his theater act. (In a later work, *Synecdoche, New York*, Kaufman names the protagonist Caden Cotard, ostensibly after the French neurologist Julian Cotard, who described a delusion—negation delirium, or Cotard's syndrome—in which a person believes he or she is dead or, in some variations, putrefying, without blood or internal organs, or immortal.)[15]

Kaufman has also incorporated works from the theater into his films, such as Anton Chekhov's *The Cherry Orchard* and Shakespeare's *Richard III* in *Being John Malkovich*, and Arthur Miller's *The Death of a Salesman* in *Synecdoche, New York*.[16] These works—like other works of literature Kaufman features, such as Franz Kafka's *The Trial* and Marcel Proust's *In Search of Lost Time*—are not merely quick cultural referents meant to heighten the intellectual credentials of his films, but function as important signs for our understanding of character, for how these plays get read in the context of the story. The use of theater in his films also provides Kaufman with a natural way of introducing the ramifications of "acting" like someone, and perhaps not acting like oneself. Does my behavior change when others are around? Do I act better? Am I more myself?

What Has Charlie Kaufman Done?

Charlie Kaufman has accomplished an unusual artistic feat, especially in terms of popular media and culture: he entertains, despite the gravity of his subjects. Kaufman blends an artist's sense of creative freedom with a philosopher's impatience with nonsense. His films are not belabored, insistent, or didactic; nor are they bitter, whiny, or suffused with unmerited self-importance; this is not to say that some of his characters do not embody these characteristics. When his work is disparaged as pretentious, even "morbidly pretentious," one fears that the viewer has failed to join Kaufman in the joke.[17] Kaufman speaks about the same topics and problems that philosophers speak of, but not in their usual tone. As a result, there is nothing that makes his work feel "philosophical" in the sense of being rarefied, abstract, dense, or otherwise unavailable. Just the opposite—and that is quite special.

Kaufman does not hide his influences—an eclectic range of thinkers in philosophy, literature, religion, science, and the arts; more importantly,

he engages with rare imagination and elegance some of the central contro-
versies in the history of Western metaphysics, ethics, aesthetics, logic, and
epistemology. Strangely, the elegance is often achieved by means of some
fantastical apparatus or playful narrative conceit. Despite the whimsy or
implausibility of these devices, Kaufman's profound, affecting, and penetrating ideas don't get lost; rather, they abound in the concentrated network of
his characters' emotional lives. Kaufman's gifts as a screenwriter include
the ability to substantiate an abstract philosophical problem in an emotionally fraught world of sensitive, often troubled, characters. He does not
dramatize philosophy, for example, by making characters spokespeople or
mouthpieces for a philosophical position. Such an approach would render
the character a mere vehicle for an abstraction, and would carry very little
interest and even less emotional resonance. Instead, he creates characters
for whom genuine philosophical problems emerge naturally from their
circumstances. In this way, Kaufman achieves what few philosophers—even
the finest—have: a compelling engagement with the intellect and the heart,
a revealing exploration of the mind and the body, an unflinching, though
often humorous—perhaps necessarily humorous—look at the fatal conflicts
of ideals and realities.

Even as Kaufman draws on complex philosophical conundra—from
skepticism about other minds to multiple personalities, from the nature of
consciousness (as memory? as will? as experience?) to eternal recurrence—
he locates these problems in the lives of flawed characters, which is to say,
human beings. Kaufman himself has said that his films are meant to reflect
the truth of human life—its struggles, contradictions, losses, and confusions,
and its occasional insights and satisfactions. Kaufman offers a counterpoint
and corrective to a long history of Hollywood romantic comedies that dramatize and distort how we really experience things. As a fabulist, Kaufman,
through his distortions, aims to give us realities and truths. In an interview
with Charlie Rose, Kaufman confessed that romantic comedies "messed me
up" because their distortions suggested false realities—fairy tales beyond
human experience—and that he wanted to write films with "truth": to create
work that may be romantic and comedic, but *also* true.[18]

One of the surprises of Kaufman's success is the way in which his critique
of romantic comedy genre conventions is not incompatible with box office
success and critical acclaim. Kaufman gives us fleshy, awkward, tormented,
but ultimately thoughtful characters who deserve love—showing that his
ideas and his style do not diminish bottom lines or dissuade rave reviews.

Why Should I Have Views about Charlie Kaufman?

If the essays collected here are as engaging and insightful as I think they are, the answer to the question why a reader should have views about Charlie Kaufman will become evident. In the course of reading, questions may evolve spontaneously into self-implicating side inquiries: Do I have views about myself? Who am I to have views? Why should I have views at all? Am I Charlie Kaufman?

PART 1: ON BEING AND NOT BEING ONE'S SELF

Charlie Kaufman has said, "I don't like talking about myself"[19] and "I don't consider myself a public person."[20] Yet asking "Who is Charlie Kaufman?" is just the right sort of question for understanding what he has done or accomplished in his work. In a less literal sense, Charlie Kaufman is the subject of his work, but not the Charlie Kaufman you think he means. He's not talking about himself, but about versions of himself, which may or may not have any correlation to his actual life. He is aware of how autobiographical experience can be transformed through art into something extremely depersonalized.

One should be careful not to commit the fallacy of watching Kaufman's films for clues to his personal life. It's better, more useful, and truer to his craft to think of the dynamic and sustained use of reflexivity in Kaufman's work. Part of what constitutes Kaufman's greatest contribution to philosophical thinking is found in the way he shows how a certain kind of self-responsiveness to one's experience can point outward to a world beyond oneself and to the created nature of everything—including oneself and others. The emphasis is not on him, but on his *manner* of self-awareness, for it is in that space that we find the philosophical tension, intrigue, and, ultimately, insight of his work.

There is certainly a way to understand Kaufman's personal experience as a catalyst for his work. "Everything," Kaufman seems to claim and to confess, "is autobiographical, whether you want it to be or not."[21] But that is not to say that Kaufman's work is autobiographical in the sense that his characters parallel his actual experience, still less that his plots map one-to-one onto events in Kaufman's personal life. Occasionally, though, the correspondence between art and life may seem extremely isomorphic, as when we encounter the character Charlie Kaufman in *Adaptation*; yet even this seemingly extreme autobiographical moment undermines itself. At precisely these points of collision between fact and fiction, art and life, we fathom another way in which Kaufman facilitates a reconsideration of philosophical notions, including his own claim that everything is autobiographical whether you want it to be or not. In other words, some of Kaufman's most seemingly autobiographical work appears to contradict his claim, sending us even deeper into fictional realms and further away from the real world.

Part of Kaufman's exploration of the autobiographical—including the nature of imitation, narration, quotation, pseudonymity, and the development of human character more generally—involves the question, or doubt, about the coherence of individual identity. "Am I me? Is Malkovich Malkovich?"[22] Kaufman takes the doubt to an extreme, sometimes literalizing it, sometimes playfully creating a symbol for it. Usually the dramatization has something to do with what we might call doubling, or doubleness. Philosophers sometimes write of the other (or Other), and the phenomenon of the other is described as alterity (*alter* is Latin for "other"). Existential and continental philosophers have been known to dwell on the way the other feels irreproachably distant from oneself—on the other side of a liminal space that can never be crossed. As a result, we are and remain unknown to each other. (God is sometimes understood as the ultimate Other.) Kaufman incorporates the sense of distance into his own, or a character's own, psyche, so the question becomes: "Am I not also distant from myself?" The question alone creates enough mystery and confusion to generate a book-length reply, for in the first place—who is asking the question? And if I am asking the question is there . . . an other in me? Do I have a double, as it were, on the *inside*?

According to Kaufman, we possess an inner alterity. We are others to ourselves—separated, divided, alienated. In his work, Kaufman explores how that alterity is made manifest; in several cases, he devotes a lot of attention to illustrating the literal manifestation of one's inner other. In film after film, Kaufman creates scenarios in which a person is forced to contend with the nature of his identity, mortality, and failings by externalizing his inner doubts, reflections, fears, and secrets. Instead of having a "voice inside my head," I have a twin in the world who is my genetic identical and yet wholly different from me, unknown to me (*Adaptation*); or I experience someone "playing" me who may or may not know me (or my character) better than I know myself (*Synecdoche, New York*); or I have someone literally inside my head—another within another, like a Russian doll, who, presuming he is conscious, has another other within him (*Being John Malkovich*); or I am a CIA agent living a double life whose confession of that "other" life remains cloaked, doubted even by the people I know best (*Confessions of a Danger-*

ous Mind); or I am a grown man who returns to his parents' dinner table only to discover that I have been replaced by a new son, who is living a kind of improved repetition of my own life (*Human Nature*); or I am forced to consider that my memory is coextensive with my selfhood, and that far from being ancillary to who I am, it is the very definition of who I am (*Eternal Sunshine of the Spotless Mind*). Furthermore, the doubleness onscreen reflects the viewer's own ambivalence toward herself. For example, when watching *Adaptation,* the viewer recognizes her alternation between confident, play-by-the-genre rules Donald and seeker of truth, beauty, and originality Charlie. In this way, the film portrays a double of the viewer's own life, an externalization and literalized metaphor of her own doubleness.

What is the point of all Kaufman's many explorations of alterity—the awareness of the other, inside or out? It is not to come to conclusions about oneself, but just the opposite: to live and think in a constant state of negotiation (perhaps more commonly, agitation) with the world, others, and oneself; to develop a kind of bravery in the midst of indeterminacy, and a form of compassion for what lies beyond comprehension. Kaufman offers the following illustration to stimulate our thinking in this direction:

> Periphery is an illusion of individual consciousness. Each of us in our own mind is the center of the universe, and everything falls off in direct relation to its proximity or importance to us. But if you move to the periphery of your own existence, you find it to be the center of someone else's. . . . Maybe it's easier to see people as peripheral. Maybe that's why we do it. It's a weird and daunting experience to let other people in their fullness into our minds. It is so much easier to see them as serving a purpose in our own lives.[23]

In "Charlie Kaufman, Screenwriter," K. L. Evans inaugurates the first series of essays—on identity, authorship, and adaptation—by examining the nature of a screenwriter's relationship to the texts he creates: for example, how Kaufman's naming his character after himself in *Adaptation* actually intensifies the character's distance from himself. A screenwriter, Evans contends, must show why imaginative writing doesn't merely reflect reality—"why a *writer* is someone who keeps his audience in the affecting atmosphere of an event whose reference is not fixed." In prose that creates for itself a form and style precisely attuned to its subject, Evans reminds us of the myriad ways in which "Kaufman is charged, or feels charged, with making viewers formally aware of the puzzling character of fiction."

In "On *Being John Malkovich*, and Not Being Yourself," Christopher Falzon analyzes the metaphysical ideas that underwrite the philosophical accounts of self featured in *Being John Malkovich*. Falzon concentrates on the "human significance" of philosophical questions and whether self-transformation is possible. Drawing from the work of Maurice Merleau-Ponty, John Dewey, and Michel Foucault, Falzon explores the notion of embodied selfhood, understood as an alternative to the historically more dominant Cartesian account.

In "The Divided Self: Kaufman, Kafka, Wittgenstein, and *Human Nature*," Mario von der Ruhr invites readers to consider an intriguing, even uncanny, scene of intertextuality between Kaufman's *Human Nature* and Franz Kafka's *A Report to an Academy*. As von der Ruhr looks closely at *Human Nature* to investigate the "complex tapestry of autobiographical, literary, popular scientific, and philosophical considerations that inform Kaufman's exploration of the movie's subject matter," he also looks to Wittgenstein as a prompt for considering the possibility—and ramifications—of didacticism in the arts and in science. These questions about teaching in turn yield salient reflections on the often antagonistic relationship between one's cognitive self and one's animalistic self. With von der Ruhr's analysis we can appreciate anew Kaufman's attempt to confront the confounding ways in which humans cope with their participation in nature, sometimes by denying, indulging, or redescribing that formidable circumstance.

In "Unauthorized Autobiography: Truth and Fact in *Confessions of a Dangerous Mind*," I examine how the double life of Chuck Barris—celebrity game show host and apparent clandestine assassin—draws us into debates at the heart of any theory of autobiography and illustrates Kaufman's understanding of the nature of authorship. Who really gets written about when one writes autobiography? Autobiography, it seems, involves disowning—or deauthorizing—the empirical as the foundation for truth. Drawing upon the work of Thomas Carlyle, we see that Barris's facts are real because they are written; their truth is tied up with their fabrication, not their correspondence to reality.

PART 2: BEING, OR TRYING TO BE, WITH OTHERS

While Kaufman's characters tend to exhibit a combination of melancholy and intelligence, most of them struggle to find the terms for experiencing a mature, adult, romantic relationship. Fighting ennui, anxiety, alienation, self-doubt, and morbidity, they still reach out for another—someone to love and to be loved by. Kaufman shows that intelligence, will, and even genuine passion cannot assure a satisfying relationship. Rather, despite their own thoughts, efforts, and feelings, these characters need other people, as we all do, who can show them their best selves and return or direct them to that preferred incarnation. The sentiment is conspicuous in Proust's book *Swann's Way*, one of the texts featured in *Synecdoche, New York*, where the narrator writes: "it is only with the passions of others that we are ever really familiar, and what we come to find out about our own can be no more than what other people have shewn us. Upon ourselves they react but indirectly, through our imagination, which substitutes for our actual, primary motives other, secondary motives, less stark and therefore more decent."[24]

As many critics, including the contributors to part 2, have noted, Kaufman's work—especially with respect to his account of romantic relationships, the nature of the film medium, and moral perfectionism—can be productively related to ideas developed by Stanley Cavell in *Pursuits of Happiness: The Hollywood Comedy of Remarriage*; *The World Viewed: Reflections on the Ontology of Film*; and *Cities of Words: Pedagogical Letters on a Register of the Moral Life*, among other works.[25] Cavell's seminal contribution to our thinking about the possibilities of human intimacy, knowledge of others, and the role film plays in self-knowledge is so pervasive in philosophy, literature, and other disciplines that for some it constitutes an established background against which Kaufman's work is set. Several contributors express this obvious indebtedness through direct engagement with Cavell's texts; others acknowledge Cavell's influence less explicitly; and still others follow after or generate new approaches to a set of texts and problems that resonate with the contours of Cavell's thinking. For readers familiar with Cavell's understanding of classic Hollywood comedies and melodramas, Kaufman's work may seem surprisingly concordant—a genuine heir to thinking about how individuals constitute and reconstitute themselves as couples; situate themselves in relation to each other; and stand in need of instruction and education by one another, which is to say, after Emerson, provocation. For readers new to Cavell, Kaufman's films—as well as the reading of those films offered here—may provide a stimulating incentive to explore Cavell's work on its own terms. Among the many lines of affinity between their works, we might consider more specifically how Cavell's understanding of "philosophy as the education of grown-ups" finds expression in Kaufman's rendering of the human situation.[26]

With Kaufman we discover how interpersonal relationships, especially romantic relationships, transform the wretchedness of human existence—in all its limitation, error, and contradiction—into something worthwhile. Waking up beside someone can be simultaneously a terror and a relief: one is both mortified by the responsibility of being committed or connected to the other, and yet gratified to have someone reflect back the truth about one's tendencies toward self-delusion and self-defeat. The other invariably, necessarily, gratefully returns one to oneself.

In "Me and You: Identity, Love, and Friendship in the Films of Charlie Kaufman," Douglas J. Den Uyl begins the second series of essays—focused on the nature of human relationships, especially romantic ones—by assessing the degree to which Kaufman's characters exhibit or lack personal integrity, and how that trait affects intimate relationships. Looking to classical notions of friendship in Aristotle and Montaigne, Den Uyl wonders if Kaufman's characters' interminable search for romantic connection bespeaks the impossibility of friendship due to insufficiently developed personal integrity.

In "I Don't Know, Just Wait: Remembering Remarriage in *Eternal Sunshine of the Spotless Mind*," William Day shows how Kaufman's *Eternal Sunshine of the Spotless Mind* should be considered part of the film genre known as remarriage comedy; but he also shows how Kaufman contributes something new to the genre. Day addresses, in particular, how the conversation that is the condition for reunion involves discovering "what it means to have memories together as a way of learning how to *be* together." One of the most innovative aspects of Kaufman's filmic representation of such a conversation is its effect on the audience: how the narrative structure "replicates for the viewer the felt contingency of memory that we attribute" to the characters we see onscreen—a couple contending with the interrelated experiences of remarriage and remembering.

In "Charlie Kaufman, Philosophy, and the Small Screen," Samuel A. Chambers considers Kaufman's work in television, in particular *Ned and Stacey*, a show for which he wrote and produced. Drawing from his research in queer theory and television studies, Chambers explores how a rather conventional setup—a marriage of convenience—becomes, in Kaufman's hands, a provocative engagement with, and challenge to, established norms of gender, sexuality, and marriage.

In "The Instructive Impossibility of Being John Malkovich," Garry L.

Hagberg demonstrates how *Being John Malkovich* contributes to philosophical notions of selfhood, language, and memory developed by classical American pragmatists, Ludwig Wittgenstein, and Avashai Margalit. In trying to figure out what it would mean to be John Malkovich, Hagberg has found a way of understanding what it means to be oneself—to define and defend "the profound phenomenon of human uniqueness," to discover "what is inviolably individual" and fundamentally private about one's experience. Ultimately, the fantasy of being another person becomes "an instructively impossible ideal."

PART 3: BEING IN THE WORLD, PARTIALLY

"I don't think my characters are a joke," Kaufman has said. "I take them seriously. And no matter how outlandish or weird their situation, their situation is real and a little tragic. I think that's what gives people something to hang onto as they watch the film. We had to find a way to make everything play on a very naturalistic level, so it didn't just turn into wackiness. I'm not interested in getting crazier and crazier."[27] Kaufman is alluding to the fact that his screenplays, especially the way they are adapted visually by directors such as Michel Gondry and Spike Jonze, often employ clunky science fiction or narrative gimmicks—traveling through a porthole into another person's brain, extracting memory with erasure machines, depicting temporal contradictions, spending fifty years on a play no one sees—but always toward a sophisticated, elegant, philosophical, poignant end. The truth of the story comes from the insight generated by the human interactions that result from the technology, not the degree to which the effects are convincing or plausible. Partly this is due to Gondry, who not just in Kaufman's films but also in his non-Kaufman work—*The Science of Sleep* (2005) and *Be Kind Rewind* (2008)—has shown his homemade aesthetic through an inventiveness with rudimentary materials (e.g., creating sets and machines made from cardboard and tape and decorated with magic marker). But the fact that Gondry and other directors can pursue this lo-fi approach to special effects—and have it succeed emotionally and intellectually—results directly from its basis in Kaufman's sense of his characters.

Not to disparage Gondry's non-Kaufman films, but rather to appreciate how Kaufman's writing complements Gondry's direction, we might consider how Gondry's non-Kaufman work sustains his standard for imaginative set design and often antic, quirky, or dreamy protagonists while also making it harder to defend this work's emotional and intellectual coherence and sophistication (when compared with the Kaufman collaborations). Gondry's work apart from Kaufman thus far does not appear to offer the same kind of raw, penetrating insight into human psychology that Kaufman is capable of. Partly, the difference may be attributed to Gondry's attention to the visual structure and the style of the film (thereby demonstrating the ways in which he excels as a cinematographer and set designer), whereas Kaufman is clearly focused most intently on the minds and hearts of his characters. One could describe some of the Gondry and Jonze conceits as childlike, even naïve, yet the simplicity of the setups—their immediacy and intelligibility—allows the emotional lives of the characters to emerge with great clarity, intensity, and complexity. "I'm interested in people and how they interact," Kaufman has said, "and, if I ever do it well, then it's interesting. It's not about FX or pyrotechnics or a string of gags for me—even though I like stuff like that—I'm more interested in the people there."[28] In Kaufman's films, the visual conceits are used to motivate the ideas that sustain the plot, support the emotional lives of the characters, and tie them to one another.

Kaufman is not a literal realist, as high-power science fiction demands of itself, but an emotional realist. It's not important that the rules of his imagined universe achieve an incontestable logic; rather, he wants to get the emotional truth of the characters to feel true to the viewers. He uses fabrication and fabulation—a playful use of "lies" and the "fake"—to achieve emotional realism. As a fabulist, Kaufman's intention is not to trick or further muddle our thinking, but to elucidate truth—perhaps penetrating and useful truths. In other words, he celebrates and magnifies the literary, metaphorical, and symbolic complexities of human experience in order to explore and expose the literal difficulties we all face: trouble expressing ourselves, sharing our lives with others, forming beliefs and making commitments, achieving satisfaction, coping with mortality. Instead of reducing everything to a theory or trying to make a point, he dwells in the layers, folds, and intricacies of the overwhelming, disquieting, but wonderful world.

Kaufman's (as well as Gondry's and Jonze's) predilection for visual and narrative conceits can be read also as an effort to rework the conventions of various genres, including science fiction, thriller, horror, and romantic comedy, to make them work in a new kind of genre—or at least type or cycle of films—dedicated to emotional realism. In the work of Kaufman and his directors, the genuineness of the characters' emotional experience counterbalances the cheapness of the tricks, unlike in conventional big-budget thrillers, horror movies, and the like, where the well-produced visuals and narrative conceits (double identity, multiple identities, lost identity, memory erasure, controlling someone's mind by taking over the body, for example, by demonic possession or by commandeering the brain) render only ersatz emotional insight.

In this way, the other genres—science fiction, romantic comedies, even thrillers and horror films—engage archetypes, conventions, and myths that make them versions of fairy tales.[29] The good guy prevails, the bad guy is punished. Order is restored, justice is served. The lover finds "the right one" (and usually there is an "only one") and lives happily ever after. For Kaufman, there is no "right one," no sense that it's "this one or no one," no final rendering of justice, no established order. The same character can continually shift from being contemptible to pitiable, intolerable to lovable. There is no clear beginning and no final resolution: life is always being lived in medias res.

In "Living a Part: *Synecdoche, New York*, Metaphor, and the Problem of Skepticism," Richard Deming commences the third and final series of essays—addressing the predicament of individual human life in the midst of society—by questioning the degree to which metaphors constitute the meaning of our personal and interpersonal reality. Deming explores how symbols that reflect our sense of separateness, particularity, and partiality function—paradoxically, uncannily—as the condition for our experience of connection with others.

In "'There's No More Watching': Artifice and Meaning in *Synecdoche, New York* and *Adaptation*," Derek Hill, author of *Charlie Kaufman and Hollywood's Merry Band of Pranksters, Fabulists, and Dreamers: An Excursion into the American New Wave*, looks at the relationship of the artist to his or her work and whether the bold effort to create something true, beautiful, or real ever mitigates the costs, compromises, and other aspects of mortality and imperfection that attend such efforts.[30] Hill finds in Kaufman a suggestion that it may not be in the creation of art that we find compensation, but in sharing it with others. The meaning of art, then, is not in the art, but in the human relationships that underwrite an experience of it.

In "Human Nature and Freedom in *Adaptation*," Gregory E. Ganssle develops further ideas he first broached in "Consciousness, Memory, and Identity: The Nature of Persons in Three Films by Charlie Kaufman" about the mutability of human nature and the possibility of self-transcendence.[31] For Ganssle, these metaphysical questions are motivated by ethical concerns about how we should, or can, live in the world as moral beings. Ganssle draws from the work of Jean-Paul Sartre and Walker Percy to assess how the characters in *Adaptation* help us think about the nature of human mutability, and how interaction with others—like adaptive processes in nature—may affect our understanding of human nature.

In "Synecdoche, in Part," David L. Smith continues his ongoing exploration of the philosophical implications of Kaufman's thinking evident in works such as "The Implicit Soul of Charlie Kaufman's *Adaptation*" and "*Eternal Sunshine of the Spotless Mind* and the Question of Transcendence" with a new work on Kaufman's newest film, *Synecdoche, New York*.[32] Smith finds that Caden Cotard, like many of Kaufman's protagonists, is searching for wholeness, reality, and truth, which eludes him. The unsatisfied desire, the compromised or failed project, however, reveals its own kind of truth about the role of human striving and the way temperament influences our perception of connectedness to others and the wider world.

In "Nietzschean Themes in the Films of Charlie Kaufman," Daniel Shaw adds new evidence to the speculation that Kaufman is a close reader of Friedrich Nietzsche and has adapted some of Nietzsche's ideas for use in his screenplays. Adding to work begun in "On Being Philosophical and *Being John Malkovich*," Shaw contends that core Nietzschean notions such as eternal recurrence, will to power, human drives, and perspectivism inform the intellectual content of Kaufman's work and enrich its philosophical credentials and insights.[33]

In "Inconclusive Unscientific Postscript: Late Remarks on Kierkegaard and Kaufman," I find a resemblance between Søren Kierkegaard's and Charlie Kaufman's responses to existential anxiety and the phenomenology of love in their capacious, philosophically nuanced, and self-knowing deployment of pseudonymous authorship. I note shared features and topics of their work, such as the possibility of learning truths from lies, metaphysical varieties of acting, the presence of doubles and proxies, and the puzzling effects of work that repeats and reflects back on itself.

Notes

1. See Michael Spadaro's website beingcharliekaufman.com.

2. A volume of essays written by several scholars has been devoted to a single Kaufman film, *Eternal Sunshine of the Spotless Mind*; the eponymous work is edited by Christopher Grau (London: Routledge, 2009). And in a single-author monograph, one of the contributors to the present volume, Derek Hill, included an analysis of Kaufman's work as part of a group portrait of contemporary filmmakers. See Hill, *Charlie Kaufman*

and Hollywood's Merry Band of Pranksters, Fabulists, and Dreamers: An Excursion into the American New Wave (London: Kamera Books, 2008).

3. For works addressing the auteur theory, see J. Dudley Andrew, *The Major Film Theories: An Introduction* (London: Oxford University Press, 1976); John Caughie, ed., *Theories of Authorship: A Reader* (London: Routledge, 1981); J. Dudley Andrew, *Concepts in Film Theory* (Oxford: Oxford University Press, 1984); Tim Bywater and Thomas Sobchack, *Introduction to Film Criticism: Major Critical Approaches to Narrative Films* (New York: Longman, 1989); David A. Gerstner and Janet Staigher, eds., *Authorship and Film* (New York: Routledge, 2003); Virginia Wright Wexman, ed., *Film and Authorship* (New Brunswick, NJ: Rutgers University Press, 2002); Barry Keith Grant, ed., *Auteurs and Authorship: A Reader* (Malden, MA: Blackwell, 2008); and C. Paul Sellors, *Film Authorship: Auteurs and Other Myths* (London: Wallflower, 2010).

4. See, e.g., Peter Bradshaw's review of *I Heart Huckabees* (David O. Russell, director, 2004), *The Guardian,* November 26, 2004 (guardian.co.uk).

5. Roger Ebert, "The Best Films of the Decade," *Chicago Sun-Times*, December 30, 2009 (suntimes.com).

6. David Edelstein, "When Dreams Came True," *New York*, December 6, 2009 (nymag.com).

7. Matt Zoller Seitz, "Directors of the Decade," *Salon*, December 30, 2009 (salon .com). Seitz also deemed *Synecdoche, New York* to represent the best "on screen dream" in film history, eclipsing *8½* (Federico Fellini, 1963), *Brazil* (Terry Gilliam, 1985), and *Twin Peaks* (David Lynch, 1989–1990). At number one in this top ten list, the film, says Seitz, "isn't so much a dream film or a film about dreaming, but a film-as-dream—one that's meant to be reacted against (or embraced) rather than decoded" ("Beyond *Inception:* Best On-Screen Dreams," *Salon*, July 16, 2010).

8. Walter Chaw, "State of Mind," *Film Freak Central*, October 26, 2008 (filmfreakcentral .net).

9. John Patterson, "Guided by Voices," *The Guardian*, November 26, 2006 (guardian .co.uk).

10. For more biographical details see Spadaro's website and Doreen Alexander Child, *Charlie Kaufman: Confessions of an Original Mind* (Santa Barbara, CA: Praeger, 2010).

11. Richard Linklater directed an animated feature film based on his own adaptation of Dick's novel (2006).

12. Lynn Hirschberg, "Being Charlie Kaufman," *New York Times*, March 19, 2000 (nytimes.com). Some biographical details are drawn from Carol Brennan's entry on Charlie Kaufman in the *Encyclopedia of World Biography* (notablebiographies.com).

13. See Spadaro, beingcharliekaufman.com, for more details on Kaufman's theater work.

14. Jeremy McCarter, "Theater of the New Ear," *New York*, August 21, 2005 (nymag.com).

15. The same Parisian neurologist, Julian Cotard, is the inspiration for the character Dr. Cottard in Proust's *Swann's Way*.

16. Michael Sragow, "Being Charlie Kaufman," *Salon*, November 11, 1999 (salon .com).

17. David Moats, "Charlie Kaufman's *Synecdoche, New York* Reviewed," *The Quietus*, May 20, 2009 (thequietus.com).

18. See "A Conversation with Screenwriter Charlie Kaufman," interview with Charlie Rose, March 26, 2004 (charlierose.com).

19. Spadaro, beingcharliekaufman.com.

20. Sragow, "Being Charlie Kaufman."

21. "Charlie Kaufman: Life and Its Discontents," interview with Tania Ketenjian, *The [Un]Observed: A Radio Magazine* (theunobserved.com).

22. *Being John Malkovich* (Spike Jonze, 1999), 00:33:26.

23. Charlie Kaufman, *Synecdoche, New York: The Shooting Script* (New York: Newmarket Press, 2008), xi.

24. Marcel Proust, *Swann's Way*, Volume 1 of *In Search of Lost Time*, trans. C. K. Scott Moncrieff and Terence Kilmartin, rev. D. J. Enright (New York: Modern Library, 2003), 175–76.

25. Stanley Cavell, *The World Viewed: Reflections on the Ontology of Film*, enlarged ed. (Cambridge, MA: Harvard University Press, 1979), *Pursuits of Happiness: The Hollywood Comedy of Remarriage* (Cambridge, MA: Harvard University Press, 1981), and *Cities of Words: Pedagogical Letters on a Register of the Moral Life* (Cambridge, MA: Belknap Press of Harvard University Press, 2004). Other relevant works by Cavell include: *Must We Mean What We Say?* (Cambridge: Cambridge University Press, 2002 [1976]); *The Claim of Reason: Wittgenstein, Skepticism, Morality, and Tragedy* (New York: Oxford University Press, 1999 [1979]); *Conditions Handsome and Unhandsome: The Constitution of Emersonian Perfectionism* (Chicago: University of Chicago Press, 1990); *Contesting Tears: The Hollywood Melodrama of the Unknown Woman* (Chicago: University of Chicago Press, 1996); *Emerson's Transcendental Etudes*, ed. David Justin Hodge (Stanford, CA: Stanford University Press, 2003); *Cavell on Film*, ed. William Rothman (Albany: State University of New York Press, 2005); and *Little Did I Know: Excerpts from Memory* (Stanford, CA: Stanford University Press, 2010).

When reviewing Kaufman's films, several contemporary critics have invoked Cavell's work; see, e.g., A. O. Scott, "Charlie Kaufman's Critique of Pure Comedy" (*New York Times*, April 4, 2004); and David Edelstein, "Forget Me Not: The Genius of Charlie Kaufman's *Eternal Sunshine of the Spotless Mind*" (*Slate*, March 18, 2004).

Work in which Cavell's ideas of remarriage and moral perfectionism are addressed include Ronald L. Hall, *The Human Embrace: The Love of Philosophy and the Philosophy of Love: Kierkegaard, Cavell, Nussbaum* (University Park: Pennsylvania State University Press, 1999); Stephen Mulhall, *Stanley Cavell: Philosophy's Recounting of the Ordinary* (Oxford: Oxford University Press, 1999); Richard Eldridge, ed., *Stanley Cavell* (Cambridge: Cambridge University Press, 2003); Russell Goodman, ed., *Contending with Stanley Cavell* (Oxford: Oxford University Press, 2005); Lawrence Rhu, *Stanley Cavell's*

19

American Dream: Shakespeare, Philosophy, and Hollywood Movies (New York: Fordham University Press, 2006); Natsu Saito, *The Gleam of Light: Moral Perfectionism and Education in Dewey and Emerson* (New York: Fordham University Press, 2006); and James Walters, *Alternative Worlds in Hollywood Cinema: Resonance between Realms* (Bristol, UK: Intellect Books, 2008).

In the year in which Kaufman's first feature film appeared, Cavell offered a sketch of some films made since the publication of *Pursuits of Happiness* that "seem to have a remarriage feel to them, sometimes emphasizing one or two salient features of the genre (for example, the principal pair's mysteriousness to the rest of their world; or the characteristic enigmatic quality of the ending; or the woman's demand or readiness for education) if not obviously taking part in the full argument" including *Moonstruck, Tootsie, Sleepless in Seattle, Clueless, Groundhog Day, Joe vs. the Volcano, Crocodile Dundee, Working Girl, Inventing the Abbotts, Four Weddings and a Funeral, My Best Friend's Wedding, Everyone Says I Love You, The Sure Thing, Say Anything,* and *Grosse Point Blank*: "An Exchange with Stanley Cavell," Rex Butler (1999), sensesofcinema.com.

26. Cavell, *Little Did I Know*, 9; see also Hillary Putnam, "Philosophy as the Education of Grownups: Stanley Cavell and Skepticism," in *Reading Cavell*, ed. Alice Crary and Sanford Shieh (London: Routledge, 2006).

27. Sragow, "Being Charlie Kaufman."

28. Rob Feld, interview with Charlie Kaufman in *Adaptation: The Shooting Script* (New York: Newmarket Press, 2002), 122. Feld: "Do you think it's a strong character or character relationships that then keep you on solid ground?" Kaufman: "Either character relationships or someone's relationship with him- or herself. I mean, how you are in the world, how you're not in the world."

29. The cultural pervasiveness of fairy-tale–based storytelling in film and elsewhere, of course, makes such work extremely important and therefore obliges our attention. Along these lines, one might consult Robert Pippin, *Hollywood Westerns and American Myth: The Importance of Howard Hawks and John Ford for Political Philosophy* (New Haven: Yale University Press, 2010). I am not condescending to fairy tales or their importance for an understanding of myth in human life, but rather am noting that Kaufman is doing something different in relation or reaction to them, which is also worthy of our consideration. Kaufman's sentiment that romantic comedies "messed me up" can be taken as part of his underlying motivation to create work that does not confound people in the same way that myths and fairy tales tend to do. While myths and fairy tales may be noted for their positive influence on human self-understanding, they might also, as Kaufman testifies, lead to various kinds of delusional, self-defeating thinking and behavior. Kaufman seems to be working to redress the negative impact of such mythic forms.

30. Derek Hill, *Charlie Kaufman and Hollywood's Merry Band of Pranksters, Fabulists, and Dreamers: An Excursion into the American New Wave* (London: Kamera Books, 2008).

31. Gregory E. Ganssle, "Consciousness, Memory, and Identity: The Nature of Persons in Three Films by Charlie Kaufman" in *Faith, Film and Philosophy: Big Ideas on the Big Screen*, ed. R. Douglas Geivett and James S. Spiegel (Downers Grove, IL: InterVarsity Press, 2007).

32. David L. Smith, "The Implicit Soul of Charlie Kaufman's *Adaptation,*" *Philosophy and Literature* 30, no. 2 (October 2006): 424–35, and "*Eternal Sunshine of the Spotless Mind* and the Question of Transcendence," *Journal of Religion and Film* 9, no. 1 (April 2005) (unomaha.edu/jrf).

33. Daniel Shaw, "On Being Philosophical and *Being John Malkovich,*" *Journal of Aesthetics and Art Criticism* 64, no. 1, special issue: "Thinking through Cinema: Film as Philosophy" (Winter 2006): 111–18.

Part 1

ON BEING AND NOT BEING ONE'S SELF

CHARLIE KAUFMAN, SCREENWRITER

K. L. EVANS

Does the film *Adaptation*, written by Charlie Kaufman and featuring a protagonist named Charlie Kaufman, chronicle Charlie Kaufman's actual experience? Is it memoir? Undoubtedly the predicament that so overtaxes the character Charlie Kaufman (Nicolas Cage), his great effort to fashion meditative journalism into a feature film, is analogous to the difficult, unpleasant, and embarrassing situation the real Charlie Kaufman finds himself in. Before it becomes the stuff of his fiction, Kaufman has in fact been hired to adapt for the screen Susan Orlean's *The Orchid Thief*, and in his imaginative rendering of this event a writer's false starts, his confusion about the nature of his project, are truthfully depicted. In evidence, too, is something of Kaufman's own mortification about his professional position or standing—chagrin deeper than that occasioned by obligation, by his having accepted an advance for work he said he could do.[1] For Kaufman, taking on the orchid script means confronting a problem bigger than the task at hand. If he is going to continue to exist as a Hollywood screenwriter, if he's going to survive or remain relevant in the economically driven moviemaking "industry," he must show why imaginative writing (even—or especially—in films, where the temptation to think otherwise is great) doesn't merely reflect or transcribe Reality—why a *writer* is someone who keeps his audience in the affecting atmosphere of an event whose reference is not fixed.[2] Kaufman is charged, or feels charged, with making viewers formally aware of the puzzling character of fiction.

For these reasons we must learn to say that *nothing* in this film is referential. Even the name "Charlie Kaufman" is used to reveal the difference between works of the imagination and everything that can or has happened in real life. We can't say that the Charlie Kaufman who, in *Adaptation*, agrees to turn *The Orchid Thief* into a screenplay is the Charlie Kaufman who, in his independent life as a screenwriter, agrees to the same, just as we can't say that the character Susan Orlean (Meryl Streep) is Susan Orlean, staff writer for *The New Yorker*, or that Robert McKee (Brian Cox) is screenwriting guru Robert McKee.[3] The difference is everywhere apparent. The difference is made obvious by the fact that the names are identical; if Kaufman had based his characters on these actual people and given them different names it would be easier to suggest a correspondence between the story and real life. As it is, the film's audience needs no reporter to inform us, as industry analyst Rob Feld does, that Kaufman is "slight and with a full head of wild hair—nothing like the overweight and balding Nicholas Cage in *Adaptation*."[4] We already *know* that Nicholas Cage as Charlie Kaufman is not Charlie Kaufman; and by the time this stale news arrives, we have enjoyed from inside the joke about who should "play" whom in a Hollywood production. When, for instance, avant-garde orchid poacher John Laroche (Chris Cooper) charms Orlean by asking, "Who's gonna play me?" in the movie about his life, then shrewdly suggests: "I think I should play me."[5]

If it's not going to remain an academic distinction, the contest, or contrast, between imaginative writing and reflective journalism should have a kind of life in the film itself. It ought to be part of the action—or, more accurately, power the action: Kaufman's preoccupation with the difference between making (*poesis*, the feat of giving form and pressure to an imagined reality) and imitating (*mimesis*, the business of reproducing or representing preexisting reality) must be what gives the film its tense, gripping quality. That is the reason Kaufman has included in the film's story line the same conditions that affect his life and are beyond his control. In *Adaptation*, both Orlean and Orlean's nonfiction account of Florida's flower-selling subculture, the widely celebrated piece of reporting titled *The Orchid Thief*, have actual existence. And yet Charlie Kaufman's adaptation of this material, the commissioned screenplay, must also exist, and on its own terms, which for Charlie means figuring out how to dramatize Orlean's prose without tapping into the "artificially plot-driven" master-patterns from which most movies are cut.

"I wanted to present it simply," Charlie tells Robert McKee, after he's begun to lose faith in his ability. "I wanted to show flowers as God's miracles. I wanted to show that Orlean never saw the blooming ghost orchid. It was about disappointment."

"That's not a movie," counters McKee. "You gotta go back, put in the drama."[6] According to McKee, a story's drama is ignited when characters' emotional or intellectual change brings about a big ending. ("Wow them in the end and you've got a hit. You can have flaws, problems, but wow them in the end and you've got a hit.") But the spectacle that ends *Adaptation* can't be emotionally involving because, in an early scene, Charlie has already itemized these routine methods of animating scripts, and so highlighted their absurdity: "I just don't want to ruin it by making it a Hollywood thing," he tells Valerie, the literary agent (Tilda Swinton).[7] "Like an orchid heist movie or something, or, y'know, changing the orchids into poppies and turning it into a movie about drug running, you know?" Charlie is sweating and twitching but sincere, and his observations are deeply insightful: "It's like, I don't want to cram in sex or guns or car chases. You know? Or characters learning profound life lessons. Or growing, or coming to like each other, or overcoming obstacles to succeed in the end." The essential idea he tries to convey is nearly incomprehensible to Valerie, but not to the film's viewers, who begin to chafe, like Charlie, at the restrictions limiting a writer's freedom to think and work spontaneously.

"Why can't there be a movie simply about flowers?" Charlie repeatedly asks, and the refrain becomes a way to describe the kind of film he wants to make, the kind nobody has ever seen before.

"I wanted to do something simple," Charlie tells his vulgar agent, Marty (Ron Livingston). "I wanted to show people how amazing flowers are."[8]

"*Are* they amazing?" Marty asks skeptically, fairly representing mainstream movie audiences' aversion to work that departs from traditional forms.

"I don't know," Charlie replies. "I think they are." Then, as the hopelessness of his task presses down upon him: "I need you to get me out of this."

Creatio Ex Nihilo

"Writing is a journey into the unknown. It's not . . . building one of your model airplanes!"[9] Charlie tells his twin brother, Donald, a "writer" who is happy to imitate earlier works, who tries in various ways to convince Charlie that good writing requires learning a set of rules or guidelines, and who, as Charlie's script orbits ever wider from some ideal Hollywood template, becomes the means of reintroducing commerce with the real world—the world with which Charlie, surrounded by reams of his own writing, appears to have lost touch—the world in which Susan Orlean might really be a lesbian or porn-star junkie, in which people really do die, or fall in and out of love, or say wise things to each other. Forgotten, of course, as Donald coaches his brother in the truth of cliché, is Charlie's early warning that these kinds of "teachers are dangerous if your goal is to try to do something new. And a writer should always have that goal."[10]

If Charlie is going to turn the orchid book into the kind of singular, inventive script he admires, if he is earnest about his desire to "grow as a writer," he must discover how it is possible to fulfill his obligation to what he calls "Susan's material,"[11] her compelling, personal observations on real-life events—what in his early stages of writing Charlie calls "that wonderful, sprawling, *New Yorker* stuff" and later, as he feels himself mired in it, "that sprawling *New Yorker* shit"—and simultaneously create something that has a life of its own, the imagined world of a feature film. He must bring *images* to life. Or, rather than imitate life, he must make something out of nothing.

This does not mean that in *Adaptation* Kaufman has taken for himself the role of God. True, at the film's close, Charlie puts the last touches on the world he's made, an orderly world wrought from an original chaos, by narrating his withdrawal from it. And in the darkness of the film's beginning it is Charlie's voice that brings about the fact of existence by constructing an account of it—an expression of remorse that, offered as a kind of apology for his existence, also formally justifies it. But as day follows darkness (for this is a *Jewish* story) and a handheld video camera captures Charlie, standing awkwardly by himself, on the set of *Being John Malkovich*, the depiction of "Charlie Kaufman, Screenwriter" that the film offers is of a man struggling for the preservation of his status *as* a man, with all the anxiety about authority that that implies: "What am I doing here?" Charlie wonders in voice-over narration. "Why did I bother to come here today? Nobody even seems to know my name. I've been on this planet for forty years, and I'm no closer to understanding a single thing. Why am I here? How did I get here?"[12] Though these unanswerable doubts only intensify Charlie's loneliness and indecision, they confirm Kaufman's identification with the fallible human material from which God eventually chooses one man to bless with redemptive purpose.[13]

Whatever gets cooked up in *Adaptation* will be man-made, but—and here is where it gets interesting—assembled in a way that suggests supernatural, rather than natural, agency. That is the reason why the film feels internally generated, much like great works of literature. In these works of the imagination something is engendered, as celebrated literary critic Geoffrey Hartman writes, "from what is barely seen or grasped . . . [the] air, as in omens, thickens, becomes concrete, theriomorphic, auguring; and to air there corresponds the airy womb of the imagination,"[14] which likewise thickens into a projection, a formation, a protuberance, like the one named Charlie Kaufman, for instance.

If we think of *Adaptation* as a story of creation (and the extent to which it resembles the book of Genesis encourages this view), it is the kind of story in which man is able to imagine people, things, and events—to bring them into existence—without needing to ground his imagination in a prior reality, and without having his imaginative powers held against him, as evidence, say, of his inability to perceive the world objectively. In the film, the second freedom is secured by the fact that Charlie's incapacity to perceive the world without predisposition or prejudice is, from the beginning, the means of establishing his existence, and so can't be understood as a disadvantage or weakness. And the first freedom, founded on the disjunction between imagination and reality (the reason, for instance, that the name "Charlie Kaufman" does not have a direct connection to the incontestably real man who goes by that name), is licensed by an initial establishing shot of original darkness, suggesting that the world *before* the world established by the space of agency was "tohu and bohu," without form and void. Nothing exists or happens before this story, that is; nothing authorizes it but the telling.

Genesis

Needless to say, beginning such a story is difficult, because it is hard to begin with this kind of beginning and not try to go further back. Charlie's numerous false starts, his trouble meeting his deadline, have to do with his realization that in order "to write about a flower, to dramatize a flower," he has to "show the flower's arc. And the flower's arc stretches back to the beginning of life."[15] Given that "probably all the organic beings which have ever lived on this earth," as Darwin hypothesized, "have descended from some one primordial form into which life was first breathed," the orchid's arc includes the entirety of life. If Charlie wants to understand the flower's evolution ("How did this flower get here? What was its journey?"), he'll have to make sense of, make story out of, the natural or artificially induced process by which *all* new and different organisms develop and relate: "Adaptation. The journey we all take. A journey that unites each and every one of us."

However profound Charlie's discovery, it is also debilitating. For what at first seems like the breakthrough he'd been looking for, the way to tie everything in the story together, in fact makes his own project that much less manageable. "Darwin writes that we all come from the very first single cell organism," thinks Charlie, puzzling over the orchid script, as usual, in the gloom and isolation of his bedroom. "Yet here I am . . . And there's Laroche . . . And there's Orlean . . . And there's the ghost orchid . . . All trapped in our own bodies, in moments of history. That's it. That's what I need to do. Tie all of history together!" He grabs a mini-recorder and, shucking off weeks of dejection, speaks with the breathless anticipation of a man who at last has something to say: "Start right before life begins on the planet. All is . . . lifeless. And then, like, life begins. Um . . . with organisms. Those little single cell ones . . . Uh, from there we go to bigger things. Jellyfish. And then that fish that got legs on it and crawled out on the land. And then we see, you know, like, um, dinosaurs. And then they're around for a long, long time. And then, and then an asteroid comes and, and . . ."[16]

But the longer this succession goes on, the more questionable it seems, and as Charlie listens to the tape-recorded playback of his new idea his mood shifts from unchecked enthusiasm to acute despair. "The insects, the simple mammals, the primates, monkeys"—Charlie's taped voice is no less fervent, but his flat, listening face lends the monologue a frantic air, and we start to hear, as he has, the absurdity of his pedestrian logic: "The simple monkeys. The, the old-fashioned monkeys giving way to the new monkeys. Whatever. And then the apes—Whatever. And, and man. Then we see the whole history of human civilization—hunting and gathering, farming, uh, Bronze age, war, love, religion, heartache, disease, loneliness, technology . . ."[17]

By stringing together sequentially the very things and events whose nonlinear arrangement he's promised to account for, Charlie exposes the gaps such chains of causation inevitably contain. From single-cell organisms he must leap to "bigger things," to "Jellyfish," and his "likes" and "ums" and "you knows" ("And then we see, you know, like, um, dinosaurs") communicate his apprehension that this will not do: that the way "the old-fashioned monkeys" evolved into the "the new monkeys" is not at all clear; that the process by which "apes" undergo the change into "man" can't be spanned by the conjunction "and"—that "apes" and "man" do not have the same nominal value, just as "Bronze Age" doesn't quite follow "farming." And yet if the links between adjacent but unlike organisms are weak, it is precisely this permeability that leaves room for something never before seen, something not from the first instance encoded.

Like Darwin, Charlie has discovered that there is no end to the number of new life forms on the planet, no end to creation, which occurs not only in the beginning but also over and over again. This fortifies his initial hypothesis that there is no limit to the number of categories artistic works can be divided into, since, as his own film will demonstrate, new kinds of films are always emerging. (McKee might be a "genius," as Donald insists, but there is something blinkered about his assertion that screenwriters must discover their inventiveness within preexisting genres, especially when this assurance is accompanied by the declaration, as Donald reports, that, "there hasn't been a new genre since Fellini invented the mockumentary.")[18] Charlie's conviction that a writer must always "try to do something new," however—that this is the way to create a "reflection of the real world," where new things are emerging all the time—has less to do with originality than with history, with his desire to overturn a trite concept of history that informs his fellow screenwriters' sense of story.

Story is the title of both McKee's 1997 best seller and his screenwriting seminar, the transformative business in which people like Donald learn, in three days, how stories begin, and—through a long chain of causes and effects that push the story along—end. They learn about the way a protagonist undergoes change and how such changes are borne out by the story's conclusion. According to McKee, a story's end always justifies its means. But what happens when a story has no end? *Adaptation*'s final or concluding scenes (already undone, as we have previously said, by its premise) makes this a film without end, a film, we might say, that is all beginning. And as Kenneth Dauber argues, it is worth pondering the meaning of a beginning without end: "Without the idea of an end, causes and effects will appear not as a chain but as a network and not even as a network but as a set of reciprocal and overdetermined influences impossible to get behind. Without an end to recast the beginning as the beginning of an end, that is, beginnings will occur not only in the beginning but over and over again at every moment, in each and every action."[19]

The idea of a beginning without end is one Dauber finds in Genesis, the history, or origin of our idea of history, most directly at odds with what McKee calls story's "eternal, universal" form—the beginning, middle, and end structure that owes more to Hellenistic culture than Judaic tradition, in which, on the contrary, the idea of an end is a late addition, in which the beginning ("In the beginning God created the heavens and the earth") goes on indefinitely, in which the beginning is "always now."[20]

In Dauber's reading, Genesis offers a genealogy that, in order to raise questions about the continuity of its "chain of 'begats,'" officially includes spaces between its links—for example, "the nonlinked link" that "relates Jesus to the Davidic line through the nonfather Joseph." By this measure Genesis itself draws attention to the uncertainty, the caprice, Darwin's theory of evolution is at pains to accentuate.[21] This is hard news for man, who must discover in even "that most seemingly deterministic of histories . . . not the certainty of existence well placed, but the burden of placing [himself] instead."[22] When Creation implies a beginning without end—a world, therefore, in which particular effects are no longer the certain or natural result of specific causes—the consequences for man's actions, what is required of him *as* a man, are significant. Without underlying laws or principles to govern his behavior, despite his skepticism or even because of it, he must figure out for himself the extent of his capacity to act in the world. Who's to say what effects his choices will have? But he is nevertheless responsible for the *means* by which these effects are achieved, for in the picture of history Genesis introduces, "there are no ends to excuse one's means."[23]

How different is McKee's picture of the world (or is it Aristotle's?), in which the final act, the big ending, the "big payoff,"[24] to turn from theology to the language of screenwriting, is what "makes the film,"[25] as McKee promises, and excuses whatever means were necessary to achieve it. A writer who can "wow them in the end" is released from any obligation to the film's system of reasoning and inference—what Charlie, who is always observant of this logic, calls the "reality of the film," and Donald, who doesn't understand this logic and repeatedly abuses it, has no words for whatsoever.[26]

For all his savvy, then, McKee's instructions are only suitable for writers who do not consider writing "a journey into the unknown," a chance to make "something new." That is why Charlie does not share McKee's poetics, or why he feels the burden of writing in a way that Donald does not—why Donald is McKee's natural heir, his right beneficiary, happy to discover a reliable method for putting together a script, and quick to make use of a set of established or fundamental beliefs. "A principle says this works," intones Donald, reciting one of McKee's tenets, "and has through recorded time."[27] But time, the dimension that enables events to be distinguished by the interval between them, collapses when, as in Genesis, "everything becomes, as it were, a beginning of everything else simultaneously."[28] In the tradition to which Charlie is intellectually beholden, we should understand, a principle is no different than a rule, and, since rule-following presupposes the existence of regular practices, a rule is no real help at all.

The Orchid Script

So, between the twin screenwriters Charlie and Donald Kaufman, it is just Charlie who properly understands writerly agency, the extent of the writer's responsibility to the world he is making. That suggests a difference in kind, and not just quality, in the scripts they produce. What sort of script does Charlie create, after all? Is what makes his script different from Donald's *The 3* the fact that it is "about flowers," as Charlie says? Or, since Charlie's film takes part in its own reproduction, since it is sustained by the internal force of its style, could we say that the script is itself a kind of flower? Isn't the orchid script come into bud, *Adaptation*, the flower whose "arc" Charlie must show?

If flowers are "God's miracles," as Charlie suggests, and thus events that appear to be contrary to the laws of nature, thinking of the script as a flower means remembering that there is no broadly applicable principle that guarantees these phenomena—that, as with all flowers that aren't simple, self-pollinating weeds, much depends on circumstance, on the spread of pollen from one plant to another, either by the wind or birds or insects. Besides, if *Adaptation* is a flower, it's not just any flower but an orchid, which, as Darwin says, requires an almost perfect contrivance for its fertilization. "No one knows whether orchids evolved to complement insects or whether the orchids evolved first, or whether somehow these two life forms evolved simultaneously, which might explain how two totally different living things came to depend on each other," Susan Orlean (Susan Orlean)[29] reports in *The Orchid Thief*:

> The harmony between an orchid and its pollinator is so perfect that it is kind of eerie. Darwin loved studying orchids. In his writings he often described them as "my beloved Orchids" and was so certain that they were the pinnacle of evolutionary transformation that he once wrote that it would be "incredibly monstrous to look at an Orchid as having been created as we now see it."[30]

Orchids have extraordinary requirements and conditions for life, in part because the schemes they use to attract pollinators are "elegant but low percentage," as Orlean writes.[31] Wild orchids, in particular, "will usually flourish and produce seeds only if they are in their own little universe with their favorite combination of water and light and temperature and breeze, with the perfect tree bark at the perfect angle, and with the precise kind of bugs and the exact kind of flotsam falling on their roots and into their flowers. Many species of wild orchids aren't propagated commercially, either because they aren't that pretty or because no one has been able to figure out and reproduce exactly what they want and need to survive."[32]

If Kaufman's script is a flower, then like several species of orchid it is going to "either live wild or die." Its success or fruition will depend on what Kaufman in an interview calls "fortuitous accidents," something going on that he's "unaware of," a recurring or unifying idea that over time comes to the fore.[33] Most screenwriters don't operate that way. (In "How to Write a Movie in 21 Days," Viki King explains that "by page 45, your hero has reacted to what happened on page 30. He is now different, and we begin to see that here, in a symbolic scene.")[34] Because Kaufman can't predict what kind of flotsam will be falling into his life, his writing process is undomesticated, impulsive: "It's a bit scary and fun" for the reason that there's no way to know "how it's going to end."[35]

Thinking about *Adaptation* as a flower or flowering thing means, for a critic, thinking about the intricate, variable contrivance that enabled its production. This is not the case if we imagine the script as Kaufman's "way to dramatize the idea of a flower," as Rob Feld posits in his interview with Kaufman and Spike Jonze. "Do you know what the device was that manages to dramatize that flower?" Feld asks, inviting from the film's writer and director the same bemused silence an earlier bit of "industry" nonsense had solicited ("Are there common themes you each find yourselves gravitating towards, or that you find yourselves accentuating as you execute the material?").[36] The fact is, the idea of "dramatizing a flower" is just, well, stupid, unless it is interpreted to suggest the process of making a different kind of life from something that already has a kind of life. The ghost orchid, *Polyrrhiza lindenii*, which grows nowhere in this country but the Fakahatchee, has a life, and John Laroche, "who'd been fooling around with ghost orchids for years" and "claimed he was one of the only people in the world who'd solved the puzzle of how to clone and grow them," had a plan to give it a different kind of life. For that matter John Laroche has a life, and when Susan Orlean decides to go down to Florida and "follow him around," recording the things he says and putting them into her book, she gives him a different kind of life. And of course Orlean's *The Orchid Thief* has a life as a "New York Times Notable Book," a best seller on the nonfiction lists, and when Kaufman adapts it into a screenplay, he must give it a different kind of life—which is all to say that what Kaufman makes must have a life of its own; and although, as with orchids, his manner of realizing this living thing might appear to have "been modeled in the wildest caprice," as Darwin writes, that "is no doubt due to our ignorance" of this living thing's requirements and conditions.

What Kaufman shares with Laroche is an interest in, and talent for, simulating the conditions in which wild things can grow. "Almost anyone who wants a wild orchid now has to steal it from the woods themselves or buy it on the black market from someone else who had,"[37] Orlean reports. But Laroche planned to give the Seminoles a laboratory where they could propagate their own wild orchids. "Sure, the Seminoles could just go into their back yard and dig up grass and twigs and sell it at the nursery," he tells Orlean. "Well, big fucking deal. On the other hand, a lab is a fucking *great* idea. It is a *superior* idea . . . I wanted to bring a little flair to the place. Screw wax myrtles! Screw saw grass! A lab is the way to make real money, not growing *grass*."[38]

Understanding Laroche means understanding how his interest in remarkable, sublime achievements, in figuring out how to manufacture "God's miracles," far outweighs his concern for fast profits. Laroche is always talking about being a millionaire, about being "*completely* set for life," but it's easy to see from what he says to Orlean that for him wealth stands for the recognition of ingeniousness and that what really matters is cleverness and imagination, being resourceful and inventive. "If you could figure out how to housebreak any wild orchid, especially a pretty one like the ghost orchid, you would probably become a rich person,"[39] writes Orlean, somewhat skeptical of Laroche's powers, and mistaken about the difference between commercialized domestication (the "How to Grow an Orchid in 21 Days" plan she imagines Laroche marketing) and what Laroche envisions for the lab—a "huge operation," a strange and exceptional place in which Laroche and the Seminoles could cross-pollinate different orchids and invent hybrids, fool around with mutation and "end up with some cool stuff and some ugly stuff and stuff no one has ever seen before," generate new living things, "and then get to introduce them to the world and, like Adam, name the living things."[40]

"See, my whole life," Laroche tells Orlean, "I've been looking for a god-damn profitable plant." For Laroche that doesn't mean finding "a really nice-looking lawn grass" and producing enough seeds to mass-market it, the way a friend of his did. "I'm not into lawn grass," Laroche says. It means making homegrown ghost orchids that rich collectors—whom he loathes, who think of him as "a criminal"—will clamor for. "I'm bad news in the plant world," Laroche tells Orlean, sounding pleased. "They want me *dead*. I'm serious . . . And to be honest, I feel the same way towards them."[41]

In a way, Kaufman is in the same boat. He must create a living thing from "Susan's material"—something new, something no one's ever seen before. And having his ingeniousness recognized (finding commercial success for the wildly inventive *Being John Malkovich*, for example) means convincing people he loathes and who loathe him, agents and industry types, to buy what he makes. Whatever he writes, moreover, must adhere to an internal logic. This logic, the "reality of the movie," can't be affected by exterior ties, as in the case of nonfiction, by what actually happens in the world, and can't depend on devices not available to writers—for instance, the "trick photography" Donald wants to use in his thriller in order to "have somebody held prisoner in a basement and working in a police station at the same time," the multiple personality "twist" Charlie tells him "there's no way to write."[42] And Charlie manages to do it. The orchid script grows, and he sells it, and it doesn't really have an end but it does have "drama," and not because he avoids the essential character of creative writing, the alarming, unpredictable, time-consuming work of the imagination, but because he's accounted for those qualities that make writing creative—proven his responsibility to the world he's made by showing there is nothing in the writing for which he is not responsible, nothing he's just found in the backyard, nothing he's simply imported from nature.

In that way, Kaufman and Laroche are the same. Orlean calls Laroche a "thief," but in this she is wrong. She thinks he's the definitive example of the sort of people who are "wrapped up in their special passion for the natural world," who are "enthralled" by the things they find there, and who "pursue them like lovers."[43] But Laroche, like Kaufman, is a creator. He'd rather make than find or steal. And when Kaufman makes characters of these real people, when he puts them in the real world of the film, behind which we never get, he gives us an Orlean who is bent on a romantic pursuit of something in nature, a Laroche who makes ghost orchids. Although Rob Feld describes *Adaptation* as a film "about a writer who becomes fixated on the woman whose experience he's trying to represent in his writing,"[44] Kaufman in fact is absorbed by nothing like Susan Orlean's actual experience, and the story he puts together features a writer who is able to survive as a writer—someone, that is, both genuinely interested in people like Orlean and Laroche and not at all interested in finding out about them.

A Goddamn Profitable Plant

The irony at the heart of *The Orchid Thief* is that it is Orlean, and not Laroche, who makes money off the ghost orchid—that this talented but fastidious New Yorker is the one who finally manages to smuggle something precious out of the Fakahatchee. What Orlean takes home is not an orchid, of course (she was so leery of getting hooked on orchid collecting she gave away every plant she was given), but the man who wants to make them, the unnaturally adaptable Laroche himself, who, like all things gorgeous and good at surviving, thrives because he takes himself out of competition, because he learns to position himself above the common fray.

Orlean, who when interviewed describes Laroche as having "a grand self-image," would no doubt find this view of him too generous. "Laroche has a vision of himself as something larger than life," she says critically.[45] But Orlean's misreading of Laroche, her condescension toward him, unchecked to the end (transformed in the film, where her disdain melts in the face of Laroche's very real attractions), is a telling instance of the distance Orlean imagines between herself and her subject, a distance she describes in her writing and also preserves *through* her writing, the kind of storytelling that deals only with "what really exists" and what actually happens.

Perhaps that is why in *Adaptation*, Orlean, unlike Charlie, has no trouble at all beginning her story. We see her fingers move gracefully over the computer keyboard as she works, and we listen to her confident, mellifluous voice describing realms unknown yet not unfamiliar: "Orchid hunting is a mortal occupation," she notes, and we believe her. "John Laroche is a tall guy, skinny as a stick." The writing comes easy because her subject is all before her. Her subject is something she happens upon—or fails to spot—in the world. For such writers the world *before* the world that writing opens up (the world itself, like Florida itself, to which Orlean keeps returning) is the one that contains riches, and an adept writer plunders them. That is why in *Adaptation* one of Orlean's sneering New York friends says of Laroche, Orlean's latest find, "Sounds like a goldmine, Sue."[46]

Accordingly the outlook and tactics of the Orlean of *Adaptation* are not unlike those of the Orlean who authored *The Orchid Thief*, the Orlean who is not Meryl Streep. Orlean has interviewed Laroche. She's logged countless hours with orchid collectors, horticulturists, and Seminole Tribe members. She's even tramped through the Fakahatchee swamps, and though we're delighted with her eloquence and her memorable, slightly haunting observations ("Laroche loved orchids, but I came to believe that he loved the difficulty and fatality of getting them almost as much as he loved the orchids themselves"), her work is affecting because it provides instruction about mysterious, alluring worlds we previously had no sense of—orchid poaching and selling and cloning—and then shows why the more we learn about these worlds the better we'll know our own. As admiring reviewer James W. Hall writes, "*The Orchid Thief* is everything we expect from the very best literature. It opens our eyes to an extraordinary new universe and stirs our passion for the people who populate the world."[47] In Hall's realist tradition, literature's best use is the heightened feeling it gives us for the world we live in, and in this way wakes us to a "new universe."

The basic premise of such work is that the untrained observer, who knows about orchids but doesn't think about them, who reads the news but hasn't a reporter's nose for the *story*, is missing something the writer can provide, some insight about the world or the people in it that follows as the consequence of the special way the facts are gathered and presented. "Sometimes this kind of story turns out to be something more," Orlean writes in the book's introductory pages, "some glimpse of life that expands like those Japanese paper balls you drop in water and then after a moment they bloom into flowers, and the flower is so marvelous that you can't believe there was a time when all you saw in front of you was a paper ball and a glass of water."[48] What makes the ball bloom is good investigative journalism and a steady hand. For Orlean there is "life"—grand, glorious, hard to decipher—and there are "characters" like John Laroche, people more eccentric and fascinating than she could ever have imagined,[49] and there is "writing," the disciplined practice of "taking true stories and making them engaging to a reader," the tradition which allows a writer to "whittle the world down to a more manageable size."[50]

The reading strategy associated with this tradition is one in which a discerning public scrutinizes a text in order to find out who its "characters" really are—and, importantly, judges them accordingly.[51] This way of thinking about writing as a lens through which to view the world is demonstrated by a *New Yorker* subscriber, who writes that Laroche "belongs to a milieu whose members turn to horticulture partly as therapy, partly as a convenient refuge from the burdens of responsibility." This verdict isn't delivered with Orlean's light hand (hey, *New Yorker* reader, don't say "milieu"), but this subscriber shares Orlean's sense that books like *The Orchid Thief* help readers form sound opinions, start them on a path of judgment, and discover how writing can be used, practically, as a tool for revealing 𝕏 the world around them.

There is another way to think about literature, however, that is just as useful, though based on a concept of writing to which Orlean appears hostile. This is one in which the writer as "fabulator," as Gilles Deleuze says, the writer in his endless capacity for invention, confronts readers with the fact that the text is an invention. (Naming one of his characters "Charlie Kaufman" is one strategy Kaufman has for confronting his readers. That way, as Kaufman says, the movie's viewers are "constantly being taken out of the movie. Even though [they're] watching the movie as a story that plays as a story, there's this constant nagging thing that's, 'Is this real, is it not real?' I like that.")[52] Fabulators obstruct readers from making judgments about characters and instead enable them to think about characters *as* characters, an idea so unsettling that readers, forced to reposition *themselves*, see newly. The glimpse is not of a "new universe" but an old universe more adequately viewed.

That is what a conceptual reading of literature would teach. Literature that "exceeds closed, psychological, or personal narratives and opens itself up onto the endless conditions of its creation," writes Anthony Larson, elegantly summarizing Deleuze, "achieves the form of a concept."[53] When literature responds to the problem of its own creation, we might take this to mean, it becomes something larger than life, not a reflection of life but a *conception* of it. That is why writing that is not simply personal or historical but conceptual has the benefit, as Nietzsche also argues, of enlarging and strengthening its readers—just as, rather than "whittle it down," this literature enlarges and strengthens the world. This is not to suggest that producing or even encountering this work isn't hard. For Deleuze and Nietzsche (and for Spinoza, through whom this intellectual tradition might be seen to stretch all the way back to Genesis) the burden presented by an ontology of the middle, of perpetual being, or being that lacks an end to recast its beginning as the beginning of an end, is, as Larson writes, "that the process of composition must seize itself through itself and in itself without recourse to any 'supplemental' or transcendental category."[54] In everyday terms, this means that Charlie Kaufman, struggling to compose the orchid script in the darkness of his room, cannot rely for guidance on a morality or material reality that exists outside of the one created and sustained by his composition process. That's why it's so funny—and, for those of us who suffer similarly, mortifying—that the world he must neglect in order to write is always tempting him, as the first scene in which we see Charlie in front of his typewriter reveals: "To begin. To begin. How to start," he thinks. Then, "I'm hungry. I should get coffee. Coffee would help me think. But I should write something first. Then reward myself with coffee. Coffee and a muffin. Okay, so I need to establish the themes. Maybe banana nut. That's a good muffin."[55] As the transcendent banana nut muffin scene makes clear, writing is hardest when one cannot turn for any real comfort to something exterior to, or outside of, the world the work itself generates.

This is not Orlean's view of writing. For Orlean, writing is not what one is able to do only in the absence of an antecedent referent, but what one generates in order to refer back to something that happened or existed before the writing. Orlean's writing draws attention to or gives further details about something that predates it. *Life.* The reason fiction holds little interest for her likely has to do with what she sees as a fiction writer's loose attachment to past events. As a nonfiction writer, Orlean says, "You have to deal with what really exists. That is a greater challenge than thinking, 'Gee, it would have worked out better if he had gone to jail for a year; I think I'll just make him go to jail for a year.' Instead, this is reality."[56] Fiction writers—people who *create*—are obliged to little more than whim, Orlean seems to suggest. This is perhaps one reason she consistently depicts Laroche as someone driven by impulse, not insight. "I think he's a person who can't seem to live within the conventional bounds that most of us feel comfortable living within," she reports. "And it is probably something to do with needing attention. He can't just succeed, he needs to succeed in a complicated, interesting, unusual way."[57] Here Orlean is unwittingly right about evolution's criteria for success, but wrong about Laroche, who has already quite ably articulated that although he's a "shrewd bastard" and could have been "a great con man," it's finally "more interesting to live your life within the confines of the law. It's more challenging to do what you want but try to do it so you can justify it."[58] Given Orlean's blindness to Laroche's voluntary—and thus righteous— submission to prevailing conditions, we can imagine her impatience with the idea of the "reality" of a fictional world, one that needs to be obeyed as closely as the reality she calls her own.

It may therefore not come as a total shock to discover that Orlean's thoughts about writing are shared, essentially if not characteristically, by Donald Kaufman. How else might we make sense, in *Adaptation*, of Donald's eager discovery of the paper-ball passage in Orlean's book, after Charlie has asked for his help with the orchid script? "I feel like you're missing something," Donald tells his brother, and then takes *The Orchid Thief* from his bag. "Look. I did a little research on the airplane." He reads: "Sometimes this kind of story turns out to be something more . . ."

"For God's sake," Charlie responds. "It's just a metaphor."

"But for what? What turned that paper ball into a flower? It's not in the book, Charles."

"I don't know. You're reaching."

"Maybe. But I think you actually need to speak to this woman. To know her."[59]

So begins the contest between Charlie's way of knowing Orlean and Donald's—which, in the mock ending of *Adaptation*, Donald wins, and thus which, in the never-ending beginning that is *Adaptation*, Charlie wins. Charlie's way of knowing Orlean depends on *not* finding out about her, on remaining altogether ignorant of her sexual history, recreational drug use, love life, and so on. This shrinking from the actual is established by the scene in which Charlie shares an elevator with Orlean—whom he does not address, though he has come to find her. The scene is an iteration of an earlier scene in which Charlie bumps into Valerie, who is having lunch with Orlean. Valerie tells Charlie that he should join them, that Orlean is dying to meet him. But Charlie flees after falteringly excusing himself ("I'd love to meet her, too, but I don't want to be . . . beholden. And . . . Because once you meet somebody that you're writing about it becomes very hard to . . . separate").[60] Viewers who feel frustrated by Charlie's inability to reach out to the tantalizingly near Orlean have perhaps forgotten Henry James's warning that "the minimum of valid suggestion serve[s] the man of imagination better than the maximum"[61]—that as strong as the temptation to support oneself with facts may be, the writer's capacity for invention comes from the endless capacity for invention that is language.[62]

Compare the elevator scene's staging of the relation between Kaufman and the object of his interest that can never be reached with Orlean's desire to see a ghost orchid. "If it was a real flower, I wanted to see one," Orlean writes in *The Orchid Thief*; "I wanted . . . to see this thing that people were drawn to in such a singular and powerful way." Seeing the blooming ghost orchid is something she desperately wants, because seeing one would "complete the cycle," as Orlean reports, or "make sense of everything [she'd] been doing in Florida."[63] In other words, even when her subject remains elusive, her story is still *about* something, something with physical reality, of practical or aesthetic value. In *Adaptation* Charlie says he thinks Orlean's story "is about disappointment," and that is because what are beautiful to him are stories about nothing—stories, as Flaubert says, sustained by the force of their style, that have no subject, or in which the subject is almost invisible.[64] But in *The Orchid Thief* Orlean says it is "just as well" she never sees a ghost orchid because that way "it could never disappoint" her and would "remain forever something [she] wanted to see."[65] Orlean uses language to describe events, even unrealized events. She does not think of herself as a writer who, by expressing that which has *up until the time of expression* remained unexpressed, invents or creates things. Sure enough, Orlean's book is full of such writing, moments of seeing or hearing of which only a writer is capable; but Orlean mistakenly thinks these moments derive from real life—that "life" is what "is so interesting."[66]

Not coincidentally, this is also what McKee tells the workshop audience in which, in *Adaptation*, Charlie Kaufman finds himself. Charlie has asked about the validity of screenplays that have no "inciting incidents" to which protagonists must react (thus throwing their lives out of balance and necessitating a restored balance which, according to McKee, they "may or may not achieve"). This question infuriates McKee, who bellows at Charlie, "If you can't find that stuff in life, then you, my friend, don't know crap about life!" Here "that stuff" refers to the kind of stirring event McKee has already catalogued—"genocide, war, corruption"—together with everyday calamity: "Every fucking day somewhere in the world, somebody sacrifices his life to save somebody else. Every fucking day someone somewhere makes a conscious decision to destroy someone else! People find love! People lose it! For Christ's sake, a child watches a mother beaten to death on the steps of a church! Someone goes hungry! Somebody else betrays his best friend for the love of a woman!"[67]

McKee's evisceration of Charlie's stance on filmmaking or storytelling disorients both Charlie and the film's viewers because it is so compelling, so true: such a list represents the realist's best response to the fabulist's stammered dreams, the final suppression of the writer who feels he has seen and heard things that haven't already happened, as it were—things that, for a moment, only the writer is capable of seeing. This argument must be resisted, however; and *Adaptation* constitutes that resistance. In the Aristotelian tradition in which McKee and his acolytes work, stories are lived before they are told.[68] But in Genesis, creation begins with a word, behind which man never gets.[69] Only when we do not side with McKee, Susan, and Donald, that is, but find in Charlie's narrative strategy exactly that willingness to traverse "the livable and the lived"[70] so essential to imaginative literature, can the dream of the artist take hold.

Notes

1. See "Q & A with Charlie Kaufman and Spike Jonze," by Rob Feld in Charlie Kaufman, *Adaptation: The Shooting Script* (New York: Newmarket Press, 2002), 115–30. In the interview Kaufman says, "The movie's pretty accurate in its depiction of my false starts and my confusion, and how I just had to plug away because I was hired and because they had paid me a certain amount of money to proceed, and so I had to. I would have dropped it a hundred times if they didn't give me that advance money, but I felt obligation." Ibid., 123.

2. For the scholarly source of this idea, see Geoffrey Hartman, *Criticism in the Wilderness: The Study of Literature Today* (New Haven: Yale University Press, 1980), 22–25. In his investigation of literary criticism, Hartman implicitly contrasts the kind of criticism in which a detective-critic, "confronted by a bewildering text . . . acts out a solution, [tries] various defenses, various interpretations, then [pretends] to come to an authoritative stance" with the criticism he admires, the kind of criticism-as-writing that puts a tremendous demand on readers and that often causes "perplexity and resentment" because "it does not see itself as subordinated in any simple way to the books on which it comments." The resentment is to be expected because such criticism does not explain imaginative literature but "makes us formally aware of [its] bewildering character." For Hartman, the image/phantasm with which critics ought to concern themselves—that which is "engendered from what is barely seen or grasped" in the work, "that does not recall natural process so much as supernatural agency, not formation but transformation . . . the visible in the invisible, an absence that can turn into a devastating presence"—has come "out of nothing" other than the writer's employment of language and thus "cannot be explained or grounded by the coordinates of ordinary perception, by stable space-time categories."

3. For a splendid philosophical account of the difference between fiction and memoir (why we cannot say that the character Charlie Kaufman "is" Charlie Kaufman, or why a piece of imaginative writing cannot be considered a transcription of Reality) see Bernard Harrison's "Imagined Worlds and the Real One: Plato, Wittgenstein, and Mimesis," in *The Literary Wittgenstein,* ed. John Gibson and Wolfgang Huemer (New York: Routledge, 2004), 92–108.

4. Kaufman, "Q & A with Charlie Kaufman and Spike Jonze," 119.

5. Kaufman, *Adaptation: The Shooting Script,* 61. Since the shooting script appears to be identical to the film, I cite the pages on which quoted dialogue occurs, rather than the time code.

6. Ibid., 70.

7. Ibid., 5.

8. Ibid., 51.

9. Ibid., 12.

10. Ibid.

11. Ibid., 51.

12. Ibid., 3.

13. Abraham, that is—the patriarch of the Israelites. God makes Abraham, and not his brothers, instrumental in bringing divine blessing after God's creation had been marred by man's persistent wickedness.

14. Hartman, *Criticism in the Wilderness*, 23.

15. Kaufman, *Adaptation: The Shooting Script*, 40.

16. Ibid., 41.

17. Ibid., 42.

18. Ibid.

19. "It is worth pondering the meaning of a beginning without end, of a causality that is ceaselessly, even ruthlessly, efficient alone," writes Kenneth Dauber in "Beginning at the Beginning in Genesis," from his coedited volume with Walter Jost, *Ordinary Language Criticism: Literary Thinking after Cavell after Wittgenstein* (Evanston: Northwestern University Press, 2003), 331–32. In Dauber's brilliant reading, Genesis, the first genealogy to disqualify material, final, and formal causes, shows us how "the point of genealogy is not to establish continuity but to assure us that such newness and discontinuity as the line from Abraham to Ephraim represents are continuous enough" (334). Dauber's discussion of the "nonlinked link," for instance that which "relates Jesus to the Davidic line through the nonfather Joseph," clearly anticipates a comparable argument in this essay—see for example Dauber's suggestion that if the link between King David and Jesus is weak, it is also "what gives the birth of Jesus its revolutionary moment. Without spaces between the links to raise questions about the continuity of the chain, what space is there for something to occur that is not merely there in the first link? To speak theologically, without room for skepticism, what possibility is there of faith?"(332–33).

20. Ibid., 343.

21. Ibid., 332. I should be clear that this point about the relation between Darwin's theorizing and the writing in Genesis ("By this measure Genesis itself draws attention to the uncertainty, the caprice, Darwin's theory of evolution is at pains to accentuate") does not appear in Dauber's essay.

22. Dauber, "Beginning at the Beginning," 332.

23. Ibid., 331.

24. Kaufman, *Adaptation: The Shooting Script*, 56. This is what Caroline (Maggie Gyllenhall) calls *The 3*'s surprise finale, in which viewers learn that the cop, the killer, and the girl all one person—Kaufman's lighthearted mockery of films like *Fight Club* (David Fincher, 1999), in other words.

25. Ibid., 70.

26. Ibid., 31. Instances of Donald's abuse include his decision to make the cop, the killer, and the girl the same person. When Charlie asks Donald how he's going to do this, Donald's answer is "trick photography." "Okay, that's not what I'm asking," says a frustrated Charlie. "Listen closely. What I'm asking is, in the reality of this movie, where

there's only one character, right? Okay? How could you . . . What, what exactly would . . ." (Then, according to the shooting script, "Donald waits blankly." Charlie gives up and says:) "I agree with Mom. Very taut. *Sybil* meets, I don't know . . . *Dressed to Kill.*" Ibid.

27. Ibid., 11.

28. Dauber, "Begining at the Beginning," 331.

29. In these last two sections of the essay I talk often about the real-life Susan Orlean and her book *The Orchid Thief.* Given the likelihood of confusion between these Orleans I've tried to clearly mark the movement between film and book.

30. Susan Orlean, *The Orchid Thief* (New York: Ballantine Books, 2008 [1998], 47.

31. Ibid., 46–48. About these low yielding schemes, Orlean writes: "There are orchids that smell like rotting meat, which insects happen to like. Another orchid smells like chocolate. Another smells like an angel food cake. Several mimic the scent of other flowers that are more popular with insects than they are. Some release perfume only at night to attract nocturnal moths." In a recent study of one thousand wild orchids for fifteen years, Orlean notes, "only twenty-three plants were pollinated."

32. Ibid., 24–25.

33. Kaufman, "Q & A with Charlie Kaufman and Spike Jonze," 125.

34. King quoted in Ian Parker, "The Real McKee," *The New Yorker,* October 20, 2003. Parker, like fellow *New Yorker* staff writers Tad Friend and Adam Gopnik, does not sound at all like someone who thinks of writing as a transcription of reality. His knowing but kind essay on McKee is not out of keeping with Kaufman's sensibilities, in other words, and suggests an ear perfectly tuned to the logical gap separating a person's conclusions from the propositions that form the basis of his or her argument.

35. Kaufman, "Q & A with Charlie Kaufman and Spike Jonze," 125.

36. Ibid., 119. Obviously these kinds of questions are ridiculed in the film, though in an interview with Tim McHenry published in the back of the 2000, 2002, and 2008 editions of *The Orchid Thief,* Orlean herself is asked such questions ("If there was one question you wished an interviewer would ask, but never has, what would it be?") and goes about the business of answering them.

37. Orlean, *The Orchid Thief,* 25–26.

38. Ibid., 24.

39. Ibid., 25.

40. Ibid., 17, 201. The last quote is actually something Orlean says about another orchid collector and smuggler, Lee Moore the Adventurer, but Orlean says herself it seemed as if the two men were "cut from the same flammable cloth" (199). Lee also tells Orlean, "I'm always looking for something new. That's been my goal all along. New things, really special things" (200).

41. Orlean, *The Orchid Thief,* 81.

42. Kaufman, *Adaptation: The Shooting Script,* 31.

43. Orlean, *The Orchid Thief,* 136.

44. Kaufman, "Q & A with Charlie Kaufman and Spike Jonze," 119.

45. Orlean, *The Orchid Thief*, 290, an interview between Susan Orlean and Tim McHenry.

46. Kaufman, *Adaptation: The Shooting Script*, 25.

47. Orlean, *The Orchid Thief*, 55. James W. Hall, from Orlean, *The Orchid Thief*, promotional quote in front matter.

48. Orlean, *The Orchid Thief*, 6–7.

49. Ibid., 287: "I don't think I could have imagined a character as eccentric and fascinating as John Laroche," Orlean writes. Significantly, this nonliterary use of the word "character" is the same one adopted in the film by Valerie, the literary agent: "Laroche certainly is a fun character," she says. Kaufman presses further on the difference between what he means by "character" and what Orlean and Valerie mean when, in *Adaptation*, he has a different-sounding Orlean, an Orlean turned—soon absurdly—into a character, report her conversation with Valerie to Laroche, who says charmingly, "No shit I'm a fun character."

50. Kaufman, *Adaptation: The Shooting Script*, 55.

51. For a brilliant critique of this kind of realist reading strategy and the verdicts it encourages, see Anthony Larson, "First Lessons: Gilles Deleuze and the Concept of Literature," in *Literature and Philosophy: A Guide to Contemporary Debates*, ed. David Rudrum (New York: Palgrave Macmillan, 2006), 13–23. Here Larson elegantly describes what Deleuze sees as the problem with *this* kind of "practical" use of literature, a kind of professionalized or teacherly use of literature Orlean frankly admits appeals to her: "There is also a part of me that likes the pedagogical part of writing," she says in the McHenry interview, "the challenge of bringing knowledge to readers, material they didn't know they would actually want to know" (Orlean, *The Orchid Thief*, 220).

52. Kaufman, "Q & A with Charlie Kaufman and Spike Jonze," 128.

53. Larson, "First Lessons," 21.

54. Ibid., 20.

55. Kaufman, *Adaptation: The Shooting Script*, 2.

56. Orlean, *The Orchid Thief*, 287.

57. Ibid., 289.

58. Ibid., 289, 30.

59. Kaufman, *Adaptation: The Shooting Script*, 75.

60. Ibid., 58.

61. Henry James, *The Aspern Papers* (Mineola, NY: Dover, 2001), vii.

62. Larson, "First Lessons," 18.

63. Orlean, *The Orchid Thief*, 280.

64. This is something Flaubert says is true of the "most beautiful works": "What seems beautiful to me, what I should most like to do, would be a book about nothing, a book without any exterior tie, but sustained by the internal force of its style . . . a book which would have almost no subject, or at least in which the subject would be almost invisible, if that is possible. The most beautiful works are those with the least matter."

Quoted in Kenneth Burke, *Counter-Statement*, 2nd ed. (Berkeley: University of California Press, 1968), 6.

65. Orlean, *The Orchid Thief*, 281.

66. Ibid., 286.

67. Kaufman, *Adaptation: The Shooting Script*, 69.

68. Alasdair MacIntyre, *After Virtue: A Study in Moral Theory* (Notre Dame, IN: University of Notre Dame Press, 1981), 197. Ian Parker, in "The Real McKee," quotes MacIntyre's sentence incompletely, leaving off its crucial ending: "Stories are lived before they are told—except in the case of fiction."

69. Dauber, "Beginning at the Beginning," 335.

70. Gilles Deleuze, *Critique et clinique* (Paris: Minuit, 1993), 11. Cited in Larson, "First Lessons," 19.

ON *BEING JOHN MALKOVICH* AND NOT BEING YOURSELF

Christopher Falzon

In *Being John Malkovich*, the first of Charlie Kaufman's screenplays to be made into a feature film, the protagonist, Craig Schwartz (John Cusack), finds a portal into the body of actor John Malkovich (John Malkovich), allowing him to inhabit it for fifteen minutes. Craig describes the experience to his sexy and condescending coworker Maxine (Catherine Keener), whom he lusts after: "It raises all sorts of philosophical-type questions, you know . . . about the nature of self, about the existence of a soul. You know, am I me? Is Malkovich Malkovich? I had a piece of wood in my hand, Maxine. I don't have it any more. Where is it? Did it disappear? How could that be? Is it still in Malkovich's head? I don't know! Do you see what a metaphysical can of worms this portal is? I don't see how I could go on living my life the way I've lived it before."[1]

Kaufman's film does indeed raise "philosophical-type questions" about the nature of self, including: What kind of self could possibly make this journey?[2] Paired with the philosophical aspects of *Being John Malkovich* is its dark and deadpan comedy, as the protagonist finds himself in a series of increasingly absurd situations that explore the consequences of entering the portal. There is no reason why comedy should preclude serious philosophical questioning, especially because showing the ridiculous consequences of an argument is a potent form of critique. In Kaufman's hands, Craig's progress represents a kind of reductio ad absurdum; his eventual fate calls the existence of the very self that makes the journey possible into question. *Being John Malkovich* is also a comedy that addresses serious personal and interpersonal concerns, in which the human significance of these "philosophical-type questions" emerges. Craig's questioning of the nature of self is not posed as an abstract question but as a radically immanent existential crisis. While Craig's longing, and his judgment, are often portrayed as pitiful, ultimately we discover that his fate is entirely tragic.[3] But this tragedy is also part of the comedy. As viewers, we see how certain metaphysical presumptions about the nature of the self lead to absurd conclusions—the conditions for much of the film's comedy, and most of its tragedy. In this essay, I critically explore the metaphysical ideas that underwrite the notions of self in *Being John Malkovich*, ideas that not only inform Kaufman's film but are called into question through it.

According to Murray Smith, *Being John Malkovich* is a film that "exploits some of the absurdities implicit in our confused and often paradoxical ideas about consciousness."[4] In particular, the film dramatizes situations in which characters believe in a conception of the self as a conscious subject, essentially distinct from the body. The idea of a mind-body dualism goes back to the fourth century BCE when Plato, among others, argued for a separation between ideas and material substances. In modernity, the idea is associated with the seventeenth-century philosopher Descartes; and partly because of his work's widespread influence in European philosophy, dualism has become part of everyday thinking.

One of the more bizarre implications of the Cartesian self—that some interior part (e.g., mind, soul, self) can leave behind its "host" body and occupy another—is the basis for the film's central conceit: that one can enter a portal and take a "ride" in the body of actor John Malkovich. And yet the film is ultimately concerned less with what makes us ourselves than whether self-transformation is possible. Many of the film's characters yearn to escape their lives. The Cartesian notion of self seems to suggest the convoluted, though possibly appealing, notion that one can escape one's physical frame to become someone else—and yet somehow also remain who one is. We see some of the darkness of the comedy in Kaufman's understanding that the move to another body is not really a mode of escape at all, but rather a chance to merely imprison the self in someone else's body. This foolish exchange is at the heart of Craig's tragic fate.

Still, there are times when Craig seems to experiment with the nature of the Cartesian self—moving beyond merely riding in Malkovich to actual control over his body. When Craig's mind makes this connection with Malkovich's body, it seems we are presented with a new, hybrid self.

Perhaps because ideas of the Cartesian self can be used to demonstrate such apparently absurd conclusions, it is not surprising that many philosophers have attempted to undermine the theoretical basis of Descartes' notion of self. Thinkers as different in outlook and methodology as John Dewey, Maurice Merleau-Ponty, and Michel Foucault share an anti-Cartesian approach. Their common insight, echoed in the film, is that escaping from the Cartesian idea of self requires taking our embodiment seriously—and understanding it differently than Plato and Descartes have. To that extent, the film *Being John Malkovich* illustrates not only the problematic implications of believing in a Cartesian notion of the self, but also orients us toward an alternative—embodied—conception of the self. Whether this embodied self itself makes self-transformation possible is a question I will consider further.

Cartesian Comedy

In *Being John Malkovich*, Kaufman takes the idea of the Cartesian self as his intellectual touchstone. In this view, the self is understood to be a unified subject existing over time, one that is conscious and has experiences, memories, and so on: an essentially nonphysical mind. According to Descartes' "dualist" view, human beings are composed of two very different substances, mind and body; but the mind is the more important of the two, because it is essential to individual identity. Somewhat strangely, the self (or mind) is said to be associated with a particular body, and yet not necessarily tied to it. The mind can exist apart from the body, and presumably even inhabit another body. *Being John Malkovich* is among the recent contributions to a tradition of Hollywood "mind-swap" films, such as *All of Me* (Carl Reiner, 1984), *Big* (Penny Marshall, 1988), and *Switch* (Blake Edwards, 1991). In fact, these films may be understood to comprise a genre, "the Cartesian comedy."

In Kaufman's film, Craig, a failed street puppeteer, has been forced to get a proper job at the Lestercorp filing agency, where he discovers the mysterious portal into John Malkovich. When Craig passes through the portal into Malkovich, he doesn't travel as the fully embodied Craig, but rather, as it were, the essential Craig: his conscious, nonbodily self. According to this logic, Craig continues to be Craig even after he enters Malkovich; the self remains distinct from whatever body it happens to occupy. As Walter Ott puts it, on the Cartesian view "it is as if each human body had another, much tinier human being inside it, a 'homunculus' somewhere in the skull."[5] This homunculus experiences the world through the body by receiving signals from the body's sense organs and, in turn, controls the body's nerves and muscles. *Being John Malkovich* exemplifies Ott's characterization of the Cartesian self. While he is in Malkovich's body, Craig does not directly observe the world but sees what Malkovich's eyes present to him. His point of view is not Malkovich's but of someone who is within Malkovich, behind Malkovich's eyes, observing what Malkovich sees. On-screen, a cutout frame that limits the film viewer's field of vision, along with muffled audio, helps create the illusion of seeing the world through Malkovich's eyes, from the point of view of the homunculus, Craig. This Cartesian homunculus, it should be emphasized, is a nonbodily creature. What has happened to Craig's body during his time in Malkovich, along with "the piece of wood in my hand, Maxine," is a question that the film both alludes to and cheerfully leaves unanswered.

Initially Craig solely observes what Malkovich sees, but he gradually finds—or is it learns?—that he can influence what Malkovich does. However, even when "active" in this way, the Cartesian self remains distinct from the body. Craig does not directly act on the world; rather, he gets the body he occupies to do things by forming an inner intention, a will, that causes the body to act. Malkovich is in effect being "possessed" by Craig, the alien entity within, a scenario that would not be out of place in a horror film. We find yet another Cartesian aspect of the film in the impossibility of directly encountering the mind of another person. All we have access to is another's body. For this reason, we have to infer the existence of a mind "behind" the body, and we can always be mistaken about "who" is there. It might be someone other than we think it is—if indeed anyone is there at all. Craig exploits this feature of the Cartesian metaphysics at play in the film to seduce Maxine. While she is indifferent to him, she enjoys having sex "with" his wife, Lotte (Cameron Diaz), during Lotte's visits inside Malkovich, because Lotte is "inside" him and, as it were, inside Maxine. When Craig replaces Lotte inside Malkovich during their trysts, Maxine doesn't notice the difference. These scenarios suggest that selves and bodies are separate entities. On the face of it, Craig's puppetry provides an instructive metaphor for this view of individual identity, in which the mind controls the body as a puppeteer operates the puppet: behind the scenes, pulling the strings. There is certainly no shortage of puppetry allusions to Craig's occupation of and control over Malkovich, including Craig's statement that Malkovich is just another puppet he can control.[6] As we will see, however, there are a number of different ways of understanding the puppetry metaphor.

So far Kaufman's film looks to be telling us about what we most essentially are, the nonbodily Cartesian mind that survives the transition into Malkovich, allowing Craig to remain Craig. But the film is less about finding than about escaping ourselves, about the search for transcendence.[7] Craig and many of the other characters are desperate to escape from themselves, and to be John Malkovich is to have the opportunity to become someone else. From this perspective the puppetry metaphor takes on a different significance, that of transcending oneself. Craig himself characterizes the appeal of puppetry for him as "the idea of becoming someone else for a little while. Being inside another skin. Thinking differently, moving differently, feeling differently."[8] The portal into Malkovich appears to make this escape from oneself possible in reality. This idea of wanting to escape from ourselves implies that who we are is something confining or entrapping. The self that one is escaping from here is broader than the Cartesian self. It can be understood in terms of the ensemble of practices, the distinctive patterns of behavior, that go to make up the life one pursues within a certain milieu.

Craig wants to escape from a life that is narrow, stifling, and cut off from others. He is emotionally distant from Lotte and has no wider audience for his puppeteering (his overly erotic street puppetry only gets him beaten up by passers-by). Even when he is talking about the attraction of puppetry, as a way of getting into another person's skin, he is doing so by himself, to a puppet he has made that resembles Maxine. Various images of physical confinement reflect Craig's confined, claustrophobic life. He works in his tiny workroom, in the cramped apartment he shares with Lotte. His filing job is on the seven-and-a-halfth floor of the Mertin-Flemmer building, its low ceiling forcing those working there to crouch down.[9] Craig's desire for self-transcendence is bound up with a wish to connect with others. He wants to be recognized for his puppetry, to be famous; he also wants to be desirable to Maxine, who has contemptuously rebuffed his advances. The portal seems to afford him the possibility of such an escape. And Craig is not alone in his desire to escape himself. When he tells Maxine about the portal she recognizes a business opportunity and suggests they sell rides in Malkovich. It turns out that there are plenty of people willing to spend money to escape their mundane lives and spend time being someone else—anyone else, but especially someone famous (even if no one in the film is quite sure what film roles Malkovich has actually played).

For these characters, escape from a claustrophobic life is bound up with escape from confinement within their physical frame, the body that locates them in a particular form of life. Craig characterizes the appeal of puppeteering as a mode of transcendence in frankly physical terms. He likes the sensation it gives him of "being in another skin," prefiguring the literal escape from his own skin into Malkovich. Meanwhile Lester (Orson Bean), chairman of Lestercorp, looks to Malkovich in order to escape his very mortality. He was the first to discover the portal, and he has been using it to transfer his consciousness from body to body for some time. In this way Lester aims to avoid not only his own death but also the loss of sexual vigor that comes with age.[10] It is worth noting that Kaufman presents a strictly secular, nonreligious conception of transcendence. The portal is a kind of technology, and it is not a passage to another world, to a postlife liberation, but a way of remaining in this one. At the same time, as we've seen, being able to escape through the portal into Malkovich presupposes an unworldly, nonbodily Cartesian self, a kind of soul, even if a secularized one. As this self, one is able to leave behind one's existing form of life and physical limitations.

Pursuing the theme of self-transcendence in the film thus brings us back to the Cartesian self, now as aiding or underwriting transcendence.[11] But the film also depicts the failure of this transcendence; and it shows that this failure arises from the very notion of a Cartesian self. This conception of self allows us to say that Craig remains Craig even when he is within Malkovich's body, but it also means that he remains trapped within himself. He becomes an immaterial ghost, cut off from interaction with the world and others, distinct from the body, with direct access only to himself. The most striking image of this self-confinement appears in the film when Malkovich himself, having discovered that Craig and Maxine are selling rides in him, tracks them down and demands to go through the portal himself.[12] Entering his own portal does not lead to him becoming an inner observer of his own experiences, as we might expect. Instead, he becomes no less than a witness to the Cartesian self's self-absorption. He remains himself, but everyone in the world is turned into a version of him, and all language is reduced to the endless repetition of his name, "Malkovich." The film thereby dramatizes visually the self-enclosure attending the Cartesian self. To be such a self is to only have access to a world that has been reduced to a reflection of oneself, in which there is no escape from oneself.

This self-enclosure becomes Craig's fate in the film's denouement. Craig ends up in the body of Emily, the child of Maxine and a Lotte-driven Malkovich. There, he is reduced to a bodiless, impotent ghost, unable to influence Emily's behavior and without access to any experiences except those that filter in through her senses. His attempts at self-transcendence thus end in utter self-confinement. In the context of the film's plot, Craig ends up in Emily because he tries to reenter Malkovich too late, after Malkovich's crucial forty-fourth birthday (when he is no longer "ripe"). And yet, Kaufman seems to be hinting, this fate is not simply the result of Craig's poor timing or bad judgment but has to do with the nature of the self that is involved. Craig's situation with regard to Emily is essentially no different to his situation when he first enters Malkovich. The devices used to emphasise Craig's Cartesian distinctness, the vision-limiting cutout and muffled audio, merely become more pronounced with Emily. In each case Craig is reduced to being an inner observer. He may be able to influence Malkovich's actions, but even here he remains confined, reduced to an inward wish that somehow makes Malkovich's body move. There is no real escape from the Cartesian self.

If the Cartesian self's complicity in the failure of self-transcendence serves to call that understanding of the self into question, the film further questions this notion of the self because the experience of being a detached, inner self that it portrays is so manifestly at odds with everyday experience. What we are presented with—Craig's experience of standing behind and observing what is presented through Malkovich's (and eventually Emily's) eyes—is remote from the ordinary experience of seeing, where one seems directly present to the world; and formulating a wish that gets translated into Malkovich's bodily activity is far from our ordinary experience of actively engaging with the world. Descartes himself is aware that this is not how things are with us in our experience. As he notes in his *Meditations*, "I am not merely present in my body as a sailor is present in his ship."[13] He recognizes that in our actual experience, mind and body are less separate, more mingled, than his dualist account suggests they should be. But as Ott points out, it is difficult to see how he could offer any other picture, given this account.[14]

Not only does the Cartesian self leave one reduced to a ghostly inner self; from the point of view of this self, the body amounts to a form of exterior confinement, a "prison for the soul." Craig ends up trapped in a child's body. Kaufman's comedy thereby draws out the full tragedy of Craig's fate. His failure to escape himself is compounded because in his attempts to transcend his physical frame, he has come to be trapped in the very thing he sought to escape. But once again, Craig's situation at the end of the film is not essentially different from his situation when he first enters Malkovich.

Here also the body is imprisoning. Riding in Malkovich is like being forced to wear a mask or a confining helmet. There is a long history of such thinking about the body in philosophy, from Plato to Descartes and beyond, where the body is seen as shackling or weighing down the soul, and as something that we need to escape.[15] But it may be that we need to escape not only from this view of the self as something distinct from the body, but also from the conception of the body that corresponds to it. This view remains contrary to experience. Just as we do not ordinarily experience ourselves as radically separate from our bodies, the body as something imprisoning seems very much at odds with our ordinary experience.

Being Malkovich

So *Being John Malkovich* both makes use of a Cartesian notion of self as an avenue of self-transcendence and calls it into question, not least because this self turns out to involve a new kind of confinement. But the film also orients us toward an alternative conception of self. The theme of transcendence is not abandoned, but it becomes evident that genuinely escaping from ourselves is going to require moving beyond the Cartesian conception of the self, along with the body that corresponds to it, toward an embodied notion of self. In this, the film echoes philosophical efforts to escape Cartesianism from thinkers ranging from Dewey to Merleau-Ponty and Foucault. A common theme for these critics is that escaping from the Cartesian self requires a transformation in the categories of mind and body themselves. Merleau-Ponty, for example, argues that we are best understood neither as a disembodied consciousness nor as merely bodies, objects in the world; and furthermore, not as a combination of these two disparate things, which is Descartes' dualist position. Rather, as one commentator puts it, "Merleau-Ponty aims to establish how subjectivity—the complex property of being an interpreter and an agent of the world yet being within that world—depends on corporeality, that is, on being a body."[16] For Merleau-Ponty, far from taking a ride in my body, I "am" my body; the body is something that I "live." He arrives at this conception of the "lived body" through careful analysis of experience, the hallmark of his "phenomenological" approach. For him, the reflective construction of the human being as a combination of mind and body distorts a more fundamental experience of ourselves as integrated minds and bodies. His aim is to capture, within philosophical reflection, this more primordial unity. When we "return to our senses" we see that the body is not lived as a thing among other things, but experienced as a necessary condition for perceiving. It is the background, the point from which we observe.[17] Moreover, the body is the perspective from which we organize our perceptions. Rather than viewing the world from "nowhere," from a position of Godlike detachment, we are embodied perceivers. The body provides us with the ability to act, use objects in the world, change things there, respond to situations emotionally, and so on; and it is as active bodies, interacting with the world, that we find it intelligible as a forum for action.[18]

For both Merleau-Ponty and Dewey (though Dewey does not provide a phenomenological analysis), the body is itself organized around habits, patterns of behavior that are the present products of past experience. For Merleau-Ponty, in acquiring habits the body incorporates behaviors and indeed instruments into its structure, enlarging its capacities: "To get used to a hat, a car or a stick is to be transplanted into them, or conversely to incorporate them into the bulk of our own body."[19] Dewey also gives a central place to bodily habit, to habits of feeling, thinking, and acting that make us the selves we are. Habits "constitute a self . . . they form our effective desires and they furnish us with our working capacities."[20] In these terms he rejects a dualistic account of action, in which an inner will leads to an outward act. Rather, it is the existence of dispositions that gives acts their voluntary quality; it is only when we can perform an action that we can decide to do it: "the act must come before the thought, and habit before an ability to evoke the thought at will . . . failure to recognize the essential bond between will and habit only leads to a separation of mind from body."[21]

Being John Malkovich echoes this move beyond a Cartesian self toward an embodied conception of human being because this is the path that Craig himself takes. Initially, in Cartesian mode, he is merely taking a ride in Malkovich, and he remains clearly distinct from Malkovich's body, even when he learns to influence its behavior. But Craig goes beyond influencing Malkovich. He learns how to stay in Malkovich's body for as long as he wants, and from this point onward there is a distinct change in how he is presented in the film. In particular, the film no longer provides viewers with the internal point-of-view shot that denotes Craig's distinctness from Malkovich. As Scott Repass notes, what is essentially the disappearance of the person John Malkovich is represented visually in this way: "Once Craig takes control of Malkovich's body, we are no longer given constant access to the internal point-of-view shot. Craig is no longer simply riding in Malkovich; he has actually become Malkovich."[22]

Craig now seems to be much more than the "will behind the actions of the Malkovich vessel."[23] He seems to *be* Malkovich's body, to be incorporated into it while also transforming it, forming a new hybrid self in which mind and body are an integrated totality. Through his consummate mastery of Malkovich's body he is finally able both to impress Maxine and win her over and to achieve fame as a puppeteer; but this body is not merely an external instrument for realizing his desires and projects. To be a puppeteer is precisely not to operate the body like an internal puppeteer pulling the strings, but to acquire a complex set of skills and capacities that make it possible for one to perform the relevant actions. And a large part of our sense that Craig has become this body comes from the way Malkovich has acquired the bodily manner and capacities associated with Craig—his look, how he talks and carries himself, and his formidable puppeteering skills. For his part Craig clearly identifies with this body. When Craig-as-Malkovich watches a television documentary on his new career as a famous puppeteer, he says, "It's really good. I look really amazing," drawing no distinction between himself and Malkovich's body.[24]

Despite this, Craig-as-Malkovich is sometimes characterized in terms of the puppetry metaphor, or variations thereof. He explains to Maxine how he is able to stay in Malkovich's body by saying that it is a matter of "making friends with the Malkovich body," imagining it as a "really expensive suit" that he enjoys wearing rather than an enemy to be subordinated.[25] He then performs what he calls the "dance of disillusion and despair," which we saw him make a puppet perform in the film's opening scene. What he is doing now is evidently another form of puppetry, though as he points out triumphantly, "You see, Maxine, it isn't just playing with dolls." Maxine agrees: "My God, it's playing with people."[26] Yet the puppetry metaphor itself is surprisingly flexible. We can also see it as suggestive of a more embodied view of the self. The puppets themselves are never presented as things being manipulated, but appear infused with remarkable feeling and humanity—as if animated from within.[27] Indeed, they are explicitly characterized as more than just separate entities. When Craig-as-Malkovich is shown in the TV documentary teaching a master class in puppetry, he tells a student trying to make the puppet weep, "You yourself are not weeping. Until the puppet is an extension of you, it's just a novelty act."[28] This characterization of puppeteering recalls Merleau-Ponty's account of acquiring skill in the manipulation of instruments as a matter of "incorporating" them into the body, expanding its capacities. This in turn gives a different character to puppeteering as a metaphor for Craig's occupation of Malkovich. It no longer suggests a dualistic picture, which would reduce the human being to a "novelty act," but one where "being inside someone else's skin" implies a much more intimate arrangement.

But even if Craig can be seen as coming to be incarnated in Malkovich's body, he also eventually leaves. Lester and his geriatric friends, who have all been planning to occupy Malkovich on his crucial forty-fourth birthday, force him out. They kidnap Maxine to pressure Craig into relinquishing Malkovich. This is when unambiguously dualistic elements reappear in Craig's portrayal. As he is sitting in a bar deciding whether to leave Malkovich, Craig's internal point-of-view shot reappears, suggesting that he is starting to withdraw.[29] Kaufman's film thus seems to move between two fundamentally different views of the human being. The initial dualistic view of Craig as a mind able to take a ride in Malkovich's body gives way to the embodied conception of Craig-as-Malkovich; and then as Craig leaves Malkovich there is a return to the dualistic view, reinforced as Craig ultimately finds himself trapped within Emily. At one level this is an impossible combination of views. To be able to enter or leave Malkovich presupposes an essentially nonbodily self, but for the embodied notion of Craig-as-Malkovich, the body is a necessary part of oneself, and passing into or out of a body is impossible. Yet this is not necessarily a problem for the film. Rather than presenting a world in which the action is bounded by the particular theoretical perspective of Cartesian dualism, it offers one in which the perspective of Cartesian dualism is itself part of the action. The film is concerned with self-transcendence, and it shows that truly escaping ourselves requires escaping from the Cartesian conception of the self. It is because "philosophical-type" positions are themselves part of the action that the film can motivate the viewer to reflect on the Cartesian self and can echo various challenges to this self in philosophy itself.

Not Being Yourself

Yet escaping from entrapment within a Cartesian self is only a prerequisite for self-transcendence. The question of whether transcendence is possible now reappears in relation to the embodied self. Even in his extra-Cartesian, embodied form, Craig seems to be trapped within himself. He may have managed to wholly occupy Malkovich, but in another of Kaufman's many jokes at his expense, Craig only succeeds in turning Malkovich into a version of himself. Malkovich-as-Craig comes increasingly to resemble Craig, looking thinner and acquiring Craig's hairstyle, hesitant mannerisms, and depressed demeanor, along with his puppeteering skills. As David Ulin puts it, "Craig seeks to inhabit Malkovich because he thinks this will make him more like the actor—confident, desirable, cool. The joke's on him, though, for the opposite happens: Malkovich becomes like Craig."[30] Once again Craig remains Craig, but at the cost of his self-transcendence. Here the film touches on a more general problem concerning transcendence, which David L. Smith has identified as a recurring concern in Kaufman's films: can we *ever* change in a fundamental way, ever escape from ourselves, given that our choices and actions are determined by the kind of person we are, the repertoire of behaviors that constitute our identity? How can we change ourselves if we ourselves are doing the changing?[31]

Are we doomed, then, to self-entrapment, even if we manage to escape from the Cartesian self? Here it is useful to turn our attention to the other side of self-entrapment, to what is suppressed. Self-entrapment is bound up with the suppression of difference, the subordination of everything we think and do to the patterns of behavior that make us who we are. In other words, there is an element of power, of control, in this scenario. In *Being John Malkovich*, where escape from oneself continually turns into self-entrapment, this element of power is laid bare. As Jesse Fox Mayshark notes, in the film the search for transcendence becomes a search for control.[32] Craig's struggle for transcendence involves taking over Malkovich's body, hijacking and exploiting it. Kaufman himself has suggested that the film might be more aptly called *Using John Malkovich*.[33] Here, the ever-versatile puppetry metaphor takes on yet another meaning, as a metaphor for control or manipulation. Craig wants to turn Malkovich into a puppet in the sense of mastering him. At the same time, if we accept the idea that Craig becomes embodied in Malkovich, this mastery has a distinctive character. It does not involve objectifying Malkovich, reducing him to a thing or instrument, denying subjectivity to him. On the contrary, this mastery involves subjectification, giving a certain organization to Malkovich's body, turning him into a certain sort of subject. Only as a subject with particular capabilities is Malkovich useful for Craig's purposes. A complicating factor here is that while the film has Craig entering into Malkovich, eventually taking him over completely, an embodied notion of self, strictly speaking, precludes a literal transfer of Craig's mind into Malkovich's body (presupposing as that does a Cartesian notion of self). However, that process of transference might itself be more broadly interpreted as the transfer of habits and patterns of behavior to another body through various forms of training, through which it is turned into a usable kind of subject.

Clearly, the notion of a subjectifying form of mastery is bound up with an embodied conception of the self, of the sort that finds a significant formulation in Merleau-Ponty. It is Foucault, however, who is known for developing a notion of power as subjectifying; and there are affinities between Foucault and Merleau-Ponty in terms of their account of the human being. Foucault similarly wants to get rid of the Cartesian idea of self, the non-bodily "author-subject" behind the scenes, but without reducing the human being—or body—to an inert object. For Foucault we are embodied, active subjects, whose bodily capacities are at the center of our agency, making our activity possible. He shares Merleau-Ponty's stress on the body as that which situates us in the world, the standpoint from which we engage with the world. In particular, for Foucault Merleau-Ponty provides the important idea that knowers are "necessarily situated, because knowledge grows out of perception, which is the work of an embodied and therefore essentially situated perceiver."[34] However, in keeping with his phenomenological focus on experience, Merleau-Ponty approaches the question of knowledge from its basis in individual perception and ignores the social and historical aspects of being a situated body. More broadly, as Lawrence Hass points out, Merleau-Ponty's analysis lacks any sense of the body as part of a political field, subject to various forms of influence and coercion through cultural systems and norms that shape the body and its forms of experience. Foucault's work arguably provides this missing dimension.[35]

It is precisely because we are embodied beings, situated in the world, rather than Cartesian selves distinct from the body, that social power, investing itself materially in bodies through forms of training and discipline, can turn us into certain kinds of subjects. It does so by inculcating particular habits, rewarding behavioral dispositions, and supporting certain ways of acting. The idea that the body is organized around habits, prominent in Merleau-Ponty and also Dewey, reappears in Foucault. C. G. Prado has highlighted striking parallels between Foucault and Dewey in this regard. Prado cites Dewey's view that "habits . . . constitute the self." It is the continuing operation of habits that give us a character; and the "basic characteristic of habit is that every experience enacted and undergone modifies the one who acts and undergoes [it]," so that it is a somewhat different person that has subsequent experiences.[36] And as Prado notes, this is exactly Foucault's understanding of subject formation. That is, "governed actions instill habits, and habits cumulatively make subjects."[37] Foucault's talk of power "creating" subjects becomes intelligible in these terms.

The idea of self-formation as the inculcation of habits, prominent in Foucault's account, provides a way of expanding the meaning of what the film presents. Craig's literal entry into and takeover of Malkovich, through which Malkovich is turned into a certain sort of subject, can be interpreted more broadly as a matter of Craig's imparting certain behavioral disposi- tions, habits, and skills to Malkovich through forms of training. The film itself acknowledges that the puppeteering so central to Craig's identity is a complex set of bodily skills that in reality needs to be imparted through train- ing and discipline. In the TV documentary we see Craig-as-Malkovich, the master puppeteer, training others to become puppeteers. This is the process that has been telescoped in Craig's own case into his literal entry into and takeover of Malkovich. We thus have a new way of viewing that occupation, as a shorthand version of the process of subjectification through training and habit-inculcation; and that occupation consequently provides a prism through which to reflect more generally on the process of subjectification.

The first thing to notice is that there is nothing in the training of others, to be puppeteers or whatever, that automatically entails their subordina- tion, or the suppression of difference. In general, imparting skills through socialization, education, and training is the everyday process through which the social world shapes individuals and habituates them, making it possible for them to emerge as coherent subjects, able to function with a reasonable degree of competency. Such training is not oppressive in itself. The problem arises, however, if the body receives all of its form or character from external forces, if it merely reproduces existing cultural forms; and if any behavior that transcends these forms, or is able to challenge the external forces, is precluded. This amounts to what Foucault characterizes as a state of domi- nation, where individuals are reduced to a function of social requirements. Here, to employ Foucault's inversion of the traditional formula, the "soul is the prison of the body."[38] The corresponding situation in the film is the complete subordination of Malkovich's body to patterns of behavior that Craig imposes and the disappearance of Malkovich as a distinct person. In both cases the suppression of everything representing difference comes at the cost of entrapment. For Foucault, those subject to states of domination simply reproduce existing social forms, and social relations become "repeti- tious, inert and self-reproducing."[39] In the film, Craig seeks to escape himself by taking over Malkovich, but because any difference Malkovich might represent is suppressed, he ends up merely repeating or reproducing himself.

Here, the general question of how change is ever possible can once again be posed. How can we ever escape ourselves, if all our choices and acts are determined by the kind of people we are, the habits of thought and action that constitute our identity? In the film, since everything that Malkovich does is determined by Craig, how can Craig do anything but perpetuate himself through Malkovich? In terms of Foucault's account, if we are the product of socially imposed forms that determine our very subjectivity, how can we ever escape these forms? Aren't we condemned to entrapment and repetition?

But such entrapment is not a foregone conclusion. As noted, education and training do not automatically entail subordination. To suppose so presupposes that the individual is essentially passive and yielding, a blank slate that can be imprinted by dominating social forces. But there is every reason to suppose that one is dealing with a material that is intrinsically active and resistant. The long work of socialization, training, and discipline would be unnecessary if one were simply passive and yielding. The very idea of subordination becomes meaningless if there is no resistance to overcome. A better model would be that of a dynamic interplay between body and culture. Individuals may be shaped by and express themselves through socially imposed forms of selfhood, but their training also presupposes an active being, with various capacities for action that are able to be developed, organized, and enhanced. That process of development involves getting individuals to incorporate forms of behavior though repetition and application, and they are always capable of challenging those forms and modifying them in turn. Even if a state of subordination happens to be established, there is always the possibility that it will be resisted and challenged. And in this context, resistance consists precisely in striving to not be oneself, contesting imposed forms of selfhood, and experimenting with different ways of being. In other words, it involves self-transcendence. Moreover, as Craig discovers in the film, to participate in the subordination of others also carries with it the danger of falling into entrapment and repetition under the domination of a single standpoint. However, one may also resist this entrapment indirectly, by reforming one's attitude to that which is different, being open to alternative standpoints that challenge prevailing ways of doing things and that raise the possibility of doing those things differently.

Although the film focuses on the male protagonist whose participation in the subordination of others ensures his failure to escape himself, it also points to this indirect means of escaping confinement in the figure of Craig's wife, Lotte. Initially at least, Lotte pursues a course much like her husband's. Confined to a domestic role in a loveless marriage, frustrated and restless, she seizes the opportunity to go through the portal and take the ride in Malkovich. Like Craig, she finds that she can control the Malkovich body, and uses Malkovich to have sex with Maxine. Unlike Craig, however, she does not seek to turn Malkovich into an embodied Lotte-subject, to subordinate him and reduce him to a version of herself. Rather, she finds in the experience of being in Malkovich the possibility of a different way of being, a different standpoint on the world—a distinctively male one. Here the difference that Malkovich represents is acknowledged; and in the light of this experience of an alternative way of being, Lotte wants to change her own. Initially Lotte construes this self-transformation as a matter of self-discovery and self-actualization. She thinks that in Malkovich she has found herself at last ("For the first time everything felt just right") and decides that she is going to consult Dr. Feldman (her allergist) about sexual reassignment surgery. When Craig protests, she says, "Don't stand in the way of my actualization as a man."[40] But this transformation is less about discovering and actualizing an essential, underlying male identity than it is about escaping who she is by trying out different possible ways of being. Lotte abandons the idea that she is "really a man"; she does not go through with the idea of turning herself into one. Instead, she reinvents herself as a lesbian.

Such self-transcendence remains a transformation of oneself as an embodied self.[41] It is possible to the extent that the self one happens to be, the particular way the body is organized, the standpoint from which we engage with the world, does not exhaust our possibilities. Self-transcendence involves a readiness to not be oneself, to experiment with forms of thinking and being that go beyond what is consistent with one's current notion of personal identity. For Foucault this is the work of "detaching oneself from oneself" that he identifies with freedom and that he contrasts with the idea that we have an essential identity that determines and limits in advance what we can legitimately be.[42] Freedom as self-detachment is facilitated if we don't insist on subordinating everything we encounter to our existing standpoint, if we recognize alternative ways of being and acting. These alternatives in turn highlight the specific character of our own standpoint and encourage exploration of different possibilities for ourselves. Lotte, through openness to the different way of being that Malkovich represents, achieves the self-transcendence that is denied to Craig—or that Craig denies himself. Her encounter with Malkovich is a transformative experience, whereas Craig's efforts to master Malkovich only result in self-confinement.

In the end Lotte not only achieves self-transcendence but also "gets the girl," ending up with Maxine in a cunning subversion of the traditional Hollywood ending. Maxine, having tired of Craig, and pregnant with Emily, is all too ready to take up with Lotte. Maxine herself does not participate in the various struggles for self-transcendence that drive the film. As a character she is complete, self-assured, and autonomous. She has no desire to escape from herself and is interested in the portal to Malkovich only as a moneymaking opportunity. She does enter the portal once, but only in order to escape from Lester after he has taken her prisoner. Nonetheless she plays a pivotal role in the film; she is the point around which the film's events turn, the femme fatale who tempts both Craig and Lotte.[43] Craig's path remains one of abject failure. He both fails to attain the object of his desire and fails to escape from himself. In the end, he cannot even escape the Cartesian self. He ends up an impotent ghost imprisoned within a little girl's body. Kaufman's masterful final scene sums up the situation.[44] Seven years after the film's main events we see Lotte, having achieved self-transformation, sitting happily with Maxine, the girl of her dreams, with Emily looking on. Craig, utterly trapped, looks on helplessly through Emily's eyes, unable even to turn away.

Notes

I would like to thank David LaRocca for his very helpful comments and suggestions on an earlier draft of this essay.

1. Charlie Kaufman, *Being John Malkovich*, directed by Spike Jonze (1999); 00:32:08–00:32:44.

2. As pointed out in the introduction to this volume, although his screenplays were directed by a number of different directors—*Human Nature* (Michel Gondry, 2001), *Adaptation* (Spike Jonze, 2002), and *Eternal Sunshine of the Spotless Mind* (Gondry, 2004)—Charlie Kaufman and his distinctive voice have come to be recognized, and it has become appropriate to refer to a film he has written as a "Charlie Kaufman film."

3. Kaufman himself has said, "I don't think my characters are a joke. I take them seriously. And no matter how outlandish or weird their situation, their situation is real and a little tragic." Michael Sragow, "Being Charlie Kaufman" (interview), *Salon*, November 11, 1999 (salon.com).

4. Murray Smith, "Consciousness," in *The Routledge Companion to Film and Philosophy*, ed. Paisley Livingston and Carl Plantinga (London: Routledge, 2009), 46.

5. Walter Ott, "It's My *Heeeeaaaad*! Sex and Death in *Being John Malkovich*," in

Movies and the Meaning of Life: Philosophers Take on Hollywood, ed. Kimberley Blessing and Paul A. Tudico (Chicago: Open Court 2005), 63.

6. *Being John Malkovich*, 01:01:16.

7. A theme noted by Jesse Fox Mayshark, *Post-Pop Cinema: The Search for Meaning in New American Film* (Westport CT: Praeger, 2007), 142.

8. *Being John Malkovich*, 00:23:52–00:24:04.

9. These images of confinement are noted by Ott, "It's My *Heeeeaaaad!*" 61–62; and also Colm O'Shea, "Out of His Head: Metaphysical Escape Attempts in the Screenplays of Charlie Kaufman," *Bright Lights Film Journal*, February 2009 (brightlightsfilm.com).

10. On the desire to escape physical limitations in the film, see, for example, Daniel Shaw, "On Being Philosophical and *Being John Malkovich*," in *Thinking through Cinema: Film as Philosophy*, ed. Murray Smith and Thomas Wartenberg (New York: Blackwell, 2006), 114; and William Young, "Otherwise than *Being John Malkovich*: Incarnating the Name of God," *Literature and Theology* 18, no. 1 (2004): 98.

11. It is not in fact surprising that the Cartesian self should be involved with this form of self-transcendence. In his *Meditations*, Descartes himself arrives at his conception of the self through a process of escaping from one's physical frame. In his version, the mode of escape is not a quasi-technological portal but a more spiritual technology, the meditative therapy of systematic doubt. By rejecting any beliefs about the world that might be mistaken, he is in effect withdrawing mentally from involvement in the things around him, even his own body. All these things may not exist. Certain only of his own existence as a thinker completely separate from involvement in the world, Descartes moves quickly to the conclusion that his essential self is to be identified only with his mind. By the end of the *Meditations*, this mind has, as it were, made the passage into a new body. Descartes now reformulates the human being in dualistic terms, with the body now understood as an external thing attached to the mind, and the mind as distinct from any physical or bodily existence.

12. *Being John Malkovich*, 01:06:52–01:08:00.

13. René Descartes, *Meditations on First Philosophy: with Selections from the Objections and Replies*, 2nd ed., ed. John Cottingham (Cambridge: Cambridge University Press, 1996), 56.

14. In addition to the Cartesian mind's detachment from the body, one is also alienated from others, who are also minds separate from their body. The presence of their mind can only be inferred from the physical body we see before us. Once again this seems a distorted view of what it is to have a body. Rather than saying that one encounters a body and infers a mind, one would ordinarily say that one simply encounters a person. As Ott puts it: "any view that turns your best friend in to the object of an inference, however well-founded, is one that no one but a philosopher could take seriously" (Ott, "It's My *Heeeeaaaad!*" 69).

15. See Hubert Dreyfus, *On the Internet*, 2nd ed. (London: Routledge, 2009), 4.

16. Kevin S. Decker, "Knockout! Killer's Kiss, the Somatic, and Kubrick," in *The*

Philosophy of Stanley Kubrick, ed. Jerold Abrams (Lexington: University Press of Kentucky, 2007), 97.

17. As Merleau-Ponty notes, far from being an object external to me, like a tree that I can turn away from, it is the object that never leaves me. See Maurice Merleau-Ponty, *Phenomenology of Perception*, trans. Colin Smith (London: Routledge and Kegan Paul, 1962), 150.

18. See Lawrence Hass, *Merleau-Ponty's Philosophy* (Bloomington: Indiana University Press, 2008), 83–85.

19. Merleau-Ponty, *Phenomenology of Perception*, 145. See also Hass, *Merleau-Ponty's Philosophy*, 87–88, 90–91.

20. John Dewey, *Human Nature and Conduct*, cited in Richard Shusterman, *Body Consciousness: A Philosophy of Mindfulness and Somaesthetics* (Cambridge: Cambridge University Press, 2008), 190. For a discussion of parallels between Merleau-Ponty and Dewey, especially in connection with the notion of habit, see Victor Kestenbaum, *The Phenomenological Sense of John Dewey: Habit and Meaning* (Atlantic Highlands, NJ: Humanities Press, 1977).

21. John Dewey, *Human Nature and Conduct*, cited in Shusterman, *Body Consciousness*, 194. As contemporary pragmatist Shannon Sullivan argues, habits are what constitutes the body as a self. Before acquiring habits through our transaction with our environment, a self does not exist. From the start our "bodying" is organized by habit, and it is thus habit that provides us with "will and agency." See Shannon Sullivan, *Living across and through Skins: Transactional Bodies, Pragmatism, and Feminism* (Bloomington: Indiana University Press, 2001), 31.

22. Scott Repass, untitled review of *Being John Malkovich*, *Film Quarterly* 56, no. 1 (2002): 35.

23. As Shaw characterizes him; see Shaw, "On Being Philosophical," 115.

24. *Being John Malkovich*, 01:26:17. This is pointed out by Joshua McDonald, "*Being John Malkovich* and Claims of Body Ownership," *The California Undergraduate Philosophy Review* 1, no. 1: 5 (csufresno.edu).

25. *Being John Malkovich*, 01:18:04–01:18:21.

26. Ibid., 01:19:44–01:21:38.

27. Repass, untitled review, 31. As Repass notes, the puppets almost become characters themselves, which is emphasized cinematographically by presenting the puppets in extreme close-up, often with only the puppet-theater sets in the background, so that they appear in scale with their surroundings.

28. *Being John Malkovich*, 01:26:40–01:26:56.

29. Ibid., 01:36:35.

30. David S. Ulin, "Why Charlie Kaufman Is Us," *Los Angeles Times*, May 14, 2006 (latimes.com).

31. See David L. Smith, "*Eternal Sunshine of the Spotless Mind* and the Question of Transcendence," *Journal of Religion and Film* 9, no. 1 (2005): 2 (unomaha.edu/jrf).

32. Mayshark, *Post-Pop Cinema*, 143.

33. Interview on BeingCharlieKaufman.com, originally posted in 2000. Cited by Shaw, "On Being Philosophical," 115.

34. Hubert Dreyfus and Paul Rabinow, *Michel Foucault: Beyond Structuralism and Hermeneutics*, 2nd ed. (Chicago: University of Chicago Press, 1983), 166.

35. See Hass, *Merleau-Ponty's Philosophy*, 93.

36. John Dewey, "Experience and Education," cited in C. G. Prado, "Foucault, Davidson, and Interpretation," in *Foucault and Philosophy*, ed. Timothy O'Leary and Christopher Falzon (Oxford: Blackwell, 2010), 111.

37. Prado, "Foucault, Davidson, and Interpretation," 111.

38. Michel Foucault, *Discipline and Punish*, trans. Alan Sheridan (Harmondsworth: Penguin, 1977), 30.

39. Michel Foucault, *The History of Sexuality*, vol. 1, trans. Robert Hurley (Harmondsworth: Penguin, 1978), 93.

40. *Being John Malkovich*, 00:40:43–00:41:49.

41. It is worth stressing that this is a thoroughly this-worldly transcendence, a matter of Lotte's changing herself as an embodied, sexual being. Her experience of being in Malkovich certainly has mystical-religious overtones, but these remain colored by a decidedly this-worldly eroticism. As Christopher Hyde notes, "after her second ride in Malkovich (and her first sexual encounter with Maxine), she lands alongside the Turnpike and lies looking upward, serene and enchanted, in ecstasy"; and we are reminded of Baroque representations of ecstatic visions, like Bernini's St. Teresa, where the ecstatic vision is also more than a little suggestive of the erotic. See Christopher Hyde, "The Inconceivable Universe: The Borgesian Neobaroque in Charlie Kaufman's *Being John Malkovich*," *Barroco* 3, no. 3 (Fall 2009) (revistabarroco.com).

42. Foucault identifies freedom with the capacity to detach oneself from oneself, to no longer be ourselves, at a number of points, e.g., in "What Is Enlightenment?" in *The Foucault Reader*, ed. Paul Rabinow (New York, Pantheon 1984), 46.

43. Here also standard Hollywood formulas are challenged, for Maxine, the seductive femme fatale, does not get punished; she ends up living happily ever after. See Mayshark, *Post-Pop Cinema*, 144.

44. *Being John Malkovich*, 01:41:18–01:42:06.

THE DIVIDED SELF

Kaufman, Kafka, Wittgenstein, and *Human Nature*

MARIO VON DER RUHR

When Charlie Kaufman's *Human Nature* was released in 2001, it met with a mixed response, not only from those who had previously applauded *Being John Malkovich* and were curious about Kaufman's next project, but also from professional film critics, whom the movie connoisseur rightly expects to contribute more than a shrug of the shoulder, or observations too cursory or incidental to deepen their (critical) appreciation of it—unless, of course, it is the kind of movie that invites comparison to a cheap, off-the-peg suit: just about adequate for an evening's entertainment in town, but otherwise unremarkable and not worth talking about. What saves *Human Nature* from an unflattering verdict, it seems to me, is not so much what its critics have to say about it—indeed, they often say disappointingly little—as the complex tapestry of autobiographical, literary, popular scientific, and philosophical considerations that inform Kaufman's exploration of the movie's subject matter.

Some of these, including the autobiographical and literary influences, provide useful background information for a better understanding of the movie, and should be noted for the record. The remainder, especially some of the movie characters' philosophical assumptions about the nature of language, love, and evolutionary biology, invite further critical reflection and are worth highlighting for this very reason. That the screenplay is the product of such a diverse range of intellectual stimuli and influences is not always apparent, however; nor do descriptions of the movie as "an acquired taste," "uniquely offbeat," "a dash of the avant-garde fused with humour," or "a crazed, joyous romp" do much to show why its appeal to potential audiences should be greater than that of, say, a tub of popcorn.[1] Roger Ebert, too, finds that "the movie has nowhere much to go and nothing much to prove," indeed that if "it tried to do more, it would fail and perhaps explode," though he is happy to concede that "at this level of manic whimsy it is just about right."[2] Ebert's final verdict on *Human Nature* is that it is "slight without being negligible," as it raises interesting questions about the relation between natural human impulses and the "inhibitions" of civilization, though he does not elaborate on how exactly the movie illuminates that relation.[3] And Kaufman himself? He certainly agrees that there is a sense in which his movie really does have "nowhere much to go," openly admitting, "I don't know where the characters are going to go or what the screenplay's going to do. For me, that's the way to keep it alive and make it interesting and worthwhile."[4] This does not mean, however, that he is merely experimenting with a set of strange characters placed in slightly surreal scenarios. It is rather that his creative endeavors are not driven by an ideological agenda, let alone a *theory* about any of the phenomena explored in his work. "I don't subscribe to anything," he once said in an interview. "I sit there and I try to think about what seems honest to me."[5] While Kaufman does have something to say to his audience, he is reluctant to pander to the prejudices of social convention, cinematographic fads, or the parameters of scholarly theory. Instead, his mission is to embark on an imaginative quest for new perspectives and ways of looking at the familiar, no matter what fashionable -isms or -esques his viewers may subsequently choose in characterizing his work. And when, in this connection, critics such as Warren Curry remark on "the absurd, somewhat esoteric, elements of the script," they are unwittingly highlighting Kaufman's own conviction that the terms *real* and *surreal*, far from expressing a sharp dichotomy, may actually condition each other in a way that deepens, rather than obscures, our relation to the phenomena or experiences in question.[6] As Kaufman puts it: "Realistic and naturalistic are not the same thing. And I think it's interesting to play with surrealism or dream logic and try to create a poem, a metaphor, something that conveys a feeling or makes something happen in your gut that you don't necessarily intellectually understand."[7] On this account, *Human Nature*, too, is much more akin to a metaphor than it is to a conventionally naturalistic depiction of, say, a human relationship, an individual's attitude toward his natural impulses, or a scientist's conception of animals. And this much is surely right: the power of a (good) metaphor or poem lies precisely in its capacity to move, even to yield insight, in a way that is not translatable into a series of mundane factual statements or captured by hypotheses deduced from some highfalutin theoretical framework—into something, in other words, that belongs predominantly in the domain of reason, rather than feeling.

Regardless of whether *Human Nature* succeeds in providing such insight, one merely needs to think of poetry, music, painting, and sculpture to appreciate Kaufman's skepticism about rational deliberation as the only, or even the most reliable, avenue to understanding the human predicament. Indeed, one recurring motif in *Human Nature*, revealed in the transient affections and loyalties of its main characters, is that the very experiences that affect an individual most deeply, including those of love, sexuality, and loss of trust, also seem to be the most resilient to rational explanation and resolution. (I shall return to this theme later.) As for the role of art in human life, Kaufman would no doubt have applauded the Austrian philosopher Ludwig Wittgenstein, who rightly observed: "People nowadays think scientists are there to instruct them, poets, musicians etc. to entertain them. That the latter have something to *teach* them; that never occurs to them."[8] For readers unfamiliar with the movie, it should be pointed out that Wittgenstein receives an honorary mention in it toward the end, when Nathan (Tim Robbins) comments on the apish grunts ("Ugnh") of his formerly more civilized apprentice, Puff (Rhys Ifans): "Oh please, is that as articulate as you can be after all the time I spent teaching you? We've discussed Wittgenstein, for God's sake. Not that you ever had anything enlightening to say on the subject."[9] As such, Nathan's cryptic reference to Wittgenstein doesn't contribute much to the development of the plot, but then Kaufman can hardly be expected to abandon his own artistic vision for an ad hoc emulation of Louis Malle's *My Dinner with André* (1981) merely because one of his characters has just mentioned the name of a European philosopher.

What, then, is the point of this name-dropping? Is it decorative verbal confetti that had better be cut from the script? Kaufman's hint at his characters' inability to speak with any depth about this thinker? An ironic revelation of Kaufman's own cursory reading of Wittgenstein? Or clever signposts for those who, like Kaufman, are deeply puzzled by the movie's central themes and want to dig deeper than the constraints of the story line and a ninety-minute time frame will allow? The film itself does not tell us which, if any, of these readings comes closest to the truth, but it confronts the audience with an important question: Which of them would make *Human Nature* the more interesting movie?

Autobiographical Aspects

While it is true that *Human Nature* is, among other things, "a study of three characters in war against their sexual natures," it is also a reflection on the phenomenon of love more generally and a critical response to the standard depictions of love relationships in mainstream American cinema.[10] That reflection, as Kaufman candidly admits in an interview, is ultimately rooted in a series of intensely personal experiences: "I thought, shit, I'll write a small movie and it'll be about love, because I was falling in love at the time [with actress Mercedes Ruehl], and I wanted to celebrate that and at the same time look at relationships realistically."[11] A realistic portrayal of human relationships, Kaufman believes, must eschew the kind of romanticization and idealization that is being propagated by mainstream Hollywood cinema: "I think that people have expectations of themselves and other people that are based on these fictions that are presented to them as the way human life and relationships could be, in some sort of weird, ideal world, but they never are. So you're constantly being shown this garbage and you can't get there."[12]

There are two ways of taking this criticism: one plausible, the other seriously misguided. If Kaufman's point is that most movies about human relationships tend to disseminate illusions about what it really means to be in love, that they draw an oversimplified picture of the experience and seem oblivious to the difficulties surrounding a life à deux, then it is well taken. If, on the other hand, his criticism is directed against the portrayal of characters who transcend themselves and their natural proclivities in the direction of a particular ideal, whether of love, friendship, heroism, or self-effacement, then it misses its target, since artists such as dramatists and playwrights—unlike sociologists, historians, or journalists—may well be guided by a vision of life in which human actions are both contrasted with, and measured against, such ideals. Indeed, if Wittgenstein's comment on the edifying nature of art is even partly true, a certain kind of idealization in art may not only be acceptable, but positively required, at least insofar as the artist has anything of interest to say to his or her audience.

Returning to the autobiographical dimension of Kaufman's *Human Nature*, two further considerations should be mentioned. One concerns Lila (Patricia Arquette), who is depicted in the movie as an attractive female whose physical beauty is nevertheless marred by excessive body hair, evoking images of apes or chimpanzees. The medical term for this well-documented condition is *idiopathic hypertrichosis*; it was first diagnosed in the seventeenth century and is a rare affliction, with fewer than a hundred cases reported to date. Like Lila in *Human Nature*, some of the afflicted chose to travel around the country as part of a circus act, under such names as "Jo-Jo the Dog-Faced Boy," "Lionel the Lion-Faced Man," "Jesus the Wolf-Man," and "Annie the Bearded Woman."[13] As Kaufman explains, his own knowledge of these so-called feral people was not merely gleaned from books, but was also based on personal experience: "I was taken there by the subject matter. Y'know, these are very dark and despairing issues. Without going into too much personal detail, I was immersed the last few years in lots of sadness, some of it involving an actual feral person. And there's nothing funny about it. I wasn't going to mock it or diminish it by playing it for laughs."[14]

It is perhaps not surprising that this encounter, together with Kaufman's interest in behavioral psychology and his critical attitude toward the relentless conditioning of animals for the purposes of scientific experiment or human amusement, should have resulted in his writing a screenplay in which the juxtaposition of human nature and animal instinct is a central theme.

Equally pertinent in this context is the influence of Franz Kafka's short story *A Report to an Academy*, which, probably unbeknownst to most viewers of the film, provides *Human Nature* with a narrative frame for the presentation and portrayal of its central characters—Lila, Nathan, Puff, and Gabrielle (Miranda Otto)—and the uniformly fragile relationships into which they are driven. By paying homage to Kafka and concealing the gesture to all but the cognoscenti, Kaufman is adding yet another layer of meaning to his already richly metaphorical project, and invites us to explore connections, not only between his own and Kafka's interests in the ape motif, but between various features of Kafka's biography and their fictional analogues in some of Kaufman's screen characters.

Kafka's *A Report to an Academy*

Kafka's short story about a humanized performing ape who has been summoned by a learned academy to deliver a detailed report on the life he was leading before his capture and forcible adaptation to the ways of civilized society was first published in Martin Buber's journal *The Jew* in 1917, and was subsequently included in the collection of Kafka's short stories entitled *A Country Doctor*. Like Kaufman's screenplay, Kafka's story was partly influenced by personal experience, including a visit Kafka had made to a variety show in Prague. As Kafka's translator Stanley Corngold explains:

"Kafka very likely knew of the vaudeville act titled 'Peter, the Human Ape,' which opened at the Ronacher Theater in Vienna in December 1908. Advertisements claimed that Peter acted 'just like a human being, has better table manners than most people, and behaves so well that even more highly evolved creatures would do well to model themselves on him.' He smoked, drank, ate on stage, pedaled a bicycle, and rode a horse."[15]

In Kafka's story, which combines satirical comment on the civilizing process with somber reflection on the vicissitudes of cultural assimilation, the ape from the Viennese vaudeville act reappears as "Red Peter" (alluding to a wound the fictional ape sustained on his cheek during his capture), and the training process itself is seen as an elaborate metaphor of subjugation, conditioning, transformation, and loss of identity. Not surprisingly, Kafka thought such behavior toward animals condescending and indefensible. Unable to see them as anything other than his fellow creatures, he lived as a strict vegetarian and was able to confront even fish without a guilty conscience. Kafka's friend and editor Max Brod tells the story of how they were both visiting an aquarium in Berlin and how Kafka, gazing at the fish in their illuminated tanks, started talking to them: "Now at last I can look at you in peace, I don't eat you anymore."[16] Like Lila in Kaufman's *Human Nature*, whose life is virtually saved by the look of a mouse ("The way that mouse looked at me. It didn't care if I had hair all over my body. I was just what I was. I felt so free")[17] and the realization that "animals have eyes that don't judge,"[18] Kafka was drawn to the animal world precisely because it signified a realm in which, for once, he was not being scrutinized or evaluated.

Kafka once confessed, "I have never been under the pressure of any responsibility but that imposed on me by the existence, the gaze, the judgment of other people."[19] This statement may sound odd, for why should Kafka have felt apprehensive about such judgment, indeed unnerved by the mere *existence* of other people? And yet he often found their presence hard to bear, even when they were members of his own family: "I cannot live with people; I absolutely hate all my relatives, not because they are my relatives, not because they are wicked, but simply because they are the people with whom I live in close proximity."[20] There was a taciturnity about Kafka's being that invariably made social intercourse an ordeal, prompting him to retreat or withdraw.[21] In *Letters to Felice*, he recalls a typical episode: "Wasted another evening with various people. I bit my lips to stop my attention from wandering, yet in spite of all my efforts I wasn't there at all, but was definitely nowhere else, either; so perhaps I didn't exist at all during those two hours? That must be it, for my presence would have been more convincing had I been asleep in my chair."[22] At first glance, Kafka's demeanor appears excessive and irrational, but as Elias Canetti has pointed out in his superb analysis of Kafka's *Letters to Felice*, one must remember that Kafka's self-image was tainted by all manner of insecurities about his physical appearance and bodily constitution.[23] "It is certain," he confided to his diary on November 22, 1911, "that a major obstacle to my progress is my physical condition. Nothing can be accomplished with such a body."[24] Thinking of himself as "the thinnest person I know (and that's saying something, for I am no stranger to sanatoria)," he felt particularly embarrassed about exposing his physique in public; in a letter to Felice Bauer, he wrote: "What was it like at the mixed baths? Alas, this is where I have to suppress a remark (it refers to my appearance in the bath, my thinness). In the bath I look like an orphan."[25]

But outer appearance was not the only aspect of his corporeality that troubled Kafka. In addition, he was constantly worrying about the function of particular organs, became a hypochondriac, and was plagued by insomnia—ills that he sought to remedy by embarking on a rigid regimen of physical exercises: leaping up and down the staircase, swimming, taking extended walks in the country, and working out naked in front of an open window; fresh air became for him the sine qua non of a healthy constitution.[26] Moreover, and as Kafka himself realized, his commitment to writing—the only conceivable way out of his existential predicament, as it were—entailed a wholesale renunciation of other goods, both physical and intellectual:

> When it became clear in my organism that writing was the most productive direction for my being to take, everything rushed in that direction and left empty all those abilities which were directed towards the joys of sex, eating, drinking, philosophical reflection, and above all music. I atrophied in all these directions. This was necessary because the totality of my strengths was so slight that only collectively could they even half-way serve the purpose of my writing.[27]

Kafka's admission that he "atrophied" in relation to his sexuality is, of course, an understatement, as his protracted aversion to sexual intimacy—he saw it as "punishment for the happiness of being together"—took a long time to overcome.[28] Not surprisingly, his relationship with Felice Bauer, too, became increasingly more complicated and eventually, as far as he was concerned, impossible to sustain. In spite of an official engagement in July 1917, the relationship, which Elias Canetti has aptly described as "the story of a five-year-long withdrawal," came to an end in the fall of 1917, when Kafka realized that he had no feelings left for her.[29] Such erosions of affection are tragic, not only because the existence of feelings eludes the control of the will, but because love without feeling seems to be merely an attenuated form of love: genuine concern about the other's welfare, maybe, but not *need* of the other, where this need is understood to be in quite a different category from the "need" for a walk, a cigarette, a can of beer, or even sexual pleasure.

In order to forestall possible misunderstanding, I should say that this sketch of Kafka's biography is not intended to show that the human relationships depicted in *Human Nature* are Kaufman's deliberate and creative variations on the theme of Kafka's personal life. The movie is not about Kafka, after all, but focused on the nature and complexity of human relationships, and it would be stretching credulity to claim otherwise. What does make Kaufman's allusion to Kafka such a valuable interpretive tool, however, is that it invites the moviegoer to explore not merely the structural analogies between *Human Nature* and *A Report to an Academy*, but the ways in which the tragedy surrounding Kafka's relationship to Felice illustrates Kaufman's own puzzles about the nature of love, sexual desire, and unconditional commitment to another. It is only to be expected that, in articulating these puzzles, *Human Nature* does not blandly reproduce, but merely gestures toward, Kafka's work and biography.

In Kaufman's screenplay, for example, the relation between Nathan and Lila assumes a tragicomic tone, and the narrative scaffolding of Kafka's short story (ape becomes man) is inverted to one in which a man is first raised *as* an ape, then turned (by Nathan) into a civilized man, and then reversed again, as Puff is reconditioned (by Lila) to return to the primitiveness of his former life, only to finally rejoin civilization, testify before a learned academy, and become a public celebrity. Now all this—Kaufman's allusion to Kafka, the shared narrative frame of an "ape's" report to an academy, the shared motif of existential angst seeking rescue and relief in writing, the authors' use of the animal world as a metaphor of moral innocence and unconditional acceptance—may be interesting enough, but it does not yet go to the heart of the matter, which is the absurdity of the narrative frame itself and the implications of this absurdity for what Kaufman's screen characters say about their relation to both the animal world and civilized society. For even though Lila, Nathan, and Puff offer some valuable insights into that relation, they also make claims that on close inspection turn out to be either false or conceptually confused; and it is these confusions for which Kafka's "Report to an Academy" provides a forceful corrective.[30] To begin with, and as Kafka's narration makes clear, the Academy's request for Red Peter's report on his life *before* his entry into civilization is in reality a contradiction in terms: a *report* involves conceptualization, linguistic ability (a report on the intensity of a toothache, for example, would require one to say such things as "It is excruciating," "It is stronger today than it was yesterday, but not quite as bad as it was on Monday," "Much better, " or "It is nearly gone"), and hence a level of awareness missing from the narrator's life as an ape. As Kafka's protagonist puts it: "Naturally, today I can use human words only to sketch my apish feelings of the time, and so I misstate them; but even if I cannot arrive at the old apish truth, my recital at least leans in that direction, there can be no doubt."[31] Paradoxically, then, the very abilities that the learned academy is taking for granted in inviting the narrator to deliver a report about his prelinguistic state also reduce the request for such a report *ad absurdum*.[32] The deeper significance of this absurdity lies in the realization that, contrary to a common view, the difference between animals and humans is not a matter of degree, but one of kind—as radical, in fact, as the rift between Red Peter's simian existence and his subsequent life as a human(-ized) being. Friedrich Nietzsche put the point as follows:

> Consider the herd grazing before you. These animals do not know what yesterday and today are but leap about, eat, rest, digest and leap again; and so from morning to night and from day to day, only briefly concerned with their own pleasure and displeasure, enthralled by the moment and for that reason neither melancholy nor bored. It is hard for a man to see this, for he is proud of being human and not an animal and yet he regards its happiness with envy because he wants nothing other than to live like this animal, neither bored nor in pain, yet wants it in vain because he does not want it like the animal.[33]

What Nietzsche says here might seem hasty, for while it may be granted that afflictions like melancholia or severe depression, say, are wrongly ascribed to animals (only in fairy tales and cartoons does the idea of a cow for whom life has become problematic or pointless make any sense) it seems plainly false to suggest that dogs, for example, cannot get bored.[34] Indeed, the sense of boredom seems to fall under one of the countless modes of feeling, perception, realization, and recognition that we *share* with other animals. And aren't these shared forms of consciousness precisely what entitles the dog owner, for example, to assert with confidence that his pet *feels* bored, *thinks* he is going to receive a treat, *knows* that the food is hidden in the cupboard, *recognizes* the caretaker, or *realizes* that he cannot have his way with the dog trainer?[35] Does this not show, therefore, that Nietzsche's distinction between animals and humans is much too sharp to be plausible? Not quite. In response, Nietzsche might argue that (a) while it is easy to see what kinds of criteria might inform the judgment that a dog is bored (for example, the dog's posture, responsiveness to stimuli, gaze, behavior in other circumstances, and so on), we have no clear idea about what would prompt us to say the same of a cow in the field; and that (b) the objection misses the point of his remark, which is not to deny that animals feel and think, but to point out that, while they share in *some* forms of consciousness, they are nevertheless excluded from others. As Norman Malcolm has rightly noted, although the attribution of thought to animals typically involves a transitive verb taking a propositional phrase as its object, "we do not thereby imply that the animal *formulated* or *thought of* a proposition, or had a proposition 'before its mind.'"[36] In other words—and the observation applies just as much to people as it does to animals—we must be careful not to draw hasty inferences from grammatical form to psychological reality, but acknowledge that, while animals may well be said to *think* in the sense described, they do not *have thoughts*.[37] Malcolm explains the distinction by means of an example involving his own dog: "Once I owned an Airedale dog who hated a bath, and it came about in the course of time that whenever he saw preparations for a bath underway he would go into hiding. I have no hesitation in saying that he 'realized' he was going to be given a bath, or in saying that he had 'learned from experience' that certain preparations were followed by a bath. But certainly I would not attribute to him the thought 'Here we go again! Another of those horrible baths.'"[38]

The upshot of Malcolm's observation is that (a) thinking takes a variety of forms; (b) to the extent that humans engage in nonpropositional or nonlinguistic thought, they have more in common with animals than has been suggested by proponents of an "absurdly over-intellectualized" view of human life;[39] and (c) insofar as "it would sound funny to say of a dog, a monkey, or dolphin, that the thought that *p* occurred to him, or struck him, or went through his mind," there is a genuine gap between humans and animals, one connected with language, meaning, and distinctly human significances.[40] *Human Nature* does not express a clear view on the nature of animal thought and consciousness, but if Nietzsche's remark about animals is read against the background of Malcolm's observations, the latter can provide a helpful starting point for further discussion of the issue.

For the characters in Kaufman's story, Nietzsche's diagnosis of the human predicament is difficult to dispute, for aren't they all members of the species homo sapiens? And don't even Lila and Puff, in spite of their occasional and naïve idolizations of nature, refuse to abandon their "civilized" form of life for an existence entirely *au naturel*? Kaufman illustrates their ambivalent attitude by clever juxtaposition—for example, Lila's book *Fuck Humanity* versus her subsequent return to the human world (her sexual desires over-whelming her, she naturally wants a *man*, not an animal, to satisfy them); or Puff's eulogy on "the joy of living in a pure state of being" versus his all-too-ready acceptance of haute couture and French cuisine.[41]

Indeed, the movie owes much of its momentum and panache to Kaufman's fascination with these conflicts in his characters' psychologies and to his skill at switching between perspectives, no matter which end of the nature–civilization spectrum the protagonists happen to be gravitating toward. Not surprisingly, these internal divisions also affect and transform the characters' interactions with one another, including their love relation-ships. (I will say more about this later.) *Human Nature* may profitably be read as a series of cinematic variations on the passage from Nietzsche's *Untimely Meditations* quoted above, and at the same time as a (humorous) exposé of a certain kind of intellectual naïveté about the natural world.[42] That naïveté is, of course, not unique to Lila, nor does Kaufman portray her as either emotionally or intellectually inferior to other characters in the movie. On the contrary, we have already seen that some of her views on the animal world also express those of Kafka and Nietzsche—for example, the thought that animals neither judge nor show ingratitude and, when domesticated, tend to exhibit a fidelity to their masters that is rarely found among humans. If Lila feels drawn to such animal responses, as she clearly does, it is not merely because they are entirely unreflective or uncalculating—"natural" in the best sense of the word—but because they gesture toward the possibility of an unconditional acceptance that even her lover (Nathan) is reluctant to extend to her. Elsewhere, however, Lila combines an almost childish romanticization of nature with an equally childish criticism of civilized life: when, during a hiking expedition with Nathan, they stumble upon Puff, the apish human, she readily elevates the latter to a symbol of true freedom and inner purity: "I don't understand you. This is fascinating. Here's a human being totally uncontaminated by civilization."[43]

But how, exactly, does civilization "contaminate" the individual? Lila's remark carries faint echoes of Jean-Jacques Rousseau's charge that "man is born free, but everywhere he is in chains" and of the familiar critique of civil society as a source of oppression, social inequality, warfare, artificially multiplied needs, and a host of other evils allegedly absent from the so-called state of nature. But while she may be right in saying that the civilizing process involves the loss of a certain kind of innocence and the repression of various natural instincts, Lila's confident description of Puff's (apish) life as happy, and Puff's dogmatic assertion that "words are evil,"[44] surely go too far.

Puff is not, after all, an animal grazing in a field, but a human being, with potentialities for thought and action that far transcend mere animal existence and that can therefore bestow on his life a unique and distinctive kind of meaning. As Nathan rightly observes about Puff: "Is he happy? Never to know the love of a good woman, never to read *Moby-Dick* or marvel at a Monet?"[45] It is precisely these potentialities for personal growth and self-fulfillment that place Puff's "uncontaminated" happiness in the same category as that of a lunatic in a mental institution who believes himself to be an ape, throws food at the nurses, defecates when and where he pleases, and leaps about the room as though he were in the jungle. The proper response to such a life would be pity, not applause—and certainly not emulation. With Nietzsche's grass-chewing cows, things are very different. So long as they are not maltreated, starving, etc., they are not to be pitied because, as cows, they could not be leading a different kind of life. What matters, then, is not so much how things feel from the inside—the deluded lunatic may be the most contented person in the asylum—but how far the individual is removed from leading a life worth living, with its value being measured against a stronger currency than that of a crude, psychologized, sentimental conception of happiness.

Similar things could be said about Lila's and Puff's attitudes toward language. Words can certainly be used as instruments of deceit, as Kaufman's characters amply demonstrate, but the possibility of deception itself presupposes that the majority of speakers generally tell the truth and mean what they say. Indeed, why else would the liar even try?

Apart from the fact that language was not "invented" for this or that purpose (unlike, say, a can opener), the use to which it is put on a particular occasion—for the propagation of a lie or a declaration of love—is largely a matter of motives and intentions, not some mysterious, magic power inherent in the words themselves.[46] Lila and Puff both know, of course, that there would be no Lila—not *this* Lila, at any rate—without language, and that her life would be unthinkable without it, whether she decides to become a nature writer or tries to make sense of her first encounter with Nathan ("I cannot believe how in love I am with this man"),[47] whether she lies to him about what she really thinks and feels or provides the police with false testimony concerning Nathan's murderer.

Like all of Kaufman's characters, Lila and Puff do not always believe what they say, nor are their actions always consistent. But then, Kaufman might add, this is exactly what one would expect from such complex beings as humans, who are frequently driven by instinct and feeling, prone to sentimentality and self-deception, and given to compensating for poor self-understanding by fanciful rationalization. It is tempting to think that the solution to this predicament must lie in a healthy skepticism about human self-transcendence; but, as the Nietzsche–Nathan retort already indicates, this would be hasty. For what if the analogy between humans and other animals turns out to be more limited than Lila and Puff think, and the full realization of our natures requires just such self-overcoming?

At this point, Kaufman's characters wisely avoid an extended intellectual debate about evolutionary biology and genetic determinism, though the screenplay does contain a telling exchange between Nathan and his father that (unwittingly?) reveals the futility of any attempt to explain distinctively human capacities and attitudes in terms of genetic similarities with other species:

> FATHER: The ape is our closest biological relative—specifically the pygmy chimp. A single chromosome separates us. But you know what truly separates us?
> NATHAN: No, papa. What?
> FATHER: Culture. Civilization. Refinement. Without it, we might as well be living in pens and throwing our feces about, masturbating in public.[48]

The exchange is illuminating, both as an example of the extent to which Nathan's own attitudes perfectly reflect those of his father and as an illustration of how a combination of scientific fact and fallacious reasoning can result in false analogies and pseudo-explanatory myths. As the philosopher John Dupré has pointed out: "It is often remarked that our genomes have turned out to be 98.4 percent identical to those of a chimpanzee. We are invited to conclude that we are, contrary to our inflated expectations, 98.4 percent identical to chimpanzees. But if this means anything (which I rather doubt) it is surely false. The correct inference is, of course, that neither we nor chimpanzees are identical to our genomes. That this conclusion is usually not drawn speaks volumes for the contemporary power of gene mythology."[49] Curiously, Dupré's conclusion applies with even greater force to the pygmy chimps mentioned by Nathan's father: "It is ironic," Dupré notes, "that among one of our two closest relatives, the bonobos (or 'pygmy' chimpanzees), males, females, young, and old engage frequently in sexual relations of all kinds (homosexual, heterosexual, genital, oral, manual, etc.). It has been suggested that bonobos are unique in the animal kingdom in the extent to which casual sex is a fundamental part of their social interaction."[50]

In Kaufman's narrative, Puff reports that he once believed himself to be just such a pygmy chimp, and his inability to keep his sexual urges under control is an allusion to the bonobos' craving for casual sex. But far from showing that human sexual behavior is determined by a gene pool shared with pygmy chimps, the permanent tension between Puff's sexual propensities and his environment's insistence on restraint merely confirms that human sexual conduct is more plausibly explained in terms of *cultural* factors, rather than genomes; again, to quote Dupré, "Victorian country gentry almost surely engaged in less sexual activity than, say, contemporary British holidaymakers in Ibiza, and not because of any difference in their genes. Human culture is much more rapidly mutable and flexibly responsive to its situation than is the human genome."[51]

Admittedly, the exchange between young Nathan and his father could be read differently—for example, as the latter's stubborn refusal to see things as they really are, which is that our behavior *is* invariably the product of evolutionary biology, "selfish" genes, neuroses, unconscious urges, or similarly elusive causes. In that case, he would be indoctrinating young Nathan with an idealized view of human nature and, at the same time, setting the stage for his son's subsequent disagreements with Lila over the very same issue. Once again, Kaufman leaves the interpretation up to the audience, but it should be clear from what has been said above that any moviegoer who believed Nathan's father to be seriously deluded about the roots of human sexual behavior may be just as confused as the popular gene mythologists in Dupré's examples. And so, it seems we are swinging back in the direction of Nathan and his ostensibly noble aim of bringing civility and cultivation, not only to mice in a lab but also to Puff, Lila, and indeed the world at large: "My thesis is that courtesy, decorum, manners, are all sadly lacking from our daily intercourse, and rudeness, vulgarity, meanness are the norm."[52]

In order to reverse this erosion of civility, Nathan proposes a comprehensive reeducation of the crude and unrefined—beginning modestly, as it were, at the low end and working upward: "Ergo, if I can teach table manners to mice, then I can teach them to humans. If I can teach table manners to humans, then maybe I can make the world a bit safer."[53] That the entire scheme is absurd, however, comes out in Kaufman's clever use of irony—for example, in the description of Nathan's experiment as part of a "federally funded" sociological research project, or in his portrayal of mice punctiliously following human dinner table etiquette—and in the further development of the story line, which culminates in Nathan's death at the hands of the very being (Puff) whom he had tried so hard to initiate into the world of high culture (from the delights of fine foods and tango dancing to the creations of Beethoven, Melville, and Yeats).

More specifically, Nathan's project is flawed for several reasons. First, his treatment of animals is not an enhancement of their natures but a travesty, since it forces them to perform an artificial behavioral routine that, among other things, panders to Nathan's aversion to disorder, spontaneity, unpredictability, and chance. Second, from the fact that he is able to reliably condition mice in a lab with the aid of electric shock therapy—a procedure he also applies to Puff later on—it does not follow that human beings can be similarly conditioned, at least not if the latter are thought to be free and self-determined in a way that animals are not. Third, while such conditioning may well result in outward conformity to a certain mode of conduct, it does not (yet) produce the right kind of motive or inner disposition: the beaming shop owner who tells his customers to "Have a nice day!" usually does so because it is good for business, not because he is truly delighted to see them. Fourth, exquisite table manners may happily coexist with the most heinous criminal intent, as the case of the unsavory Dr. Hannibal Lecter in *The Silence of the Lambs* (Jonathan Demme, 1991) demonstrates only too well.

Indeed, it is not at all obvious that cultural sophistication and refinement are even necessary, let alone sufficient, conditions of truly civilized and humane behavior. "Hitler liked Wagner, Mozart, and Verdi as well as Beethoven. He was very musical," Hermann Goering once remarked in an interview; and when he was asked whether he had read any of the great philosophers, he proudly reported: "I read them all, including Kant, Schopenhauer, Nietzsche, Hegel, and Feuerbach."[54] Toward the end of *Human Nature*, Puff tells a spellbound congressional committee that "human beings have become so enamored of their intellectual prowess that they've forgotten to look to the Earth as a teacher. This is hubris, my friends."[55] He then vows, amid much applause, to keep his promise to Lila and return to the wilderness for spiritual decontamination. Followed by a caravan of radio and television crews and ecstatic citizens, Puff proceeds to take off his clothes in public and soon disappears into a nearby forest . . . until his co-conspirator Gabrielle secretly comes to pick him up in her car and they both drive off into the unknown.

Thus, Puff's public expressions of regret over Nathan's death, his elaborate ode to the Earth, his solemn promise to Lila to return to nature—these were all part of a grand illusion whose origins lie not in the educational endeavors of a civilized culture, but in an animality that has not (yet) overcome itself. If it had, then Puff would understand what Kafka understood when, in spite of his deep respect for apes and other animals, he nevertheless refused to idolize their animality: "What is terrible about war is the dissolution of all existing certainties and conventions. The *animalistic* and physical overgrows and suffocates everything spiritual. It is like a cancer. Man no longer lives for years, months, days, hours, but only for moments. Even those, he no longer lives. He only becomes aware of them. He merely exists."[56]

Human Nature and Love

One of Kaufman's motivations in *Human Nature* is to "look at relationships realistically," to provide a counterpoint to the romanticized and cliché-ridden depictions of love's entanglements in mainstream Hollywood cinema.[57] But what does a realistic portrayal of a love relationship involve? Kaufman does not spell this out, but a closer look at *Human Nature* suggests that an attuned sensibility for the complexities of human psychology and the refusal to pander to common expectations about a happy ending are essential desiderata. However, its story—like any story—of a human relationship is also informed by critical appraisal or judgment, as can be seen from the distinctions we draw between love and infatuation, mature and immature love, dignified love and servile love. In fact, even the claim—popular among certain evolutionary biologists—that these distinctions are "in reality" no more than abstract social constructs, designed to repress and control our natural, nonrational urges and desires, or abstract rationalizations of phenomena whose meaning would otherwise remain disturbingly elusive, is far from being value-neutral. Thus, the subtlety or shallowness with which a filmmaker portrays a human relationship is crucial for the audience's perception of its character, so a considerable degree of discernment is demanded on both sides of the author–audience divide. What, then, does *Human Nature* reveal about the reality of human relationships, or their "realistic" quality? Given the movie's tragicomic tone, one should not expect a happy ending, nor does Kaufman deliver it. On the contrary, one character (Nathan) ends up dead, another (Lila) is in prison, a third (Puff) is a murderer, and a fourth (Gabrielle) is one who lives under the illusion that her lover (Puff) is an innocent man who has never wanted anyone but her. The fact that the movie closes with Gabrielle and Puff driving off to a French restaurant does nothing to subvert this reading, though it is true that the satirical accent in which Kaufman speaks of his protagonists does much to conceal the true meaning of their actions (unlike, say, Woody Allen's 1989 film *Crimes and Misdemeanors*, whose comic dimensions never undermine the seriousness of its leitmotif).

As for the vicissitudes of love, a closer look at the main characters' interrelations prompts an equally disenchanting verdict, since none of them exhibits a love that is more than self-referential, conditional, and immature. Lila is a case in point. As the movie progresses, her attitude toward Nathan undergoes a transformation from genuine affection, even obsession, to servile subordination, and then to essentially remorseless complicity in his murder. Even when she is still allegedly in love with Nathan, she seems more than ready to abandon him at the drop of a hat or, more accurately, the sight of a naked Puff: no sooner does she see Puff rushing by in the forest than she tears off her clothes and chases after him, leaving Nathan behind as one who no longer matters.[58] In Kaufman's movie, the incident is played for laughs; in reality, a woman acting like Lila would be considered seriously disturbed and in urgent need of psychotherapy. Later on, as Lila senses that Nathan is drifting away from her and she becomes increasingly afraid of losing him, she resorts to the kind of insincerity—or self-delusion—that can only lead to a loss of self:

LILA: Do you like my new look?
NATHAN: It's nice.

LILA: I'm trying, you know. I'm trying to be what you want. All I want
    is to be what you want.
NATHAN: You're exactly what I want.[59]

By this point in the story, Lila's love for Nathan has become servile, and with
scenes like this Kaufman perceptively shows just how easy it is for lover and
beloved to become estranged when the former becomes desperate and the
latter responds with a misguided sense of pity. Rather than honestly admitting that his feelings for Lila have changed, Nathan is content to play along
and tell her what she wants to hear, which in turn encourages her to act the
part of a Lila that, in reality, she is not. And when two lovers start to say
to each other "the kinds of things one says when in love" rather than what
they *really* think and feel, then, as Lila and Nathan soon realize, they are
already en route to selling their souls and becoming as inauthentic in their
relationship as bad actors in a mediocre play.[60]

In truth, Nathan has already betrayed Lila with Gabrielle—who, ironically, will later betray *him* with Puff—but pity and cowardice prompt him
to continually postpone his confession. When he finally makes it, and Lila
breaks up with him, neither Nathan nor Lila seems ruffled by the experience
for long; it is almost as if they think it "natural" to fall in and out of love, to
transfer affections from one person to another, from one moment to the next.
In fact, nobody in Kaufman's movie seems overly concerned about the past
and how to integrate it into the present so as to make some kind of unity of
their lives. Everything, so *Human Nature* seems to be telling us, is in a state
of flux, and human relations are no exception. As Nathan asks in his state
of postmortem detachment: "What is love, anyway? From my new vantage
point, I realize that love is nothing more than a messy conglomeration of
need, desperation, fear of death, and insecurity about penis size."[61] Not surprisingly, Kaufman's central characters all conform to Nathan's diagnosis in
their interrelations with one another, with Puff serving as a kind of paradigm:
unable to control or sublimate his "natural" sexual urges, he continues to
treat women—whether they be a waitress in a restaurant, a prostitute in a
brothel, or "regular" lovers like Lila and Gabrielle—primarily as objects of
his sexual desire, moving from one woman to the next like an ape swinging
from one tree branch to another.

The initial impression of Puff as a rather droll and innocent figure is
soon dispelled by the realization that he is, in fact, the exact opposite: morally benighted, deceitful, and deeply fragmented. No sooner has he shot

Nathan, accepted Lila's sacrifice (she wants to take responsibility for the murder so he may go free), and sworn to live out his life in nature (only after testifying before Congress) than he becomes oblivious of his promise and elopes with Gabrielle, telling her, "You know I've wanted you forever."[62] And while Lila may well have other reasons for going to prison than Puff's future well-being, the primary motive behind her sacrificial act has become tainted with irony, since Puff no more cares about his earlier promise to her than he cares about the man he has shot.

In his first draft of *Human Nature*, Kaufman depicts Puff's reaction to Nathan's death and Lila's insistence that she take the blame for it in a way that removes all doubt about the kind of person he is: "I won't let you do that. I shot the bastard. And I'm glad."[63] The line may have been removed from the final script, but its basic truth is still evident in much of what Puff says and does. In response to those who see in *Human Nature* an overly cynical and thoroughly depressing view of human relationships, Kaufman might say that the stark truth about human nature is exactly as the movie depicts it, indeed that even the French philosopher and religious mystic Simone Weil couldn't have expressed it better when she observed: "Human love is not unconditional. I can become much dearer to the vultures than to any human being, and any human being, even the most beloved, can become much dearer to the vultures than to me."[64] However, even if it is true that human love is never unconditional and that former lovers may become "dearer to the vultures" than to each other, it does not follow that the love relationships portrayed in *Human Nature* are the only kinds that are either real or possible. The inference would be warranted only if human nature had to run along the mechanical tracks of a deterministic psychology, or if there were no reason to think that love could take human beings out of themselves in the way that it frequently does. Either way, it is both regrettable and ironic that, in its stern rejection of Hollywood romance, *Human Nature* should focus its lens on human relationships that are mostly casual, superficial, and uninspiring.

Corollary: Wittgenstein and Kaufman's Mirror

Wittgenstein wrote: "I must be nothing more than the mirror in which my reader sees his own thinking with all its deformities and with this assistance can set it in order";[65] one wonders whether Kaufman, too, would not be prepared to adopt this motto for his own work, at least insofar as it can deepen his audience's understanding of life's complexities. Now Wittgenstein's remark clearly presupposes that his readers' thinking is deformed and that his writings will allow them to recognize those deformities for what they are. But the problem, as Wittgenstein himself realized, is that readers may look into his mirror and, instead of seeing the confusions of their own thinking, merely find their views reiterated, and so walk away unperturbed. In that case, they would have learned nothing, and the artist would have cast pearls before swine. To what extent, then, does Kaufman take his movie *Human Nature* to be such a mirror? Does he set his viewers' thinking about themselves, love, human relationships, civilization in order? His audience may applaud *Human Nature* for exposing the messiness of human relationships, but are they likely to detect in its characters aspects of their own reasoning or subterfuge? The difficulty is that if the moviegoers are merely presented with a buffet of possible attitudes, viewpoints, and ways of thinking, but no indication which, if any, of these is being promoted, they are bound to help themselves to it as their individual lifestyle preferences suggest and leave the theater none the wiser. For a screenwriter who wants to provide nothing more than some light entertainment, this is fine. For one whose aspirations tend toward the creation of art, it results in a fiasco.

Kaufman may object that he is neither an educator nor a moralist, and certainly not a certified social reformer, but simply an explorer of human relationships. Indeed, doesn't the discussion of *Human Nature* just presented show that his exploration has much to offer, especially to those who come to it not merely with a bag of popcorn, but with the desire to probe more deeply into Kafka, Nietzsche, Wittgenstein, and evolutionary biology? While this hypothetical response is well taken, it cannot quite remove my unease over Kaufman's reliance on the sexual motif, which caters all too obviously to the expectations of a culture already suffused with the cult of the body and increasingly relaxed attitudes toward casual sex. But perhaps this troubling feature of contemporary society, too, is something to which Kaufman's mirror is drawing attention. This would not only align his own artistic intentions with those of a writer like Kafka, but would also confirm once more Wittgenstein's dictum that the arts, including filmmaking, "have something to *teach*" us.

Notes

I am greatly indebted to David LaRocca for his numerous perceptive comments on the substance and style of an earlier draft of this paper, and to an anonymous reader for additional critical comment.

1. Warren Curry, Review of *Human Nature*, *Filmcritic*, April 7, 2002.

2. Roger Ebert, Review of *Human Nature*, *Chicago Sun-Times*, April 12, 2002.

3. Ibid.

4. Quoted in Stephen Appelbaum, "Life's Little Dramas," interview with Charlie Kaufman, *The Scotsman*, May 9, 2009.

5. Ibid.

6. Curry, review.

7. Appelbaum, "Life's Little Dramas."

8. Ludwig Wittgenstein, *Culture and Value*, trans. Peter Winch (Oxford: Blackwell, 1998), 42. Italics added.

9. *Human Nature* (Michel Gondry, 2002), 01:15:18.

10. Ebert, review.

11. Dave Franklin, conversation with Charlie Kaufman at www.beingcharliekaufman.com. According to the administrators of the site, Kaufman probably wrote this exchange himself.

12. Appelbaum, "Life's Little Dramas."

13. *Human Nature*, 00:35:10; see also the Wikipedia entry on hypertrichosis.

14. Franklin, conversation with Kaufman.

15. *Kafka's Selected Stories*, trans. and ed. Stanley Corngold (New York: W. W. Norton and Co., 2007), 78.

16. Max Brod, *Franz Kafka: A Biography* (New York: Schocken, 1947), 74. Quoted in Peter Stine, "Franz Kafka and Animals," *Contemporary Literature* 22, no. 1 (Winter 1981): 35.

17. *Human Nature*, 00:05:06.

18. Ibid., 00:08:46.

19. Franz Kafka, *I Am a Memory Come Alive: Autobiographical Writings*, ed. Nahum Glatzer (New York: Schocken, 1974), 192. Quoted in Stine, "Franz Kafka and Animals," 61.

20. Franz Kafka, *Letters to Felice* (Harmondworth: Penguin Books, 1978), 408. See also Elias Canetti, *Kafka's Other Trial* (London: Penguin, 1982), 23.

21. Canetti, *Kafka's Other Trial*, 27.

22. Kafka, *Letters to Felice*, 312–13. See Canetti, *Kafka's Other Trial*, 27.

23. Canetti, *Kafka's Other Trial*, 27.

24. Kafka, *Letters to Felice*, 6. See also Canetti, *Kafka's Other Trial*, 20.

25. Letter to Felice Bauer, January 10, 1913, *Letters to Felice*, 268. Canetti, *Kafka's Other Trial*, 19–20.

26. Canetti, *Kafka's Other Trial*, 24–25.

27. Letter to Felice Bauer, January 3, 1912, *Letters to Felice*, 7. Canetti, *Kafka's Other Trial*, 20–21.

28. Quoted in Peter Stine, "Franz Kafka and Animals," 64.

29. Canetti, *Kafka's Other Trial*, 61.

30. It goes without saying that, insofar as Kaufman shares any of his protagonist's confused beliefs, Kafka's story also provides an (ironic) corrective of the screenwriter's views.

31. *Kafka's Selected Stories*, 79.

32. For an excellent discussion of this point, see Gregory B. Triffit, *Kafka's Landarzt Collection* (New York: Peter Lang, 1985), 189–202.

33. Friedrich Nietzsche, "On the Advantage and Disadvantage of History for Life," in *Untimely Meditations*, trans. Peter Preuss (Indianapolis: Hackett, 1980), 8.

34. I am grateful to an anonymous reader for pressing this objection.

35. For a sharp formulation and insightful discussion of the problem, see Norman Malcolm, "Thoughtless Brutes," in *Thought and Knowledge* (Ithaca: Cornell University Press, 1977), 40–58, esp. 53.

36. Ibid., 50.

37. Ibid., 51.

38. Ibid., 53.

39. Ibid., 49.

40. Ibid, 49–50.

41. *Human Nature*, 01:11:36; 01:25:45.

42. See Nietzsche, "On the Advantage and Disadvantage."

43. *Human Nature*, 00:28:20.

44. Ibid., 01:17:50.

45. Ibid., 00:28:53.

46. For a penetrating philosophical discussion of this topic, see Ludwig Wittgenstein, *Philosophical Investigations*, trans G. E. M. Anscombe (Oxford: Blackwell, 1999).

47. *Human Nature*, 00:19:16.

48. Ibid., 00:07:45.

49. John Dupré, *Darwin's Legacy* (Oxford: Oxford University Press, 2005), 96–97.

50. Ibid., 118.

51. Ibid., 116.

52. *Human Nature*, 00:14:08.

53. Ibid., 00:14:15.

54. Leon Goldensohn, *The Nuremberg Interviews*, ed. Robert Gellately (New York: Alfred A. Knopf, 2004), 106, 108.

55. *Human Nature*, 01:21:00.

56. G. Janouch, *Gespräche mit Kafka* (Frankfurt: Fischer, 1968), 175. Quoted in Gregory B. Triffitt, *Kafka's Landarzt Collection* (New York: Peter Lang, 1985), 201 (author's translation from the German; italics added).

57. Franklin, conversation with Kaufman.

58. *Human Nature*, 00:25:40.

59. Ibid., 00:41:53.

60. Ibid., 00:47:18.

61. Ibid., 00:20:28.

62. Ibid., 01:25:45.

63. *Human Nature*, First Draft (May 20, 1995), 102, online at beingcharliekaufman .com.

64. Simone Weil, *First and Last Notebooks*, trans. Richard Rees (Oxford: Oxford University Press, 1970), 323.

65. Ludwig Wittgenstein, *Culture and Value* (Oxford: Blackwell, 1998), 25.

UNAUTHORIZED AUTOBIOGRAPHY

Truth and Fact in *Confessions of a Dangerous Mind*

DAVID LAROCCA

Chuck Barris says he was a hit man for the Central Intelligence Agency. Meanwhile, everyone else knows him as the iconic host of the 1970s game show *The Gong Show* and creator of *The Dating Game* and *The Newlywed Game*. Was the "godfather of reality TV" a secret agent for the United States government with thirty-three kills?[1] Is Barris telling the truth or is he lying? What if the answer to these questions is "It doesn't matter"? Or, rather, that the "drive to truth," as Nietzsche calls it, obscures what is most important and most interesting in Barris's case: how an understanding of "an unauthorized autobiography" yields insights into the nature of authorship and autobiography in general.[2]

Barris wrote an autobiography called *Confessions of a Dangerous Mind*. Charlie Kaufman wrote a screenplay based on Barris's self-described "unauthorized autobiography," and George Clooney later bought Kaufman's screenplay and directed a film with the same title, starring Sam Rockwell as Chuck Barris. The meaning of authorized biography is easily intelligible, but what in fact is an *unauthorized* autobiography? Is Barris not in a position to speak for himself? What would his work need in order to be authorized? With the author of an autobiography questioning his own position as author, readers' suspicions of the fabulous qualities of his stories are heightened. In this way, we are drawn into debates at the heart of any theory of autobiography. Who really gets written about in an autobiography—is it the author, or merely some idea the author has of himself? Does the truth of an autobiography have anything at all to do with the facts of a life?

Barris's autobiography, Kaufman's screenplay, and Clooney's film, all existing under the same title, demonstrate that we are not comparing an actual life with a fictional life. Rather, the fiction is the life; it is the real thing. Story is wholly other than what happens in the real world. And even autobiography—the most personal, potentially the most revelatory, of one's unmediated experience—appears to be just another incarnation of story. Barris does not root his truth in the empirical. Rather, it is the disowning—or de-authorizing—of the empirical that becomes the foundation for his story-telling. The point is precisely that these are not the kind of facts one checks by seeking them out in the world. They are facts because they are written; their truth is tied up with their authorship, not their correspondence to reality.

If Barris's story had to be based on facts—facts that are empirical and verifiable—in order to be "authorized," then we would not have a story. Rather, we would have a natural history. Just because Barris says "This really happened" doesn't mean it did; especially when reading autobiography, readers should not be distracted by the notion that facts cannot bear truth when fabricated. What is interesting—what makes the work more than just a series of observational reports—is the way the author renders facts for his own account, not the way they align with an impartial or collective judgment. Moreover, we ought to dwell on the way the work is put together, how a story emerges out of, and in spite of, things happening one after another. The real mystery here, the real clandestine phenomenon, is not that something happened, but that a writer finds a story in that happening—or in something that didn't.

The Earnest Confessor

Among the many famous confessions in the history of Western literature, St. Augustine's *Confessions* and Rousseau's *Confessions* stand apart; appearing in 398 and 1782, respectively, they are at once deeply personal and masterfully wrought. In these works, the authors are taken at their word, understood to be faithful and competent interpreters of their life's affairs, full of candor and self-knowledge, willing to account for successes and faults, loves and lies, insights and delusions with equal justice. If they are delusional or deceptive, vain or vicious, we are meant to think they are aware of it and need no correction from contemporaries or latter-day critics. The confessions are made earnestly, and we are to accept them as genuine acts of self-disclosure. For exactly this reason the tone of these *Confessions* is at odds with the autobiographical project—if we think of autobiography as a genre not where truth is revealed, but where it is made. While works of autobiography are said to be based on one's life, they are works of fiction. If we find truth, it will be in the fiction. Yet there are cases—genre-defining, epoch-making works such as Augustine and Rousseau's confessions—rendered with such exquisite poise that we may be unintentionally convinced that the author's apparent forthrightness is also a sign of truth beyond fiction, as if we are privy to truths aside from their literary manifestation. Still, once it is pointed out, Augustine and Rousseau's works convincingly come to life as tracts devoted to personal propaganda; each draws a self-portrait didactically. These authors teach the reader how to read them (that is, to take them at their word) and then tell the reader what they want her to know. The result is a highly constructed, highly orchestrated auto-portrait.

The pursuit of counterfactuals to discredit Augustine's and Rousseau's descriptions is pointless: dates, locations, much less the nebulous aspects of emotional distress, moral lapse, religious offense, or even criminal deed cannot be deemed false by reference to something outside the text. A competing document—say, an alternate version of the story given by someone else—does nothing to change the literary import or philosophical impact of these confessions. We may gain additional perspective by consulting other sources, but the insight and power of the autobiographer's claims will not be diminished or otherwise discredited. In an autobiography, the veracity of authorship is simply the author's word. Doubting the author's capacity to tell his or her own story merely reminds the reader of the work's fictitious nature. Even deliberate fabrications and distortions only intensify the way in which the work is created. It is for this reason that in works as artful and compelling as Augustine's, we may recognize how a man prostrated by his sins, confessing his wretchedness, may yet live under the threat of exhibiting spiritual pride.

Every narrator is unreliable. Lying, scheming, murderous Chuck Barris is on the same page as St. Augustine and Rousseau when it comes to the unreliability of his autobiographical account. It's just that Barris is more self-conscious—and self-mocking—about the circumstance that autobiographers find themselves in; in fact, he makes his awareness of his unreliability part of the gimmick of the book. Barris is not trying to convert us to Christ, but to the story of his double life. Augustine's story is not in the service of getting us closer to the truth of Augustine, but to the truth of Christ. Barris's story—his double life—merely seems to reinforce our disbelief in the worldly truth of his account. With Barris, we don't get closer to anything—certainly not the "real" Barris. What we mainly get is an expression of how autobiography is a literary, artistic, fictional act, and how any attempt to create it reflects our fundamental unreliability as narrators of our own stories and experiences. In this context, unreliability does not compromise the authority of authorship—something one can have more or less of—but appears among its constitutional attributes.

Every narrator is unreliable because narration has nothing to do with describing reality—the way things really are. Nevertheless, such unreliability doesn't undermine the potential significance of the autobiography—in fact, it may contribute to our understanding of the work and the person it portrays. As Stanley Fish notes, "While autobiographers certainly insist that they are telling the truth, the truth the genre promises is the truth about themselves—the kind of persons they are—and even when they are being mendacious or self-serving . . . they are, necessarily, fleshing out that truth."[3] "That truth," then, may be a fiction, but it is not, as it were, a lie. It can be revelatory of a deeper truth. Since an autobiographer must compress his story, much will necessarily be left out—yet what he leaves out can be as important as what he puts in. And changing the story, or getting it "wrong," or simply fabricating it, makes all the difference when approaching the subject under description. But to read character—to discern the truth of our author—don't we have to go to the facts against which we can measure what is changed, what is "wrong," and what fabricated? Fish contends: "You cannot fault the author of an autobiography for failing to be objective, or for substituting his story for the story of his subject. He is his subject, and his performance, complete with the quirks and blindnesses of his personality, is not a distraction or deviation from the story of his life but an extension of it. Autobiographers cannot lie because anything they say, however mendacious, is the truth about themselves, whether they know it or not. Autobiographers are authentic necessarily and without effort."[4]

An author's duplicity, conscious or not, doesn't undermine the authenticity of the work; by Fish's account, the autobiographer can do nothing to be inauthentic. Such an understanding of the authenticity of autobiographers deflects the tendency to see doubleness in its several forms (double-crossing, leading a double life, being two-faced or duplicitous, assuming an alter ego) away from terms of truth and falsity, and toward an appreciation for the way that alternation is interesting, revelatory, and possibly profound. The two lives that Barris describes—game-show host and CIA assassin—operate in alternation and interrelation, each life providing surprising insights into the other. When a panel at Princeton University convened on PBS and declared that Barris "symbolizes everything that's wrong with television,"[5] we find

Barris negotiating the unexpected ironies of his double life, experiencing the "strange dichotomy of being crucified by my peers [in Hollywood] for attempting to entertain people and lauded by my peers [in the CIA] for killing them."[6] (Uncannily, in comedy, succeeding at a live show is often referred to as "killing" the audience.) Reflecting on the nature of another kind of double life, Charlie Kaufman has said of the screenplay for *Adaptation:* "Crediting the script to myself and Donald Kaufman is important to understanding the movie. So we don't want to say that Donald is an invention."[7] Yet of course Donald is an invention, a literalization of what is "other" than the character Charlie, a writer who is "boisterous, blithe, and unreflective."[8] As a writer, Barris too may have appreciated the literary possibilities of creating an alter ego, a fictive self who was sent by his government to kill enemies of the state. But with Barris, the two are in one: Barris as game-show host and Barris as assassin are described as self-same—the same man under different aspects or moods. By contrast, in *Adaptation* the two are literalized as two different characters, Charlie and Donald. (Furthermore, the conceit of Donald's screenplay *The 3* goes one further to claim that three are in one—a trinity fit for Hollywood.)

When George Bernard Shaw learned of Archibald Henderson's intention to write a critical, but authorized, biography of the Irish playwright, Shaw wrote to the young man: "A thorough biography of any man who is up to the chin in the life of his time as I have been is worth writing as a historical document; and, therefore, if you still care to face it, I am willing to give you what help I can. Indeed, you can force my hand to some extent, for any story that you start will pursue me to all eternity; and if there is to be a biography, it is worth my while to make it as accurate as possible."[9] At one point, given the collaborative nature of the project, Shaw himself suggested the title *G. B. S. Biography and Autobiography.*[10] The work's dual status and dual authorship, though, would do nothing to render it any more "historical" than if it were solely biographical or strictly autobiographical. The very idea of "accuracy" in accounting for one's life misses the point of telling it: namely, the life emerges precisely from the depiction one makes of it, and that depiction is always a distortion. Shaw himself seems to be aware of this point, and thus appears to be of two minds on the nature of autobiographical works. Just a few pages after we find him lending his support for the creation of an accurate historical document, Shaw says, "All autobiographies are lies," and glosses his remark: "I do not mean unconscious, unintentional lies: I mean deliberate lies. No man is bad enough to tell the truth about himself during his lifetime, involving, as it must, the truth about his family and friends and colleagues. And no man is good enough to tell the truth in a document which he suppresses until there is nobody left alive to contradict him."[11] Henderson follows up with a summary that almost gets Shaw's meaning right: "The true, the real autobiography will never be written; no man, no woman—Rousseau, Marie Bashkirtseff?—ever dared to write it."[12] Better to say: The true, the real autobiography will never be written because it cannot be written.

Sigmund Freud uses a lexicon that roughly engages the terms in Shaw's note, but to quite different effect: "A psychologically complete and honest confession of life," he says, "would require so much indiscretion (on my part as well as on that of others) about family, friends, and enemies, most of them still alive, that it is simply out of the question."[13] So Freud, like Shaw, believes that he is not "bad enough to tell the truth about himself." (Of course, that Freud sees a confession as so problematically indiscreet is itself a very telling moment of confession on his part.) Yet even if Freud took the risk of writing "a psychologically complete and honest confession" of his life, perhaps incriminating and embarrassing himself and others along the way, it would not be worth the trouble or the pain, since he concludes definitively, "What makes all autobiographies worthless is, after all, their mendacity."[14]

Stanley Fish, Chuck Barris, and Charlie Kaufman offer a corrective, or redescription, of autobiography's quality: an autobiography is always prone to mendacity because any person's attempt to come to terms with life will likely involve deceptions, falsehoods, or divergence from an account of absolute or complete truth. Again Fish: "Autobiographers cannot lie because anything they say, however mendacious, is the truth about themselves, whether they know it or not. Autobiographers are authentic necessarily and without effort."[15]

The Confessor, Retailored

The reason one can't tell the truth in one's autobiography is not because one has access to the truth and has decided to withhold it. Rather, the truth as such—even one's own truth—is not accessible. Shaw, like Freud, presumes that the truth can be told—historically, accurately, completely, honestly—if only we were not so afraid of giving offense to others or harming reputations. Parsimonious disclosures of autobiographical truth were, for them, a matter of decorum—not existential revelation or even character definition.

In this light, it is highly consequential, then, that in reading Chuck Barris's *Confessions of a Dangerous Mind*, Charlie Kaufman noted Barris's adoration of Thomas Carlyle, nineteenth-century Scottish essayist, satirist, and historian and author of *Sartor Resartus: The Life and Opinions of Herr Teufelsdröckh*. Kaufman, in essence, discovers in Carlyle the proper antecedent to Barris's approach to autobiography, one that discredits Augustine's, Rousseau's, Shaw's, and Freud's faith in the possibility of confessing, or suppressing, "real truths" about oneself. Carlyle sees that "lives" in Plutarch's sense are necessarily constructed, sewn and patched together, stitched and otherwise mended bits of disparate fabrics. Ironically, a life that is "cut from whole cloth" forthrightly admits its fabricated existence. All writing, though autobiography is especially illustrative on this point, is a patchwork.

Carlyle is mentioned in Barris's autobiography, Kaufman's screenplay, and Clooney's film. Kaufman discerned Barris's love of Carlyle and amplified Carlyle's importance in the screenplay, and subsequently Clooney sustained Carlyle's presence and influence in the film (creating what feels like a cameo in the form of a conspicuously displayed plaster-cast bust).

In the first few pages of the screenplay, Barris says the following to an interviewer; in the film, the passage is read early on as voice-over narration: "I remembered something Carlyle wrote: 'There is no life of a man, faithfully recorded, but is a heroic poem of its sort, rhymed or unrhymed.' I realized my salvation might be in recording my wasted life, unflinchingly. Maybe it would serve as a cautionary tale. Maybe it would help me understand why."[16] To record, or—even more strongly—"faithfully" record, a life may sound a bit too close to Shaw's notion of accurate historical documentation. Barris's deviation, and where we find him acting as the proper inheritor of Carlyle, comes in his recognition that a self-inscribed life is a "heroic poem," even if written in prose. Barris's intent and his tone reflect his commitment to an "unflinching" look at his life very much at odds with Shaw's sense that an autobiography can't properly be written (either because one is too good, or one is too bad), and with Freud's panic over the mendacity of auto-writing. Barris is speculative about whether his autobiography will "serve as a cautionary tale." If it is a heroic poem, then of course it cannot be such a tale. And neither can it help him "understand why." In short, Barris finds in Carlyle the right patron saint for his outlook, but doesn't quite get the implications of the view he's attracted to. Barris wants to write a heroic poem about his life, but he struggles to find and articulate a reason why he should. Carlyle is saying that the commitment to the task of poetizing one's life is enough of a reason.

In the screenplay, Kaufman conceives another scene featuring Carlyle:

INT. BAR—NIGHT
Barris sits drunkenly at the bar. He talks to a drunken guy next to
    him.
BARRIS: So I figured I'd skip town. I intend to be important, y'know,
    I can't be saddled with this. But then I remembered something
    Carlyle said: "Do the duty which lies nearest thee."
BARFLY: Who's Carlyle?
BARRIS: Dear God, why do I even bother?
BARFLY: Hey, fuck you, you condescending prick.
BARRIS: Hey, fuck you.
BARFLY: Hey, fuck you.
BARRIS: Hey, fuck you.
The guy punches Barris. A fight ensues.[17]

The quote from Carlyle appears in *Sartor Resartus,* a genre-mixing book (pseudo-biography, pseudo-autobiography, and pseudo-history) exhibiting an unexpected mix of satire, mysticism, philosophical rumination, poetry, and more. In the work, an unnamed English editor has charged himself with the task of writing the biography of an obscure German philosopher, Diogenes Teufelsdröckh. The Editor, as he is called, travels to a remote part of Germany, talks with the philosopher, gathers his papers (often filed haphazardly in paper bags labeled with names from the zodiac), and spends much of the book commenting on how wearisome the project is. Carlyle, then, has written a book about a biographer who sets out to write a biography, but ends up writing autobiographical prose and compiling myriad autobiographical fragments by the philosopher himself. In the attempt to tell a story about Barris's life, related things happen for Barris, Kaufman, and Clooney. Barris writes an autobiography, Kaufman adapts it into a screenplay, and Clooney further adapts and supplements the screenplay—but does not engage Kaufman in the adaptation process. (At the beginning of the film an intertitle reads: "This film is taken from Mr. Barris's private journals, public records, and hundreds of hours of taped interviews," and Charlie Kaufman is credited as screenwriter; at the end of the film, a title reads: "Based on the book *Confessions of a Dangerous Mind* by Chuck Barris.") Kaufman is like

Carlyle, trying to makes sense of Barris's Teufelsdröckhean autobiographical remarks and philosophical claims even as he is making some of them up himself. Barris, like Teufelsdröckh, obscures his story by writing passionately and vividly about the reality of his experiences even as he presents a work comprised of incredible claims and loyal to "fiction's inherent need for narrative compression."[18] At last, it is as if Clooney bought the rights to make a film about Teufelsdröckh, but didn't want to collaborate with Carlyle in offering a reading of the main character. *Sartor Resartus* translated means "The tailor, retailored." The allusion is to Teufelsdröckh's lifework, a so-called Philosophy of Clothes. The metaphor is apt, for Barris and Kaufman are both writers rewritten. First Kaufman selects, edits, arranges, and adds to Barris's remarks, creating a patchwork fabric drawn from pieces of Barris's book *Confessions of a Dangerous Mind*. Later, Clooney redacts Kaufman's script, culls a wide range of additional documentary sources, and films a series of first-person reminiscences and reflections by people who knew Barris. And the "duty which lies nearest thee" is much as Carlyle describes it: "Inasmuch as all Speculation is by nature endless, formless, a vortex amid vortices: only by a felt indubitable certainty of Experience does it find any centre to revolve round, and so fashion itself into a system."[19] In the context of Teufelsdröckh's Philosophy of Clothes, the idea of a "system" is akin to the creation of texts by means of other texts, just as one makes clothes cut from cloth. All the authors here are in the business of invention and assembly, including the activity of quotation, the duty to convert conviction to conduct (as Teufelsdröckh says), and the generation of new texts.[20] In these new fabrics and innovative fabrications we find fictions that reveal truths. In the combination of these discrete elements—parts from Barris, Kaufman, and Clooney, among others—*Confessions of a Dangerous Mind*, like *Sartor Resartus*, is recognized as an unending project, one that is unfolding and enriched with each iteration. All of the authors involved, real and imagined—Carlyle, his fictional editor, his fictional philosopher, Kaufman, and Barris—are redacted in some way. Their work is continually undergoing transformations as new "editors" or tailors come to fashion new works from existing materials; my own essay necessarily illustrates the point, contributing as it does to that ongoing series of additions, deletions, and transformations. As a community of fabulists and fabricators, all sharing remnants and thread, we neither draw away layers of fabric to reveal the truth nor drape lies in obscuring cloth, but spend our time on the surface, cutting and stitching, dwelling on the multifarious arts of illusion—where the truth really lies.

Among the examples that illustrate the generative quality of fabrication, consider another instance where Carlyle is invoked in the book, screenplay, and film. Here, in an excerpt from Kaufman's screenplay, Barris responds positively to a quote he recognizes as Carlyle's:

INT. LA SCALA—EVENING
The waiter leaves. Keeler sips his drink, stares at Barris.
KEELER: "Whatsoever thy hand findeth to do, do it with thy whole might. Work while it is called, for the night cometh wherein no man can work."
BARRIS: That's Carlyle!
KEELER: Yes.
BARRIS: It's amazing you should quote him. He's my hero.[21]

In the book *Confessions of a Dangerous Mind*, Barris writes the final line this way: "You read Carlyle? Carlyle's one of my heroes."[22] In the film, we find another version of the dialogue:

KEELER: Let me read you something [he opens a book, then reads aloud]. "Whatsoever your hand finds to do, do it gladly, because there is no work, love, knowledge, or wisdom in the grave."
BARRIS: Who is that, Carlyle?
KEELER: No, it's the Old Testament. It's God.
BARRIS: It's amazing you should quote him. He's my hero.[23]

Barris's reply in the film is, of course, funny but also self-consciously intertextual, letting the viewer know that someone (Clooney?) knows that Carlyle's lines from *Sartor Resartus* are quoted from and inspired by a verse in Ecclesiastes.[24] The film takes a cue from Kaufman's use of Carlyle, then reverts to the earlier source—the text, as it were, Carlyle quoted from.

Kaufman's awareness of the layers of quotation—Carlyle quoting the Bible, Barris quoting Carlyle, Kaufman quoting Barris—is tied to the very possibility of authorship. What kind of relationship does a writer need to have to quotation and originality, and how does that relationship affect his claims to authorship? In conversation with Patricia Watson—a character featured in the screenplay and the film—Barris confides, "Y'know, I wanted to be a writer once. I wanted to write something that someday some lesser person would quote. But I never did. I'm the lesser person, Treesh. I never said anything meaningful that wasn't said by somebody else first."[25] We are, then, all lesser persons, for we are all quotations, as Plato said and Emerson said after him, quoting Plato. Even when Barris is discovered to be a writer—as in a late scene in the film where Patricia Watson reads aloud to Barris, quoting from a letter he wrote to her—we hear, in her voice, Barris's confession: "'I'm not at all the person you and I took me for.' Hmm. Sounds like an epitaph. Your handwriting too. You see, Chuck, I save everything. All of your lovely notes. Mmm. You know what? I like Carlyle best, too. I really do. Yeah."[26]

Authorship after Carlyle

In Barris's adoration of Carlyle, Kaufman finds a clue to his own work, not just to understanding Barris. Kaufman, like Carlyle, revels in the strata that emerge in creative experiment—for instance, in the self-conscious or meta-diegetic ways an author writes a book about an editor editing the work of another writer. In this way, *Sartor Resartus* is a perfect antecedent to Kaufman's work, as it is to Barris's: Carlyle deauthorizes himself in order to reauthorize himself (by making Teufelsdröckh a kind of pseudonymous character and his writing a self-parody of Carlyle's own Teutonic-existential-mystical-philosophical-poetic authorial style). Even as Kaufman recognizes in Carlyle some of his own metaphilosophical tendencies, he finds in Carlyle a way to understand Barris's efforts at writing a confession; that is why Kaufman amplifies the theoretical implications of Carlyle's presence in the screenplay. In the wake of Carlyle's work, especially *Sartor Resartus,* we come to see that "unauthorized" does not mean *unofficial, undocumented,* or *unverified,* but rather is a way of acknowledging how a work is drawn from diverse sources, is necessarily and usefully eclectic, a patchwork of quotations and references, a quilt of themes, ideas, and metaphors stitched together—only to await another pair of scissors and a threaded needle. Kaufman stylizes and emphasizes Barris's lack of earnestness—the way his story is faintly ridiculous—to help us see the doubleness not just of Barris's identity as televised host–secret assassin, but also of his book, *Confessions of a Dangerous Mind.* Barris's book remains unstable: it is sometimes pure fiction—the fantastic revelry of an anxious performer who fears being "gonged" at any moment for lack of talent—and at other points seems to reflect a confident effort to call attention "unflinchingly" to that very lack of talent. Barris relieves himself of Augustine's and Rousseau's implicit or assumed earnestness and exhibits his lack of concern for any hope of creating a historical document (Shaw) or honoring the propriety of withholding scandalous details (Freud). Barris's playful experimentation, his apparent break with long-standing and dominant traditions of autobiographical form, however, does not mean he lacks seriousness about his authorship. Just the opposite.

"Would you rather be known as an author or as a TV game show producer?" came a question from the audience when Barris was promoting his book *The Big Question* (a novel about an octogenarian ex–game show host who created *The Dating Game* and thought it was a "catastrophe" and the "biggest disappointment" of his life when the movie based on his book *Confessions of a Dangerous Mind* "tanked").[27] Barris replied: "That's the easiest question of all. I would love to be known as an author. But I don't think it's written that that's the way it's going to be. I just think on my tombstone it's going to say 'Gonged at last.' And I'm stuck with that."[28] Within the first few pages of his book *Confessions of a Dangerous Mind*, Barris presents the reader with a man in emotional despair coming to terms with his physical decay. The reader sustains the somatic and scatological descriptions long enough to feel genuine pity. And then—"I awoke with a start": he wakes up! The whole thing is a dream sequence! Can you believe it? An autobiography that begins with a dream sequence? Coming to the text with a conventional sense of what autobiographies are supposed to do and offer, the reader may feel betrayed by the narrator—already tricked, already lied to, suddenly disoriented by the prospect that the author is untrustworthy and unreliable. Maybe the story is a dream all the way through; how can one ever be sure it isn't? Despite his apparent betrayal of the reader, we have in this beginning a clue to understanding not just Barris's autobiography, but the genre in general. While Barris offers an extreme case—an author who dramatizes and continually reemphasizes the degree to which he can't be trusted—he also illustrates how authorship, even by sincere authors, must be treated as an aesthetic act, not a scientific report. Barris creates something altogether different from a historical document; he writes a work of literature. Still, *Confessions of a Dangerous Mind* as a work of literature may be gonged.

The unbelievable quality of Barris's assertions—that he was a clandestine officer of the CIA, that he killed people—not to mention the dream sequences and the self-inflicted character assassinations, encourage us to stop asking the question "What really happened?" Barris's autobiography reflects back to us what we have wrongly come to expect and desire from confessions, memoirs, and autobiographies: a clear way of distinguishing between public fictions (gossip and rumor) and private truths (honest facts and candid feelings)—a sense that the author is not only committed to telling the truth, but also capable of discerning it. Barris's autobiography dares the reader to believe it as truth despite a constant self-generated attack on the author's ability to deliver it. When Barris writes about his game shows, the nature of which is the subject of speculation (are the shows scripted? are the guests actors?), he seems to make his work as a CIA assassin a similar kind of jocund staging: "The show was make-believe, camp, put-on. It was a caricature of all the amateur hours that had come before, and as such had to be played tongue-in-cheek. It was supposed to be amusing, not serious."[29] Killing people, that's serious. But in his confessions, Barris makes murder amusing, not least because he questions whether something can be both serious *and* amusing, and because he implicates himself as one of the performers trying to amuse, trying to be taken seriously, and yet being told, "You're as bad as the acts—maybe worse."[30] Being "gonged" suddenly doesn't seem so funny. Barris's game shows dispose of people, even as Barris claims he's doing the same in the back alleys of Europe.[31] Barris is a bad act doing bad acts. And he too is expendable, under continual threat of being killed, or "canceled" just like one of his shows. Barris as CIA operative, then, is presented as possibly just another contestant performing before a panel of judges who will decide his fate, targeted for elimination because he too is an amateur.

Author, *Auteur*

In 2002, two films based on Charlie Kaufman's screenplays appeared: *Confessions of a Dangerous Mind* and *Adaptation*. Both screenplays involved the adaptation of an autobiography (Barris's *Confessions of a Dangerous Mind*) or memoir (Susan Orlean's *The Orchid Thief*), but Kaufman's relationship to the production of the final films is strikingly different. Studying the contrast, we find Kaufman engaging, even struggling, with two kinds of authorship. Where Kaufman boldly, provocatively wrote himself into *Adaptation*, creating an eponymous character, and worked extremely closely in all phases of production with director Spike Jonze (with whom he had collaborated intimately on *Being John Malkovich*), Kaufman was, by his own estimation, alienated from the making of *Confessions of a Dangerous Mind* by its director, George Clooney. In an interview on the topic a couple of years after the film's release, Kaufman reflected: "I think George Clooney did take the project in a different direction from the one I had intended, but he's certainly powerful enough to take any direction he likes. That he didn't include me in the process is irksome. Of the three directors that I have been involved with I would say that the other two were preferable. Of course, they have their opinions, and some of the time they win, but I am always involved in the discussions."[32]

Years later, in another interview, Kaufman offered a gloss on his sense of being irked by Clooney: "I can tell you that George Clooney is my *least* favorite person. He's like this really charming guy who pretends he's your best friend. I had written him a 17-page note [about changes that should be in *Confessions of a Dangerous Mind*]. He didn't make the alterations. I was horrified when I saw the film. Someone can change things, as long as I'm involved in making the decisions."[33] Kaufman's blend of ad hominem attack and chagrin over Clooney's effrontery culminates in the idea that the screenwriter should be a creative force throughout the making of a film. "I was always engaged collaboratively," Kaufman stated in another interview. "I was very present and respected by the directors I worked with. I had a strong voice in the process."[34] The degree of Kaufman's autonomy and influence as a screenwriter is more unusual than Clooney's apparent impudence; in fact, institutional or "industry" ("Don't say 'industry'") standards of production suggest that Clooney did nothing untoward—he bought a script, and then made the film he wanted to make.[35] After all, a director might ask, Once the screenplay is complete, what does the screenwriter have to do with making a film? The answer to this question would clearly differ if Kaufman replied or Clooney did. Despite Kaufman's rancor, Clooney "nonetheless stated that he chose to make his directorial debut on *Confessions of a Dangerous Mind* with the 'best screenplay I'd ever read.'"[36]

Clooney's admiration for Kaufman's screenplay notwithstanding, the conflict that arose over the creation or creative control of the film *Confessions of a Dangerous Mind* signals not just the two artists' particular visions for what it is screenwriters and directors *do* and may claim as their own, but also refracts a long history of discourse on the best ways to understand the authorship of film. In 1954, director François Truffaut wrote an article entitled "A Certain Tendency in French Cinema," in which he provocatively asserted that a film's director should be understood as its preeminent source of creation.[37] Truffaut wrote that "la politique des auteurs"—*la politique* most usefully translated as "program" or even "personal vision"—shapes a film to such an extent that other creative or functional influences, from screenwriters to producers and even actors, are secondary to the authorial dominance of the director. Many theorists, notably André Bazin, questioned the fundamental thesis of what became known as the auteur theory, noting how there are too many creative talents and contingent factors present in making a film to ascribe the work to a single person, much less a director.[38] Bazin recognized that auteur theory can easily degenerate into some form of personality cult instead of offering substantive reasons why we should connect the identity of a finished film with a director's identity: "the politique des auteurs is the most perilous for its criteria are very difficult to formulate."[39]

Understandably, almost immediately following Truffaut's pronouncements a critical backlash formed among screenwriters who, like Bazin, recognized how auteur theory would threaten their status as contributors to filmmaking and transform their claims to authorship.[40] More recent attempts to correct imbalances inaugurated by auteur theory include *The Schreiber Theory: A Radical Rewrite of American Film History*, in which David Kipen contends that the schreiber—or writer—is a better indicator and even predictor of a film's character and quality.[41] Addressing a long history in which the role of screenwriters has been diminished, Kipen may be guilty of overcorrection. Yet the alternation between the extremes of auteur theory and schreiber theory suggests that the debate over the meaning of film authorship is lively and contested because it is crucial to any sense of speaking about the phenomenology and ontology of film: how many disparate elements become arranged into a coherent work, and who should be understood as the work's creator.

For Kaufman, unlike Barris, authorizing a text is intimately tied up with his understanding of authoring a text: "Someone can change things, as long as I'm involved in making the decisions."[42] Barris, by contrast, baits our interest in the possibility that even he, perhaps especially he, is not in a position to speak for himself or write definitively about his life. On Kaufman's account, though, the alteration of a work, or at least the preservation of his freedom to do so, is part of what makes it authorized by him. Clooney, then, appears to have deauthorized Kaufman, denied him the kind of relation to his work that Kaufman believes is constitutive of his status as author. Consequently, the film *Confessions of a Dangerous Mind* is an unauthorized work of a different kind. While Barris's book taught us to appreciate the presence of truth inherent in an autobiographer's always unreliable account of his life—to fathom its literary significance—Clooney's film reminds us that the claims for authorship, perhaps especially in film, are under continual negotiation.

Moving from the single author and his book to the community necessary to make a motion picture, we can ask anew: Who authored the film *Confessions of a Dangerous Mind*?

Part of a response to this question will return us to the ways in which Kaufman works to make his films more literary, that is, as texts that do not seek external reality to justify their truth. Yet that response intensifies the need to define the conditions and parameters involved in adapting a screenplay. For instance, what does it mean to be loyal to a text when adapting it? Kaufman clearly is invested in how his screenplays are read, understood, and ultimately visualized by actors and directors. Contrast Kaufman's concern on this point with the blithe pronouncement of screenwriter-director James Cameron (*The Terminator, Aliens, Titanic, Avatar*) that when he gets to the set he lets actors know that "one hundred percent" of his self-authored screenplay is open for revision, even deletion.[43]

In the case of *Confessions of a Dangerous Mind*, we find a cascade of adapters: Barris writes a work (an autobiography); Kaufman uses Barris's autobiography to create another text (a screenplay); and Clooney draws from work by Barris and Kaufman, among others, to produce yet another text (a film). Considering Kaufman's irritation with Clooney's adaptation, we might ask whether Clooney adapted Kaufman's work (viz., the screenplay) in the spirit in which Kaufman wrote it. Did Clooney understand (or even care about) Kaufman's tone or intention with respect to his subject? As in *Adaptation*, Kaufman dwells in his screenplay *Confessions of a Dangerous Mind* on the nature of authoring and authorizing work as it relates to movements away from reality. Drawing from Barris and at times from Carlyle, Kaufman seeks to unsettle seemingly well-founded beliefs about the relationship between fact and truth—to disown truth's purported reliance on the way the world is, to fathom there is another kind of truth—literary truth—for us to consider.

Clooney, to Kaufman's chagrin, moves decidedly against a literary understanding of Barris's book and Kaufman's screenplay in favor of a literal understanding of the story—for example, how near or far it is to the truth of what actually happened. Clooney tries, rather boldly, to increase the correspondence between the "true" or "real" story that he suspects is lurking about in Barris's and Kaufman's literary works; for instance, Clooney drops in documentary footage of people who knew Barris (Dick Clark et al.) as his own way of authorizing his film. Return again to the intertitle Clooney adds at the outset: "This film is taken from Mr. Barris's private journals, public records, and hundreds of hours of taped interviews." (Barris's book is acknowledged during the end credit sequence, after Kaufman is noted as screenwriter, and after Clooney is identified as director.) Clooney believes that the authority of his film derives from its awareness of the history or reality that exists apart from it, and that informs the fictionalizations he dramatizes in the course of the film. His film is "taken," as if it were a form of dictation and not, say, an interpretation or a literary creation. Where Kaufman dissociates himself, and therefore his screenplay, from any concern with mimesis, Clooney registers the extent of his commitment to have his film imitate life. These are indeed contrasting visions of authorship, authority, and adaptation.

It is with a view of this contrast that we should assess the nature of Kaufman's alarm with respect to Clooney's finished film: when Kaufman wants to be involved in making changes, he is not being megalomaniacal, but careful to do what he can to encourage a director to appreciate the spirit in which the screenwriter creates, and to adopt the tone he aims for. Kaufman's disappointment derives, then, from having imagined a different kind of film than the one Clooney made—where imitation of reality, or accounting for historical facts, has no purchase on the notion of authorship and authority. As Kaufman's approach aligns with Carlyle's, it also resonates with Plutarch's: "I have chosen rather to epitomize the most celebrated parts of their story than to insist at large on every particular circumstance of it." As Plutarch's "design is not to write histories, but lives,"[44] so Kaufman hoped for a literary film, something he achieved in his collaborations with Spike Jonze and Michel Gondry, and later on his own as director of *Synecdoche, New York*. Because of his successful collaborations, Kaufman seems surprised that he wouldn't continue to have productive engagements with other directors—and be asked to contribute to the process of adapting his work from screenplay to screen. After watching *Confessions of a Dangerous Mind* rendered through Clooney's direction, we can only conjecture what Kaufman might have contributed had he been drawn into the creative fold, as with Jonze and Gondry. We don't have access to those seventeen pages of suggestions Kaufman sent to Clooney, but we may wonder whether one of the recommendations might have been to consider how the film would have a better chance of conveying or reflecting the truth of Chuck Barris's autobiography if it didn't try to imitate, re-create, or otherwise verify the life Barris actually lived. The proviso, then, would be to create—to adapt—with an appreciation for fiction's capacity to reveal truth.

Notes

In July 2010 I presented an earlier version of this chapter at Swansea University, Wales, in the Department of Political and Cultural Studies and the Department of American Studies, which offers a master's degree in the study of Hollywood film. I thank Mario von der Ruhr for the invitation to speak, and members of the audience who offered stimulating critical comments; I hope the finished version of the chapter reflects my understanding of their discerning remarks.

1. King Kaufman, "Chuck Barris," *Salon*, March 6, 2001 (salon.com). Charlie Kaufman, screenplay for *Confessions of a Dangerous Mind*, third draft (revised), May 5, 1998, 6 (beingcharliekaufman.com); hereafter Kaufman (1998).

2. Friedrich Nietzsche, "On Truth and Lies in a Nonmoral Sense," in *Philosophy and Truth: Selections from Nietzsche's Notebooks of the Early 1870s*, ed. and trans. Daniel Breazeale (Atlantic Highlands, NJ: Humanities Press, 1979), 84.

3. Stanley Fish, "Sarah Palin Is Coming to Town," *New York Times*, December 7, 2009 (nytimes.com).

4. Stanley Fish, "Just Published: Minutiae without Meaning," *New York Times*, September 7, 1999 (nytimes.com).

5. Chuck Barris, *Confessions of a Dangerous Mind: An Unauthorized Autobiography* (New York: Hyperion, 2002), 176.

6. Ibid., 181.

7. Quoted in Jonathan Vankin and John Whalen, *Based on a True Story: Fact and Fantasy in 100 Favorite Movies* (Chicago: Chicago Review Press, 2005), 186.

8. Ibid., 186.

9. Quoted in Archibald Henderson, *George Bernard Shaw, His Life and Works* (Cincinnati: Stewart and Kidd Co., 1911), iv.

10. Ibid., 5.

11. Ibid.

12. Ibid.

13. Letter from Sigmund Freud to Edward L. Bernays, August 10, 1929, in *Letters of Sigmund Freud, 1873–1939* (London: Hogarth Press, 1960), 391.

14. Ibid.

15. Stanley Fish, "Just Published."

16. Kaufman (1998), 6. Carlyle's line appears in the *London and Westminster Review* (No. 12, 1838) as part of his remarks on the publication of the *Memoirs of the Life of Sir Walter Scott* (Edinburgh, 1837).

17. Kaufman (1998), 15–16. The quote from Carlyle appears in Book II, Chap. IX of *Sartor Resartus*.

18. Bruce Duffy, *The World as I Found It* (New York: Houghton Mifflin Co., 1987), ix. Related to narrative compression in fiction, a note in the title sequence at the beginning or end of a film may state that the work is "based on" or "inspired by" a "true story."

Occasionally, often at the end of a film, there is more explanation, such as "Characters and events have been fictionalized for dramatic purposes." Here "fictionalized" means that some form of narrative compression has occurred, as well as other kinds of distortion or deviation from the way things "actually" or "literally" happened. Intriguingly, these notes may be understood in two radically different ways (and yet while appearing antagonistic, they also seem to create a useful tension): on the one hand, the notice may be meant as a hedge against the claim that the film is presenting itself as history—something no work that aspires to be fiction should wish to be associated with, or accused of; and on the other hand, the notice seems like an appeal to the viewers' sense that the authority of historical or literal verisimilitude lends the film a greater degree of reality and truth, and therefore importance.

19. Thomas Carlyle, *Sartor Resartus: The Life and Opinions of Herr Teufelsdröckh* (London: Chapman & Hall, 1891), Book II, Chap. IX, 135.

20. Ibid.

21. Kaufman (1998), 94–95.

22. Barris, *Confessions*, 129.

23. *Confessions of a Dangerous Mind* (George Clooney, 2002), 01:13:12.

24. Ecclesiastes 9:10, King James Version: "Whatsoever thy hand findeth to do, do *it* with thy might; for *there is* no work, nor device, nor knowledge, nor wisdom, in the grave, whither thou goest."

25. Kaufman (1998), 114; *Confessions of a Dangerous Mind*, 01:36:27.

26. *Confessions of a Dangerous Mind*, 01:39:23.

27. Chuck Barris, *The Big Question* (New York: Simon & Schuster, 2007), 147.

28. "Barris on Barris," *Book Passage*, May 17, 2007, Corte Madera, CA (video online at fora.tv).

29. Barris, *Confessions*, 161.

30. Ibid.

31. In the film *Confessions of a Dangerous Mind* (01:39:00), Barris says, "I dispose of people. I am disposable."

32. Nik Huggins, interview with Charlie Kaufman, *Future Movies*, May 30, 2004 (futuremovies.co.uk).

33. Howard Feinstein, interview with Charlie Kaufman, *Indie Wire*, October 24, 2008 (indiewire.com). Kaufman's italics.

34. Anne Thompson, "Cannes Welcomes Charlie Kaufman," *Variety*, May 9, 2008 (beingcharliekaufman.com).

35. Charlie Kaufman, *Adaptation: The Shooting Script* (New York: Newmarket Press, 2002), 10.

36. Ibid.

37. François Truffaut, "Une certaine tendance du cinéma français," *Cahiers du Cinéma*, no. 31, January 1954.

38. André Bazin, "De la Politique des Auteurs," *Cahiers du Cinéma*, no. 70, April 1957.

39. Bazin, translated in Donald E. Staples, "The Auteur Theory Reexamined," *Cinema Journal* 6 (1966–1967): 1–7.

40. William Goldman, for instance in *Adventures in the Screen Trade* (New York: Warner Books, 1983), is one of the screenwriters who voiced opposition to auteur theory.

41. David Kipen, *The Schreiber Theory: A Radical Rewrite of American Film History* (Hoboken, NJ: Melville House Publishing, 2006).

42. Feinstein, interview with Kaufman.

43. James Cameron, guest on *Inside the Actors Studio*, season 16, episode 4, February 23, 2010.

44. Plutarch, *Lives*, ed. Arthur Hugh Clough, trans. John Dryden (New York: Modern Library, 2001), 139.

Part 2

BEING, OR TRYING TO BE, WITH OTHERS

ME AND YOU

Identity, Love, and Friendship in the Films of Charlie Kaufman

Douglas J. Den Uyl

The films of Charlie Kaufman are masterpieces of humor and insight. They also collectively represent a significant study of what it means to try and sustain a relationship with another person. At one level the films might be said to be generally concerned more with the problem of personal identity than with relationships. This problem of identity is reflected in various forms of self-doubt, as in Kaufman's representation of himself in *Adaptation*, or appears as an issue of how to organize one's own mental furniture, as in *Eternal Sunshine of the Spotless Mind*, *Being John Malkovich*, and especially *Synecdoche, New York*. Although the problem of personal identity is interesting in itself, what one realizes in watching these films is how critical personal identity is for understanding one's relationship with another.

By "relationship" I mean a strong and stable form of connectedness to another person. In popular films generally, connectedness is usually expressed though depictions of love and romance—what might be called the search for "true love." There is certainly no lack of such relationships in Kaufman's films. Romantic relationships and their success or failure are part of the plot in all the films just mentioned. There are exceptions, however. Charlie's relationship with his brother in *Adaptation* is more prominent than his romantic interest. But generally the characters in Kaufman's films discover each other, fall in love, sleep together, are unfaithful, break apart, and exhibit all the other characteristics one would associate with love and romance. In most of these relationships, however, there is togetherness without connectedness, and even when there is connection it seems fragile and in danger of pulling apart (as it often does).[1] The viewer senses the characters' search for something that would cement their relationships and, ideally, remove the self-doubt, alienation, and loneliness that threaten intimate connection.

Kaufman points us to the "something" without actually showing us an example of it. Indeed, he might even believe the elements needed for true connectedness are almost impossible to find. Those elements are nonetheless strongly suggested by his films. The elements are obscured, however, by our general propensity always to attach love to romance, sexuality, or companionship. There is another way to think about love, and it is the form implied through the struggles of his characters. That other form of love is friendship. Because friendship is commonly overshadowed by romantic love in our culture, it will serve us well to take an independent look at the concept and phenomenon.[2] However, it is not just any understanding of friendship that shall inform our reflections, but classical friendships as depicted primarily by Aristotle and Montaigne.[3] I do not claim that love and friendship can never be conjoined. Indeed, the issue is whether successful love depends on friendship, so as our discussion progresses, talk of love will reemerge. The task of reconciling the two, however, is difficult, and the modern vocabulary of love often diverts our attention from what that combination would require.[4] For the time being, then, I will set aside that vocabulary.

Classical Friendship

The first thing to note about classical friendships is that they fall under the rubric of what is sometimes called moral "perfectionism." There are various ways of describing what perfectionism means, though all of them are at least loosely associated with self-realization, self-discovery, and self-mastery.[5] The aim of perfectionism does not require that at some point a person becomes perfect.[6] The object is not the unobtainable perfect person but rather, as Aristotle might put it, using the best condition of which we are capable as an aspirational standard for, and thus guide to, our own development. The application of perfectionism to film has been pioneered by Stanley Cavell. He frames the approach as follows: "Perfectionism concentrates on this moment. First, it recognizes difficulties in the moral life that arise not from an ignorance of your duties, or a conflict of duties, but from a confusion over your desires, your attractions and aversions. . . . Second, it proposes that such muddles essentially stand in need of the perception of a friend. Third, it underscores that for one to confront another with her confusion, especially when she has not asked for advice, requires the justification of one's moral standing with her."[7] Cavell is making these comments in his analysis of *The Philadelphia Story* (George Cukor, 1940), but the remarks resonate strongly for the films we are considering here. Kaufman's films depict our tensions, drives, and inner conflicts in a form that calls upon the viewer to consider ways for those tensions to be resolved or equilibrated. And as Cavell suggests, the first step on this road to "perfection" involves becoming intelligible to ourselves. Aristotle refers to friends as "other selves" and asserts that friends are critical to our own self-understanding (and we to theirs). In this respect Charlie Kaufman's use of a fictional twin brother (Donald) in *Adaptation* as a metaphor for insight into himself is an effective way to cast the Aristotelian idea. Although Charlie and Donald are twins, they are also opposites in many ways. What then is essential to self-discovery through friends? What can one discover about him- or herself through an experience with another person?[8]

INTEGRITY

The first thing to recognize about friends being other selves is that there must be selves. That statement would seem to imply a double bind. One cannot become a self without the presence of friends, but one can only have friends if there is a self from which to appreciate others. Yet aren't we all already selves? The answer to that question from a classical perspective is, basically, no. While there is definitely a "me" and a "you," each of us as selves is an accomplishment, not a starting point. The starting point is that bundle of drives, insecurities, and uncertainties noted by Cavell and depicted by Kaufman. But we are also naturally disposed toward an extension of our goodwill to others with a need to have such returned to ourselves. We observe that disposition in situations where we find the company of others pleasant or where they help us in some way. Goodwill exists in both those contexts, and when it is present we might be said to be among friends. Aristotle refers to friendships in these cases as friendships of utility and friendships of pleasure.[9] Our goodwill can be extended to those we enjoy being around or who help us in various ways, and we can receive the like from them as well.

Friendships of utility and pleasure are not, unfortunately, the sorts of relationships sufficient in themselves to secure the depth and stability we seek. If they were, the problem of stable relationships would be much easier, because most of the time we deal with people for reasons of pleasure or utility. However much goodwill there may be, such friendships pretty much conclude when the pleasure or utility ceases. Consequently, though they can be counted as forms of friendship, they lack the stability needed for the kind of enduring relationship we would expect from those who are true friends. As one commentator notes, pleasure and utility offer us nothing by way of increased understanding of our own value, and understanding our own value is the necessary ingredient in a deeply meaningful relationship with others.[10] On this basis, the degree of permanence in our own sense of value is proportionate to the degree of stability we are likely to have with others. The more we understand our own value the more we can appreciate like value in others, and understanding their value aids in appreciating our own. Such value does not diminish if the stream of useful or pleasurable things is interrupted. More important, what becomes pleasurable and useful for friends is a function of how they come to value themselves. The reverse, where little more can be said about a person than what is pleasing or useful, is not for Aristotle a sufficient basis for being a self.

As it turns out, then, for stability and permanence to emerge in a relationship one has to have already achieved a solid sense of integrity—that is, a well-integrated sense of self. Integrity results from melding our dispositions, appetites, talents, propensities, and goals into one coherent whole. Ancient thinkers tended to believe that the virtues such as courage, justice, temperance, and prudence were both our guide to self-development and what we actually exhibit once we accomplish it. This is why Aristotle says that "good people will be friends because of themselves, since they are friends insofar as they are good. These, then, are friends unconditionally; the others are friends coincidentally."[11] Because of Aristotle's use of terms like "good" and "virtue," such friendships are referred to as "friendships of virtue" or "character friendships." But terms like "virtue" and "good" to our ears carry with them moral overtones that may not have been a part of Aristotle's own usage or relevant to our discussion here. Consequently, we shall speak of "character friendships" rather than "friendships of virtue," and we will think of "virtue" more in terms of the excellence of character than in terms of "doing the right thing" or following the "right rule."[12]

Although I have chosen to use the term "integrity," Aristotle himself speaks of "self-sufficiency," which he ties to happiness: "Now happiness, more than anything else, seems complete without qualification. For we always choose it because of itself, never because of something else. The same conclusion also appears to follow from self-sufficiency. For the complete good seems to be self-sufficient. What we count as self-sufficient is not what suffices for a solitary person by himself, living an isolated life. We regard something as self-sufficient when all by itself it makes a life choice worthy and lacking nothing; and that is what we think happiness does."[13] From this passage we should notice two points: first, what has highest value for Aristotle is tied up with the good, the complete, the unqualified, or what is chosen for its own sake. Integrity, then, involves the kinds of things that one chooses for their own sake. Second, self-sufficiency must not be understood to mean living without others.[14] I prefer the term *integrity* primarily because it does not suggest an absence of others. But the term *self-sufficiency* also has its uses, at least initially, because our goal is to figure out how to talk about friendship without talking about needing others.[15] Is such a thing possible?

Aristotle indicates that talking in terms of needs will actually lead us *away* from an understanding of the nature of character friendships.[16] For classical thinkers, the essence of friendship was not about satisfying needs, as is characteristic of our thinking about friendship in the modern world.[17] Indeed, one tends to believe these days that the best sign of a friend is that he or she is there to help when something goes wrong. C. S. Lewis has, however, succinctly summed up the proper understanding of conferring and receiving benefits from a classical perspective on friendship: "But such good offices are not the stuff of Friendship. The occasions for them are almost interruptions. They are in one way relevant to it, in another not. Relevant, because you would be a false friend if you would not do them when the need arose; irrelevant, because the role of benefactor always remains accidental, even a little alien, to that of Friend."[18] Although helping one's friends is certainly a part of character friendships, as is companionship and pleasure, character friends are united on the basis of something other than their ability to confer benefits. The relationship is cemented based upon each person's clear sense of who he or she is and what he or she values and thus how the other is a reflection of those very same understandings. In this respect self-knowledge is the critical ingredient of integrity and thus of character friendships. And isn't it the case that self-knowledge is what virtually all of Kaufman's main characters seem to be in search of?

On this reading of character friendships, we desire such friends because they give us insights into ourselves and not because they are best at aiding us in some way. Friendship for Aristotle turns out to be the most significant contributor to self-knowledge.

Now we are not able to see what we are from ourselves (and that we cannot do this is plain from the way in which we blame others without being aware that we do the same things ourselves; and this is the effect of favor or passion, and there are many of us who are blinded by these things so that we judge not aright); as when we wish to see our own face, we do so by looking into the mirror, in the same way when we wish to know ourselves we can obtain that knowledge by looking at our friend.[19]

The process of gaining self-knowledge or integrity is not as simple as looking at one's face in the mirror. It requires instead the use of our human intelligence to bring order to our own selves by recognizing in the other the kind of person we ourselves want to be. That sort of recognition requires judgment and reflection. If all we needed was companionship when attending a movie, for example, virtually anyone might do. But we want to attend with our friend because that person better than anyone else will have the sort of reactions that we are not just likely to agree with, but also that we will find insightful and broadening. For although as friends we share a common framework of some sort, she nevertheless notices what I do not. Indeed, she might say things I disagree with, but because she says them, I can avail myself to claims to which I would have otherwise been deaf. Even the feeling we would get in the two cases reflects the difference: we are invigorated by the company of our friend; we are merely comforted by a companion.

The use of our intelligence in this context does not make friendship a theoretical activity or demand that true friends relate to each other only on a theoretical basis.[20] Intelligence is instead more broadly conceived by Aristotle to include thinking something through and having practical reasoning and insight.[21] Our intelligence can be directed toward ourselves in a way that seeks to harmonize our desires and dispositions and weigh alternatives for their contribution to our flourishing as persons. With respect to others, however, mutual interactions based on intelligence will normally occur through discourse.[22] Through talking, living together, and acting jointly we discourse with our friends in ways that deepen self-knowledge and strengthen integrity. We "see" ourselves in others not through acts of imitation but through acts of understanding. Through their discourse with each other, friends share their active intelligence.

Another attribute of character friendship is equality. Aristotle tells us that equality is one of the marks of a character friend because inequality brings dissimilarity.[23] Dissimilarity obviously serves as an impediment to there being an "other self"; Aristotle here is referring to substantive matters of circumstance or nature and not relatively trivial matters of personality. In cases of inequality, such as between parent and child, master and servant, and teacher and student, friendship will be more challenging or impossible. The issue of equality, however, need not detain us at all. Kaufman's films are remarkably egalitarian in their outlook, perhaps because they center on romantic relationships. The usual societal roles that might prove to be impediments to the equality needed for friendship are simply not obstacles for Kaufman. We need look no further for an example than Caden's love of Hazel in *Synecdoche, New York*, where Caden is the brilliant playwright and winner of a MacArthur genius award and Hazel is a box-office ticket taker. There is not the slightest sense in the film that their stations in life have any bearing on their love affair or their friendship. But the love affair, like all love affairs, does pose other sorts of problems for friendship besides equality, and to that issue we do best to turn to Montaigne.

FREEDOM

Montaigne's conception of friendship at its highest would share the main characteristics posited by Aristotle.[24] For Montaigne, friends "mingle and blend with each other so completely that they efface the seam that joined them, and cannot find it again."[25] Yet Montaigne considers a dimension that is not as clearly expressed in other classical conceptions of friendship—namely, freedom. For Montaigne the issue of freedom comes up precisely because of the problem of eros, or romantic sexual love. In exploring the connection between friendship and eros, Montaigne (and Kaufman following him) is in search of what he regards as freedom—a kind of self-directedness and mastery over our choices and actions. Eros, unlike friendship, is largely a distraction from freedom.

Montaigne describes three differences between eros and the sort of character friendships we have been considering: voluntariness, satiation, and constancy.[26] Eros differs from friendship because it is "more active, more scorching, and more intense. But it is an impetuous and fickle flame, undulating and variable, a fever flame, subject to fits and lulls, that holds us only by one corner."[27] Physical attraction is essentially an involuntary pulling irresistibly "by one corner" of ourselves. Eros is inconstant and subject to lulls when we are satiated. Friendship, by contrast, is voluntary, beyond satiation, and constant. Should we ever be pulled into marriage because of eros, Montaigne's insight here is no more optimistic: "As for marriage, for one thing, it is a bargain to which only the entrance is free and a bargain ordinarily made for other ends. For another, there supervene a thousand foreign tangles to unravel, enough to break the thread and trouble the course of a lively affection; whereas in friendship there are no dealings or business except with itself."[28] If our search is for freedom, friendship is a kind of pure and unmixed form of it. The problem with eros, as so many of Kaufman's characters remind us, is that either through the neediness it engenders within us or the "foreign tangles" it creates around us, we become dependent rather than self-sufficient. In this respect Aristotle's self-sufficiency is Montaigne's freedom.

The comparison of freedom in Montaigne to self-sufficiency in Aristotle is a way to overcome an apparent tension in Montaigne's thought. Some have held that his praise of friendship is inconsistent with his praise of solitude in an essay by that name and in other places where he seems to eschew the company of others.[29] Yet I would regard any praise of solitude as an appeal to the primacy of integrity, that is, as an appeal to avoid distractedness in order to achieve self-understanding. If others who are present are distractions, as many are, it is better to be alone. In any case, as C. S. Lewis noted, "every real Friendship is a sort of secession."[30] Friends separate from others and thus create their own brand of solitude, so friendship and solitude are not really estranged. Moreover, solitude gives us the opportunity to introspect, which is necessary for organizing our passions in integral ways that make us suitable for friendship. Paradoxically, then, withdrawing oneself can actually better prepare one for engagement with one's surroundings—and others—than can constant interaction.[31]

Throughout his *Essays* Montaigne focuses upon the very real and human dimensions of our lives, which revolve mainly around our passions and physical nature. It is thus not for the sake of withdrawing from the world that Montaigne writes, but rather for our proper engagement with it.[32] Precisely because we are not only thinking beings but also beings of flesh and blood, there is for Montaigne an ideal form of friendship that encompasses it all—one I believe Kaufman holds out as an ideal in his films: "If such a relationship, free and voluntary, could be built up, in which not only would the souls have this complete enjoyment, but the bodies would also share in the alliance, so that the entire man would be engaged, it is certain that the resulting friendship would be fuller and more complete."[33] These words from Montaigne bring us back to the question of "love," which we chose to set aside earlier on. It is now possible to look at the issue of love through the lens of friendship and perhaps find both freedom and stability. In his films,

Kaufman does seem to be in search of Montaigne's ideal, and we seem called to that ideal whenever we view them. We are not so called because these films are depictions of perfect friendships; they are rather more often depictions of the obstacles to it. But we frequently get a clearer picture of what perfect friendships might be by seeing how people relate to their impediments.

The Perfectionist Turn

FRIENDSHIP IN ADAPTATION

Cavell suggested, as noted earlier, that making ourselves intelligible—to others, but especially to ourselves—was the primary difficulty of the morally perfected person, and that this process involves a sorting out of the confusion we often have over our desires, attractions, and aversions. Put this way, sorting out confusions over desires could be described as the principal occupation of Kaufman's lead characters. We might begin by reflecting on Charlie from *Adaptation*, a character who is riddled with insecurities and physical passions that effectively paralyze him throughout the film. This confusion about, or inability to deal with, his passions is in contrast to his twin brother, Donald, who seems quite at home with himself and easily matches his actions with his desires. Of course, Donald is meant to be the more "primitive" of the two characters and is barely elevated above a simple base-level set of appetites. Like a creature who has survived millennia because its lack of complexity allowed it to adapt, Donald seems much more able to function in the world than his more sophisticated brother, Charlie. They both have the same passions, but the passions are dealt with differently: as Charlie masturbates, Donald scores with women. Donald is less internally conflicted, less emotionally tormented. Thus Donald has a kind of integrity that Charlie lacks. Yet something is also missing from Donald, which allows us to develop a certain respect—and sympathy—for Charlie as a person.

Donald is a kind of nuisance to Charlie and is often dismissed by him. They are not exactly character friends. Donald clearly admires Charlie and even seeks to imitate him by becoming a screenwriter, and we, the viewers of the film, witness some growth on Donald's part during the course of the movie. But in the end it is mainly Charlie who gains intelligibility and integrity through his interaction with his brother, Donald. The point is symbolized in Donald's death at the end of the film, which leaves Charlie on his own, as if the process of integrity had been completed and Charlie is now possessed of the requisite self-sufficiency he lacked so evidently at the beginning of the film. In the wake of Donald's death, has Charlie somehow internalized some of Donald's attributes? Ironically, one realizes by the end of the film that much of what took place was a version of Donald's own script about which Charlie had been so critical all along! Charlie has more than internalized Donald; the two have become one. That is a fitting device for bringing home the idea of how much of our self-realization comes through another.

One may wonder whether this sort of analysis applies to Charlie, who tells us early in the film that life is not about personal growth, overcoming obstacles, hooking up, car chases, or other such Hollywood clichés.[34] Charlie is interested in originality and expresses this value throughout the film, including using it as a basis for criticizing Donald's script. Barely a minute passes from the point where Charlie expresses his distaste for Hollywood clichés, however, before we are introduced to the representative of pure nature, John Laroche. Laroche is listening to a book on tape of Darwin's *Origin of the Species*, and we hear Darwin's point that "all corporeal and mental endowments will tend to progress toward perfection."[35] We are from that point forward compelled to wonder what "perfection" might mean in this film and how our prejudices, like Charlie's, are likely to move in the wrong direction. For we are inclined to believe that Charlie's passion for originality and intellection is the path to perfection. In fact, however, it is Donald who successfully finishes and sells his script while Charlie agonizes and flounders over his. The lesson is a hard one: success comes within the world and not outside of it. Consequently, one must adapt oneself to one's surroundings in some fashion to develop at all. Amelia, Charlie's "girlfriend," makes this point when she says she is going to "solve this Charlie Kaufman mess once and for all."[36] What she effectively advises is that Charlie get "out of his head" and look at the bigger picture. This is what Charlie needs and what he eventually learns from Donald by the end of the film. Indeed, it is only after Charlie understands that he must make his way in a world larger than his own inner mental one that he can finally tell Amelia at the end of the film that he loves her.

Charlie's obsession with his inner life is starkly contrasted with Donald's apparent lack of one. We want to believe that Charlie's sensibilities are "higher" than Donald's, but our search for the meaning of perfection or success forces us to recognize some truth in what Donald represents. If so, the lesson being taught in this film is Montaignesque in character. Whether one refers to passions or actions, both must function in a context that is very much of *this* world, not some other. However, we do not want to make two further mistakes, namely to assume that Donald is our model of the perfected person or that we can arrive at intelligibility of ourselves without the use of our mind. With respect to the first of these two cautions, we have already noted Donald's own inadequacies as indicated by his need to imitate Charlie. Donald senses that his perfection lies in the further development of his mind.

The second of our two cautions is more complicated. The principle for thinking about the issue can be found in the following words spoken by Laroche at the flower show as he reflects upon the relationship between orchids and the insects they use for pollination.

> What's so wonderful is that every one of these flowers has a specific relationship with the insect that pollinates it. There's a certain orchid looks exactly like a certain insect. So the insect is drawn to this flower—its double, its soul mate—and wants nothing more than to make love to it. And neither the flower nor the insect will ever understand the significance of their lovemaking. How could they know that by doing their little dance the world lives? But it does. By simply doing what they were designed to do something large and magnificent happens. In this sense, they show us how to live. How the only barometer you have is your heart. How when you spot your flower you can't let *anything* get in your way.[37]

These words reiterate the perfectionist context in which we are now working. It is the attraction of another self that draws the insect and that elicits love from it. Furthermore, the fulfillment of a thing's own nature is connected to its perfectibility, and that must be the standard for something to be living its own life. But the passage also points to blind, unthinking attraction as the basis for the movement of life, perhaps suggesting—if we want to take these words as expressing the main point of the film—that the problem with Charlie is that he thinks too much.

We do not, however, have to read the film exactly this way. That is, we do not have to read it as a tribute to instinct over reason. We are not, after all, insects, and it may be that we, unlike them, need to *understand* our relationships with others in order for the connection with them to be secure and meaningful. Kaufman films compel us to realize that relationships must be understood to succeed, and that neither instinct on the one hand nor retreating into oneself on the other is a recipe for success. The symbol for instinctual nature in this film, namely Laroche, is fittingly eaten by unthinking beasts at the end of the film. Laroche possesses intelligence and knowledge, but that knowledge is instrumental to his passions, not informing of their shape and direction.[38] Susan makes this clear to us when she asks Laroche, after listening to his story about his love for fish and then his sudden decision to be "done with fish," whether if one really loved something would not some of that love linger.[39] A human love is one that is defined in part by its intelligibility, and intelligibility would make the love linger. But for Laroche love is attraction, with intelligibility having no function beyond finding effective ways to serve the appetite. Susan's problem is the opposite: she is looking for passion. In a way, she gets too much of it in the end, not just in her affair with Laroche and with drugs, but as the instigator of the attempted murder as well. In her case she completely abandons to disastrous effects the aids already present in her world that secure reasonable control of the passions.

The relationship between Susan and Laroche is the other romantic interest in the film besides the one between Charlie and Amelia. In many respects it is the more prominent of the two. As just noted, Susan searches for passion, while Laroche is a man continually driven by it. It would seem like a perfect fit, but from the perspective of classical friendship using passion alone for the basis of a relationship is a recipe for failure—not simply because the passion may diminish but, more importantly, because the relationship would lack the stabilizing guidance of self-understanding.[40] This insight into love is given by Donald toward the end of the film. Donald's truth is the one that Charlie finally comes to realize for himself. When Charlie mentions to Donald how a girl Donald loved, Sarah Marshall, laughed at him (Donald) about his love behind his back Donald says, "It was mine, that love. I owned it. Even Sarah didn't have the right to take it away."[41]

For love to work, then, it has to be one's own. Something being one's own is, in turn, predicated upon one having a strong degree of self-understanding. That is exactly why integrity matters so much in love relationships. Appetites, in themselves, are internal forces that move us rather than we them. Through the ages, philosophers have noted how the passions influence our thinking, behavior, and sense of ourselves. One is passive with respect to them, yet what one wants most from one's passions is for them to emanate *from* oneself, thereby reflecting one's individual identity—and, by extension, one's individual freedom. Through Donald, Charlie begins to understand that love is something that must come from within him as a function of who he is as a person of independent integrity. He must be perfected in this way before his love can become manifest. Once Charlie understands that and realizes what he is about, he is able to tell Amelia he loves her and finish his script. Those two actions are not unrelated; both stem from Charlie's newfound self-ownership and self-possession. Hence, it is not the absence of passion we are after, but rather developing those passions that motivate us toward courses of action that we can confidently say are our own. At the end of the film, we hear Charlie in voice-over (a film attribute his scriptwriting teacher, Robert McKee [Brian Cox], disapproves of) say, "I don't care what McKee says, it feels right."[42] That was something he could not have said before he improved his own sense of self-possession and became able to intelligently meld his passions with his projects.

CAN WE BE JOHN MALKOVICH?

Based on the discussion above, the answer to the question "Can we be John Malkovich?" is no. But *Adaptation* is not the only one of Kaufman's films that brings us to that same answer. One of the patterns one finds in these films is the difficulty the main characters have in "getting their heads together." Perhaps the most dramatic instance of this is *Synecdoche, New York*, where Caden's play is a metaphor for his life and particularly his mental life. But besides Caden (and Charlie in *Adaptation*), similar concerns about one's mental state can be found with Craig in *Being John Malkovich* and with Joel in *Eternal Sunshine of the Spotless Mind*.[43] In the context of Kaufman's meditations on mental life, two main issues emerge: coherence and self-respect. Both are important components of the sort of integrity described above. Of course, such films as *Being John Malkovich* and *Eternal Sunshine of the Spotless Mind* toy continuously with the relationship between one's mental state and the problems for well-being that result from a fractured mental life. *Synecdoche, New York*, however, is perhaps most explicitly about the intricate connection between coherence and self-respect.

In *Synecdoche, New York* we are encouraged to treat Caden's play as a metaphor for the life of the mind, for Caden tells us that "theater is the beginning of thought. It is truth not yet spoken."[44] Caden is eager to work on his play because he can finally put his "real self" into something. The problem is that he does not know who his real self is.[45] Caden never does find his "real self," as the woman auditioning to play him reiterates toward the end of the film: "he's strived valiantly to make sense of his situation, but now he's turned to stone."[46] Yet whatever Caden's failings, he functions like a mirror for us all as he traverses a litany of obstacles in his search to make sense of his life. The things Caden has had to sort out seem numerous and varied—from marriage to learning how to talk to his daughter (which Caden eventually does, through a translating machine).[47] Looking at the particular things Caden is forced to manage, we see that they bear a striking resemblance to the obstacles we face in our own lives. Yet Caden's problems do not stem simply from the variety of things with which he has to cope. His mental life builds upon itself such that the world, and the world created by his mind, become completely indistinct. Caden ends up living "in a half-world somewhere between stasis and antistasis where time is concentrated, chronology confused."[48]

The task of managing the enormous complexity of things thrown at us by modern life and the passing of time is further complicated by our ability to spin mental worlds out of the empirical worlds we confront and then use those newly created mental worlds to filter our experience still more. The question then becomes: What could possibly limit this process of creation and insufficient fulfillment? The film offers death as the only fixed limit. The hoped-for limit, namely intelligibility of the self, is nowhere to be found.[49] But why is that? Paradoxically it is because Caden's whole focus is upon himself and nothing else. Indeed, just before Sammy (who also plays Caden in the play) jumps to his death, he tells Caden that he (Caden) has never looked at anyone but himself. It might seem from my earlier discussion that Caden's incessant introspection was the right course. In fact, however, Kaufman's films remind us that we are meant to extend ourselves out into the world. Our minds are actually designed to engage the world out there; and without, as it were, a "reality check" they spin out of control. The cost of losing control over our minds—again somewhat paradoxically—is self-respect. A self is not built out of thought alone, but also from incorporating actual experiences and engagements with the world. The classical admonition to "know thyself" was not a call to retreat into some interior world, but to reflect upon how to function within the one we find beyond ourselves.

If self-respect is a function of the self-knowledge that comes from striving toward the integration of our thoughts, actions, and passions with the world around us, then its critical role in love and friendship is obvious. Aristotle confirms the centrality of self-respect when he tells us that the sort of person who makes a good friend must be a "self-lover" and that the good person is also a self-lover.[50] Aristotle does not mean by "self-lover" what we might call a selfish person, one who seeks only what is advantageous or lives only for his or her feelings. He means instead that one thinks of oneself as worthy of respect. Caden is much admired by people like Claire and Hazel, but he does not admire himself, as we witness through his continual propensity to cry during sex.

But Caden (and Charlie) are not the only ones deficient in self-respect in Kaufman's films. Despite his knowing that puppeteering is his life, Craig in *Being John Malkovich* also suffers from a lack of self-respect—as do the people waiting in line to get into Malkovich's head and out of their own. Joel too, in *Eternal Sunshine of the Spotless Mind*, lacks self-respect, even if he does not display the level of despair we find in Caden and Charlie. But Joel perhaps more than any other of Kaufman's characters reminds us of another dimension in the quest for self-respect, namely that the world out there is filled with connections we make with other people, not just with things and circumstances. *Eternal Sunshine of the Spotless Mind* shows us that the endeavor to erase someone from our lives with whom we have been close, even if that person is less than a full "other self," affects the very substance of who we are. The dire consequences that torment Joel as Clementine is being purged from his memory result in a disorientation that he fights against as much for the sake of his own self-understanding as for any pleasure the memories may contain within themselves. The forgetful are in fact not blessed, nor do they "get the better of their blunders," because others link to so many parts of ourselves that the endeavor to disown them constitutes a virtual unraveling of one's identity.[51] Clementine, who has supposedly forgotten Joel, indicates all of this through her uneasiness with Patrick's imitations of Joel as Patrick pursues her.[52] The links from one part of life to another are thus not easily disentangled. If, as Clementine tells us at the end of *Eternal Sunshine of the Spotless Mind*, finding "peace of mind" is the goal, then erasure of our connections is no substitute for the self-respect that comes from reflecting upon and understanding them.[53]

At the end of *Eternal Sunshine of the Spotless Mind*, Clementine and Joel recognize that they are not perfect and have some way to go to realize that "peace of mind." Most people find themselves in this predicament. They are seekers living in a less than fully perfected state of being. Consequently, we might say that Kaufman is generally more interested in what sustains love than what brings it about, unlike what is customary in so many romantic love stories. Moreover, in contrast to the usual love story, dramatic tension in Kaufman's depictions of a relationship is less centered on issues of sexual infidelity per se, and more on uncertainties connected to self-identity and its effect on the real compatibility of the lovers. Films such as *Human Nature* and *Being John Malkovich* give much attention to exploring the connection between infidelity and identity. *Being John Malkovich* could be described as one long example of infidelity, yet the viewer senses clearly that this is not what really troubles the characters. Though primal passions can initially create conflicts, as when Craig, who is married, starts hitting on Maxine early in the film, such attractions serve more as setups for later examinations of how self-understanding can affect a relationship.[54] In *Being John Malkovich*, the way personal identity influences the nature of a relationship is significantly more prominent than the usual problems of sexual jealousy.[55] Almost everyone in that film comes to look at himself or herself differently by the end of the story after having experienced numerous identity-shaking events (such as passing through brain portals).

Kaufman tends to portray the mind and body in a Cartesian fashion: as distinctly different entities capable of placing unique demands upon us. Perhaps the Kaufman film that is most focused on the physical self and its instincts, drives, and passions is *Human Nature*, a Rousseauian tale of how civilization corrupts our natural selves and distorts our natural passions. Indeed, we're told by Puff that human beings have become so "enamored of their intellectual prowess that they have forgotten to look at the earth as their teacher."[56] But the problem with nature as our teacher, as the film itself demonstrates, is that it is not at all clear what nature teaches. Our drives and passions are themselves imprinted by the circumstances and conventions our minds have created. Even Puff, who was essentially reared in the wild, cannot escape civilization in the end and returns to it, albeit in a corrupted condition, with his latest accomplice, Gabrielle. It would seem, then, that we have the task of managing our intellectual and physical selves jointly—not as separate but as equal parts somehow joined together, as integrated aspects of one life. Romantic sexual love is a good vehicle for exploring any problems with our passions because it seems so purely physical. Kaufman uses the physical to point us to the dimensions of mind present therein, just as whenever he turns to what seems to be solely mental, the physical is always prominent as well. The integrated person would thus seem to be one whole created by a managed combination of both the physical and the mental.

Conclusion

I have argued that imbedded within Kaufman's films is a kind of ideal, perhaps only tacitly expressed, but nonetheless definitely prefigured. The ideal is perfectionist in nature in that it concerns the proper integration of desires, mental states, circumstances, and persons into a coherent form of self-understanding. The characters in his films are not depictions of the ideal itself but of individuals groping toward it. Whatever degree of success they have in approaching this ideal, it is still the basis upon which any success is measured. The ideal is rooted in a form of personal integrity that serves to stabilize a person's relationship with herself and with others. It is grounded in the sorts of things Aristotle says are necessary for friendship but which, in Kaufman's hands, seem to carry an additional dimension of Montaigne's model of combining friendship and eros. More broadly considered, Montaigne's model life could be described in the following way: "The greatest virtue, then, is the moderation born of reason and self-knowledge that allows one to enjoy life's pleasures to the fullest, precisely because one does so within reasonable bounds and without unreasonable demands or fantastic hopes and fears."[57] Kaufman's characters take us through the challenges one must face if we are to "enjoy life" in the controlled fashion that is free of the fantastic. We may be like Caden in repeatedly proclaiming, each time as if for the first time, that we "know how to do this play now"; but that is just what it means to approach our lives in human fashion: thinking about how to do our play. The most significant challenge to doing one's own play, however, arises when one tries to connect with others. For that, perhaps we all sing the words of the song sung during the closing credits of *Synecdoche, New York* and written by Kaufman himself: "And somewhere, maybe someday, maybe somewhere far away, I'll find a second little person who will look at me and say: 'I know you. You're the one I've waited for.'"[58]

Notes

I wish to thank Emilio Pacheco, Aeon Skoble, Margarita Molteni, and Douglas Rasmussen for the various insights they have given me through discussions of some of these films. I especially want to thank Ruth Abbey for her helpful comments on an earlier draft and David LaRocca for useful suggestions on some finishing touches.

   1. The opening of *Being John Malkovich* is a case in point. The marriage seems relatively normal, though there is bit of a strain concerning full-time employment. The issue of employment, of course, pushes against art, which we are to regard as superior. But the relationship seems stable and solid enough, though it flies out the window almost as soon as Craig meets Maxine for the first time early in the film.

   2. For the ancient Greeks there was a distinction between *philia* and *eros*. The former is often translated as "friendship," but it would have been regarded as a form of

love by them and not as something different from love. We, however, are too used to separating the terms to ignore it here, so I maintain the separation.

3. This is undoubtedly a contentious claim. Timothy Fuller, for example, places Montaigne squarely in the modern camp in "Plato and Montaigne: Ancient and Modern Ideas of Friendship," in *Friendship and Politics*, ed. John von Heyking and Richard Avramenko (Notre Dame, IN: University of Notre Dame Press, 2008), 206–11. In Fuller's case, "modern" here seems largely to refer to giving up on the notion that there is a single telos for human beings and that a variety of lives can qualify as good. I use a different standard for making the division between classical and modern, as discussed later in the text. Lorraine Smith Pangle, however, seems to pair Montaigne with Aristotle much as we would here. See Pangle, *Aristotle and the Philosophy of Friendship* (Cambridge: Cambridge University Press, 2003), 64–78.

4. See, in this connection, Ruth Abbey and Douglas J. Den Uyl, "The Chief Inducement? The Idea of Marriage as Friendship," *Journal of Applied Philosophy* 18, no. 1 (2001): 37–52.

5. For an account of this, see Douglas B. Rasmussen, "Perfectionism," in *Encyclopedia of Applied Ethics* (Oxford: Elsevier, forthcoming 2011), a revised and expanded version of his 1997 entry for *Encyclopedia of Applied Ethics* (San Diego: Academic Press, 1997), vol. 3, 473–80.

6. "To perfect, to realize, or to actualize oneself is thus not to become God-like, immune to degeneration, or incapable of harm; it is rather to fulfill those potentialities and capacities that make one human." Rasmussen, "Perfectionism" (1997), 474.

7. Stanley Cavell, *Cities of Words: Pedagogical Letters on a Register of the Moral Life* (Cambridge, MA: Harvard University Press, 2004), 42. The perfectionism of which Cavell speaks here is connected to Emerson rather than to Aristotle and Montaigne. Hence some aspects of this account may not exactly fit the theories of these two thinkers. Still, Aristotle and Montaigne lay the basic groundwork for understanding perfectionism in friendship, and I contend that the passage just cited from Cavell fits Kaufman's project perfectly.

8. A similar set of questions can be found in Rod Long, "The Value in Friendship," *Philosophical Investigations* 26, no. 1 (January 2003): 73–77.

9. The citation used here and elsewhere in the paper is from Aristotle, *Nicomachean Ethics*, trans. Terence Irwin (Indianapolis: Hackett Publishing Co., 1999). All citations are from the Irwin translation, though some are taken from the anthology *Other Selves: Philosophers on Friendship*, ed. Michael Pakaluk (Indianapolis: Hackett Publishing Co., 1991), 1156a1–1156b3.

10. See Talbot Brewer, *The Retrieval of Ethics* (Oxford: Oxford University Press, 2009), 247.

11. *Nicomachean Ethics*, 1157b4–5.

12. Aristotle says that only "decent people" can be character friends and "base people" cannot (ibid., 1167b5–15). These sorts of statements also should be interpreted in light of what is said in the text below.

13. Ibid., 1097b1–15. I have recently discovered that a fuller account of integrity, which seems quite compatible with my own, can be found in George W. Harris, *Agent Centered Morality* (Berkeley: University of California Press, 1999), esp. chaps. 3 and 4.

14. Indeed, this is also another one of the sections where Aristotle refers to the friend as another self.

15. I treat a version of this problem in "Friendship and Transcendence," *International Journal for Philosophy of Religion* 41, no. 2 (April 1997): 106–8. I address it again with respect to film in "Civilization and Its Discontents: The Self-Sufficient Western Hero" in *Philosophy and the Western*, ed. Jennifer L. McMahon and B. Steve Csaki (Lexington: University Press of Kentucky, 2010).

16. *Nicomachean Ethics*, 1169b3–5, 8–10.

17. Francis Bacon is a good example; see Pakaluk, *Other Selves*, 202–7. In Bacon's case friends are largely about being useful to each other (for example, in business), and thus are mainly of instrumental value.

18. C. S. Lewis, *The Four Loves* (New York: Harcourt Brace, 1960), 69.

19. This passage is cited in Brewer, *Retrieval of Ethics*, 254. It comes from the *Magna Moralia* (1213a15–22), which Brewer notes is under dispute with respect to Aristotle's authorship. I doubt, however, that there is any question that it is Aristotelian, even if not directly from Aristotle. The passage is cited here not only to make the present point, but also because it seems especially pertinent to what I say about Kaufman later in the text. As Brewer notes, "the capacity to love ourselves and the capacity to love others arise together as the result of our struggles to perfect the ubiquitous human relationships that Aristotle calls *philia*" (258).

20. Indeed, Aristotle makes clear that sharing activities (doing things together) is necessary for friendship (*Nicomachean Ethics*, 1157b6–15), though of course theoretical activities can be among them.

21. See, for example, Ronna Burger, "Friendship and Eros in Aristotle's *Nicomachean Ethics*," in *Love and Friendship*, ed. Eduardo Velasquez (New York: Lexington Books, 2003), 47. Burger also notes here that "friendship with another is the extension of inner harmony," reinforcing my point on the connection between wholeness and completion and integrity.

22. See, in this connection, David O. Brink, "Eudaimonism, Love, and Political Community," in *Human Flourishing*, ed. Ellen Frankel Paul, Fred D. Miller, and Jeffry Paul (Cambridge: Cambridge University Press, 1999), 262–65.

23. *Nicomachean Ethics*, 1159b4–6.

24. I am not alone in noticing this. David Lewis Schaefer treats it this way, for example, in his "Michel Montaigne and His Imaginary Friend," in *Love and Friendship*, ed. Velasquez, 75. I do not, however, share Schaefer's understanding of the differences between Montaigne and Aristotle, discussed on the pages following the one cited, specifically with regard to self-sufficiency. More on that later in the text.

25. Michel de Montaigne, "On Friendship," *The Complete Works of Montaigne*, trans. Donald M. Frame (Stanford: Stanford University Press, 1943), 138.

26. This section is taken largely from Abbey and Den Uyl, "The Chief Inducement?" 43–44.

27. *Complete Works of Montaigne*, 137.

28. *Complete Works of Montaigne*, 137–38.

29. Schaefer makes this point in "Michel Montaigne," 75, as does Pangle, *Aristotle and the Philosophy of Friendship*, 72.

30. Lewis, *The Four Loves*, 80–81.

31. See, in this connection, Ruth Abbey, "Circles, Ladders, and Stars: Nietzsche on Friendship," *Critical Review of International Social and Political Philosophy* 2, no. 4 (Winter 1999): 50–73.

32. Schaefer makes this point, though to a different end; see "Michel Montaigne," 77. He does raise here what may be more of an issue between Montaigne and the other ancients as to whether Montaigne's self-sufficiency is less otherworldly.

33. *Complete Works of Montaigne*, 138.

34. *Adaptation* (Spike Jonze, 2002), 00:05:45.

35. Ibid., 00:06:52.

36. Ibid., 00:12:40.

37. Ibid., 00:23:45–00:24:50.

38. Laroche does, however, have a focused intelligence. It would be a mistake to suggest that some important aspects of integrity are not present in Laroche. Aristotle, however, rightly draws a distinction between cleverness and practical wisdom, where cleverness incorporates the idea of efficient use of instrumental reason. *Nicomachean Ethics*, 1144a25–29.

39. *Adaptation*, 00:29:00.

40. At one point Susan gives the sensible advice that having a passion will "whittle the world down to a sensible size" (00:52:57). But however true that may be, Susan loses control of her life, caught up by the end in an extramarital affair, using hard drugs, and being an accomplice to murder.

41. *Adaptation*, 01:54:00.

42. Ibid., 01:49:00. Charlie says, "Kaufman drives off after his meeting with Amelia for the first time filled with hope. I like this. This is good."

43. I do not include Malkovich himself here because his mind was essentially invaded. Besides, one of the main reasons the film works is because Malkovich is actually a man possessed of integrity relative to his invaders.

44. *Synecdoche, New York* (Charlie Kaufman, 2008), 00:39:12.

45. Ibid., 00:37:09.

46. Ibid., 01:45:52.

47. Ibid., 01:20:00.

48. Ibid., 01:45:45.

49. The message is ostensibly depressing, but there are so many problems and ob-

stacles present in this film that it becomes a parody of itself and life in general. I found myself chuckling rather than depressed in the end.

50. *Nicomachean Ethics*, 1169a12.

51. *Eternal Sunshine of the Spotless Mind* (Michel Gondry, 2004), 01:16:40.

52. Ibid., 01:05:50–01:06:22.

53. Ibid., 01:42:51.

54. *Being John Malkovich* (Spike Jonze, 1999), 00:19:30.

55. Ibid., 00:41:24–00:43:30.

56. *Human Nature* (Michel Gondry, 2001), 01:24:44.

57. Pangle, *Aristotle and the Philosophy of Friendship*, 72.

58. *Synecdoche, New York*, 02:01:43.

I Don't Know, Just Wait

Remembering Remarriage in *Eternal Sunshine of the Spotless Mind*

William Day

"Meet me in Montauk." This line near the end of *Eternal Sunshine of the Spotless Mind* presents a problem for Charlie Kaufman's film and for his viewer. The problem for Kaufman's film (as distinct from the finished film as seen) is that he didn't write the line—in any event, it doesn't appear in his shooting script—and it undermines various of Kaufman's remarks about what he takes to be important and exciting about his screenplays. For the viewer, the problem is that Kate Winslet's whispery, echoey "Meet me in Montauk" is felt at the moment of its utterance to be a lover's command or promise of a rendezvous that is meant to remind us of, and in some sense explain, the apparently chance meeting of Joel (Jim Carrey) and Clementine (Winslet) out in Montauk that we witness at the beginning of *Eternal Sunshine.* On further reflection, however, we come to believe that this meeting out in Montauk couldn't be the result of a promise of a rendezvous, since (as Kaufman says) "Clementine's not there":[1] the Clementine who voices those words is "really Joel talking to himself."[2] Even if *Joel* could remember it (and doesn't the scene immediately after the "Meet me in Montauk" line, with the computer's virulent "beep" and Dr. Mierzwiak's "Okay," show us that Joel's memory of this whispered promise has been erased?), one can't expect Clementine to remember to keep a promise she didn't make.

To spend even a few moments considering this problem is necessarily to get caught up in the nature of film narrative. How does a movie work on us? Is the experience of its discontinuous presentation of a world—the effect of the technique, familiar since the early days of film, of cutting from one shot to another—at bottom the piecemeal experience of a narrative that is to be (usually quite easily) puzzled out? If so, does our inability to solve this narrative discontinuity in *Eternal Sunshine* present us with terms for criticizing it? Surely if any screenwriter's work were about the audience's puzzling out the experience of its discontinuous presentation, it would be Charlie Kaufman's movies, and none more than *Eternal Sunshine*. The screenplays themselves seem to tell us this. So does Kaufman: "We'd done test screenings [of *Eternal Sunshine*] and people often got lost, but for the most part don't mind it, which is what I always thought. It's like having a moment of epiphany. You're lost, and then it's, like, Oh! to me is the greatest thing in a movie. Some audiences don't want that, but I don't care. I like it so I want to do it in the movies that I'm working on."[3] But faced with our problem, in which the promised epiphany is followed by frustration and bafflement as we consider the narrative placement of the words "Meet me in Montauk," should we, by Kaufman's own criterion, be left disappointed with this film?[4] (Kaufman himself may be disappointed, since the line may not be his. Would he erase the line from our memories if he could?)

At least two other writers, noting the narrative discrepancy of the Montauk line and Clementine's otherwise inexplicable appearance on the beach, settle on describing the connection between the line and her appearance as "magical."[5] ("Magical" is how Joel, on the beach, describes Clementine's very name.) This can sound like a cop-out, apologetics masquerading as criticism. But what is promising in this solution—in fact, more true to an experience of the film than the alternative—is the suggestion that we might learn to read a Kaufman movie without giving veto power to the determinations of and fascination with narrative puzzle-solving that Kaufman identifies as a prime motive in the writing of his screenplays. (We could call this the test of faithfulness to a Kaufman film, that we read it through our experience of it rather than allow Kaufman's challenge to himself in writing the screenplay to do the reading for us.) What still needs saying is how we should make sense of our experience of *Eternal Sunshine* once we have sorted out its narrative as best we can, found our efforts to comprehend it frustrated by one or more inconsistencies, and wondered whether such "magical" moments might be our best clues to making another sort of sense of it. I believe that we can make sense of it, and that the important narrative in a film like *Eternal Sunshine* is the one that, one might say, the film is remembering for us, or for which it stands as a meme brought to life in our viewing. In the specific case of *Eternal Sunshine*, the narrative being remembered bears more than a resemblance to the narrative genre identified by Stanley Cavell as the Hollywood comedy of remarriage.[6] My aim in saying this is not to reduce our experience of *Eternal Sunshine* to a genre *formula* (which is not, in any event, how Cavell or I understand a film genre), but to guide a reading of the film that helps articulate the viewer's sense that the events in the great middle of the film—the events that, narratively, are Joel's thoughts of and projections onto his memories, all of which (those thoughts and projections as well as those memories) are then erased—nonetheless *do* something. And they do something not just to the principal pair, but to us; indeed, our experience of what those events do to the principal pair rests on what they do to us.

The sense of a connection between *Eternal Sunshine* and the Hollywood comedies of remarriage from the 1930s and '40s was among the first critical reactions to Michel Gondry and Charlie Kaufman's film registered in the popular press.[7] The connection has since been observed by philosopher Michael Meyer in what he calls his "ethical reading" of *Eternal Sunshine*.[8] But in each instance the mythos of the remarriage comedy has been no more than invoked, either in misunderstanding (as with Meyer's piece) or in recognition that more needs saying.

The characteristic story arc of remarriage comedies is the telling of a couple's journey from estrangement back together, a journey they accomplish through the uniquely human and uniquely philosophical form of intercourse we call conversation. What the remarriage conversation is about, amid the false starts and detours and occasional raised voices, is the nature of men and women: both the differences in their nature (which the couple may feel as the unspecified and unspecifiable but nonetheless palpable obstacle to their finding a way back together) and the nature of their desires, or the nature of human desire itself, which is the quintessentially philosophical wonder. (Philosophy, which begins in wonder, comes to wonder eventually about its own motivations, about what it seeks, what its desire is.) The forms of desire that these couples talk about and otherwise express—and here the dialogue in *Eternal Sunshine* can serve us as illustration—are not only sexual desire (Clementine: "This is a memory of me, the way you wanted to have sex on the couch after you looked down at my crotch"), but also include the beginning of desire in childhood (baby Joel: "I want her to pick me up. It's weird how strong that desire is") and, perhaps most keenly, the desire or wish to be *alert* to one's desire, which is to say, to change. Consider this exchange between Joel and Clementine at the bookstore, near the end of the film:

CLEMENTINE: Too many guys think I'm a concept, or I complete
    them, or I'm gonna make them alive. But I'm just a fucked-up girl
    who's looking for my own peace of mind. Don't assign me yours.
JOEL: I remember that speech really well.
CLEMENTINE: I had you pegged, didn't I?
JOEL: You had the whole human race pegged.
CLEMENTINE: Hmm. Probably.
JOEL: I still thought you were gonna save my life, even after that.
CLEMENTINE: Mmm. I know.
JOEL: It would be different . . . if we could just give it another go-
    around.
CLEMENTINE: Remember me. Try your best. Maybe we can.[9]

Note how Clementine, through her denial, pegs Joel's interest in her to his conviction in her ability to save his life, to make him alive, to wake him up. The desire given form in remarriage comedy films is just such a longing for a self transformed.[10] That longing often takes one or another of the principal pair down false paths—to an inappropriate partner, say (think of Clementine's fling with Patrick, her "baby boy"), or to places as desperate as Lacuna, Inc., the memory-erasure service; but it also leads the pair to the discovery that finding your changed self, the desired change that Emerson baptizes your "unattained but attainable self,"[11] requires a life of conversation with your other self—that is, with the one you find to be a fit partner in remarriage.

Where, then, is the remarriage conversation in *Eternal Sunshine*? If not on the Montauk train at the beginning of the movie (where Joel has next to nothing to say and Clementine, as George Toles has observed, is transparently flirtatious in an effort to distract herself from some felt mourning mood),[12] and if not in Joel's hallway at the end of the movie (where the few choice words they find to say to each other bear the scars and love marks of a remarriage conversation long since begun), then their conversation of desire is nowhere if not in the kaleidoscopic center of the film, in the scenes that take place in Joel's head.

That these scenes depict Joel and Clementine in conversation—even if it's not yet clear how this is to be explained or how we are to understand it—is, I simply assert, evident to us in the viewing of the movie. It may be that this impression is stronger at first viewing. But that the principal pair are talking and acting together, doing things together, are matters that we cannot, as we watch them, or on reflection, simply forget. If that claim required evidence, one could point to how often those who discuss *Eternal Sunshine* fall into speaking of Joel and Clementine in these scenes as acting in tandem (or not), offering reassurance to each other, and so on. More to the point, one could note how those who wish to hew the narrative line find that they must *remind* themselves that it's all happening in Joel's head, as if their eyes are out to deceive them.[13] My point is that the viewers' natural inclination here shouldn't be read as a sign of failure or forgetfulness on their part; it seems a sign of failure in the storytelling only if we assume we know what kind of story is being told, independent of the evidence of our eyes.

Among the first facts of this particular film is that what we see in the middle of it, as we venture with the principal pair through Joel's memories, is not a Clementine-simulacrum that Joel has dreamed up. What we see, still and throughout, is Kate Winslet. As we measure Joel's and Clementine's responses to each other, what matters in eliciting our response, what matters in our registering of emotion, is that it is *her* repertoire of responses, her startlingly expressive possibilities, that we are measuring. That fact is part and parcel of the internal relation between human actors on film and the characters they vivify. As Cavell puts it, "the screen performer is essentially not an actor at all: he *is* the subject of study, and a study not his own."[14] The import of this for cinema, one of a handful of facts about the projected image that we invariably overlook, can be brought out by considering counterfactual alternatives to *Eternal Sunshine*, versions of the film that were never made. In one imagined alternative, Michel Gondry casts two different actresses for the same role, like Luis Buñuel before him (in *That Obscure Object of Desire*, 1977), assigning Clementine to one and memory-Clementine to the other. In another, he infuses memory-Clementine's words with a characteristically distorted or possibly otherworldly sheen, something like the effect Bach achieves by adding strings under the singing voice of Jesus in the *St. Matthew Passion*. In another, Gondry simply continues or intensifies the blurry visual manipulations of Clementine that appear now and then early on in Joel's memory journey—for example, at the end of the scene at the flea market. It's clear that each of these alternatives would have resulted in an altogether different film, even a film more like the one Kaufman envisioned—that is, a film about Kaufman's stand-in, Joel.[15]

To the extent that we try to read *Eternal Sunshine* according to these imagined alternatives, allowing the narrative to "correct" our visual, visceral experience, we set ourselves against, or force ourselves to deny, being moved by the film in the way we are moved, and so miss what the film has to show us. Before turning to how the film works on us through Joel and Clementine's remarriage conversation, I might summarize what *Eternal Sunshine* shows us or reminds us about cinema as follows. (1) In watching a film, what we see projected is a world (even if it is a world that is past),[16] but not, except under certain conditions, a *memory* of a world; and only (again) under certain conditions is what we see a view from inside the world of someone's mind. It seems accurate to an experience of Kaufman's films to say that *Being John Malkovich* satisfies—or better, constructs—these conditions, whereas *Eternal Sunshine* does not, or not unequivocally. (2) A corollary to this notion is that everything we see in a film *happens*, even when we agree that, narratively, it didn't happen (that it was his dream before waking, or her drunken perception through the alcohol, or his fantasy of a night out together with her, etc.). One could say that everything in a film is filmed.[17] (3) A corollary to this corollary is that everything that happens in the world of the film helps to inform our understanding of that world, and every action in the world of the film helps to inform our understanding of the actor (the person performing the action). Every action has its consequences, even when the actor in the narrative (because asleep, or drunk, or imagined by someone else) is oblivious to his or her actions and to their consequences.

Reading the middle of *Eternal Sunshine* as an extravagant remarriage conversation between Joel and Clementine—or again, as the emblem, or meme, of such a conversation brought to life in our viewing—helps us to begin to unravel the narrative puzzles that seem to multiply as we consider the logic of memory-erasure. (Why must Joel think each memory as it is being zapped?[18] How do we account for the continuity of Joel's memory throughout its erasure? Why is memory-erasure resisted or confounded by memories of childhood?) In the mythos of remarriage, the obstacle to the pair's getting back together is not some force outside of their relation (e.g., a domineering father) and not some clinical, legal, or otherwise defined condition that one of them suffers (e.g., depression, loss of consortium). The obstacle lies rather in some aspect of the human condition of separateness, coupled with what might be called the dynamics of human relationships. In simplest terms: I cannot become you, and neither can I remain what I am (and likewise for you). Working out the possibility of remarriage, finding a way back together, far from depending on some general ethical insight thus requires a conversation that is about, and so enacts, the particular fault lines and glories and misconstruals and transfigurative possibilities of this pair's particular relationship. But in so doing, the conversation of the principal pair in the best of Hollywood remarriage comedies takes as its condition, and thereby reveals, further aspects of the human, and so shows its basis to be philosophical, a mutual meditation on our common lot.

Joel and Clementine are literally on the adventure of their lives as they search for places to hide (and always, importantly, to hide *together*) from "the eraser guys." But they don't begin their trip through Joel's memories together as equal partners. We can distinguish three stages in the partnership of their odyssey through the middle of the film. At first, Joel is alone in the work of remembering. Clementine does little more than act her part in his memories and is, to that extent, no different from others who appear in them. But soon, somewhere under a blanket or on the frozen Charles, Joel resolves to remember his memories of Clementine beyond his present experience of them (his last, our first). His resolve is able somehow to awaken Clem from her mostly dogmatic reenactment of their past and to enlist her talent for adventure and what she herself calls her "genius" in the effort. In this mode of alertness they race through a hodgepodge of locales: memories (in the woods, on the couch), memory fragments (hallways, rows of bookshelves), and hybrid or improvised memories (Clem as Mrs. Hamlyn, as a childhood sweetheart) where they seem most free to work out their own ways of being together and (one wishes to say) construct new memories together. This is the stretch of the erasure procedure during which Stan (Mark Ruffalo) says ironically or unknowingly that Joel is "on autopilot," and it ends shortly after Howard (Tom Wilkinson) arrives and brings the memories of his patient back under control (the memories of his patient Joel, if not of Mary [Kirsten Dunst]). In the last stage of their backward journey, Joel and Clementine are no longer trying to escape their forced march through their (now again) shared memories. But they have mastered how to break out of their roles from time to time to continue the remarriage conversation in a place or time warp that is all its own. Here they are cognizant somehow both of their (future) history together (their getting bored and feeling trapped with each other, their breaking up), which lends to these early memories their poignancy and weight, and of their (just past) adventures through Joel's populated mind. As they find themselves back at their first meeting on the beach at Montauk, they know that their adventure of a night, as if of a lifetime, has reached its end. The moment prompts Clem to suggest that they "make up a good-bye" and to whisper to Joel the promise or invitation "Meet me in Montauk."

Thus we have not simply the story arc of a travel adventure, where each new locale yields its measure of excitement, but a tale of the principal pair's coming to learn how to travel together through memory—which is to say, to discover what it means to have memories, and to have them *together*. Learning this is nothing less than their learning how to be together again. It is *Eternal Sunshine*'s innovation of the remarriage conversation. Consider some of the highlights.

Joel's first words to Clementine from inside his head but outside his memory (that is, reflecting or commenting on a memory) are not part of an effort at conversation with her. As he drives up alongside Clementine after she's left him—adding to this scene of a memory the fantasy of a car falling from the sky and crashing behind her one-legged walking body—Joel speaks only to deny what he feels ("I'm erasing you, and I'm happy!") or to acknowledge what he feels but without imagining that Clem has a reply ("You did it to me first! I can't *believe* you did this to me"). Soon thereafter follows the earlier, precipitating episode at the flea market, where Joel turns away Clem's wish to talk about having a baby, a paradigmatic conversation of marriage:

> JOEL: Clem, do you really think you could take care of a kid?
> CLEMENTINE (scoffing): What?
> JOEL (muttering): I don't wanna talk about it here.
> CLEMENTINE: I can't hear you. I can never the fuck understand what
> you're saying. . . . You can't just say something like that and say
> you don't wanna talk about it!

Their next memory-scene enacts a parody or tragedy of crossed theories of communication. Clementine, on the bed and leaning over closed-eye Joel, says, "I'm an open book. I tell you everything. Every damn embarrassing thing." After a beat, she draws the moral preemptively—"You don't trust me"—as if only by turning the conversation explicitly to him can she lure Joel into speech. And he takes the bait, offering his contrasting theory: "Constantly talking isn't necessarily communicating." Clementine responds as one might expect: "I don't constantly talk. Jesus! People have to share things, Joel. That's what intimacy is." Then she reminds us of the pitfalls of her theory, and of intimacy, by sharing, "I'm really pissed that you said that to me." But Joel recognizes and expresses, albeit to his journal, the complementary pitfalls of *his* theory of communication in the following scene at

Kang's, when he asks in voice-over, "Are we like those poor couples you feel sorry for in restaurants? Are we the dining dead?" Here their conversation is rudimentary, no more than functional: "How's the chicken?" "Good." "Hey, would you do me a favor and clean the goddamn hair off the soap when you're done in the shower?"[19] We might summarize these opening scenes of Joel's memories and commentary by saying that the gulf we're shown between Joel and Clementine is not the result of their failure to adopt a particular theory or approach to communication—neither his nor hers—despite what some interpreters of the film have suggested.[20] If the trick to remarriage were merely an openness to communicating, then all members of happy couples would be interchangeable. Further, the gulf between Joel and Clementine in these scenes is, one wants to say, as palpable as reality, despite the occasional blurriness of the figures or distortion of their voices. We don't experience it as a *view* of a gulf, as if from Joel's standpoint alone. What would the view from inside Clementine's head—say, during *her* erasing of their relationship—add to our understanding of that gulf? (Would it offer a less sympathetic view of Joel than the unsympathetic view we have from him?) We know enough to understand how Clementine could come to find Joel's displeasure with her moralistic and entrapping, and how Joel could come to view Clementine's seductive "promise" to carry him "out of the mundane" as unsustainable (even as we understand that this promise is his projection onto her). Something else, something more than a mutual openness about their respective feelings, is needed to change the conversation.

Perhaps the most striking aspect of the central stage of their adventure—when Joel and Clementine are actively searching for a place to hide from the forces of the outside world, here presented as the machinery of a kind of forgetfulness—is that it is framed by their revelations to each other about particular, formative moments from their childhoods.

Two singular features of the remarriage mythos find their expression in the middle scenes from *Eternal Sunshine*: the relocation to a place apart, and the suggestion of the principal pair having a childhood together. (1) The two need to find a place apart, a place that Cavell (following Northrop Frye in his discussion of Shakespearean romantic comedy) dubs "the green world," so that they can move beyond their ongoing discord to a place of repose where conversation of the most profound sort, a kind of philosophical dialogue of desire, can happen.[21] In classical Hollywood remarriage comedies featuring couples of sufficient wealth and Manhattan addresses, the green world is given the name "Connecticut." In *Eternal Sunshine*, this mythical locale gets renamed "Joel's head." But especially here in the middle of the film, Joel's head contains scenes of woods and fallen leaves, frozen rivers, snowy beaches, and rainfall not only outdoors but also indoors—a midsummer night's dream's worth of natural mysteries and forest magic. It reminds me of no film world so much as the Connecticut forest night populated by leopards in Howard Hawks's *Bringing Up Baby* (1938), a world that like Joel's head includes whimsical games, chase scenes, wildlife, and sexual imaginings. (2) As in *Bringing Up Baby*, the middle adventures in *Eternal Sunshine* have a decidedly childish playfulness, but with the innovation that we see Joel and Clementine not only acting like children but *as* children, and we also see the adults in different combinations playing at childhood (Carrey's Joel as baby Joel) and at adulthood (Clementine as the neighbor-lady Mrs. Hamlyn). What they gain in these performances of their having grown up together as childhood sweethearts, or as phallic-stage boy and sexy babysitter, are ways for them to act out the fantasy of a life together as if from before history, before they are required to enter the social and sexual realms of adulthood proper with its endless complications, "this mess of sadness and phobias," as Mary finds herself describing it without knowing why exactly.[22] What must happen for them to (in Mary's words) "begin again" is not that they literally return to childhood, infantilizing themselves ("so pure and so free and so clean," the illusion peddled by Lacuna, Inc.), but that they recast their childhood and remember it as theirs *together*, by bringing it and its better ghosts to life in conversation—which is, after all, all that remains of it to *be* shared. As Cavell says of the playful couple in *Bringing Up Baby*, "it is as though their [Valentine's Eve] night were spent not in falling in love at first or second sight, but in becoming childhood sweethearts, inventing for themselves a shared, lost past, to which they can wish to remain faithful."[23]

It should not be a surprise, then, that the first retreating memory of Clementine that Joel wants to keep is one of hers, which is to say, a memory that is his *because* it was hers. He remembers the time under the blanket when she tells him the story of her ugly Clementine doll from childhood, the one whose imagined transformation would magically make her pretty. And Joel remembers his response: he kisses Clementine tenderly, over and over, and repeats "You're pretty," as if his words at that moment are the long-awaited executor of the wished-for transformation.[24] What about this memory reawakens in Joel the desire to remember Clementine? Is it that it is warm while the earlier ones—that is, the first to be erased—were unpleasant? But then Joel is doubly shortsighted, first in ordering the procedure on account of the bad memories and now in wanting to call it off on account of the good. (Does Joel in his memories have the excuse that the bad memories of Clem are already gone, erased? Then is this midoperation buyer's remorse a necessary consequence of the Lacuna procedure?) Rather, the doll memory—not Clementine's of the doll, but Joel's of her retelling and of his heroic gesture: the memory we see—reminds Joel of the possibility, or at least of the early promise, of their "inventing for themselves a shared, lost past" through their remembering, recalling, together.

This is one place where Kaufman's understanding of *Eternal Sunshine* and of what it reveals about memory is surprisingly confused. In an interview, Kaufman, discussing the achievement of Lydia Davis's remarkable novel *The End of the Story*, about a woman's uncertain retelling of the details of a relationship long since ended, explains that she "was talking about the way that memories don't exist as tape recordings. You have a memory of your first date with this person, and you have a memory of your first date with this person after the relationship is over. The end is coloring the beginning, but you still assume it's the same memory if you don't think about it. You're a completely different person, it's a completely different memory."[25] Kaufman's enthusiasm for the radical contingency of self and memory would seem made for his film's response to this contingency, which is to exhibit and explore the transformative effects (as in the doll memory scene) of giving voice to one's memory, recalling or retelling something to another. One might even expect Kaufman to embrace the thought that this is what screenwriters like Kaufman do.[26] But moments later, in discussing the doll memory scene and how "even that's just Joel's memory, too," Kaufman retreats to a variant of the tape-recording model: "When you have a friend tell you a story, you visualize it. No way is it what they visualize, but then it becomes part of your memory of your friend, and it's completely manufactured, it's completely fictitious. Or, at least, a fictitious version of something that they're telling you."[27] The assumption here is that, when you tell me you went to the shore and it was snowing there, my understanding you consists in my forming an image (a private affair). The error in this assumption is that, if understanding rested on something essentially private (private images), then it would make no sense to speak of my image or visualization as in conflict with yours.[28] The moral is that, even if your words suggest an image to me, I am not stuck with it: I may ask to hear more ("Was it beautiful?"), and you may give further voice to your memory ("It was almost a dry snow"). If Kaufman sees (rightly) that memory is not a tape recorder, that this model gives us a confused picture, then why, in describing a memory of a friend's or lover's story, does he invoke the category of the fictitious, as if his memory stood in contrast to the friend's or lover's "recorded" memory? Perhaps because he continues to be seduced by the picture of a memory recorded faithfully somewhere inside. (And perhaps because one person's radical contingency is another's solipsism.)

If to be human is not so much to have fixed memories as to have, or to be, occasions for remembering, then what I remember is not so much "colored" or tainted by what I am now as it is occasioned by it, called for at times and in ways that I can come to understand, or try to. The occasionality of memory is one reason that humans talk and have things to say to one another. We might observe this fact rather than run from it. If I remember something that you do not, or not in the way that I do, or that doesn't include you, that may be a fact about us. But it is no more than a fact about us, which is to say it is not our fate. For I can still tell you, and then it will be your memory, too—yours because of mine, of course, but also mine because of yours, because this occasion for my remembering is bound to you, just as my memories of you bind me to you. One could say, in the spirit of Wittgenstein: there is no private memory—that is, no memory that I could not share with another (though I may be unwilling to share it with you, or with anyone living, or at this particular time and place, or because to share this really means to *confess* it, and so on).

I said earlier that *Eternal Sunshine* is a tale of the principal pair's coming to discover what it means to have memories and to have them together, that this becomes their way of learning how to be together again. That Clementine shows herself in need of this education, by going first in having her memories erased, imagining that her happiness lies in starting over rather than in going back—a trait she shares with the heroines of classical Hollywood remarriage comedies—is simply a further clue that the story unfolding before us in these middle scenes is not just Joel's. As we watch Clementine begin to awaken within Joel's memories and to join in the search for a hiding place in answer to his resolve to remember her, we can feel that she is stepping out of her entire Lacuna-induced amnesia as well. After a hodgepodge transition that includes the two of them darting on the ice in search of the way to Dr. Mierzwiak's office, with Clementine (in voice-over) commenting on various intercut memory scenes ("Oh, look at me. Hey, I look good there!"; "What did we see that day? Oh, look! Hey! We're going to see my grandma"), they arrive in a wood, filmed in natural light and without special effects—both of them, finally, fully present and engaged in the task at hand.

The nature of their conversation that begins here is unlike any so far. To be sure, it has its moments of petty annoyance and of less than petty recrimination. But these merely lend authenticity to answering moments of patience and sympathy and apology, and to the overriding sense of a profound and easy familiarity. The feeling of having *space* (at least world enough, and time) to talk and to listen pervades this forested hillside. Thus, when old patterns of bickering arrive—

> JOEL (after trying Clementine's suggestion to wake himself up): It *did* work, for a second, but I couldn't—
> CLEMENTINE: See?
> JOEL: I couldn't *move.*
> CLEMENTINE: Oh, well, isn't that just another one of Joel's self-fulfilling prophesies? It's more important to prove me wrong than to actually—
> JOEL: Look, I don't want to discuss this right now, okay?

—what happens next isn't the continuation of an old argument, an argument about the argument, as before ("You can't just say something like that and say you don't wanna talk about it!"). Instead, what we get is just more talk, a hint of friendly recrimination answered by an apology answered by its acceptance: a new excuse to be doing something together:

> CLEMENTINE: Fine. Then what? [Pause] I'm listening.
> JOEL: I don't know. You erased *me.* That's why I'm here. That's why I'm doing this in the first place.
> CLEMENTINE: I'm *sorry.*
> JOEL: You—You!
> CLEMENTINE: You know me. I'm impulsive.
> JOEL (after a sigh): That's what I love about you.[29]

We almost don't notice that the precipitating and (despite all) irreversible act that sets the whole drama in motion—Clementine's erasing Joel from her memory—has just been forgiven, perhaps even redeemed.

Joel and Clementine's sense of at-homeness with each other carries over effortlessly from the wood scene to the scenes of Joel's childhood. As Mrs. Hamlyn, Clementine interacts with baby Joel and reveals the tender and tolerant, but not spoiling, childcare-giver that Clementine knew she could be when Joel voiced his doubts at the flea market.[30] But no less revealing of what they are working out in this scene is the awkward moment when Mrs. Hamlyn, now as Clementine, tries to comfort crying Joely by lifting her dress and whispering, "My crotch is still here, just as you remembered it." Joel looks and replies, "Yuck." This attempt to soothe a Joel longing for his mommy may in fact remind him and us of nothing so much as the impossibly treacherous and, it seems, never completed journey from childhood sexuality to adult playfulness. It is the moment that stops the erasing machine and forces Stan to call Dr. Mierzwiak. (Clementine's earlier words alluded to here—"This is a memory of me, the way you wanted to have sex on the couch after you looked down at my crotch"—elicited a curious reply from Joel's memory: "What?" That line, brilliantly improvised by Jim Carrey, seems to carry the suggestion that Joel's ownership of his desire is an ongoing problem, here no less than in the masturbation scene of his humiliation.)

The reimagining of Clementine and Joel's childhood together comes to an end with the scene of his deepest humiliation, when he was goaded by other kids to smash a dead bird with a hammer. Clementine's touching, almost too poignant, rescue of Joel, edited with alternating shots of their adult and childhood selves, is the bookend to Joel's chivalrous response to Clementine's retelling of her longing to transform her ugly doll. (Young Clementine wears the same dress and cowboy hat, and sits in the same cushioned chair, that we saw in the photo in the doll memory scene.) After Joel is rescued, in one of the film's most simple yet surreal moments, we watch the kid couple walking together as we hear the adult couple in voice-over, as if situating ourselves between these times, or outside of time altogether. Their conversation turns on adult Clementine's elemental words of comfort to a Joel whose age is left unclear. (Joel: "I'm so ashamed." Clementine: "It's okay. You were a little kid.") By the time the little kids arrive at Joel's childhood house, the adults' words have moved beyond any lingering awkwardness or indifference or enmity from earlier in the film and arrived at the sublimity of the mundane. Talk of life and death mixes easily with expressions of keen empathy and domestic happiness. (Joel: "That's where I live. Lived. I wish I knew you when I was a kid." Clementine: "Do you like my pink hat? Here, look, feel better. You can really kill me this time.")

In a scene a few moments later that appears to mark their transition from resistance to resignation in the face of Dr. Mierzwiak's efforts, Joel and Clementine are out on snowy Montauk and spot the beach house where they met. (Clementine calls out simply, "Our house!") The somber music we hear in the background seems mismatched with the shots of them in the snow— running through it, throwing it, rolling in it, dragging one another across it. The music suits Joel's mood: he knows now that places tied to memories of Clementine are places where she will soon disappear, and he tugs and drags her in a direction roughly away from "their" house. But Clementine playfully resists, remaining faithful to the mood and the revelations of the previous, childhood scenes, and she throws snow in his face. ("It's fluff," she says: another improvised line. The entire unconstrained spectacle seems to undermine our ability to tell Joel from Jim and Clem from Kate.) On his back and covered in snow, Joel yells, "This is a really bad time for this!" Yet by the time they find themselves on the beach again a few scenes later, reliving the day they first met and knowing it to be the end, and Clementine asks, "What do we do?"—not from uncertainty, but because whatever they are to do takes two—Joel has mastered the mode of their existence and can answer, in the same mood as Clementine back on the snowy beach: "Enjoy it."[31]

What "it" is, the mode of their existence, about which Clementine had said, "This is it, Joel. It's gonna be gone soon"—whether it is the existence of things in the head, or of things on film, or an existence that we are enjoying as we hear these words spoken—is none too clear. Several commentators on *Eternal Sunshine* notice that Mary twice quotes Friedrich Nietzsche (quoted in her *Bartlett's*), and they take this as permission to read the film through Nietzsche's positing the eternal return of the same, what is sometimes referred to as his doctrine of eternal recurrence. The suggestion of a link might be revealing if it were not used to distort Nietzsche. So, for example, Nietzsche's idea can be introduced to advance the thought that we should affirm the good times irrespective of the bad to follow, since Nietzsche's claim is that we should live as if (or, as it is often misread, because) we will suffer each of these moments innumerable times more. And this thought is understood to lead to a kind of happy fatalism that eschews the human habit of, and our entwinement in, regret. Thus *Eternal Sunshine's* closing scene, with its answering pairs of "Okay"s following all that Joel and Clementine have discovered about their past from the Lacuna tapes, is read as their resolve to confront without despair the "disappointment, resentment, and even hostility" that, as their past reveals, inevitably lie ahead of them.[32]

If, however, we return to the closing scene of their last adventure in Joel's head, their first meeting out on Montauk, we find that Joel and Clementine's decision to "enjoy it" has led them back to their beach house, where they reenact Clementine's breaking in, Joel's nervousness as she looks for liquor and heads up the stairs to find the bedroom, and his scared, abrupt leave-taking. But before he leaves, he lingers, reflecting on the memory:

> JOEL (in voice-over): I thought maybe you were a nut, but you were exciting.
> CLEMENTINE (off camera): I wish you'd stayed.
> JOEL (speaking on camera): I wish I'd stayed too. *Now* I wish I'd stayed. I wish I'd done a lot of things. Oh, God, I wish I had— [He pauses.] I wish I'd stayed. I do.[33]

"I wish I'd done a lot of things. Oh, God, I wish I had—." We imagine Joel continuing with a list, terminable or interminable, of all his regrets, the fixed price of memory. But instead, Joel stops himself to speak the simple and obvious one: "I wish I'd stayed. I do." If Joel is affirming something here, it most certainly is not the end of regret. (Is the Joel we've been following, then—the one whose adventures are all "gonna be gone soon"—fated to be supplanted by a wiser Joel who will say "Okay" to everything, including to his inevitable running out on Clementine again? One can choose to affirm this.) Rather, Joel is affirming something here *in* his regret, and affirming it to Clementine, or to someone who hears his "I do" as Clementine did in an earlier scene (it is in their future, after their second first night of courtship):

> CLEMENTINE (in voice-over, answering the phone): What took you so long?
> JOEL (talking to her on the phone): I just walked in.
> CLEMENTINE: Mm-hmm. You miss me?
> JOEL: Yeah. Oddly enough, I do.
> CLEMENTINE: Ah! [Laughs.] You said "I do." I guess that means we're married.
> JOEL (laughing): I guess so.[34]

For Joel to say that he misses Clementine, to regret that he's not there or that she's not here, is, again, to be bound to her in memory. (The truism on which Lacuna is founded: you can't regret what you can't remember.) Similarly, Joel's saying in so many words—as he reexperiences his first failed night with Clementine—that he regrets walking out on her, and his saying this *to* her, is a new effort at binding himself to her, marrying her to his memory, for better for worse. It is his giving up, as if for both of them, the wish to forget. The payoff of Nietzsche's teaching of eternal recurrence is not that one thereby foregoes regret, but that one comes to see what it would mean to affirm it completely, to live without regretting regret. It is a vision of freedom, and one unequivocally opposed to Lacuna's head game of starting anew.[35]

But what does it mean to say that Joel marries Clementine to his memory again, that he remarries her, when he doesn't, after all, or after he wakes up, remember her? Is there anything beyond their "magical" rendezvous at Montauk to indicate that they remember something, anything, of their night adventures in Joel's head?[36]

The question is complicated, well beyond any typical film premise, by the intrusion of the Lacuna tapes into their lives. The tapes don't return Joel's and Clementine's memories to them, but they do, of course, return to Joel and Clem the fact of their having a past together, as well as a picture of that past. The picture may be askew, but it is also shared: they each hear snippets of the other's recording. And while each is devastated by those snippets, neither of them seems to misread or be under any illusion about what they hear. The words on these tapes are part of their remarriage conversation. One reason Clementine wants Joel's tape to keep running when she comes to his apartment (beyond its being, as she says, "only fair") is that she wants to hear what he thought and said about her, why he had her erased. They are the words of the man standing before her at a time when his mind was differently placed, or displaced; and they seem to express not only pre-erasure thoughts but private, clinical thoughts, as if Joel were speaking to his analyst, thoughts offered in the hope that some cathartic effect might be had in giving voice to them. The words on the tape offer a different kind of journey through Joel's head. It's hard to imagine how they could be redeemed. Clementine's decision to get up and leave Joel's apartment seems, however, nonjudgmental (she has a tape of her own, after all); she must leave because of her own state of mind, which she calls "confused." The contrast between their experience of the past forty-eight hours (on the train, on the Charles) and the words on the tapes is too stark.

But of course, something happens out in the apartment hallway:

JOEL: Wait.
CLEMENTINE: What?
JOEL: I don't know. Just wait.
CLEMENTINE: What do you want, Joel?
JOEL: Just wait. I don't know. I want you to wait for . . . just a while.[37]

They wait for about ten seconds. How one understands the words that follow, culminating in Joel's and Clementine's film-ending, reciprocating "Okays," depends on how one makes sense of those ten seconds of waiting. What could they possibly be thinking, and what might they be remembering? At a comparable moment near the end of Max Ophüls's *Letter from an Unknown Woman* (1948), a man who is reading a letter addressed to him from the mother of his son—a woman whom he had long since forgotten—finishes reading it, puts the letter down, looks into the camera, and waits. What follows is a montage of short scenes from his past (and from earlier in the film) that show him with the woman in question and thereby show us what he is thinking, as though his gaze had called up these scenes for us to recollect along with him. And in Mervyn LeRoy's *Random Harvest* (1942), an amnesiac who longs to remember his former wife, though she is also his present wife, has his memory jogged when he returns on a business trip to the town where they first met and to the cottage where they once lived. Here we can follow his thoughts because he is shown actively pursuing the trail back to his former life, and we are reminded of its sights and sounds pretty much when he is and as he is; nothing of his progress is hidden. But in the narrative of *Eternal Sunshine* there are no traces of a road back to the remarriage conversation that they had in Joel's head (unless showing up in Montauk together is such a trace), and neither Joel nor Clementine is given the power by the camera to call up those scenes for us while we all wait the ten seconds. Do we imagine that their heads might hold those scenes anyway? Mostly I think not. Do we nevertheless call up those scenes on our own as we try to bridge the chasm of those ten seconds, as if we could—and as if it mattered that we could—ransom those earlier, forgotten memories for them? (How could it matter to us? And how are we able to so much as try?) Like Paulina in *The Winter's Tale*, who conjures the statue of her mistress Hermione to life, we who watch *Eternal Sunshine* (this needn't be true of all) seem compelled to enliven the forms up on the screen with memories—and, if the trick is to be perfect, not with our *own* memories, however much it appears that we alone (and not Joel or Clementine) hold the key.

If it is right to say that the viewer's experience of *Eternal Sunshine* as it comes to an end is one of projecting the principal pair's forgotten fantasy-past onto them, or (better) of remembering that past *for* them, returning it *to* them—if that is the magic that those ten seconds of just waiting can accomplish—then this experience of the film also makes clear how that fantasy-past matters, how it *does* something (to Joel and Clementine, because of what it does to us). As I have said, *Eternal Sunshine* stands as a meme, or bears the mark or pattern, of remarriage, and its contribution to the genre is the story of coming to discover what it means to have memories together as a way of learning how to be together. (Why the longing to bind ourselves to others in and through memory has such power over us, and why film is the natural medium to conjure up and expose this longing, are questions whose answers must await another occasion.) But just as there is a contrast between a freedom from memories (Lacuna's promise) and a freedom through memories, so there is a difference between how Joel and Clementine's past is returned to them in the film and how *we* return their past to them. Viewers of *Eternal Sunshine* cannot bring the story to an end, cannot unify the pre- and post-erasure memories, by introducing a recording the way Mary does. We cannot supply the missing memories by returning *in fact* to an earlier scene, since what is recorded on the DVD (say) is not a *memory* of what happens in the film any more than it is an interpretation of it. (Memory is not a tape recorder.) We can supply only what we have in memory, what *we* have seen and felt. And what we have seen and felt is not a given: we may forget things, forever miss other things, fail to appreciate the importance of still other things on a first or fortieth viewing. Not the least virtue of Charlie Kaufman's narratively puzzling screenplay is that it replicates for the viewer the felt contingency of memory that we attribute to Joel and Clementine's experiences. But it replicates as well the felt sense that what we remember is always paired with an *occasion* for being remembered. When we remember Joel and Clementine's past for them in the scene in the hallway, so that Clementine can sigh and sob a little and Joel can say "Okay" and they can, with eyes open, begin to imagine a life together again, we do it but once. It is no more, but no less, than an opportunity that awaits us with any given screening. It is what Joel and Clementine are waiting for.

Notes

I want to thank David LaRocca for the invitation to write on *Eternal Sunshine* for this volume and also for his comments and guidance in shaping the paper.

1. Charlie Kaufman, quoted in Rob Feld, "Q & A with Charlie Kaufman," in *Charlie Kaufman, Eternal Sunshine of the Spotless Mind: The Shooting Script* (New York: Newmarket Press, 2004), 135.

2. Kaufman, commentary to the DVD *Eternal Sunshine of the Spotless Mind* (Spike Jonze, 2004), 00:59:57.

3. Kaufman, in Feld, "Q & A," 137.

4. C. D. C. Reeve spots another kink in the narrative chronology when Clementine, driving back from the Charles, is "outraged" at Patrick's calling her "nice," despite the fact that our ability to understand why she is outraged rests on the film's earlier scene of the later (i.e., second) meeting of Joel and Clementine out on Montauk. See Reeve, "Two Blue Ruins: Love and Memory in *Eternal Sunshine of the Spotless Mind*," in *Eternal Sunshine of the Spotless Mind*, ed. Christopher Grau, Philosophers on Film series (London: Routledge, 2009), 29.

5. Ibid., 29 ("Wishful thinking, notoriously, is magical thinking"); George Toles, "Trying to Remember Clementine," in Grau, *Eternal Sunshine*, 116 ("It is as though the Clementine memory composite lodged in Joel's head . . . has set off a magical echo in the *real* Clementine").

6. Stanley Cavell, *Pursuits of Happiness: The Hollywood Comedy of Remarriage* (Cambridge, MA: Harvard University Press, 1981); see also Cavell, *Cities of Words: Pedagogical Letters on a Register of the Moral Life* (Cambridge, MA: Harvard University Press, 2004). Among the films Cavell identifies as members of this genre are *The Philadelphia Story* (George Cukor, 1940), *The Lady Eve* (Preston Sturges, 1941), *It Happened One Night* (Frank Capra, 1934), *Adam's Rib* (George Cukor, 1949), and *The Awful Truth* (Leo McCarey, 1937).

7. See David Edelstein, "Forget Me Not: The Genius of Charlie Kaufman's *Eternal Sunshine of the Spotless Mind*," *Slate*, March 18, 2004 (slate.com); A. O. Scott, "Charlie Kaufman's Critique of Pure Comedy," *New York Times*, April 4, 2004 (nytimes.com).

8. Michael J. Meyer, "Reflections on Comic Reconciliations: Ethics, Memory, and Anxious Happy Endings," *Journal of Aesthetics and Art Criticism* 66, no. 1 (2008): 77–87. Meyer, however, takes from Cavell's description of the narrative of remarriage little more than the pair's dedication to "remarriage reconciliation" (82) and "a discerning disposition to recommitment" (83)—in other words, an ethical gesture sympathetically and repeatedly offered. Nothing in Meyer's telling of the remarriage mythos explains *how* the principals arrive at this ethical gesture, or how they are able to make this gesture to each other (as if all that stood in their way was to recognize that they *ought* to make it), or what change allows them to keep making it. In sum, Meyer leaves out from his telling and thinking the central feature of the genre, the couple's ongoing remarriage conversation. This explains Meyer's mystifying identification of *Eternal Sunshine*'s "green world," the locale in a remarriage comedy where society is kept at bay so that remarriage talk can happen, with "the scene on the beach at Montauk in the coda" (87n37)—that is, a thirty-second scene with no dialogue.

9. *Eternal Sunshine of the Spotless Mind*, 01:22:11–01:23:00.

10. For an illustrative reading of another post-classical Hollywood remarriage comedy where sexual desire is emblematic of the principals' longing for transformation, see my "*Moonstruck*, or How to Ruin Everything," in *Ordinary Language Criticism: Literary Thinking after Cavell after Wittgenstein*, ed. Kenneth Dauber and Walter Jost (Evanston: Northwestern University Press, 2003), 315–28.

11. Ralph Waldo Emerson, "History," in *The Collected Works of Ralph Waldo Emerson*, ed. Robert E. Spiller, Alfred R. Ferguson, et al. (Cambridge, MA: Belknap Press of Harvard University Press, 1971–), vol. 2, 5.

12. See Toles, "Trying to Remember Clementine," 136–39.

13. Compare, for example, Meyer, "Reflections on Comic Reconciliations," 79: "It is crucial to begin by noting that for the bulk of the film (the entire story of Joel's erasure process, which reveals most of what we know about their friendship) it is strictly speaking not Clementine, but Joel's memory of Clementine, that is on-screen." (Note the self-conscious cautiousness of "strictly speaking.") For director Michel Gondry's different take on these scenes, see the commentary to the DVD release of *Eternal Sunshine* at 01:00:15. Gondry's remarks here are mostly transcribed in Christopher Grau's Introduction to his *Eternal Sunshine*, 11–12.

14. Cavell, *The World Viewed: Reflections on the Ontology of Film* (Cambridge, MA: Harvard University Press, 1971), 28.

15. See Kaufman, in Feld, "Q & A," 136 ("In a way Joel is maybe a stand-in for me, you know?"); also 139 ("Well, I guess that goes back to what I was saying about this really being Joel, not Joel and Clementine that we're watching"). Michel Gondry's contribution to the film evidently brings Kaufman pleasure even as it changes what he thought he wanted. This is too neat a parallel to the kind of pleasure that Clementine's responsiveness brings to Joel (to Joel's journey through his memories of Clementine that he thought he wanted erased) to go unnoticed, and it suggests the extent to which unrestrained Clementine, the one who has Joel and the whole human race pegged, can be read as a stand-in for Gondry.

16. Compare Cavell, *The World Viewed*, 23.

17. As I mean this claim, it isn't negated by the apparent counterinstances of post-production special effects, computer-generated imagery, etc. If one prefers, what the claim amounts to is that everything in a film is as if it were filmed.

18. This is related to the puzzle: why is it necessary to "map" Joel's brain back in the Lacuna offices, which requires that Joel think his memories of Clementine *then*, if he must also think them *now*, in his own bed?

19. *Eternal Sunshine of the Spotless Mind*, 00:38:29–00:38:35, 00:42:18–00:42:37, 00:44:50–00:45:37, 00:46:08–00:46:49.

20. Reeve thinks that Clementine is, from her first appearance in Joel's memory, the singular adult in the relationship: "She already has the sort of heart that Joel, through suffering, must acquire. Capable of intimate disclosure, eager to have children, able

to understand that lovers must learn to take the bad with the good, she is already an adult, already aware of what she's like" (Reeve, "Two Blue Ruins," 22). This reading of Clementine contrasts markedly with Kaufman's own wishes for his character and for our response to her: "What I wanted when I wrote this thing was for you to think that she was horrible. The challenge that I set myself was to think that she was horrible, and then think otherwise at the end, which is the beginning" (Kaufman, in Feld, "Q & A," 141).

21. Compare Cavell, *Pursuits of Happiness*, 49.

22. Compare ibid., 31.

23. Ibid., 127.

24. The doll memory scene was a late substitute for a scene that Kaufman says "didn't play well, I don't know why," a memory of Clementine reading from *The Velveteen Rabbit* (Kaufman, in Feld, "Q & A," 140). What I offer in this and the following two paragraphs helps to explain why Clementine's retelling of her childhood memory of the ugly doll plays well at a point in the story where her reading from a children's book does not.

25. Ibid., 139.

26. Compare ibid., 136.

27. Ibid., 140.

28. My thinking on what it means to understand another's words is indebted to the later Wittgenstein. See Ludwig Wittgenstein, *Philosophical Investigations*, 2nd ed., ed. G. E .M. Anscombe and Rush Rhees, trans. G. E. M. Anscombe (New York: Macmillan, 1958), esp. §§138–84.

29. *Eternal Sunshine of the Spotless Mind*, 00:58:35–00:59:19.

30. Reeve argues convincingly, as Freud would have argued, that the ease with which Clementine takes on the role of Mrs. Hamlyn and others from Joel's childhood is the result of a prior, reverse association that was part of his initial attraction to Clementine: "Joel's childhood contains avatars of Clementine; his adult relationship with her [contains] infantile residues" (Reeve, "Two Blue Ruins," 24).

31. *Eternal Sunshine of the Spotless Mind*, 01:12:57–01:13:12, 01:14:47–01:15:13, 01:26:21–01:26:27.

32. Troy Jollimore, "Miserably Ever After: Forgetting, Repeating and Affirming Love in *Eternal Sunshine of the Spotless Mind*," in Grau, *Eternal Sunshine*, 56. Jollimore's essay is not without its virtues: he notes the Emersonian mood pervading much of the film (and even moments of the shooting script that don't appear in the film), and he recognizes that Nietzsche, in proposing the idea of eternal recurrence (citing *The Gay Science*, §341), is interested not in the thesis that our lives will repeat but in what our response to that proposal tells us about our attitude toward the lived present. But even if Jollimore did not twice make the bogus claim that Nietzsche affirms a "rigid determinism" (49) (apparently forgetting Nietzsche's explanation in *Beyond Good and Evil* §21 that such a view misuses "cause" and "effect" and that "the 'unfree will' is mythology"), he is consistent in misreading Nietzsche's "most profound" and "most troubling" view of affirmation (57) as requiring of Joel and Clementine that they "must frequently re-

mind each other of the importance of valuing the present moment, and of *refusing to allow past-directed regrets* or future-directed fears to undermine this valuing" (52; my emphasis). But we are about to see the importance for Joel of allowing regret, and the voicing of regret, into their remarriage conversation.

33. *Eternal Sunshine of the Spotless Mind*, 01:29:04–01:29:28.

34. *Eternal Sunshine of the Spotless Mind*, 00:13:36–00:13:51.

35. The logical and emotive link between freedom and affirming regret was observed over a century ago by William James. See James, "The Dilemma of Determinism," in *The Will to Believe, and Other Essays in Popular Philosophy* (New York: Longmans, Green & Co., 1897), 145–83.

36. At one point early in their conversation on the train back from Montauk, Clementine asks, "Do I *know* you? . . . I've *seen* you, man!" We might imagine that her recognizing Joel reveals a trace of a memory of their earlier relationship. But her surmise is correct: she did see him where she thought she had, at the Barnes and Noble where she works, after her erasure but before his. It was this encounter at the bookstore that drove Joel to Lacuna.

37. *Eternal Sunshine of the Spotless Mind*, 01:42:17–01:42:28.

CHARLIE KAUFMAN, PHILOSOPHY, AND THE SMALL SCREEN

SAMUEL A. CHAMBERS

It goes almost without saying that Charlie Kaufman is best known for his work on the big screen. In 1999 he was nominated for an Academy Award for his first screenplay, the breakthrough *Being John Malkovich*, and then in 2004 he went on to win the Academy Award for *Eternal Sunshine of the Spotless Mind*. Of his six films to date, he has also produced five of them, and in his most recent, *Synecdoche, New York*, Kaufman made his directorial debut. It therefore seems both utterly unsurprising and completely appropriate that the contributions to this volume on Kaufman's philosophy devote the majority of their attention to Kaufman's work in film. Nonetheless, it would be a serious mistake to overlook Kaufman's contribution to the small screen. After all, the blurb for the series in which this volume appears says the book will "illuminate and explore philosophical themes and ideas that occur in popular culture," and there can be no doubt that television is an outstanding medium for exploring popular culture. Hence, this chapter offers a detour of sorts, as it puts aside Kaufman's better-known projects in cinema in order to argue that Kaufman's work in television makes a signal contribution to his overall engagement with popular culture as a mode of philosophical inquiry.

Kaufman produced twenty-two episodes and wrote three episodes of the critically acclaimed but commercially unsuccessful *Ned and Stacey*. While *Ned and Stacey* appears to be a typical situation comedy, the situation itself—a marriage of convenience between the two lead characters, arranged for his career advancement and her desire for a nice apartment—makes possible a provocative engagement with norms of gender, sexuality, and especially marriage. The show thereby offers an exemplary context not only for exploring the unique qualities of Kaufman's work on television but also for engaging with the philosophy of Kaufman around questions such as relationships, marriage, and identity. In particular, this chapter analyzes *Ned and Stacey* using some of the tools of queer theory. It offers an analysis and engagement with questions of "the normal" that surround gender, sexuality, and marital relations. And it uses the episodes written by Kaufman as the central spoke with which to spin a set of engagements with the philosophy of Kaufman. In so doing I argue that *Ned and Stacey* provides viewers with a "Kaufmanesque"[1] portrayal of gender and sex roles that in turn offers a more radical political critique, one more compatible with a "queer" vision, than the significantly more successful, and more obviously "gay," shows that would follow.

One New York Apartment, One Male-Female Relationship, No Desire

Ned and Stacey aired for one full and a second partial season on Fox, from 1995 to 1997. Kaufman was not involved with the show during the first season's twenty-four episodes, but he produced all twenty-two episodes of the second season. The show was canceled and taken off the air exactly halfway through season 2, right after the airing of episode 35 (the third and final episode written by Kaufman). The final eleven episodes were never shown by Fox, but did air in first-run syndication, first in Australia and then later on the USA network in the United States. The first season was released on DVD in 2005, but its lackluster sales have resulted in no DVD release for season 2. In critical television studies the Internet Movie Database (IMDb) has become something of a standard reference for sourcing credits for contributions to television shows and episodes, especially when there are no officially released DVDs. In this case, IMDb only gives Kaufman credit for writing two episodes of the series, "Computer Dating" (episode 28) and "Where My Third Nepal Is Sheriff" (episode 35). However, currently circulating video files of season 2 show a clear on-screen single writing credit for Kaufman on episode 30, "Loganberry's Run," and both plot and dialogue in that episode appear very much to be Kaufman's.

Before turning to either the particular episodes that Kaufman wrote or the general themes that the show explored, I should first give a précis of the show and position it in an important context. Every airing of the show (other than the pilot) gave its setup in the credits, which included a voice-over as follows:

NED: Why Stacey?
STACEY: Why Ned?
NED: It was business.
STACEY: *Strictly* business.
NED: Here's the deal: to get a promotion, I needed the wife.
STACEY: See, to get a life, I needed his apartment.
NED: So what the hell, we up and got married.
STACEY: The only thing we have in common? We irritate each other.
NED: Right! Enjoy the show.

So Ned and Stacey have a classic marriage of convenience, but with a number of modern twists, many of which are played for the necessary laughs of any situation comedy. But the marriage of convenience structure appears to make the show unique within the sitcom genre. That is, here we have something very different from the typical workplace, family, or group of friends situation. This may be one reason that Kaufman was attracted to the project: he took up the job on *Ned and Stacey* during the time that he was unsuccessfully shopping his own sitcom with the not-very-salable title of *Depressed Roomies*, and immediately following his work on a short-lived sitcom, *The Trouble with Larry*, about a man (Bronson Pinchot) who was kidnapped by a baboon during his honeymoon and returns ten years later to discover that his wife (Courteney Cox) has remarried.[2] It is hard to imagine Kaufman working on *Cheers* or *Friends*.

Despite its distance from the standard sitcom fare, *Ned and Stacey* has one unignorable comparison: the smash hit *Will & Grace*, which began airing the very next season (1998) on NBC. The list of similarities is almost eerie. In both shows:

- The action centers on the lives of two late twenty-something urbanites—one male, one female—living in Manhattan.
- Debra Messing plays the female lead.
- The title of the show is made up of the names of the two lead characters.
- The main set is the apartment with the following layout: open kitchen on the left, couch in the middle, office-like area to right rear, balcony center rear.

I am not alone in drawing this comparison; indeed it is not much of an insight at all, since the connections are obvious both to any fan of *Will & Grace* who looks back at old episodes of *Ned and Stacey* and to any fan of *Ned and Stacey* who went on to watch *Will & Grace*. Indeed, reviews of *Ned and Stacey* on Internet sites repeatedly make the case for the show by comparing it to *Will & Grace* and by showing the latter to be an inferior product.[3] My own concern is not with which show is "better" in some sort of broad aesthetic sense, but in the different ways that these two very similar shows deal with gender roles, sexual identity, and questions of normality.

Before exploring these differences, I first need to suggest one last, and crucial, comparison. This one, however, I cannot merely point to, but must argue for. Both shows, I contend, are structured around *the absent space of desire* between the lead characters. In *Will & Grace* this is an obvious point, built into the very structure of the show: it is taken as given that as a gay man, Will cannot desire Grace. Part of the comedy in their roommate "situation" spins off of the fact that their relationship can only be platonic, and therefore all the trials and tribulations of their romantic relationships with others can center on a friendship, rivalry, and camaraderie that never risks becoming sexually charged—their tensions are never sexual tensions.

At first glance *Ned and Stacey* might appear to be working on quite the opposite premise, as it would be easy, at least at first, to assume that the numerous conflicts between Ned and Stacey are based upon sexual tension. When read this way, the show would seem to be operating according to the age-old trope of an unrequited spark of romantic attraction, with two characters who seem as though they cannot stand each other ("The only thing we have in common? We irritate each other") only because of their mutual attraction. This delayed romance strategy is a standard sitcom theme—perhaps most well known in recent television history by the Sam and Diane relationship on *Cheers* and recently parodied so brilliantly on *Community*. *Ned and Stacey* does in fact include this theme, but it works not within it, but against it. Ned and Stacey may well be connected by more than circumstance and mutual self-interest, but that bond is at most one of friendship, not romance. While season 1 might appear to operate according to the logic of deferred romance, the conclusion of season 1 and beginning of season 2 actually reject that possibility. Season 1's finale culminates with the destruction of Ned and Stacey's sham marriage, as Ned kicks Stacey out of the apartment. In a final scene that at first appears to follow the script of romance realized, Ned kisses Stacey, but then immediately yells at her yet again to "get out!" At the beginning of season 2 Ned and Stacey are, in fact, pulled back together by an attraction of sorts. But this is an attraction of equals and peers, and possibly friends; it is not the romantic spark of potential lovers. At the foundation of the relationship between Ned and Stacey lies *philia,* not *eros.*[4] And it is precisely the fact that, like Will and Grace, Ned and Stacey are never headed toward the telos of a romantic relationship that allows *Ned and Stacey* to experimentally explore and critically investigate gender roles in a manner far more radical than most other shows (including *Will & Grace*).

Television and the Normal

With respect to his better-known film work, Kaufman has been praised for his understanding of the importance of television and the characters that emerge within its terms: "He may be the first artist to grasp the fluky profundity of nutso TV."[5] But Kaufman always manages to bring a twist, a turn, a certain torque to his treatment of even the most straightforward or banal of subjects. We see this in the added wrinkle that comes to *Ned and Stacey* during its second season, the season that Kaufman produced and for which he earned his solo writing credits. This season operates under a somewhat bizarre form of the marriage of convenience plot, since at the end of the first season Ned and Stacey agree to get a divorce. Thus the entire second season works within a slightly altered but significantly different set of rules concerning marital roles. I have chosen to compare *Ned and Stacey* to *Will & Grace* not merely because the comparison seems obvious, or because others have drawn it before, but precisely because the *differences* between the two shows highlight what I want to argue is so politically salient (in terms of queer politics) about *Ned and Stacey.* And what makes *Ned and Stacey* Kaufmanesque may be precisely that which enables it to challenge the "normal" with respect to roles of gender and sexuality.

At its inception and throughout its eight-year run of both critical (it won sixteen of its total of eighty-three Emmy nominations) and capitalist (in the Nielsen top twenty for half of its initial network run) success, *Will & Grace* was rightly praised for blazing paths in the portrayal of lesbians and gay men on TV. The Wikipedia entry for the show states matter-of-factly that it "is the most successful television series with gay principal characters."[6] Indeed, there is nothing to argue with in this claim, as the show was unquestionably successful and it was the very first to feature as its lead male character an out gay man. Nonetheless, and as I have previously argued, by giving us an upstanding, straight-laced, and entirely normal character, who the viewers and almost all characters who surround him already know without doubt to be gay, *Will & Grace* rarely if ever engages with, much less challenges or resists, *heteronormativity.*[7]

Heteronormativity is not the same as homophobia. Homophobia describes a very real phenomenon: the individual (or mass) fear (or hatred) of homosexuals (or homosexuality). However, heteronormativity is a concept that points to something that may often be related to, but is always analytically distinct from, homophobia. And it is a different sort of "something"; whereas homophobia is a phenomenon or experience, a concrete event that occurs in the world, heteronormativity is a *condition* of the world in which we currently live. It is the condition wherein heterosexuality is not only more common, typical, or prevalent (because the vast majority of people in the world self-identify and live their lives as heterosexuals), but also *normalized*. To say that heterosexuality is "normalized" means to indicate the extent to which the presumption of heterosexuality is built into languages, practices, institutions, laws, and expectations of behavior. This means that the concept of heteronormativity describes an extremely broad set of conditions: from the federal tax code, which allows only "single" or (heterosexual) "married" status, to the mere but ubiquitous fact that every stranger you meet will very likely presume (without even giving it a single conscious thought) that you are straight. Heteronormativity therefore explains why, as Eve Sedgwick famously argued, the closet is not just a narrow issue or problem that gay people have to deal with once in their lives (when they choose to come out or not), but a generalized and foundational structural feature of the world we live in.[8] Because it reinforces and generalizes the presumption of heterosexuality, heteronormativity is a power, a normalizing force, which helps to constitute a world in which gay people must either repeatedly make the decision to declare their sexuality (often to people who will likely protest that they did not want to hear such a declaration), or allow those very people to continue assuming that they are straight (and therefore run the risk of later being accused of "hiding" or "lying"). Straight people, by contrast, never have to come out as straight and are never accused of "shoving their sexuality in everyone's face" as they live their lives.

Thus, while *Will & Grace* broke new ground in the positive portrayal of gay characters on television (and therefore made an important contribution to lesbian and gay identity politics), it almost never revealed, explored, or resisted heteronormativity. Of course, my analysis up to this point raises an obvious question: What does any of this have to do with *Ned and Stacey*, a show without any gay characters at all? In response, I have no intention of trying to defend a strong thesis about the subversion of heteronormativity and the radical queer politics of *Ned and Stacey*, since the show does not effect such a critique (and surely its lack of gay characters is one of the reasons it does not do so). Nonetheless, and very significantly, *Ned and Stacey* does grapple with questions of "the normal" and "normalization," and precisely in its differences from *Will & Grace* the show contributes to a critique of normalization that very much supports, enhances, and resonates with the project of queer theory and politics.[9]

The best approach to understanding *Ned and Stacey*'s engagement with questions of "the normal" is to analyze the way that the structure and plotting of the show allows for the exploration of sex and gender roles. That is, because Stacey is a "wife" who is not really a wife, and Ned is a "husband" who is not really a husband, the situation comedy of the show is able to throw into starker relief precisely what is potentially constraining and limiting (although also empowering) about these roles. To start with, and to put it simply, partially because they intentionally play the roles of "husband" and "wife" both Ned and Stacey are able to articulate their opposition and sometimes revulsion at those roles themselves. In other words, Stacey not only fails to be a real wife but also fails to desire being a wife or mother. Numerous episodes make this point directly, as Stacey rejects exactly the "trophy wife" role that she is forced to play in the service of Ned's success in his corporate advertising job. For his part, Ned simply never expresses any desire whatsoever to be a husband or father; his goals are not just at odds with the presumptions and demands of these roles, but also beyond, or external to, such roles.

Thus, both Ned's and Stacey's relation to the standard heteronormative roles of love and marriage stands some distance from the position of Will and Grace, both of whom repeatedly narrate their desire for love, marriage, and family. Indeed, Will and Grace both, in their unique ways, follow and repeat a number of heteronormative patterns. Whereas Ned and Stacey use the arrangement of their fake marriage to pursue goals outside of the heteronormative ideal, the roommate pairing in *Will & Grace* seems designed only to defer and delay the eventual resumption of Grace's (and Will's, in his own way) pursuit of romance, marriage, and "family." Moreover, the story arcs of *Will & Grace* often seem designed to overcome the putative "difference" of the show, that is, that Will is a gay man; as has been argued before, the show puts enormous energy into showing how very "normal" Will is, despite his sexual orientation.[10] Because of this, *Will & Grace* often apes heteronormative roles and goals. Will and Grace are not the perfect heterosexual couple, but neither has become what they hope one day to be—and that final goal appears to fall much closer to the telos of heterosexual romance and reproduction than one might at first imagine given the setup of the show.

This comparison leads to a rather striking, if at first difficult to see, contrast. Ned and Stacey turn out to be much more radical characters with respect to gender roles; that is, their relationship is in many ways more disturbing to "the normal" than that of Will and Grace. That is to say, it is much more troubling to dominant norms and perceived standards that Ned and Stacey would not only pretend to be married but also *not really want to be married* than that Will would be gay and therefore naturally incapable of desiring a typical heterosexual narrative. Put another way, Will and Grace, as characters, are natural types that deviate ever so slightly from the normal. Ned and Stacey, by contrast, are characters who are only *playing the role* of the natural types "husband" and "wife," and while the roles they play are utterly normal, the fact that they are playing them proves much more disturbing to the ideal of normality and the processes of normalization. Role-playing itself creates a space for a certain amount (though surely an extremely limited and precisely delimited amount, given the context of a thirty-minute network sitcom) of commentary and critique of heteronormative roles.

Kaufman in Action on the Small Screen

These general theses are exemplified, in various ways, in the three episodes of *Ned and Stacey* written by Kaufman. In these episodes we witness Kaufman's unique sense of humor, but we also see how Kaufman's sense of identity and society inflects the show so as to focus *Ned and Stacey's* engagement with question of normality around sex and gender roles. Kaufman wrote three episodes of the first half of season 2 (episodes 4, 6, and 11). There is no need to summarize the full plot of each episode; instead, I will pick out a key scene or a key story line from each episode and examine it in light of the arguments I have developed above.

For purposes of developing the argument within the structure I have elaborated here, I will take up Kaufman's three episodes out of chronological order. The writing credit for Kaufman that immediately precedes *Being John Malkovich* is for the final episode he wrote of *Ned and Stacey,* and titled, bizarrely but unsurprisingly, "Where My Third Nepal Is Sheriff." The episode deals with the theme, familiar to Kaufman fans, of trying to live up both to our own image of who we should and can be and to society's expectations. This episode focuses on the character of Eric Moyer, Stacey's brother-in-law and Ned's coworker and best friend. Eric and Ned have planned a great adventure/getaway/vacation to Nepal, but Eric is overcome by fears of the unknown and cannot bring himself to get on the plane. Since he has the week off anyway, Eric spends his days sitting on the couch watching VHS tapes that Ned has (somewhat magically) sent back documenting his glorious experiences in Nepal. Eric feels he has failed himself, failed to be the man that he wants to be: one eager for adventure, new experiences, and challenges. Moreover, in the process, he fails to live up to the standards of being a husband. This side effect occurs because Eric's wife, Amanda, has planned a visit from a very old friend, whom she has not seen in many years, to coincide with the week that Eric is away. Amanda hopes to impress her friend, but instead she has to deal with Eric's depression, which leads him not to bathe, cook, or dress himself and to mindlessly rent porn videos at the local video store. This episode is important for what it is *not* about; it is significant for the way it avoids an obvious heteronormative narrative. Rather than Eric's finding it within himself to be the *husband* that he should be, the episode focuses instead on Eric being the *person* that he wants to be. Eric has an epiphany and decides to go to Nepal after all. When he tells Amanda that he has to "follow my heart" and "just live," she says, "I love it when you're like this. . . . Just go to Nepal and follow your heart." The scene seems to end with the standard exchange of "I love yous," but then Eric sticks his head back in the door and says, "Oh, honey, I'll be gone for about two weeks, so if you could return those pornos—thanks." Compared to standard sitcom (and dramatic) fare on television, almost all of which almost always finds a way to be about romance or family, this episode is important for its avoidance of, and resistance to, the obvious narrative. The overall arc of Eric's story has absolutely nothing to do with romance, with his love for or relationship with Amanda, with being a good "father" (Amanda and Eric have one child, who makes no appearance in this episode) or a good "husband."

We see a similar set of narrative choices in the first episode Kaufman wrote for the show, "Computer Dating," and here again Kaufman seems drawn to focus on Eric, who is otherwise a minor character on the show. The title of the episode is a play on words, since rather than using computer technology to find dates, the episode deals with Eric's apparently romantic attachment to the new computer system, named the Omegatron, that Ned has installed at Amanda's muffin shop. Here Kaufman plays with an obvious narrative of love and romance, the temptation to betrayal, but he not only plays it for laughs through the device of the computer (as is to be expected on a sitcom) but also refuses to fold it back into the standard narrative. Hence, while Eric genuinely worries that he's done something wrong in sneaking into the office to "talk with" the computer, Amanda refuses to doubt Eric's fidelity even for a second.

This episode also explores a central and repeated theme in the show: the rivalry and competition between Ned and Stacey. To reiterate, the metaphorical glue that holds these two characters together is not romance but friendship, and the conflicts between them are therefore not those of potential lovers but those of friends. Hence, Ned and Stacey are extremely competitive when it comes to career success, and in this episode Kaufman pushes that competition to a peak. Stacey starts dating one of Ned's clients, a young tech geek (inventor of the aforementioned Omegatron) who also runs a multimillion-dollar computer company. One would thus expect a typical love triangle, with Ned jealous that Stacey has fallen for a younger, richer man. But the conflict comes later, when Stacey accidentally pitches an ad campaign to the young CEO. We then discover that the conflict is located in career rivalry, not romantic jealousy. The fact that the geeky CEO chooses Stacey's ad over Ned's annoys Ned greatly; the fact that Stacey's ad (produced by Ned, of course) ends up winning Ned a CLIO award drives Ned to the heights of frustration and animosity. The key here is that this heightened conflict has nothing to do with romance or a delayed telos whereby Ned and Stacey will finally become a couple. The competition and conflict emerge strictly within the terms of *philia* rather than *eros*. Stacey frustrates Ned not because he wants her, but because he wants the success that she has earned—and, in a cruel twist of irony, has earned *for him*. The last thing Ned wants to do is accept the CLIO award, as it symbolizes Stacey's success, not his. Ned tries to get back at Stacey by submitting dozens of articles (unsuccessfully) to the airline magazine for which Stacey regularly writes. They are both striving for success in their work, and this competition creates the conflict that drives the humor of the episode.

Finally, in the opening scene of the middle episode written by Kaufman, "Loganberry's Run," we see a microcosm of this entire argument. The scene opens with Ned hanging up the phone and announcing to Stacey with all of the excitement usually reserved for a birth or a marriage: "That's it, we've got a date in divorce court, January 7." Stacey positively squeals her response as she jumps up and down: "Yes! Yes!" They are both so thrilled about the news that they agree to throw a "divorce party." Of course, joy and consensus cannot last long, and when Stacey criticizes Ned's choice of music for the party—"[Salsa music] for a divorce party, where were you raised?"—Ned angrily calls it all off. He exclaims, "Why don't we just forget the divorce . . . we're staying married forever!" He then storms out of the room and the show cuts to the opening credits. In some ways this is a simple and straightforward opening scene, taking a standard narrative and running it in reverse. But given that the narrative centers on the romantic telos of marriage, the very center of heteronormativity as it operates in the world today, this brief scene captures an essential element of *Ned and Stacey*'s critical interrogation of sex and gender roles.

The Kaufmanesque Masquerade

This set of scenes and story arcs are woven together by the precise manner in which Kaufman engages with the question of roles, and his unique approach to roles and role-playing also links his work on *Ned and Stacey* with his much better-known work on such movies as *Being John Malkovich*, *Adaptation*, and *Synecdoche, New York*. In all of these cases, Kaufman shows viewers a particular sense of "masquerade." While the dictionary definition of "masquerade" would tell us that, as a noun, it means "a false show or pretense" and that, as a verb, it involves "pretending to be someone one is not,"[11] there is a rich theory of masquerade that goes well beyond these meanings. As Judith Butler has argued, in Jacques Lacan's psychoanalytic writings we get a productively ambivalent understanding of masquerade. In one sense, masquerade can be understood as an appearance that deviates from one's being. This is just a fancier way of expressing the dictionary definition: you masquerade as something you in fact are not. But Lacan suggests something far more radical as well: what if the masquerade itself is that which creates the *impression of a prior being*. Masquerade would not be fake; role-playing would not be pretense. Rather, masquerade would be that which reveals to us that we are always playing roles. There is no truth in our being other than the roles that we play; indeed, to put it better, the truth of our being is nothing other than the roles that we play. According to the interpretation of Butler, who has done the most to develop Lacan's notion in the direction of a radical account of gender, this understanding of masquerade means that what is fake is not the role-playing but the very idea that there is anything other than role-playing.[12]

This idea obviously proves central to Kaufman's work on the big screen—all three of the movies named in the preceding paragraph explore the theme directly[13]—but, as I have shown in the preceding section, it also proves important to his work on the small screen. The ideas of "computer love," of tapes from Nepal standing in for the experience of Nepal, of a "divorce party" are all, when understood through the lens of masquerade, typical of Kaufman's work. In *Ned and Stacey* we get a particular and particularly important element of masquerade. Namely, the show can be understood as asking the question: What if there is no "real" husband, no "real" wife, what if there is no truth that underlies these particular family roles that we play? What if all that we have is the masquerade? To ask these questions is to critically interrogate our very idea of "the normal," and this, as I have shown, is one way to resist the force of heteronormativity.

Kaufman's writing work for *Ned and Stacey* therefore plays an important part in the show's overall engagement with questions of the normal. Kaufman's touch of the masquerade, when applied to *Ned and Stacey*, gives the show a certain critical force: the show proves significant for the space it creates to think differently about sex and gender roles, about our very idea of what "the normal" is, and about the power that that idea has as it circulates in society. To see what Kaufman does with the characters of *Ned and Stacey* in the three episodes he wrote and the twenty-two episodes he produced tells us a lot about not just how he creates an aesthetic object (as with his movies) but also how he relates to and engages with the world.

Numerous scholars have argued that the television series is a different sort of cultural artifact than the film. The serial nature of television not only means that its themes and issues are repeated but also gives it a sort of everydayness that is important when we think about the *work* that popular culture does.[14] For these general reasons, *Ned and Stacey* makes up a crucial, even if minor and largely neglected, component of Kaufman's oeuvre. But more than this, we find in this early television work some of the quintessential attributes of his later film work: stories about our ongoing efforts to realize ourselves fully, to come to terms with our identities, and to establish and negotiate our relationship to the world. But we also find in *Ned and Stacey* a unique, if initial, attempt to challenge pervasive, but largely unseen, aspects of culture. We may think we are laughing along with a conventional sitcom about a marriage of convenience, but in Kaufman's hands, the story becomes a serious (if still very funny) engagement with more complex, often difficult, and sometimes darker elements of culture—including the power of normalization. Ned and Stacey's ambivalence about marriage and their aversion to each other leads us to rethink our own commitments, to question who we think we are, perhaps even to wonder whether we are or should be "married" after all.

Notes

My thanks to Rebecca Brown and David LaRocca for their outstanding critical insights and editorial suggestions on earlier drafts of this chapter.

1. George Clooney has claimed that "one of these days, the term Kaufmanesque will be just as familiar in Hollywood as Mametspeak." Mike Sager, "The Screenwriter," *Esquire* (December 2002): 136.

2. "Charlie Kaufman," *Encyclopedia of World Biography*, 2005 (notablebiographies .com).

3. Customer and viewer reviews on Amazon.com and the Internet Movie Database (imdb.com) both make this argument explicitly.

4. One symbol of this *philia* is expressed in the final scene of the second episode of season 2, when Stacey finally returns to the apartment (her boyfriend having kicked her out). Ned has, unsurprisingly, transformed Stacey's old room into a study, so she is forced to sleep at her desk. But in a scene more moving than "the kiss" at the end of season 1 (the live audience reacts more strongly here), Ned brings Stacey a blanket and a pillow. This three-episode arc confirms that the previous kiss was itself an expression of the bond of friendship. There is no romantic spark between Ned and Stacey even after they have kissed. While Stacey says that the kiss "was incredibly passionate and intense," she says so with a flat tone of curiosity. The kiss leads to nothing; it defers nothing.

5. Tom Carson, "Increasingly Berserk Developments," *Esquire* (January 2003): 36.

6. See the entry "Will & Grace" at wikipedia.org.

7. See my "Telepistemology of the Closet; or, The Queer Politics of *Six Feet Under*," *Journal of American Culture* 26, no. 1 (2003): 24–41; see also my "Revisiting the Closet: Reading Sexuality in *Six Feet Under*," in *Reading Six Feet Under*, ed., Janet McCabe and Kim Akass (London: I. B. Tauris and Palgrave, 2005).

8. Eve Kosofsky Sedgwick, *The Epistemology of the Closet* (Berkeley: University of California Press, 1990).

9. For a detailed elaboration of the differences between lesbian and gay identity politics on the one hand and queer politics on the other, along with a fuller articulation of the way in which queerness can be understood as resistance to heteronormativity, see the Introduction to my book *The Queer Politics of Television* (London: Palgrave, 2009).

10. Kathleen Battles and Wendy Hilton-Morrow, "Gay Characters in Conventional Spaces: *Will and Grace* and the Situation Comedy Genre," *Cultural Studies in Media Communication* 19, no. 1 (2002): 87–105. See also Chambers, "Telepistemology of the Closet."

11. "Masquerade," *New Oxford American Dictionary*, 2007 (oxfordamericandictionary .com).

12. Judith Butler, *Gender Trouble: Feminism and the Subversion of Identity*, 2nd ed. (London: Routledge, 1999 [1990]).

13. Jeremy McCarter, "Untangling Charlie Kaufman: Up All Night with the Director of *Synecdoche*," *Newsweek*, November 1, 2008 (newsweek.com).

14. Michael Shapiro, *For Moral Ambiguity: National Culture and the Politics of the Family* (Minneapolis: University of Minnesota Press, 2001).

THE INSTRUCTIVE IMPOSSIBILITY OF BEING JOHN MALKOVICH

GARRY L. HAGBERG

In reflecting about what it means to understand another person we can easily think in terms of a continuum stretching from complete knowledge to complete ignorance. On the one extreme, we would have no insight into, no sense of, and no conception whatsoever of what the other person's experience might be like. On the other end, we would have total and complete knowledge, the epistemic end point of other-knowledge. At this extreme—a point of other-understanding often thought to be impossible, but still the ideal toward which we aspire or against which we measure our degree of knowledge of another's life—there would be no difference between knowing about a person and *being* that person, precisely because there would (in this ideal position) be no single point of difference, no single "blind spot," between our sense of that person and that person's sense of herself or himself. This ideal condition would, in brief, be one of total transparency.

Deeply embedded intuitions about the nature of the human self can lead us to think that such transparency of the other is readily and unproblematically imaginable: we first picture ourselves a certain way, we then picture ourselves being metaphysically transported into the seat of another such self, and from that inner vantage point we would, with regard to that person, know it all. But now, having seen the profound challenges to this straightforwardly dualistic picture of selfhood by both the Wittgensteinian and pragmatic traditions, we know that this initial picture cannot be taken for granted.[1] Why this is so can be said, and it can be shown.

To be a puppeteer is to be one in control, but at a distance, of the movements of another. That distance is the distance between one person and (the model, or doll, or otherwise inanimate vehicle of) another, a distance covered by interpolated causal connections, by strings, levers, hidden hands. The picture of the homunculus is simply an image of the ultimate puppeteer; according to that fundamentally dualistic picture, a little man sits inside the mind of the bodily machine, pulling strings, moving levers, exerting the causal control of the concealed hand. A little man should require only a little space, and in *Being John Malkovich* the character Craig Schwartz (John Cusack) finally finds employment on a strange half-height floor (floor 7½) in a New York office building.

This film, as a study in competing conceptions of selfhood, self-knowledge, and other-knowledge, in placing the act of puppeteering at the very beginning, is commenting on the embedded intuitions of the conception of selfhood the Wittgensteinian and pragmatic traditions have called into question. The first comment is essentially this: Schwartz, a struggling puppeteer, in serving as the picture of homuncular causation of another otherwise inanimate (model of a) being, simultaneously serves as (here is the embedded intuition) a model of any person as the puppeteer-master of himself or herself. (The fact that he is struggling to, as we say, get control of his life—that is, succeed as a puppeteer—only underscores this idea.) It is thus, for this model of selfhood, exquisitely fitting of Charlie Kaufman to have introduced the central device of the film, the astonishing portal—one that is, after all, hidden (in this case behind a file cabinet)[2]—that leads to what we first, given these dualist-homunculus intuitions, think of as a fifteen-minute occupancy of John Malkovich's (John Malkovich) mind.

Now, given the transparency condition—the ideal position for other-knowledge—one would think that the mental occupancy that Schwartz discovers at the end of the rapid trip through the portal-tunnel would yield the total knowledge of what it is to be *Malkovich*, that is, there would be no blind spots. But instead, we find Schwartz in a spectatorial position with regard to Malkovich's experience. That is, Schwartz is enabled, as a result of this special occupancy, to *observe* what Malkovich experiences for fifteen minutes. And so even at the outset, the philosophical picture of the meta-physical transparency of self-constitutive mental content is in difficulty—it is *Schwartz* who is, while inside Malkovich's mind, seeing what *Malkovich* experiences. (I will return to this shortly, but already the film has suggested that a spectatorial position with regard to another's mental content could not itself constitute full, or for reasons we will see, *transparent* knowledge of those contents.)

But Kaufman makes his film more interesting, and so more philosophically intricate than this, and he does so in layers. First, Schwartz finds himself in Malkovich's mind, but in a complex way: while a spectator to his experiential content *as he* (Malkovich) *perceives it*, Schwartz *senses* exactly what Malkovich does. This, we would initially think, would put Schwartz in a kind of metaphysical halfway house: he views Malkovich's mental experience from, as we say in accordance with the underlying dualistic model of a human being, the inside (in a way profoundly different from the nonobservational character of much self-knowledge);[3] but he still on a sensory level experiences directly, or at first hand, or internally (these spatial metaphors all comport with the dualistic picture) the sensation that Malkovich is having. But here again, there is a gulf of distance between Schwartz and Malkovich even on the level of sensation, for the reason that it is ineradicably *Schwartz* who sees what it is like to have sensory experience identical to Malkovich (I will return to this later as well). At this early point in the film, it seems as though Malkovich and Schwartz are connected to the same stimulus-generating apparatus—but it is the *two* of them, side by side, that are so connected.

We know that William James believed, for good reason, that a Lockeian conception of sensory experience was deeply misleading. To start, as he said, with "sensations, as the simplest mental facts, and proceed synthetically, constructing each higher stage from those below it" is to falsify the genuine character of one's own experience of sensations from the outset. To believe in atomistically sealed or hermetic sensation was, for James, to abandon a true empirical method (hence his "radical empiricism"). And if, for a pragmatic conception of human experience, relations are as real for James as things related, then the idea of our sensory perception of an object *simpliciter* is a philosophical myth. "No one," James wrote, "ever had a simple sensation by itself." Were such sensation simpliciter possible, it would be possible for Schwartz, as a second receiver of Malkovich's sensation, fully to know what it was for *Malkovich* to have that sensation. But, James continued, "what we call simple sensations are results of discriminative attention";[4] and those discriminations, as they occur not only within the patterns of our attention but as they are related to other remembered and interpreted experience, serve to make those experiences what they are.

In this context James observed that, strictly speaking, repetition is impossible, for the same event or the same experience can never occur in "an unmodified brain," that is, in a historically enmeshed sensibility that remembers the previous occurrence,[5] and so relationally in a new way positions or situates the new experience. So if the pragmatists, against the classical empirical view, are at all right in what they suggest about the constitutive power of relations, then Schwartz is ineradicably at a distance (despite our picture-supported initial intuitions) from Malkovich's sensory experience as well—even though he is in a sense directly plugged into it. We think, given our intuitions concerning transparency and other-knowledge, that Schwartz, for fifteen metaphysically transported minutes, is having Malkovich's experience. But to capture the relational facts, this—like our preliminary intuitions concerning selfhood—is too simple. In fact, Schwartz is having the experience *he* would have were he connected all the time to Malkovich's sensory organs; or, he is having the experience Malkovich would have if—as we say—Malkovich were (referring to everything about his subjective sensibility) *Schwartz.* But Kaufman is putting us into a position whereby we can begin to see the deep problem concerning the very idea of being another person. If we are transposed to the other (as we are here through the portal), it is not the other that has experience identical to what we are having. It may be fed by the same brute sensations, but those sensations—to the extent that we recognize or identify them in a Jamesian world—are already *ours,* not *theirs.* Transparency of content is not actually easy to conceive of. And if we insist that this is, after all, not so difficult an imaginative maneuver for the reason that we haven't rightly placed emphasis on what is centrally important here, that is, that we *become* Malkovich for fifteen minutes (which the film does not depict), then indeed we are only papering over the real problem from the other side as it were. That is, now we have a gap-inclusive existence, cease to exist, and although we might say we thus for that duration become identical with another, in fact (to adapt what Gertrude Stein famously said of Oakland), there is no "we" there. In that case, the very idea of other-knowledge is vacated. It is in this conceptual position that Kaufman moves to the next level of this film's content (call it level two).

Schwartz, seeing opportunity in the portal, shares his discovery with his coworker Maxine (Catherine Keener) (with whom he has fallen, nonreciprocally, in love, his marriage to his wife, Lotte [Cameron Diaz], being in serious distress), and they plan to sell the experience to others. This scheme, which he believes will finally bring him some success, he reports to Lotte. And now the next level: Lotte, having insisted on trying the portal herself, develops something of an obsession, an unsatisfiable desire to repeat the experience (to the point of wanting to spend more time in the portal than out of it in regular life). And this is due to the fact that Kaufman has given Lotte a deep-seated desire to change gender.

The implicit contrast is instructive. We think—again initially easily (or, more accurately, we initially think that thinking through the thought in question would be an easy or straightforward matter)—that to change gender would mean to "be a different person." But that way of speaking, although itself harmless, can all too easily lend a false plausibility to the metaphysical notion of being a different person. A transgendered person would be, in the sense discussed above, the same person as a different gender; that is, the patterns of Jamesian attention, the sensibility, the integration of new experience with the old, the relational resonances that emerge within the historical narrative of that experience, would still be the experience of *that* person—however much matters of presentation and embodiment have changed. This is not to suggest even for a moment that the external relations that in part make us who we are would not change profoundly; the point is that, as with Schwartz within the sensory world of Malkovich, it is still *ourselves* who undergo the change. (One imagines that a transgendered person may say and feel that her post-transgendered identity fits who she truly is far better, but that contrast is only intelligible against a background of continuity.) The instructive contrast, then, is that between metaphysically being or becoming a different person, and the colloquial description "becoming a different person." The latter is readily intelligible, but should not lend illicit support to the very different metaphysical notion. This is demonstrated by Kaufman in a lucid way: Lotte, while in Malkovich (we might do well to say "in *with* Malkovich," but I will come to that), dates, falls in love with, and makes love with Maxine (the very object of her husband's extramarital affections).

Lotte, feeling more rightly, if transiently, embodied, is in a position, as was Schwartz earlier, to double the sensation of Malkovich, and so in a sense she fulfills her transgender dream. But only partially, since it is, as Kaufman makes clear, Malkovich's embodiment that is responding to Maxine, a pattern of responses she endorses but, here again, experiences from the spectatorial distance of level one, that is, Schwartz. The difference Lotte's case brings is that, beyond level one, her case demarcates another limit of personhood, a limit to the sense we can give to selfhood. Through a kind of re-embodiment, she gets closer to the person she dreams of becoming (of the opposite gender) and is within that displaced identity more of who, as we say, she really is, yet she cannot descend wholly into that other self, for *she* is the person now with Malkovich in a way that allows her to *present* herself as a man—but only falsely so. This is partly because Malkovich is nevertheless still there and partly because she cannot do what Schwartz (as we shall see shortly) discovers he, as puppeteer, can do at level three. She cannot control Malkovich's movements, and to the extent that she has any volitional control, it is perhaps more of a nudging influence (as we might gently direct or, more strongly, slightly push, another person's movement) than what we experience as free action. And thus Lotte's action within Malkovich is action of a heavily mediated kind.

But there is more to the second level: a bit later, Maxine is told by Lotte that it has lately—that is, through the most recent string of their encounters—in fact been Schwartz inside Malkovich, and not her. (Maxine knows that it has been Lotte inside Malkovich for their affair, so Maxine has been responding to a true dualistic composite—a dualistic composite that itself shows how utterly remote from our reactions to and involvements with persons this fantasy-case is.) Thus part of what Kaufman is showing with the interactions at this second level is the hopelessly distorted conception of a human being, a self, a *person,* that the picture of dualism paints. Were such a picture—the picture both Wittgenstein and the pragmatists did so much to unearth and loosen the grip of—anywhere near accurate, rather than encountering deep imaginative resistance to the case of Maxine reciprocating the love of the Lotte-Malkovich mind-body amalgam, we would find this very nearly as natural as her responding to, interacting with—in short, being a person involved with—Malkovich (but not a Malkovich-Malkovich amalgam, which we consider at level four). Or: what this suggests is that, despite our misleading original dualistic intuitions, we really can't make sense of dualism as a conception of the self. But that is still not all there is at this level: we learn the morally telling fact that, even though Maxine now knows it is her admiring office coworker inside Malkovich during their unions, she does not care and carries on as though there is no significant difference in play. We thus now see her as materialistic, superficial, morally detached, physicalistic—in short, the romantic equivalent of a behaviorist. That her enjoyment continues despite the switched amalgam-content shows in the highest possible relief what we mean by the word "shallow" (with a hint of paradox the word is given new depth here); it also shows that her continuing attachment, whatever we ultimately want to say about it, is not fundamentally to a person—despite the fact that there are still two amalgam-elements present in the physicalized Malkovich. Maxine's "love," if we may for the occasion adapt Shakespeare, carelessly altered when it alteration found.

It is at the third level that the instructive limits on metaphysical transplantation become still more complex. The volitional limits of Lotte in (or again, with) Malkovich were fairly clear, and the word "nudge" just above captures the inescapably mediated, or external (although, like the homunculus,[6] internally placed) nature of that influence on Malkovich's movements.

But Schwartz, as we recall, was at the time of his discovery of the portal a failed puppeteer, and this distinctive skill now allows him to pull the levers of volition in a way no one else can. Does this put him in a position of being John Malkovich? No; to sum up all the reasons considered above, it is still *Schwartz* who is pulling the levers of volitional action. And of course there is one more significant point to make here that separates him from Malkovich: when he does pull those internal levers, it is precisely Malkovich who is *not* in control. (Malkovich's reaction to this—not as a reaction to himself but rather as a reaction to another, that is, a *relational* reaction to Schwartz, within himself—now sets up one new strand of the film's unfolding narrative.) Thus whatever Schwartz as internal puppeteer is now being, it is not—and could not be—Malkovich. Then does this scenario of internal puppeteering place Schwartz in a position of being *closer* to being Malkovich? The answer to this is yes and no: yes in that, unlike Lotte, he is able to decide to perform actions within the body of Malkovich that to an external observer can appear to be Malkovich's intentional action. (For example, Schwartz could commit a crime against Malkovich's intentions and get him convicted as, if not the person, then the body, that committed the crime.) But to capture the nature of the once-removed intentional action here, we have to use the language of appearance, and we have to describe Schwartz's puppeteering action comparatively against the action that either (1) he would perform as Schwartz ("perform" can be a tellingly dangerous word here, in that it suggests that there is always a gap between the agent and the act as there is—at least in nonimprovisational contexts—a gap between the dancer and the dance), or (2) that Malkovich would naturally and unmediatedly perform, were he free of the puppeteering homunculus. So is Schwartz closer, at the third level, to being Malkovich? Yes, he is closer, in that he can do what Lotte and others cannot, but then also no, in that he can never, despite his hands being on the controls, engage in unmediated action of a kind that we persons engage in constantly (or almost constantly—there are settings in which we carefully and exactly embody, or indeed perform, mentally preconceived movements).

Kaufman shows all this in a more direct way as well: Schwartz, inside Malkovich, is (as one part of this metaphysical variant on Shakespearean mistaken identity) pretending to be Lotte (whom he has, unbeknownst to Maxine, locked up) in Malkovich while making love to Maxine with the instrument of Malkovich's body. Before Maxine's discovery (Lotte escapes and, as explained at level two above, informs Maxine that it is not she, as transplanted/transgendered self, continuing with the externally embodied affair, but rather Schwartz pretending to be her to gain access to the object of his affection, Maxine), she takes this as the continuation of her relationship with the Lotte-Malkovich amalgam. We then might ask (and here is what Kaufman shows): Has *Malkovich* made love to Maxine? Importantly, no. Has Lotte? The correct answer is: in a sense. She feels more at home, more truly herself, in a transgendered embodiment, so we might say here that more of the referent of the "she" here is present than is the referent of the "he," where "he" refers to Schwartz: he is already at home in his body, so he only gets further from who he is by occupying Malkovich in order to gain a once-removed romantic and physical access to Maxine. Has Schwartz then made love to Maxine? The correct answer is: in a sense, but not in the sense Lotte has—despite the fact that he has better command of the levers. And of course part of what is so frustrating to the ever-frustrated Schwartz (his unsuccessful marriage to Lotte, his hopeless attraction to Maxine, his knowledge that both women have rejected him while accepting each other in a way only made possible by a portal he discovered and then made available to them) is the metaphysical displacement that, however close by proxy, forever separates him from a genuine union with Maxine. And this unbridgeable distance is made all the more unbearable by the fact that he falsely only bridges it by (always fleetingly) using the instrument of Malkovich—in other words, in acting on his most sincere romantic aspirations he can only have the object of his affection betray him with another man. What Kaufman at this third level has shown is that the referent of Schwartz will always be separate from the Schwartz-Malkovich amalgam; as *persons,* neither he nor Malkovich is fully there, so he cannot know what it is to be Malkovich precisely because Malkovich, exactly coincident with the times of Schwartz- (or any other-mind-) occupancy, cannot be himself. (And again, when Malkovich is fully and solely himself, he does not control volitional levers at a distance in the way Schwartz the internal puppeteer does.) But there is a fourth level.

As the mind and body within which the metaphysical fantasy is played out, Malkovich seeks the advice of his friend Charlie Sheen (*played* by—that is, performed by or, one might in this case say, enacted with a unique privilege by—Charlie Sheen). Malkovich, as a result of his conversations and ensuing detective work (he also, instructively, does not have "mind-meld" access to his inhabitants), finds the portal. What Kaufman shows here takes us to the heart of the matter of human selfhood and how self-knowledge might, and might not, be construed. In the most memorable scene in the film, Malkovich throws himself into the portal. If the world were a place only secondary to, and not constitutive of, selfhood, and if the content of self-constitution were hermetically interior rather than relationally negotiated (as William James's successors Josiah Royce and George Herbert Mead argued) in such a way that "the world" is a phrase invariably interchangeable with, or an elliptical variant on, the phrase "the external world," Malkovich would find himself, at the other end of the portal's tunnel, in what could only be described as the most familiar, and most comfortable, place imaginable. He would find himself inside his own interior, a place already (if the Cartesian picture of selfhood were true) transparently and immediately known to him. What he finds, however, is a special kind of hell in which (1) everyone looks exactly like him; (2) everyone seems too aware of, too glaringly focused upon, him; and (3) everyone can say only "Malkovich." These are not light points.

For Josiah Royce,[7] the most fundamental contrast, indispensable to the emergence of human selfhood, is what he called the contrast between the self and the not-self. Our "self-consciousness," he writes, is "from moment to moment depend[ent] upon a series of contrast effects."[8] If the fundamental fact of self-identity were *internally contained* self-consciousness, Royce's contrast effects would be secondary, contingent, dispensable. But it is precisely such contrast effects that Malkovich, as occupant of his own interior, is denied, and it is anything but familiar and comfortable, anything but a home within which a self can live. Lacking the very possibility of a network of contrasts between self and not-self, Malkovich cannot find himself, cannot stabilize any negotiated or relational conception of selfhood precisely because no such negotiated relation is available. While it is true that we can lose ourselves in a collective, it does not follow from this that we have not first found ourselves in a community. That, and only that, Royce is suggesting, is what offers the possibility of emergent selfhood, and it is the reverse of the picture of first selfhood as hermetic interiority. The character Malkovich, as the relationally constituted individual at the center of this narrative, not only did not emerge from such a condition: this scene shows us that he could not have done so.

But second, in this special hall of self-enclosure, everyone seems too aware of Malkovich—everyone looks at him in anything but an ordinary way. Why so? George Herbert Mead employed the shorthand term "sociality" for the ability that any thing, animate or inanimate, has to enter into what he called systems or networks of interests, activities, and—indeed—the interconnecting relations that constitute those activities and make them what they are. In short, all things and beings have the ability to engage in, to connect with, the constellations of activities that are in the first instance separate from, but then later associated with, connected to, that person, thing, or "sociality." Everywhere Malkovich looks, he sees Malkoviches doing things that are not independent of him, or not independent constellations of activities with which he may engage. He is always already there, and those activities are always already the activities of Malkoviches.[9] Nothing, in Mead's sense, is a "sociality," because everything already was and has ever been Malkovich-integrated. Each Malkovich looks at him as what he in truth could never be—an intruder to himself. But this leads to yet another aspect of the fourth level.

If Malkovich finds this place a reflexive hell, he finds it (here we return to a theme introduced above) a hell *as spectator to himself.* This is an ingenious move on Kaufman's part: Malkovich does not simply emerge from the portal into himself without a difference, as though two slightly separated images of one figure seen through lenses converged to identity (as, for example, where we tell the optometrist in an eye exam, "There! Now they are perfectly together"). In that case, Malkovich would be together with, or identical to, himself, and he would thus be precisely, exactly, at home. Everything in his world would be just as it was before the portal. But this is clearly not the case. And it is not the case because the sense we have of selfhood, while it is relationally emergent, is not in this sense spectatorial; the sense of self that we in truth have is nonobservational—if we are then careful about what we mean by "nonobservational."[10] (We can in some cases reflect upon, and in a sense observe, our own present and past action as we observe the present and past action of others, but this is not to say that the sense we have of the self engaging in that reflection or doing that observing is *itself* observational.) Malkovich, in these scenes, thus cannot be himself, cannot merge into a single image. Coming from the portal, even *he* cannot be John Malkovich.

But the Malkoviches also, in that alternative hermeneutic world (not, importantly, a possible one), can only say "Malkovich." Again, why so? In saying that words only have meaning in the stream of life, Wittgenstein was asserting that words (or all words) are not contingently assigned invariant meanings by stipulating a direct referential connection to an object.

Nor are they amalgams of physical sounds and mental meanings as direct analogues of bodies and minds. Wittgenstein also said in the same spirit that to understand a sentence is to understand a whole language. No word would be available to an entity—this would not be a person—defined in an exclusively self-referential or internally contained way. But actually, this is to say too much (which further makes the point): "defined" is already a public word in *our* language, so we cannot describe what the internally contained Malkovich is doing in these already-public terms. Nor, indeed, can we do so in any other terms. Because the Malkoviches do not mark any self/not-self contrast with any one of the multitude of words we use to do that, and because they cannot so much as enter into language or reside within the expansive contexts of human linguistic intelligibility, they cannot really, in any genuine sense, speak. They, like parrots, say one word, one name—really just one sound. It is a significant moment when, in that terrifying privacy within which no differentiating language—which is to say no language—is possible, Malkovich tries, wants, to speak, and from his mouth he too can only say "Malkovich." One might be tempted here to say that, if he does not have an entry into a public language, he would at least have the makings of a private one for that world with sounds that could stand for inward referents. But that would be only to attempt, futilely, to describe an allegedly private language in public terms (like the term "defined" just above).[11] In his claustrophobic "Malkovich" world, no such development could have originated within him without those public concepts already in play.[12] Those concepts are in play now for the linguistically overpressured Malkovich, because it is after all *Malkovich* who went through the portal and is in Malkovich (at one inner remove). But the others populating that hell, if they originated there, could only be parrots. And fittingly, there is significant philosophical insight shown in the fact that they seem to say "Malkovich" *mindlessly.*

The distinct "un-worded" hell of the Malkovich-Malkovich amalgam is itself sharpened and further defined comparatively within the film; that is, the position we see Malkovich to be in as a result of combining spectatorial distance with an absence of "not-self" relations is shown more clearly through a contrast with a condition that would constitute a special kind of purgatory. When Maxine informs Lotte that she conceived at a time when Lotte was in Malkovich and thus that Lotte is, in the special sense described above, the father, a lot happens (although to understand the sense in which she is the father we have to subtract both the biological and the intentional—she did not at the time intend to impregnate Maxine using Malkovich as a kind of embodied donor). The fact that she (Lotte) was resident in Malkovich at the time of conception is as meaningful to her as it is to Maxine. They declare their mutual love and begin a life together—setting the stage perfectly for Schwartz, who is about to understand the word "frustration" with a new depth, to descend into his personalized purgatory. It turns out that, unbeknownst to Schwartz, the portal moves when it needs a new host, and it does so just as he throws himself back into the tunnel to desperately attempt to reenter Malkovich and, while in him, win back Maxine (who did after all continue the relationship with Malkovich's body earlier). At that moment, however, the portal moves to Maxine and Lotte's newborn infant, and Schwartz is condemned to a world in which he has the concepts, the vast tool set of our language, yet now no physiological ability to express them. This is of course very unlike the Malkovich-in-hell scenario in that, although Schwartz is condemned to witness as their baby the happy-ever-after life of both his beloved Maxine and his estranged wife, he will grow into the ability to speak his mind. He, like his "parents," lives (albeit prelinguistically) in our language. The parrots in Malkovich's hell do not, and could not. (One might incorrectly say that Malkovich is actually in Schwartz's position, in that Malkovich wants to speak—but that is the Malkovich of our human world trapped inside the nonverbal doppelganger of the hermetic interior world without any self-defining or self-constitutive external relations.) Schwartz by contrast is, agonizingly, in a linguistic world nonlinguistically. Or: Malkovich's hell shows something of the impossibility of a private language (so much so that the words "private" and "language" cannot be used together, as the latter contradicts the former); Schwartz's purgatory shows something of the profound frustration of being in possession of linguistic content that one cannot express.

It is time to stand back from the details of the film's narrative and consider a number of the larger issues in play here. Avashai Margalit provides a helpful way of bringing into sharp focus the experiential limitations on being another person (and thus focusing on the profound phenomenon of human uniqueness and the conditions of living a life that support our having an irreducible sense of selfhood) that I am trying to bring out through a reading of *Being John Malkovich*.[13] We have, Margalit observes, episodic and semantic memories: the former, to give one small example, is a memory of the taste of cappuccino, the latter is the memory of the meaning of the word "cappuccino." Memories of past emotions (upon which Margalit so helpfully focuses) can be in either category: we can recall the emotion felt upon experiencing an episode, or upon hearing a word (that is for some reason special). Or they could (Margalit does not go into this) be memories of both—for example, an episode in which we were complimented, insulted, or many other things by hearing a word used in description of us. But the memory of the emotion needs to be understood as a memory of how we felt at the time of, and in response or reaction to, the remembered event or episode that was that emotion's object—that is, that was the act, gesture, circumstance, phrase, word, and the like that makes the emotion in question intelligible, that makes the emotion, in its context, make sense.[14] Remembering emotions thus puts us in an experiential position to know in the present "how the things we remember were felt at the time," and this memory capacity becomes "a way of grasping the sense and the sensibility of past events needed for understanding and assessing the things we care about in the present, especially the people we care about."[15] This capacity, adapted to our present concerns, becomes as well a way of grasping the sense and sensibility of past events needed for understanding and assessing ourselves. And Margalit sees the intimate connection between emotion-memory and the motivational aspects of moral psychology: it is not so much pleasure and pain, but rather the memory of pleasure and pain that, as he says, "makes us tick."[16] I would add to this that such motivations manifest themselves as patterns of attention (as the pragmatists discussed), as ingrained preferences, as affinities, and as—to very much abbreviate—everything that goes to make up a sensibility. Thus what we attend to, prefer, or feel an affinity for in the present is (often) a result of a remembered past emotion. And this memory (as Margalit also sees clearly) need not be unidimensional: we may remember having become embarrassed by actions undertaken in the grip of what we now see as schoolboy or schoolgirl infatuation that we then saw as profound love of a depth unprecedented in human history; we may remember having been wistfully amused by remembering a naïve aesthetic preference. It is for this reason, I believe, that Margalit is wisely cautious about the very idea of identity conditions for emotions: precisely where one would draw the line in demarcating the object of the emotion in such layered cases is hardly a simple (or case-transcending) matter. (And, I want to add, given the wondrous complexity and intricacy of human experience, the vast majority of cases are layered in this respect.) This degree of complexity begins to suggest what is inviolably individual—or in a special, if dangerous, sense, private—about Malkovich's, or anyone else's, experience. Or, to put it more briefly: the same sense, if it does not enter the same sensibility, is not really the same sense at all. But Margalit's discussion, brought into service here, shows a good deal more.

Margalit explores the reasons for the Earl of Chesterfield's observation, made to his son, that a physical injury may be forgotten much sooner than will an insult.[17] In the extreme case of torture, during the episode we will dwell on the pain; in the memory of it, we will dwell, Margalit says, on the humiliation. The point is not of course that we do not or cannot remember physical pain, and often vividly, but rather this: while we remember the experience of the pain, we do not (usually) relive the sensory experience in the act of remembering. In the case of remembering the insult or the humiliation, however, we do. (One could and should give attention to positive experience as well, for example, transformative love, feelings of profound gratitude, and so on, but Margalit has reasons for exploring the negative side.)[18] In any case, it is in the act of remembering the humiliation that we (to a certain extent) relive it, and one can see at a glance how this would extend that all-too-vivid memory's life in the mind of the rememberer. Here (adapting and extending Margalit's discussion beyond what he explicitly endorses), the propositional sense of the memory—where what is remembered is really the generally accessible meaning-content of a sentence—is perhaps not so distinctive to us as individuals, and thus not so constitutive of our sensibility. But the relived memory, the content of the memory that is distinctive to us and that is constitutive of our sensibility, is inviolably ours. And where we express that content in words, in sentences, what is required to understand those words is, rather than an understanding of dictionary definitions or invariant referents, a comprehension of *us*.[19] To understand fully, or to be able to experientially reduplicate our experience, given all of the backstory of our formative experience and its resultant sensibility, would thus be an instructively impossible ideal: what we (rightly) call the full or complete understanding of another could not be a matter of transparent episodic reduplication.

The experience of poetry, Margalit suggests, is one that offers occasions for both propositional remembrance and (simultaneous) reliving remembrance. Poetry thus—to bring into play here terms from our discussion of the film above—offers a kind of bifocal engagement within which we are at a spectatorial distance (when propositionally remembering it) and "inside" the experience (when reliving it) at one and the same time; in this sense our experience of the poem would be at the same time objective and subjective, and simultaneously about poetic content separate from ourselves and about poetic content internal to ourselves (and thus is what we might call a kind of parallel reading). This would come as a surprise only to one overexcited about ontological categorical clarity and neatness: it is *we* (where that means all that is involved in sensibility) who read the poem, *we* who, interpretively and creatively, interact with it. And this aesthetic experience itself offers a lucid microcosm of our interaction and interpretative engagement with our own past.

Margalit, for good reason, is careful to separate himself from a conventionally additive way of picturing the reliving of an emotion in memory. On that oversimplified additive picture, a "cold" cognition of a past event displays the propositional content of the memory to the rememberer, but needs the missing element added to make it "hot." That missing element, on this familiar picture, precisely is the set of nonintentional feelings, sensations, and bodily changes that together transform the cold propositional cognition into the heated experience of a relived, remembered emotion. (On this model, were we in possession of Malkovich's sensory or bodily alterations, additively conjoined to the same propositional content in our minds as the propositional content remembered in his, we would be able to have his experience of remembered emotion.) But Margalit, while not denying that the feelings, sensations, images, and so forth herein described may play roles in particular cases, does deny that "these are the constitutive elements both of the emotion itself and of reliving it."[20] Why not? "Living and reliving an emotion is a thoroughly intentional business, not a matter of a blind feeling's turning a cognitive state into an emotional one. What is essential to an emotion is the involved way in which the subject is engaged with the objects of his or her emotion. Living an emotion is living an involved, not a detached, life."[21] That engagement as lived out with the objects of our emotions will be with objects that have, by their nature, boundary conditions of an indeterminate kind—that is, where the boundaries are determined by details of relevancy within the context in a way that is, while not at all a matter of whimsy or mere stipulation, not invariant across individual cases either.[22] Both the content of the engagement and its boundary will be determined in part by our sensibility, the resonances and "cross-talk" of our distinctive pasts, and resonances with layered remembered emotions as described above. Margalit writes: "From my first-person perspective, if considerable time has passed since a certain event took place, I relive the emotion triggered by it if I find myself involved now with the objects of the past emotion in the way I was involved with them then. Reliving an emotion is being tied to an original event that is constitutive of the emotion (and not just a causal trigger of the emotion)."[23] To match, indeed to replicate, the way I was involved with the complex objects of the past emotion then requires (to put it oversimply) that the referent of the first-person pronoun be the same. The "I" that we use in such cases is necessarily coextensive with the "I" that experienced the emotion at the previous time now remembered, where that emotion was the result of our human engagement, in Margalit's sense, with an object that makes that emotion intelligible and whose boundaries are at least in part themselves determined by our sensibilities. And such sensibilities in turn are, as we have seen, *ours* as well. This is not at all to say that the "I" cannot undergo change as a result of such engagements, but it is to say that there needs to be continuity across time.[24] But "not just a causal trigger of the emotion"? Margalit continues: "In that sense, reliving an emotion is different from a manifestation of a disposition acquired in the past: with a disposition, the fact that there is no particular original event plays an essential role. In a disposition, the object that triggered the disposition, say, your first cigarette that launched you on a career of a chain smoker, can drop out of mind without your disposition to smoke changing in the least. On the other hand, your love for Jerusalem is affected if you forget Jerusalem."[25]

There are circumstances, many in fact, in which we rightly and sensibly speak of two people having the same experiences, and in some of these we can also sensibly use the word "exactly." In cases where we identify parallel dispositions—dispositions that are not dependent for their determinate content on memory of a kind that is determinate-yet-sensibility-variant, we speak sensibly of the same dispositions. It is these cases that can lend illicit credibility to the picture with which this chapter began, the picture of exactly replicated experience across persons. But our experience of the most human kind, the kind that requires an active and interpretively engaged memory, where memory intermingles with present experience in a way far more complex and layered than any simple additive model could accommodate, could never, strictly speaking (and indeed as William James speaks of it), be repeated.

Margalit contrasts what he identifies as the scientific picture with the literary picture of life: "In the scientific picture, life is presented along a homogeneous axis of time, segmented into objective units of seconds, hours, days, and years. Along the axis I can plot our hedonic course and compute the integral of how well I am. At each point in time there is an answer to the question how well I feel at the moment. And by summing up all such points

I can answer the utilitarian's quintessential dream and answer his question, How happy was I in March?"[26]

Extending this picture, we would then feel ourselves equipped to answer such questions as "How happy were Americans in April?"[27] And of course, were this picture true to our life, we would be able to answer the question "How happy was John Malkovich for those fifteen minutes before being expelled near the New Jersey Turnpike?" It was Wittgenstein who was perhaps most sensitive to the multifarious ways in which false or simplified pictures can generate incoherent questions, or questions of such bewildering generality that one does not have anything like the context-specific emergent criteria for sense and for proceeding along a path of inquiry toward a resolution of which the pragmatists wrote. This is clearly not lost on Margalit. Thus the other picture: "In the conflicting literary picture of life we are the authors of our lives, and we had better make sure that they [our lives as lived and told] add up to something meaningful. Meaningful life is a life of reflective memory, not the life of blind experiences."[28] The sense we have of the self is a function of the sense we make, in just this literary way, of our lives. And the phenomenon—a distinctively human one—of remembered emotion that Margalit has articulated, as he says, goes well with the literary picture. The structuring of our life-narratives is in part to respond to, and to preserve the power of, remembered emotions as Margalit has described them.[29] That literary life, I believe (although Margalit is surely right to situate it into a set of polemical contrasts), should probably be called rather just "life" for us humans. To remove all that is distinctive to the active processes of sense-making in the name of a misapplied objectivity is, simply put, hopelessly reductive (hopeless in that it falsifies beyond recognition what it is trying to analyze). That reductive picture (it is perhaps not entirely fair to call it "scientific"—science is certainly not always reductively scientist) may well fit lower organisms, but certainly not something as wondrously complicated, and as complexly situated in time and memory, as a human being. (One can only shudder at the prospect of the profoundly alienated, disengaged, incoherent, sense-starved life this reductive picture would yield.)

Wittgenstein rather puzzlingly said, "What the solipsist means is quite correct."[30] Puzzling, because this comes (if at an earlier stage) from the author who did more than anyone in philosophical history to unsettle, to rethink, and to free us from the shackles of the picture of hermetic mental enclosure, the picture of sealed content with inward transparency. So what could this remark have meant? Perhaps that, for reasons we have seen here, experience, when understood in the more complex ways intimated above is, in this sense, private; it is content that cannot be externally replicated (for all the reasons of sensibility-determined content, the variability of the boundaries of the remembered emotion's object, and indeed the impossibility of making sense of our public words, our language, and even the content of the mind that language would convey in exclusively inward or metaphysically private terms). What the solipsist says, when taken as a claim about the hermetic enclosure and irremediably isolated circumstance of the human self, is, we now know, surely wrong. But what the solipsist might intimate—if understood in (fortunately for us social-relational, rather than Cartesian, creatures) a very different way—is that our experience is, in the first and in the final analysis, *ours*. It is an intimation given expression—or shown, if not quite said—in Charlie Kaufman's conceptually intricate film.

Notes

1. I offer discussions of the Wittgensteinian tradition in "In a New Light: Wittgenstein, Aspect-Perception, and Retrospective Change in Autobiographical Understanding," in *Seeing Wittgenstein Anew*, ed. William Day and Victor Krebs (Cambridge: Cambridge University Press, 2010), and "The Thinker and the Draughtsman: Architecture and Philosophy as 'Work on Oneself,'" in *Philosophy as Therapeia*, Royal Institute of Philosophy Supplementary Volume, ed. Jonardon Ganeri and Clare Carlisle (Cambridge: Cambridge University Press, 2010): 67–81. I discuss the pragmatic tradition, particularly in connection with literary experience, in "Imagined Identities: Autobiography at One Remove," *New Literary History* 38, no. 1 (Winter 2007): 163–81.

2. The very idea of the hidden, with regard to mental content, has been much discussed in the Wittgensteinian tradition. See, for example, Norman Malcolm, *Nothing Is Hidden: Wittgenstein's Criticisms of His Early Thoughts* (Oxford: Blackwell, 1986). (The topic and this volume are of interest regardless of whether one sees "criticism" or "extension" as the correct word for this subtitle.)

3. See on this point Jonathan Lear, "Transcendental Anthropology," in *Open Minded: Working Out the Logic of the Soul* (Cambridge, MA: Harvard University Press, 1998), 247–81. I discuss this concept (nonobservational self-knowledge) in "Narrative Catharsis," in *A Sense of the World: Essays on Fiction, Narrative, and Knowledge*, ed. John Gibson and Wolfgang Huemer (New York: Routledge, 2007), 151–66.

4. The pragmatic conception of experience weaves itself throughout James's writings, but perhaps the most relevant passages are to be found in his *Principles of Psychology*, 3 vols., in *The Works of William James*, ed. Frederick Burkhardt (Cambridge, MA: Harvard University Press, 1981 [1890]), vol. 1, 219–78. A number of these sections are

helpfully reprinted in *Pragmatism and Classical American Philosophy: Essential Reading and Interpretive Essays*, 2nd ed., ed. John J. Stuhr (New York: Oxford University Press, 2000), 54–67. For the passages just quoted, see Stuhr, 161.

5. *Memento* (Christopher Nolan, 2000) is a film that explores the exception to the rule: the fortunately rare case in which experience is still in James's sense not new, but because of severe neurological damage where the capacity for memory is compromised, it always seems so (and so, to the person if not to the body, is so).

6. Just as there is in the homunculus theory of mind-body causal interaction, there is also an infinite regress problem waiting to emerge here: if the Malkovich-seated homunculus were to move to pull the levers, does an inner, still smaller homunculus move those small hands and arms? And if so, then . . . ?

7. I discuss Royce and the significance of his views for these issues at greater length in "Imagined Identities."

8. Many of the most relevant pages from Royce are reprinted in Stuhr, *Pragmatism*; these passages, 250.

9. Anthropologists and others have discussed the notion of a "distributed self" (worthy of a full discussion on another occasion); one might see these scenes of a Malkovich-only population as a distributed self run amok.

10. That is, it is all too easy at just this juncture to unwittingly revert to a dualist picture, one where we just sense (as in sensing rather than directly perceiving a person behind us), rather than perceive, inward content.

11. This logical inability to articulate the conditions of a private language might well be depicted by a human face, clearly urgently needing and wanting to say something, but not being able to so much as emit a single sound, much less a word. This is precisely what the cameo of less than one second by Brad Pitt achieves.

12. For this reason, although this is not the place to pursue the matter, the very idea of autobiography written strictly from the inside out (and the theory of the self motivating that) would be incoherent. See the insightful essays by Ray Monk: "Life without Theory: Biography as an Exemplar of Philosophical Understanding," *Poetics Today* 28 (Fall 2007): 527–70; and "This Fictitious Life: Virginia Woolf on Biography, Reality, and Character," *Philosophy and Literature* 31, no. 1 (April 2007): 1–40.

13. Avashai Margalit, *The Ethics of Memory* (Cambridge, MA: Harvard University Press, 2002).

14. There is a moment in the film where this point is nicely illustrated: when Lotte and Maxine together fall into the portal, they see a rapid run-through of Malkovich's childhood memories. That (alone) puts them into a position from which they could (if their minds were not focused on other things more immediately pressing for them) far better understand the meaning, the content, and the constitutive resonances of Malkovich's incoming sensory experience. But this better position is of course still not one of *being* Malkovich, or of perfectly or transparently seeing his experience. See also, in

this connection, the classic antireductionist statement of Thomas Nagel's in "What Is It Like to Be a Bat?" *Philosophical Review* 83, no. 4 (October 1974): 435–50.

15. Margalit, *Ethics of Memory*, 109.

16. Ibid.

17. Ibid., 117.

18. Margalit's discussion throughout is inflected by an underlying concern with the application of issues concerning memory to the political situation in the Middle East.

19. The great gulf that separates dictionary definitions from our usage of words in contexts of human understanding (and misunderstanding) is explored in fiction by Milan Kundera in *The Unbearable Lightness of Being* (New York: Harper and Row, 1984); see especially "Part Three: Words Misunderstood," 79–127.

20. Margalit, *Ethics of Memory*, 128.

21. Ibid.

22. Determining what is, or what is not, part of a person, or part of what makes up a person, is no easier than determining the boundaries of an action or the boundaries of an artwork. The parallels can prove instructive. I offer discussions of boundary indeterminacy (as this relates to the boundaries of selfhood) in "Rightness Reconsidered: Krausz, Wittgenstein, and the Question of Interpretive Understanding," in *Interpretation and Ontology: Studies in the Philosophy of Michael Krausz*, ed. A. Deciu and G. L. Pandit (Amsterdam: Rodopi, 2003), 25–37, and "Davidson, Self-Knowledge, and Autobiographical Writing," *Philosophy and Literature* 26, no. 2 (October 2002): 354–68.

23. Margalit, *Ethics of Memory*, 129.

24. This is a considerably larger matter than it may initially appear; I offer discussions of the subject in "Self-Defining Reading: Literature and the Constitution of Personhood," in *The Blackwell Companion to the Philosophy of Literature*, ed. Garry L. Hagberg and Walter Jost (Oxford: Wiley-Blackwell, 2010), and "The Self Re-Written: The Case of Self-Forgiveness," in *The Ethics of Forgiveness*, ed. Christel Fricke (London: Routledge, forthcoming). See also the extraordinarily helpful discussion by Marya Schechtman, *The Constitution of Selves* (Ithaca: Cornell University Press, 1996).

25. Margalit, *Ethics of Memory*, 129.

26. Ibid., 133.

27. Ibid.

28. Ibid., 134.

29. I discuss these processes of sense-making/sense-finding (the contrast is not as clear-cut as that dichotomy suggests) and narrative structuring in "The Thinker and the Draughtsman" and "Narrative Catharsis." For deeply insightful and clarifying examinations of narrative's structure and content, see also recent writings by Gregory Currie and by Peter Goldie: Gregory Currie, "Narration, Imitation, and Point of View" in *The Blackwell Companion to the Philosophy of Literature*, ed. Hagberg and Jost, 331–49, and his *Narratives and Narrators: A Philosophy of Stories* (Oxford: Oxford University Press, 2010); and Peter Goldie, *On Personality* (London: Routledge, 2004), esp. chap. 5, "Per-

sonality, Narrative, and Living a Life" (104–28), and his "Narrative Thinking, Emotion, and Planning," *Journal of Aesthetics and Art Criticism* 67, no. 1 (Winter 2009): 97–106.

30. Ludwig Wittgenstein, *Tractatus Logico-Philosophicus*, trans. D. F. Pears and B. F. McGuinness (London: Routledge and Kegan Paul, 1961), 57 (§5.62): "For what the solipsist *means* is quite correct; only it cannot be *said*, but makes itself manifest."

Part 3

BEING IN THE WORLD, PARTIALLY

LIVING A PART

Synecdoche, New York, Metaphor, and the Problem of Skepticism

RICHARD DEMING

There is an old bit by absurdist comic Steven Wright in which he tells the audience, employing his characteristic deadpan monotone, that he has a map of the United States, actual size. "It says, 'scale: one mile equals one mile.' I spent last summer folding it. I also have a full-size map of the world. I hardly ever unroll it."[1] If Jorge Luis Borges were a stand-up comedian, he might have written these very lines. Indeed, as funny as Wright's bit is, there is something more telling beneath it, some kind of thought experiment put into play here about scale and representation, about something we might call a world being itself a kind of representation situated within some larger condition that warrants our attention and yet exceeds our ken. In speaking of a world, we are always speaking within a series of representations and approximations, classifications that inform and form how experience comes to us. Opportunities that bring forward the problems and possibilities of representation provide the occasion for discussing issues of the largest possible import.

Philosophical occasions can appear almost anywhere, in a series of lines from a comedian, say, or in a film written and directed by Charlie Kaufman—a film such as *Synecdoche, New York*, whose title lets us know that the movie is conscious of its troping, of its *being* a trope. Both Wright's lines and Kaufman's film offer a meditation on the means of representing things, and representations are a part of some wider, some wilder earth that we cannot represent without diminishment and yet must represent in order to locate ourselves. To deal with representations is to find that one is negotiating worldviews. These works of art enact those views, which are themselves formed by values, experiences, and belief systems and are mediated by the imagination and deployed by images and language. "What does the work [of art], as work, set up? Towering up within itself, the work opens up a world and keeps it abidingly in force," writes Martin Heidegger in "The Origin of the Work of Art."[2] The world and earth are separate things, the world always displacing an ability to engage the earth as a totality, even as it reveals some partial view of what the totality might be. As Heidegger also writes in the same essay, "The world is not the mere collection of the countable or uncountable, familiar and unfamiliar things that are just there. But neither is it merely imagined framework added by our representation to the sum of such given things." He adds, "World is never an object that stands before us and can be seen. World is the ever-nonobjective to which we are subject as long as the paths of birth and death, blessing and curse keep us transported into Being."[3] What, then, does it mean to be a part of that world, a part of that work that opens a world; what does it mean to be at work in the work of art? In theater and in movies, roles are also known as "parts"—one plays a part, and if an actor is lucky, it is a speaking part. The part speaks to and for the whole: it is a synecdoche. But to speak as a part is to be separated from the whole.

In Charlie Kaufman's *Synecdoche, New York*, the protagonist, Caden Cotard (Philip Seymour Hoffman), is a forty-year-old director living in upstate New York who, in the aftermath of his wife's moving to Berlin with their daughter to become a world-class artist, spends decades creating a piece for theater that attempts to reconstruct a model of New York City inside a vast warehouse located in Manhattan's theater district. The city's seemingly countless buildings, bridges, streets, and so forth fit unaccountably, *impossibly* inside a dilapidated warehouse with enough holes in the roof that we can see the sky beyond it (thereby both establishing the size of the warehouse and drawing attention to the illusory nature of the set within that space). All this space is necessary to Caden's desire to create a work that is "big and true and tough," something into which he can finally "put his true self."[4]

Such ambition results in the piece becoming absurdly inclusive as it absorbs more and more of the banal details of the daily lives of everyone in Manhattan and presumably the world. Why Manhattan? The film never makes this explicit, but as an island, Manhattan stands apart as a part of the larger whole of the continent.

Nothing seems too banal for inclusion in the theater piece: Cotard stops an actor walking by an alley and tells him to do it again. "People don't walk like that," he says. Then what is the actor walking like? Caden attempts to literally represent—in the sense of presenting again—New York not as a whole but in terms of its constituent parts. By doing so he creates a present tense in which he can try to discover himself—a present tense not overwhelmed by regret of the past or fear of the future. Yet this construct is a presence in which those present, the countless Others that make up the world (ours is a world of worlds), do not withdraw or stand intractable in their otherness. These actors are playing parts set in motion by the fact that Caden has represented these others within his constructed world, one that he controls and directs.

The sheer impossibility of Caden's project to put New York within a worn-out warehouse warps space, making it completely indeterminate, and indicates how, within the film perspective, relative scales and relationships are constantly shifting. In other words, the world we see represented on screen is not an exactly mimetic, objective, empirical one. Of course, this is true of a great many films. Given that *Synecdoche, New York* also seems at the start somewhat realistic—Caden's house could be anyone's house, his family and problems possibly anyone's and even perhaps everyone's—the moments that veer from some stable reality and trouble any illusion that film is formed out of an objective realism reveal that *Synecdoche, New York* presents no strict mimesis. However, the film never fully breaks with nor fully mimics what we think of as the "real world." The moments of disruption get stronger and stronger as the film progresses, and the movie shifts modes at the point where the character Hazel buys a house that is perpetually on fire.[5] Such an explicitly surrealistic gesture or image signals that the logic of the film and the audience's expectations of its condition and behaviors change completely at that moment, altering the viewer's relationship to what occurs on screen, destabilizing what distinctions one makes between the real and the surreal.

From the very beginning of *Synecdoche, New York*, the viewer is within what is usually called a subjective realm. Just like space, time is in no way stable in the film: for instance, within the same opening sequence the date is indicated by the voices on Caden's radio as the first day of autumn; then, downstairs, the newspaper Caden reads indicates first that it is October 14 and then, moments later, that it is November 2. This lack of constancy and stability is the emotional condition of the film, both for the characters on screen and in terms of the viewer's relationship to what occurs on screen. These and other destabilizing elements undo the possibility of having a coherent idea of the self, as so many of the criteria for establishing distinctions necessary for the difference between subject and object, self and Other, time and space, are dismantled. The film's unities are not unified.

Given that Caden wrestles with the problem of his identity throughout the film—so much so that in the final reel of the film he "becomes" a cleaning lady named Ellen and is directed by a voice in his ear—Kaufman seems to be signaling that because relationships are always fluid, ever partial, the conditions of the self cannot be static and unchanging. If, as the movie points out again and again, one's body itself is always changing because of time and mortality, it becomes impossible to determine an essential, unchanging self.[6] Yet the desire to have and know oneself as a coherent self persists, against all odds and all the evidence of experience. The only thing that does not change is the fruitless wish that nothing would change.

This breakdown of perspective includes more than space and time. The theater project, for instance, is financed by the MacArthur grant that Caden is awarded; however, we learn that the development of the play continues over more than twenty years, possibly as many as forty. In reality—that is, in the noncinematic world—the grant itself is $500,000, paid quarterly over five years. This is a generous sum, to be sure, even life changing, but not an amount that could provide the funds to finance an operation such as Caden's, with hundreds of actors, crew members, and incredibly authentic and elaborate sets over a period of decades. One could suggest that such details are merely background and are insignificant to our viewing of the movie—the funding simply comes from somewhere else, would be the impatient argument, and to worry about the source of revenue is a bit too literal-minded. And yet the inexhaustible grant seems of a piece with all of the stretching and warping of even the most a priori conditions on screen: time and space.

Film can provide viewers with perspectives not usually available to ordinary sense experience; this is part of its condition as a medium. In *Pulp Fiction* (Quentin Tarantino, 1994), for example, because of the reordering of narrative sequences we see John Travolta's character walking and talking even though in an "earlier" scene we saw him gunned down and killed. Watching a film, we *see* this rather than simply *remember* it, an experience that we can only have at the movies. Thus, film presents a world that looks like ours, but that does not act like our own. In his comments toward delineating an ontology of film and the medium's admixture of exhibition and self-reference, Stanley Cavell writes, "Film takes our very distance and powerlessness over the world as the condition of the world's natural appearance. It promises the exhibition of the world in itself. This is its promise of candor: that what it reveals is entirely what is revealed to it, that nothing revealed by the world in its presence is lost."[7] Cinema therefore reveals the powerlessness of its viewers. The medium's candor makes the world visible to us, the world whose being is beyond human power. Film not only allows for but creates the means for a viewer to become disembodied, to be something other than a form caught in space and in time, yet requires that the same body remain fully seated as a viewer to this spectral reality. In this way, the limitations of the body and the limited powers of what being human entails are reaffirmed.

Synecdoche, New York is not only constantly commenting on its own status as a work of art, a made thing, but also calls attention to itself as a trope that hinges on the establishing of relationships of parts and wholes; this is both what makes its subjectivity bring the world more vividly into focus and what distances it as well. The film is not unique in cinema that way, but it stands for what all cinema does in terms of expanding possibilities of perception beyond what we are usually limited to by the body and its relationship *to* and *ever within* time and space.

Caden's play never has an actual script; the actors respond to notes that the director provides every day about the sorts of things that befall the characters, thus forcing the characters to be forever in a state of discovering what they are becoming. Judging from what we see of Caden at the outset of the film, the project is out of proportion with his skills, inventiveness, and temperament. When the movie opens he is a director for a regional theater company in Schenectady, New York. The play he is developing at the beginning of the movie is Arthur Miller's *Death of a Salesman*, a drama, we are quick to note, that more or less begins at the end of Willy Loman's life, and that sets the tone of tragic inevitability and melancholia built into the movie. Miller's Loman also is a character somewhat unfixed in time, as he regularly disappears into flashbacks of earlier stages of his life. The movie, in other words, begins with a death (Loman's) and then, two hours later, ends with another: Caden's. As Hazel (Samantha Morton), Caden's assistant and true love, insists the night before she dies of smoke asphyxiation after living in a burning house for forty years, the night they finally consummate their love, "The end is built into the beginning. What can we do?"[8] This sense of inevitability is in part the idea that one's choices determine, no matter how obliquely, one's end because the shape of a life is fashioned by choices and responses to what occurs. Yet, at the same time, this fact of mortality—that because things begin they must also end—becomes a measure of what being human entails: that things will end and humans do all they can to deny and even repress this reality.

This idea of endings as the central condition of the film—film being an art form that happens over time and must always come to an end—is established at the beginning of the film when we hear coming from the radio alarm clock by the side of Caden's bed a radio talk-show host ask his guest, a literature professor from Union College, why so much is written about autumn. She describes fall as "the beginning of the end," and we immediately sense how the film establishes its prevailing, melancholic mood that the end of things is already under way. In fact, as we hear the literature professor say this, we see Caden looking at his reflection in a mirror hanging on a door across from the bed. He sits up, looking disheveled in faded t-shirt and boxer shorts; he is soft, fleshy, his light, matted hair beginning to thin. The reflection of his middle-aged body confronts the viewer, as it does Caden, presenting an antinarcissistic and unglamorous moment that Hollywood films rarely afford. Caden can barely look at his reflection: he fidgets, looks away, looks back, looks away.[9] It is a moment of pointed and intimate, vulnerable self-consciousness we viewers witness and which becomes the basis for our relationship to the character. The reflection that confronts us is not just Caden's but our own as well: given the placement of the camera we are in the position to look in the mirror onscreen—instead of seeing our own reflection we see Caden's, but he is now us, we are him. We could also be following him, watching him, as the character Sammy (Tom Noonan), we later learn, has been doing for years. Throughout the first third of the movie, Sammy appears only in quick glimpses, and we therefore watch Sammy watching Caden as we watch Caden. Sammy goes on to portray Caden in the theater piece. So if we are also following Caden, we are learning to identify with him by doubling his movements, appearing wherever he is. As voyeur, Sammy represents or stands in for the audience. What arises is a kind of estrangement from the self: the viewer is there in the theater seat as well as on-screen, identifying with and as Sammy, who in turn identifies with and as Caden. The blurring of subjectivities results in the viewer's division from the sense of self he or she entered the theater with. Because of cinema's ability to allow the viewer the opportunity to identify with and see through the eyes of figures projected onto the screen, the "I" is translated into another. The audience of *Synecdoche, New York* escapes life by watching Caden's life on-screen, the life of a man who turns to his art both to confront life and to escape it—a man who uses art to confront life in order to escape it. This escape from life doesn't entail death, but something like the discovery of truth or the experience of transcendence.

Such an effort to escape from one's life—to repudiate it and the limitations of the material, of imagination, the boundaries of our own mortality, all the conditions definitive of life—enacts, however, a thoroughgoing form of skepticism because that effort is underwritten by a belief that the givenness of life is something that *can* be denied justifiably. The measure of life is that it is determined by a series of limitations. The effort to overcome these limitations is shaped by the conviction that reality (so-called), at some level, is only a dream, a fiction. Cavell insists, "Film is a moving image of skepticism: not only is there a reasonable possibility, it is a fact that here our normal senses are satisfied of reality while reality does not exist—even, alarmingly, because it does not exist, because viewing it is all it takes." Our vision is satisfiable not necessarily by seeing reality, but by the act of seeing itself, Cavell argues, whatever the degree of illusion.[10] Caden attempts to use art to transform reality into illusion by demonstrating that he can recreate it.

A skeptical self-consciousness exists at the level of the film's understanding of its own trajectory, which becomes evident when the literature professor begins reading from Rainer Maria Rilke's poem "Autumn Day," beginning with the second stanza of Stephen Mitchell's translation:

Whoever has no house now, will never have one.
Whoever is alone will stay alone,
will sit, read, write long letters through the evening,
and wander the boulevards, up and down,
restlessly, while the dry leaves are blowing.[11]

At the beginning, we do not know that Caden will end up alone, more alone than he now feels; that he will never finish the play he hoped would encompass his whole self; that, at the end of the movie, which is also the end of his play, he will wander alone through the emptied streets of his half-finished substitute city to die, at last, in the arms of a stranger. If one goes to the movies to escape reality and one's troubles, *Synecdoche, New York* promises to bring that shunted self-consciousness back into the theater. In his staging of *Death of a Salesman*, Caden casts young actors to play Loman and his wife. "Try to keep in mind that a young person playing Willy Loman *thinks* that he is only pretending to be at the end of a life full of despair," Caden tells the lead actor, "but the tragedy is that we know that you, the young actor, will end up in this very place of desolation."[12] The dramatic irony of that moment of the film's self-reflexivity reverberates out into the movie theater. In this case, what is projected onto the screen is not an ideal. The ambitiousness of the theater piece born out of Caden's artistic vision isn't necessarily intrinsic to his character, but it arises out of his desire to replace a world where love and bodies are impermanent and things occur with no intrinsic meaning. Such a definitively human world is one that his work seeks to control, and thus deny, by replacing. Caden's efforts dramatize how a synecdoche is a form of substitution and what the cost of substitution might be.

The transience that Caden takes to be so tragic occurs not only at the metaphysical and existential level; it affects him at the emotional level as well. The feeling of things coming to an end becomes most evident from the opening, when we see Caden interact with his soon-to-be-estranged wife, Adele (Catherine Keener). At the beginning, it is clear that they are nearing the end of their marriage. We learn just how bad things are twelve minutes into the film when, while they are visiting a couples counselor, Adele confesses she has "fantasized about Caden dying, being able to start again, guilt free."[13] In any event, when Adele first appears on-screen the sequence begins with a jump cut, from Caden looking at himself in the mirror to Adele, whose cough provides an aural cue that is used to move into the next sequence. Adele's initially innocuous-seeming cough foreshadows the devastating lung cancer that eventually kills her. The end is built into the beginning. At the beginning of the film, it is clear that Caden and Adele's marriage is almost over. Their inattention and insensitivity to one another as they push by each other—on the way to the bathroom, in the kitchen at breakfast—without ever making eye contact indicates in a very real way that they have lost the ability to acknowledge one another.[14] Endings are not limited simply to the narrative played out on-screen. As is the case with any dramatic or cinematic figure, Caden and all of the characters do not exist prior to the beginning of the film. Their existence is dependent on the narrative of which they are part; their being—we might say, in a more metaphysical key—is dependent on the form that reveals them. They come into existence when the film is projected onto the silver screen or summoned through cables and wires to appear on a television set. We conjure them and their world into ours. The very last word of the film is an imperative—"die"—spoken into Caden's earpiece by an actress who has taken on his role and his identity as director. With that word, he does die, and the film itself, with all of its characters, comes to an end, as all movies must eventually end. At a certain level, we never forget the fact that all movies and the lives they depict and play out before our eyes, lives by which we come to recognize, acknowledge, and learn human behavior and the vagaries of emotion—figures we identify and learn to identify with—will inevitably, inexorably come to end when the reels finally empty out. A viewer seldom feels so palpably this progression to the end—a progression through time—while watching a movie, but this film especially foregrounds the awareness of endings, mortality, and the limits of human life. While we sit, waiting, watching, absorbed in the unfolding narrative, in a sense forgetting our own embodiedness, time on-screen moves forward by leaps and bounds and earth time passes steadily and consistently without our notice. When Caden opens the morning paper, he turns directly to the obituaries and reads some aloud. The cartoon that Olive (Sadie Goldstein), Caden's daughter, is watching is about viruses that lurk everywhere.[15] Later, Olive will begin to scream when pipes and plumbing are being explained to her and she is told that blood is running through her veins. "I don't want blood, I don't want blood," she says again and again.[16] Even Caden's surname, Cotard, indicates the profound depth of his estrangement from his own body. Cotard's Syndrome is a psychological condition in which a person believes that he or she is either already dead or the internal organs are putrefying. Caden is thus a ghost who haunts his own life, which he relocates into the vast haunted house that is his theatrical project. Consciousness of the body, *Synecdoche, New York* immediately establishes (unless such consciousness is repressed), is a daily site of horror because the body is fragile and because the body's fragility continually asserts itself.

It is telling that Caden both leaves his regional home for the big city and that he doesn't mount a production of some already written play. His decision to create his own play may be—in some sense is so unequivocally—a response to his wife's dismissal of his production of Miller's canonical tragedy as simply the reiteration of someone else's authorial vision. Despite all his work on the production of *Death of a Salesman*—a work whose ending is built into the title—Adele points out that the work is not his own. Caden develops, then, his theater piece—a work that never actually has a title—as a delayed response to her accusation. Caden's play is a reaction to his first wife in another way: she is a painter whose work consists of elaborately rendered portraits only an inch in length that one needs a magnifying glass to see. Adele is a miniaturist and Caden a maximalist. Caden's act of producing his own piece of theater—a play that he never masters—is an attempt to embody his own aesthetic sensibilities and values. To build is to dwell, in Heidegger's terms. Moreover, given Caden's fast intent to make the piece authentic, the play expresses his sense of reality and experience—paradoxically, in that he wants the play also to transcend mere subjective experience. His attempt to express that self and to create something both true and transcendent, however, is a withdrawal from self and a denial of reality or the world—in its fraught insistence on being, in its complexities and chaos—that is never free of and is always encountered by means of people's subjectivities, in its fraught insistence on being, in its complexities and chaos.

One of the questions at the heart of *Synecdoche, New York*, however, is—why? *Why* does Caden wish to create a play that is more and more a replication of the world as it is, its representation spilling out further and further, becoming more and more inclusive? Why does Caden insist that everything be as realistic as possible? Indeed, at one point Caden suggests he might title the play *Simulacrum*.[17] But we can take this claim of exact replication seriously only to a point, since Caden adds nearly unbelievable simulations to his warehouse production, such as a full-size dirigible that passes quietly over the model city-set at night while he and Sammy sit on the fire escape outside of the replica of Caden's apartment. Yet simulations double-back upon themselves; for instance, the "simulated" fire escape serves the same functionality as a "real" fire escape. It *is* the thing—or an example of the kind of thing—that it represents. Caden's imagination, however ambitious, is overwhelmingly, confiningly literal. It is doomed to be unable to change the conditions it seeks to represent.

What is it, then, that Caden is creating, building? And if this construct is something into which he can "put his true self," is he creating, building, perhaps *directing* a way of dwelling, which is to say a means of living that is beyond simply subsisting? Caden's desire throughout the movie is to find a way of belonging: his loneliness and estrangement are products of this longing. The play becomes a world that he can write himself into and over which he can theoretically exercise control. But because his play is an elaborate representation, a site that always points away from itself the more it insists on its authenticity, how can he put his "true self" into a place that is always other than what it appears (appearing as if it *is* that which it represents, New York City)? Can Caden's self be "truer" than what it is? And if so, would it still be his self? Near the end of the film, Caden tells Hazel he has settled on a title for the work: "The obscure moon lighting an obscure world."[18] The line comes from Wallace Stevens's poem "The Motive for Metaphor." The stanza reads, "The obscure moon lighting an obscure world /Of things that would never be quite expressed, /Where you yourself were not quite yourself, /And did not want nor have to be."[19]

As the movie progresses, it becomes more and more difficult for viewers to determine the boundaries between the set and Manhattan itself, just as it becomes difficult to know where Caden's life ends and the theater piece begins. Yet Caden's attempt to represent his world traps him rather than allows him to escape; and this, for all the film's humor, makes *Synecdoche, New York* a tragedy. Caden's attempt to escape the world recreates the world as he had already found it. This failure raises the question of whether his play was not a way for Caden unconsciously to make ready for his own death. In trying to repress his own mortality—of exercising (and thereby *exorcising*) a skepticism towards his own finiteness—he actually sets up the conditions for his own end by enacting his limitations, which are delineated by his own psychology.

An analogy drawn from Wittgenstein indicates the implications of the limits imposed by Caden's attempt to transcend his conditions. In the *Philosophical Investigations*, Wittgenstein writes, "Our language can be seen as an ancient city: a maze of little streets and squares, of old and new houses, and of houses with additions from various periods; and this surrounded by a multitude of new boroughs with straight regular streets and uniform houses."[20] And suppose someone decided, in some Borgesian gesture, to design an artificially constructed, idealized language that mirrored exactly, word for word, "our" language in order to discover the internal mechanisms of that language—to know it, somehow, from the outside? Why wouldn't that person simply negotiate that language, discover it? As Wittgenstein insists, we are always limited in our ability to create logical systems because we are always inside that ordinary, nonidealized, labyrinthine language. Being caught within, one would never be able to see existence all at once, or as a whole. So if one were trying to create a model, the words, the ideas, the constitutive concepts needed to create—to discuss, think through, revise—this representative, mimetic language would be the very words one was trying to model. Caden attempts to mediate the city by way of the language that comprises the daily notes he provides the actors about their performances and what is about to happen to their characters on any given day. In both cases—the city, the language—it becomes impossible to get outside what one is trying to represent. One is always part of that representation, however, because the representation is how the subject—Caden or Wittgenstein or we—builds itself into that which is larger, messier, asystematic. If the end is built into the beginning, which could almost be a definition of tragedy, then Caden's vulnerability comes from his own blindness to his limitations. The tragedy lies in the fact that the audience sees what Caden refuses to see.

Caden uses the living city of New York and his experiences in it as the basis for building a substitute city, a New York City according to Caden's vision of it. But why not just live within the real city, as it were, and negotiate it? What does the doubling afford him? His wish to put himself into something real manifests as the transfiguration of his entire life into a simulacrum rather than "reality." But why is this, as he insists his work ought to be "true"? In what ways is the theatrical piece, its set, its players, all more "truthful" than the truth—at least the facticity—of the "mere real world" of New York? Why isn't the world real and true enough? The answer may have something to do with the nature of art, that art can offer some hope of reality and truth, some certainty that the world on its own is incapable of. At some level, the implication is that the world as it is is insufficiently truthful because since it is not a made thing, a consciously crafted space, it is not imbued in every asset with meaning—it does not enact its own meaningfulness. Art transforms real things into enacted meaning. It may be that the gift and the debt of a skepticism of the world's ability to mean itself, to express itself as it is, is art itself.

The title of the film gives us some indication that the play is what it seems to be: a very elaborate, almost herculean trope in which the parts of New York are made to stand for a much vaster whole. Or the individuals themselves are meant to suggest the whole of humanity as being some vast tapestry or text of voices and lives. At one level, the play seems inclusively representative by having actors portray "real people," specific real people in New York. But the totality of this representation creates a comprehensive environment in which Caden dwells. The people who are portrayed with the most specificity are the people in his life—himself, his second wife, his love interest, and so forth. One exception to this is the dramatic figure Ellen Bascombe (played by the character Millicent Weems, who is herself played by actress Dianne Wiest). Ellen is—or so it seems—the housekeeper who takes care of Adele's New York apartment. However, the audience never actually sees Ellen. Caden answers to her name when he drops by Adele's apartment upon discovering that his ex-wife has returned, decades later, from Berlin. A neighbor of Adele's approaches him as he stands at the door to the apartment and asks him if he is Ellen because she is supposed to give the key to Ellen. He says he is Ellen, takes the key, and takes Ellen's role as housekeeper.[21] Ellen, as far as we can tell, never actually appears, and Caden becomes her. Later, when Millicent offers to become Caden when he is out of ideas, Caden is free to become Ellen more continuously. Ellen serves as an escape from Caden's own life, and that escape is also a negation of his own life.[22]

What's the difference between the "real world" and the "simulated world"? As Arthur Danto has suggested, the difference between art and "mere real things" is that works of art offer "embodied meanings." "What I have in mind," he writes in defining the phrase, "is what the thought is that the work expresses in non-verbal ways. We must endeavor to grasp the thought of the work, based on the way the work is organized."[23] The world in its suchness "merely" exists—it doesn't call out for meanings. In attempting to recreate New York as art Caden is attempting to imbue that new world with meaning. The truth that Caden seeks to enact with his play and its dazzlingly exhaustive and detailed set and cast of characters is in reality a higher order of the understanding of experience by which sense and then, subsequently, value are forged. Otherwise, the world as we experience it simply is, it cannot help but be the way it is and thus can be neither true nor false. At every point *Synecdoche, New York* distances us from "the real" even as its protagonist insists on creating the real.

At a certain level, Caden seeks to build a world that he can step outside of, yet this created world is one in which he already feels estranged, lonely, abstracted because of its lack of connection to the world it represents. Or rather, because Caden attempts to forge such a *literal* connection between these worlds, he fails to generate any sense of truth—such as a nonliteral work of art might afford. Caden seems to be operating under the belief that he can create the world anew; and, by having a direct hand in its formation despite its being patterned after another form, despite the fact that he is not its origin, he can be more fully a part of it—we can presume because he was consciously shaping it. Yet for his world to be "true" and honest and tough it must also replicate the conditions of Caden's estrangement; to believe otherwise is to presume that one has no responsibility for the world one finds oneself in. Caden's play as well as Kaufman's film suggest that one always makes a dwelling and inhabits it; Caden takes that condition and attempts to make it literal, thereby revealing something about the function of art and image-making. Even as viewers, the audience—for the movie's audience is also the audience of Caden's theater project—plays its part, and thus the actors their parts as well. Caden struggles into existence and then slips from it as everyone in the movie does, as everyone watching the movie will do. Finally, as Wiest's voice-over, which simultaneously directs Caden's life and narrates the final act of the movie, reminds us, "The specifics hardly matter. Everyone is everyone."[24] One always has a part in building the world wherein one finds oneself. Therein lies a responsibility to others and for others. It may be a perpetually fragmented, largely undefined, stuttering part that we live, but as we see with Caden, one is always taking part in the parting of the world from our sense that we are always to be found there. To represent the world is to be flung outside it, to live apart in the hope of making its fugitive, impossible meanings into something, by hope, by sheer luck, through which consciousness can be made visible to each self. Such an attempt to make one's self-consciousness visible to others, to be responsible to transforming consciousness itself into a legible text, reveals a longing at last to belong.

Notes

1. Steven Wright, *I Have a Pony* (Warner Brothers, 2005). CD.

2. Martin Heidegger, "The Origin of the Work of Art," in *Poetry, Language Thought*, trans. Albert Hofstadter (New York: Harper, 1971), 44.

3. Ibid.

4. *Synecdoche, New York* (Charlie Kaufman, 2008), 00:37:00.

5. Ibid., 00:20:00–00:22:00.

6. "We are all hurtling toward death," Caden tells his assembled cast, "yet here we are, for the moment, alive. Each of us knowing we will die; each of us secretly believing we won't." Ibid., 00:42:38.

7. Stanley Cavell, *The World Viewed* (Cambridge, MA: Harvard University Press, 1979), 120.

8. *Synecdoche, New York*, 01:41:48.

9. Ibid., 00:01:00–00:02:00.

10. Cavell, *The World Viewed*, 188–89.

11. Rainer Maria Rilke, "Autumn Day," *The Selected Poems by Rainer Maria Rilke*, ed. and trans. Stephen Mitchell (New York: Vintage, 1989), 11.

12. *Synecdoche, New York*, 00:10:32–00:10:46.

13. Ibid., 00:12:19.

14. Ibid., 00:02:00–00:05:00.

15. Ibid., 00:04:09.

16. Ibid., 00:07:50–00:08:20.

17. Kaufman's allusion to Jean Baudrillard's thinking on simulacra seems both intentional and unavoidable. See Baudrillard, *Simulations*, trans. Paul Patton (New York: Semiotext, 1983).

18. *Synecdoche, New York*, 01:43.30.

19. Wallace Stevens, *The Collected Poems of Wallace Stevens* (New York: Knopf, 1954), 288.

20. Ludwig Wittgenstein, *Philosophical Investigations*, 3rd ed., trans. G. E. M. Anscombe (Englewood Cliffs, NJ: Prentice Hall, 1953), 8.

21. *Synecdoche, New York*, 01:11:00–01:12:43.

22. Ibid., 01:45:30, 01:50:30.

23. Arthur Danto, *Abuse of Beauty* (Chicago: Open Court, 2003), 139.

24. *Synecdoche, New York*, 01:56:07. And with the narration, Wiest is an actress playing an actress playing a director speaking words into the earpiece of an actor (Hoffman) playing a director who becomes an actor in his piece, words written by the film's screenwriter, who is also its director.

"There's No More Watching"

Artifice and Meaning in *Synecdoche, New York* and *Adaptation*

Derek Hill

Don't Say Pitch

If writing is a "journey into the unknown," as screenwriter Charlie Kaufman (Nicolas Cage) tells his aspiring screenwriting brother Donald (also played by Nicolas Cage) in *Adaptation* (2002), it is also a painful one.

The character Charlie Kaufman in *Adaptation* wants nothing more than to remain true to what he perceives as the best way to adapt Susan Orlean's best-selling nonfiction book *The Orchid Thief* into a film. But when he attempts to write, hunched over his makeshift desk—a chair with his electric typewriter placed on the seat—the camera focuses on the blank page before him, a taunt that sends him spiraling into panic. The scene is played for laughs, but the fear that Charlie is experiencing at that moment is all too real for anyone facing a deadline.

"To begin," Charlie says in voice-over, wanting to be anywhere other than in front of his typewriter. "To begin. How to start? I'm hungry. I should get coffee. Coffee would help me think. But I should write something first, then reward myself with coffee. Coffee and a muffin. Okay. So I need to establish the themes. Maybe banana-nut. That's a good muffin."

We then cut to Susan Orlean (Meryl Streep) in her cozy, softly lit New York apartment. She is seated at a handsome desk, the shelves around her filled with books (unlike Charlie's room, which is spartan and devoid of reading materials) and, more significantly, Orlean actually appears to be enjoying the process of writing, something that Charlie never seems to do. Then we see a series of action-packed scenes depicting the stories Orlean is telling in her book *The Orchid Thief*: Victorian-era orchid hunter William Arnold, drowning in Venezuela; a slow pan through jungle terrain in Borneo, where another hunter vanished; another cut to an emaciated, dysentery-afflicted man barely alive in China, who is preyed upon by poachers and viciously beaten to death, his prized orchids ripped from his pouch. The scenes from Orlean's book, as visualized by screenwriter Charlie Kaufman, director Spike Jonze, and director of photography Lance Acord, are dynamic and visceral. And for Charlie, suffering from writer's block, it is yet another crippling projection of how he believes other writers produce, and a reminder of how he doesn't. While Charlie can only stare at a blank page, Orlean easily conjures up final draft copy. The notion is a lie, of course. All writers deal with writer's block, all writers know the terror of staring at a white piece of paper or the stark white field on a computer screen.

Adaptation was Charlie Kaufman's second collaboration with director Spike Jonze, an ambitious follow-up to their feature film debut *Being John Malkovich*, which itself was groundbreaking for an American commercial film in its casual disregard for narrative conventions and its gleeful fusion of comedy, surrealism, and postmodernist distancing effects. *Being John Malkovich* was a creative shock to the Hollywood system in many ways. The film garnered generally strong reviews from critics,[1] and the film's eccentricities attracted a small but fervent cult audience, making it a modest success at the U.S. box office.[2]

Needless to say, expectations were high for *Adaptation*. *Human Nature*, the second film made from a Kaufman script and his first collaboration with former music video director Michel Gondry, had been given a token theatrical release earlier in the year and had been a bust artistically, critically, and at the box office. For the most part, the general public had taken no notice, so *Adaptation* would conceivably be viewed as the legitimate follow-up to *Being John Malkovich*.

Adaptation would not drift under the radar as Gondry's film had. Supplied with a larger budget and A-list Hollywood stars in key roles, and distributed by a major Hollywood studio—Columbia Pictures—the film was likely to have broader exposure; and that exposure would help further Kaufman's unique approach to storytelling. *Adaptation* is also more ambitious and complex than *Human Nature* in terms of its narrative structure. Perhaps because of that ambition and complexity, it is debatable whether the film remains coherent as it implodes in the last act under the weight of its cynical satire of Hollywood plot clichés. But what *Adaptation* begins—and what Kaufman's directorial debut, *Synecdoche, New York*, continues—is the depiction of central characters struggling to portray "real life" in their respective artistic modes. This struggle is Kaufman's own as well, as both films show artists in crisis as they attempt to explore ways in which different modes of artifice portray (or impede the portrayal of) real human emotions and insight. We watch Kaufman's characters grapple with the nature of their modes of art, asking the identical question that Kaufman himself asks: What is my responsibility to my craft and my role as a human being within the play of life? Just as Kaufman's characters struggle with the tension between art and commerce, the films themselves, situated firmly within the commercial marketplace, play out that exact tension.

It should be noted here that the idea of "authenticity" as it pertains to film is not the same as it is defined in philosophy, although both definitions are applicable to this essay and to the Kaufman films discussed. The idea as it relates to philosophy, specifically existentialism, stems from the concept of how one lives with self-awareness (authentically) within the world—being conscious of the choices one makes—as opposed to living within the constructs of a community's rules (inauthentically) as established by government, church, family, and other institutions. To live authentically is to live with bravery, questioning one's existence within these systems and choosing to tread outside the lines, sometimes even taking a moral stand that is beyond the legality of what is permitted in the society (for example, civil disobedience in the name of civil rights). To live inauthentically is to live without questioning one's self within the parameters of the community, choosing to exist without cognizance of one's place within it. It is to live with blinders on, to accept the rules of the community as it stands. The authentic being is the person aware of his or her responsibility within the world: as John Macquarrie writes in his book on existentialism, "Either he is himself, he is existing as this unique existent, standing out from the world of objects and going out from any given state of himself; or he is not himself, he is being absorbed into the world of objects as just another object, he decides nothing for himself but everything is decided for him by external factors."[3]

How the concept of authenticity is dealt with in the medium of film is an entirely different issue.[4] The stylistic mode of Italian neorealism, one of the most influential film movements since the end of World War II, is for many still the ideal of how to capture authentic reality with the camera. Proponents of the movement employed nonactors or non-showbiz performers to play working-class characters and filmed on "real" locations (as opposed to sets). Despite the effort to highlight realism, neorealism was never truly as "pure" or objective as many of the original adherents insisted it was—for instance, Roberto Rossellini, in his masterworks *Rome, Open City* (1945), *Paisan* (1946), and *Germany Year Zero* (1948), utilized melodramatic plot elements to heighten emotional power to varying degrees despite the otherwise stark, gritty, "realistic" visual style. Neorealism, nevertheless, proved a startling contrast to the mythic, almost incantatory power of German Expressionism, which generally accentuated bold stylistic strokes over the neorealists' humanism—a motive that often resulted in films that appeared more like documentaries than dramatic narratives.

But the concept of realism in films, of authenticity, has radically changed since the postwar emergence of neorealism and its assimilation into commercial filmmaking worldwide. A film like Martin Scorsese's *Taxi Driver* (1976) is regularly referred to as "realistic" by viewers and reviewers.[5] The film is directly influenced by Italian neorealism in its sense of place and through lead actor Robert De Niro's method acting style, which strives to represent realistic human behavior. But the film is also infused with moody, expressionistic flourishes that move it away from straight naturalism. Despite the fact that Scorsese deviates from a strict neorealist approach, *Taxi Driver* effects a powerful, heightened sense of authenticity and realism.

Steven Spielberg's war drama *Saving Private Ryan* (1998) is a similar case. The film's opening D-Day battle scene, notable for its ferociousness in detailing the carnage and horror of the Allied forces storming Omaha Beach, was upon its theatrical release routinely talked about and praised by reviewers and audiences for its vivid realism and accuracy. A panel discussion on the PBS program *The NewsHour with Jim Lehrer* with historians and veterans of the war commended the film for its realism and how it drastically differed from previous war films, which had never shown combat so graphically.[6] The violence in *Saving Private Ryan* is undoubtedly brutal and does not flinch from showing us blood spurting, limbs being blown off, and other visceral displays of the evils of warfare that only millions of dollars and the best special-effects technicians in Hollywood can supply. Despite its impact, though, Spielberg's approach to the material is anything but naturalistic. Cinematographer Janusz Kamiński and Spielberg devised to desaturate the color palette and manipulate the shutter speed for the battle sequences, which resulted in giving the film a grittier feel: for viewers, the altered film created a greater sense of intimacy with the horrors of war and therefore was deemed more affecting and more real.

These aesthetic manipulations, however, are rarely the concern of audiences and critics, who find themselves lost within *Saving Private Ryan's* hyperrealism or *Taxi Driver*'s sweltering, psychological fever dream. Both films generate a strong emotional spell that is hard to shake; but upon reflection the "reality" of these films dissipates to reveal their very unreal, inauthentic melodramatic cores and stylistic manipulations. Authenticity is no longer strictly the province of naturalism. It never really was. Even in Rossellini's war trilogy we recognize how his use of melodrama, character, and plot devices exceeds the bounds of naturalism.

Charlie Kaufman's search for authenticity in *Adaptation* and *Synecdoche, New York* is likewise worlds away from how a neorealist would approach capturing real life on screen. Kaufman's use of fantasy and surrealism to reflect his characters' inner lives is nevertheless a search to actualize their reality on film. What makes both films (especially *Synecdoche, New York*) difficult at times is the interplay, the seamless fusion, of inner and outer life being depicted without any clear indication that we are watching an approximation of a dream or hallucination. There are no obvious optical effects (though they are there), as in countless other films, to tell us that we are entering into subjective dream space; no outrageous supernatural narrative shenanigans to remind us that we are not in this world. *Synecdoche, New York* does incorporate science fiction elements into the narrative, but the tangible reality that is put forth is indeed a recognizable, modern America, albeit one filtered through a misleading, fluctuating viewpoint. However, even when Kaufman the storyteller refuses to be transparent on a narrative level, the sincerity of his main protagonists' struggle to live authentic lives should not be in doubt.

I Will Be Dying and So Will You, and So Will Everyone Here

Synecdoche, New York, highly anticipated by critics and admirers alike due to the fact that it heralded Kaufman's debut as a feature film director, was met with praise and puzzlement when it premiered at the 2008 Cannes Film Festival. The film failed to find a North American theatrical distributor for months,[7] but was eventually picked up by Sony Pictures Classics and given a limited release, where it performed poorly.[8] Perhaps some explanation for the lackluster viewer reception has to do with the way the film avoids giving its viewers anything like a warm welcome, instead abruptly dropping them into the blunt realities, anxieties, and confusions of its protagonist, the miserable, depressed, middle-aged theater director Caden Cotard (Philip Seymour Hoffman). While the film still displays Kaufman's expert comic timing—albeit of the dry ice variety—*Synecdoche, New York* is darker and more caustic than admirers of films like *Being John Malkovich*, *Adaptation*, and even *Eternal Sunshine of the Spotless Mind* were prepared for. But for all its misery, there is almost something impressive in its unflinching cheerlessness, a non–horror film that is far more disturbing than most of what is marketed as horror these days.[9]

Like the Charlie Kaufman character in *Adaptation*, *Synecdoche, New York*'s Caden Cotard is searching for authenticity, although at the beginning of the story he doesn't articulate his desire in these terms. Well-respected and relatively successful, Caden has never put himself on the line artistically, having been content to work through his artistic preoccupations via other playwrights' work. When we meet Caden he is in rehearsals for a production of Arthur Miller's *Death of a Salesman*, one of the most popular and critically acclaimed of all modern plays. Wanting to cover new ground, and with the intention of creating a new degree of tragedy, Caden casts younger actors in the main roles, thereby making the irony immediately transparent and the losses and failures that much more visceral. Caden wants to accentuate how the young *actors* playing Willy Loman (Daniel London) and his wife (Michelle Williams) themselves have no awareness that the horrible inevitability of death awaits them in old age—that the loneliness and regrets that haunt the main character, Loman, will be the fate of the actors, as well as of those in the audience. Caden, in the tradition of modern theatrical theorists such as Antonin Artaud, Bertolt Brecht, and Peter Brook, wants to engage the audience with direct action, using the artifice of the production as a way not to lull them to sleep—with the soporific of illusion—but to wake them up!

Caden eventually realizes that in order to make great art he will have to put himself on the line. He will have to be courageous and willing to risk everything. To make profound art, he himself will have to wake from sleep. Such a creative burden is touched upon in *Adaptation* with Charlie's and Susan Orlean's respective searches for deeper meaning, but those quests are never satisfyingly resolved. *Adaptation*'s last act spirals into parody, and though it may be effective on a comedic level, it does not resolve Charlie's pursuit of authenticity. The parody only clouds things more.

I Don't Have a Resume or a Picture. I've Never Worked as an Actor.

"You have a hangover."

"Nothing matters anymore."

"Your wife just had a miscarriage."
"You keep biting your tongue."
"You were raped last night."
"You lost your job today."

In *Synecdoche, New York*, Caden uses these simple, declarative sentences as the sole direction for his actors, who are participants in a most unusual theatrical experiment: a play without a script, intended to chart everyday life in its boredom and complexity. At the same time, however, Caden's play is meant to portray the *wonder* within the mundane and, perhaps above all, a sense of the truths within art. Caden opts for a streamlined directorial approach—simply telling the actors what happened to their characters—only after having tried to work with them in a more organic fashion, always with disappointing results. On the first day, Caden attempted to guide his actors in his usual manner, nudging them toward an understanding of who their characters are through suggestion, but grew increasingly angry when they responded theatrically instead of "living" their roles. To Caden, the actors seemed phony—inauthentic—until he changed his directorial methodology.

In *Adaptation* Charlie, too, rejects a formulaic, "phony" approach to his art, initially showing disdain for Donald's approach to writing. Charlie's disdain is valid, since Donald does not seem in the least serious about his writing and only starts doing it because he does not know what else to do. Charlie constantly mocks the lessons Donald parrots from screenwriting guru Robert McKee's (Brian Cox) seminar. By the end of the film, however, after Charlie has reluctantly, and out of desperation, attended one of McKee's writing seminars, he comes to some sort of understanding that art and commerce can mix, at least temporarily. McKee opens up Charlie's mind with alternative ideas regarding the fundamentals of story structure and the mechanics that give shape to art, but it is Donald's trite but profound words that transform Charlie's relationship to his work.

"You are what you love," Donald tells Charlie as they are hiding out in the swamp from drug-snorting, gun-toting Orlean and John Laroche (Chris Cooper), "not what loves you."

Donald will pay with his life for giving such sage advice, cruelly killed in a hyperbolic parody of Hollywood action clichés. And yet Donald's sudden death can be viewed as reconciliation on a symbolic level between art and commerce, inspiration and the far less glamorous reality of the mechanics behind making art. Donald has to be killed for Charlie to move on, so that Charlie can reconcile the extremes within himself.

The problem Charlie faces, of course, is adapting Orlean's book about rogue horticulturalist John Laroche, the search for a rare species of orchid, and the criminal case that follows. But how could someone like Charlie, or anyone for that matter, possibly make a dramatic movie out of a book that does not lend itself to any sort of traditional narrative despite its engaging premise, characters, and the fascinating orchid subculture? Charlie cannot, as we quickly realize when he has lunch with the film's producer, Valerie (Tilda Swinton). But his disorienting passion for the book, for Orlean's passion for her subject, and for Laroche's obsession in the hunt is contagious and lands him the job. But Charlie quickly runs into a creative wall. He desperately wants to maintain a sense of authenticity for the subject, honoring Orlean's mesmerizing tale and trying to break free from storytelling constraints that he believes will only corrupt the purity and beauty of the text. Charlie doesn't want to be writing a Hollywood movie at all. He wants to make art.

Although the film's last act makes a mockery of Hollywood conventions, it simultaneously validates the need for symbolic dramatic closure. Jonze and Kaufman are no doubt having fun constructing a simulacrum of the ludicrous action finale. But the joke, however cleverly executed, nevertheless feels hollow, a capitulation by talented filmmakers that, yes, they too have found themselves at a creative dead-end. Just because we know the creators are in on the gag doesn't make the end any less airless.[10]

Up to that moment, though, *Adaptation* contains several key scenes that pinpoint Charlie and Orlean's inability to fully come to terms with the numinous nature of creation. Driving back from a classical music concert, Charlie and a woman he has been seeing off and on, as it were *un*romantically, Amelia (Cara Seymour), talk about the Sibelius violin concerto that was performed. Charlie liked the performance but thought that the ending of it was "weird."[11] Amelia, a performer herself, disagrees and energetically champions the performance for its passion and emotion. The scene highlights how Charlie connects with art on a cerebral and distanced level, whereas Amelia, a musician, responds emotionally and understands that to create art one must surrender to its currents—one must be receptive in order to feel its impact. That does not discount an intellectual approach to art, merely that the two extremes should ideally be wedded; whether Charlie and Amelia, representing these extremes, should be wedded is another question. Only when Charlie loses the possibility of any sort of romantic relationship with Amelia does he find the emotional momentum that helps him to deeply engage with his own work. Certain that Amelia is lost, Charlie plunges into creative action.

Orlean knows, intellectually, that she is at a remove from the obsession that grips Laroche. But knowing such a thing does not bring her closer to an experience of the passion she desires. "I want to know what it feels like to care about something passionately," Orlean says at one point. The realization is painful because it reflects her feeling that she is passionless and that she doesn't care for something in the world as she believes she should. Yet Orlean's realization, confessed in her book, makes Charlie fall in love with Orlean even as she falls in love with Laroche. Charlie understands her yearning for connection with something greater because he also desperately wants to connect with his work, as well as with another person. In *Synecdoche, New York*, Caden progressively loses all connection with loved ones. Like Charlie in *Adaptation*, Caden is unable to engage with people in any intimate way due to his depression and assorted physical maladies. But where Kaufman the screenwriter uses Charlie's neurosis for mostly comic purposes, the opposite is true in *Synecdoche, New York*. From the opening scene, where Caden wakes up in bed to the sound of the radio broadcasting a program about the first day of fall,[12] to the final scene with an elderly Caden, alone in the wreckage of his abandoned city set (the rest of his cast and crew dead or simply living their own stories), seated next to a woman who may have entered the narrative via a television commercial or a dream,[13] he is a man seriously debilitated by his neurosis. He is a walking wound, morbidly self-obsessed. As a symbol of the suffering artist, Caden would be deeply unsympathetic if not for Hoffman's ability to generate genuine sympathy from the audience by respecting his character's determination to understand the fiction that he is living.

A Million Little Strings

The struggle for authenticity is nothing new for artists of any stripe. For filmmakers, this issue stretches back to the very invention of the medium itself, when the Lumière brothers strived to capture real-life events with their camera (the resulting films known as *actualités*), in contrast to the more fantastical visions of Georges Méliès, who conjured up elaborate illusions like *A Trip to the Moon* for audiences hungry for escape from the mundane (and, in this case, the earth). The Lumière brothers and Méliès represent the extremes of the realist–fantasy debate of early twentieth-century film, and over the decades the debate has only grown murkier and more complicated.[14]

Kaufman's achievement of authenticity has never come from staying within the parameters of realism. All of his films exude heavy doses of sur-realism and hallucinatory fantasy—elements that help separate Kaufman's work from other comedic films, which is ostensibly what his films have been promoted as, until *Synecdoche, New York*. Even as the narrative structure and plot points reflect surreal ideas, the depiction of the characters is usu-ally grounded by attention to realistic decor, gritty locations, and generally unglamorous clothes and makeup for the actors—elements that likewise distinguish Kaufman's films from others with similar fantasy stylistics. The use of realist effects is something that Kaufman seems to have appropri-ated from the classic "art-house" European films of the 1960s and 1970s. The early French *nouvelle vague* films, for instance, were all shot on real locations instead of studio sets, giving their narratives a distinct illusion of naturalism while simultaneously breaking free of neorealist-type strictures with use of "jarring" editing, ironic music intrusions, and other techniques that accentuated the director's mark in contrast to the typically Hollywood seamless, "sutured" storytelling that was commercially dominant at the time. Kaufman borrows as well from the New Hollywood brigade of filmmakers (John Cassevetes, Robert Altman, Hal Ashby, Michael Cimino, and Martin Scorsese, to name only a few), all of whom distorted or redefined notions of naturalism and created films that favored drab, low-key interiors and sober acting styles over the highly lit, mannered approach more common to the studio system. *Synecdoche, New York* is almost antagonistically "ugly" at times, moving far beyond its antecedents' grit and gloom, as if Caden's self-hatred and possibly psychosomatic illnesses have infected every miserable frame of the film. But what is fascinating about the look of the film is that the director of photography, Frederick Elmes, never makes the film *look* dark or ugly or even particularly rough on the surface. Lighting schemes are bright, colors are neutral, and the film has a televisionlike synthetic sheen to it, almost subliminally drawing out the film's artificiality. Elmes, who had earlier collaborated with director David Lynch on *Blue Velvet* and *Wild at Heart*, conjured up similar synthetic hyperrealist effects for those earlier films as well.

What *Synecdoche, New York* clearly takes from European films of the 1960s, though, is an experimentation with narrative structure and ideas. Films like Chris Marker's *La jetée* (1962) and Alain Resnais's *Hiroshima mon amour* (1959), *Last Year at Marienbad* (1961), and *Je t'aime, je t'aime* (1968), are all of relevance to Kaufman's work in varying degrees, with their shifting time frames and fusion of fantasy and realism.

But one film looms largest over Kaufman's work in *Adaptation* and *Synecdoche, New York*: *8½* (1963). The great Italian fantasist Federico Fellini's masterful comedic-surrealist film about a director, Guido (Marcello Mastroianni), based on Fellini himself, who suffers a bewildering creative drought while trying to make a costly, overindulgent science-fiction picture that he has little interest in, is still astonishing today for its dream logic meshed with everyday reality, its ripe exploration of a middle-aged man's sexual fantasies, and its deft combination of comedy and pensive lyricism. Fellini's film seems an almost perfect template for Kaufman's later work, although *8½*'s Mediterranean charm and open-heartedness seem dramatically and tonally at odds with Kaufman's big-city millennial frigidity. Fellini, who had no qualms about mining his personal life for material, has, like Kaufman, been roundly criticized by his detractors for being "self-indulgent," "decadent," and "pretentious"—especially for his post-*8½* period, which found Fellini pushing the boundaries of baroque fantasies with films such as *Juliet of the Spirits* (1965), *Fellini Satyricon* (1969), and *Fellini's Casanova* (1976).

In his way, Fellini was also searching for authenticity, even though his filmmaking style at the time of his making *8½* was becoming more "artificial" and self-consciously theatrical. Stylistically, with his penchant for increasingly elaborate visual set-pieces, realism of the neorealist variety was no longer Fellini's cup of tea, although he had initially adhered to its conventions. Immediately following the Allied liberation of Rome in 1944, Fellini began working as a screenwriter on Rossellini's films (including *Rome, Open City* and *Paisan),* helping to define the stark naturalism, use of nonprofessional actors, and focus on the plight of working-class characters that typify these Italian neorealist films. Fellini, in his own early directorial efforts, would continue working in this tradition—most notably in *La Strada* (1954) and to a lesser degree in *Nights of Cabiria* (1957)—but he would grow increasingly restless with the stylistic parameters that neorealism had established. In his subsequent films Fellini, like Kaufman, utilizes stylistic artifice and fantastical tropes not to revel in superficiality, but just the opposite: as a means for burrowing deeper beneath the surface of things. The danger in this, of course, is that the more convoluted and intricate the deception, the riskier it is to remain faithful to the emotional currents and poetic moments that help make the films distinctive.

Fellini never seemed too enamored with plot, and consistently made it as minimal as possible, unlike Kaufman, who is always elaborating and fragmenting his plots, darkening the path toward any one reading of his films. His fictional surrogates in *Adaptation* (Charlie) and *Synecdoche, New York* (Caden) likewise cannot help but confuse matters—and themselves—even as they search for purity.

It must be emphasized, though, that Kaufman does not appear to be a cineaste, a filmmaker who embeds his work with direct quotes from films that have influenced him. He is not like Quentin Tarantino or even Woody Allen, two directors who, in their disparate ways, have openly acknowledged the cinematic influences that sift through their respective films as they utilize those influences to create something fresh. Kaufman's work, though vibrantly cinematic, is far removed from the kind of pastiche filmmaking currently in vogue in so much of American commercial cinema—films about films about films about films, a Möbius strip of B-movie in-jokes and technically polished jazzing about masking emptiness. The idea of always having to relate the artistic experience to another work is mocked throughout *Synecdoche, New York*. At one point, as Caden has trouble articulating his artistic aims to his cast and crew, Claire (Michelle Williams)—the actress who played Willy Loman's wife in Caden's production of *Death of a Salesman* and who will eventually become his wife—earnestly replies that his vague, abstract intentions actually do make sense. "It's beautiful," she says. "It's Karamazov."[15] In a later scene, Claire tells Caden that what he is doing is "brave" and that being part of the project for her feels like "being in a revolution."[16] Played as a blank slate booster, Claire becomes Caden's cheerleading muse, always responding to his doubt with the perfect sound-bite salvo but with little or no understanding of what she is actually saying.

Kaufman has stated in a number of interviews during the press tour of *Synecdoche, New York* that the relationship between his film and Fellini's was not intentional: "I'm influenced by things that I've seen and read, but they're not at the front of my brain when writing. We're formed by our experiences, but I'm not like Quentin Tarantino, where everything is a reference or a homage or a tip of the hat. I still can't convince people that I've never seen Fellini's 8½. People don't want to believe it."[17] Alas, whatever similarity between Kaufman and Fellini must be chalked up to chance, an unconscious symbiosis similar to that of Newton and Leibniz inventing calculus independently, or the invention of the first motion picture camera that Thomas Edison, the Lumière brothers, and Louis Le Prince have each been credited with.

I do not doubt Kaufman's claim never to have seen *8½*, but it remains a peculiar and troubling admission, since Fellini's film is a genuine classic of world cinema; but, more pertinently, it is also one of the more famous films ever made about trying to create authentic art—or not creating, as the case may be (since Guido is incapable of actually completing his production): a subject that is of considerable importance to both *Adaptation* and *Synecdoche, New York*. Considering how seamlessly Fellini meshes fantasy and waking reality in *8½*, a similar approach that Kaufman takes with the finale of *Adaptation* and the entirety of *Synecdoche, New York*, perhaps Kaufman refrained from ever seeing Fellini's film because its subject matter was simply too close to his own ideas. (Or maybe Kaufman just doesn't like to read subtitles.)

A Profound Process

Kaufman, like countless artists before him, sees the act of creating art as a courageous one. With a production such as *Adaptation*, any heroic striving for authenticity will have to contend with industrial forms and standards—to be specific, the Hollywood commercial film industry—that constrain and suppress genuine experimentation. There are practical reasons for this, of course, due to the size of film budgets: larger budgets mean more risk, so to hedge risk, studios go with what has worked in the past. Kaufman has managed to find investors, studios, and especially other creative technicians and artists willing to invest time and money to realize his projects for the screen—on his terms. Contrast this with his character, Caden, at the start of *Synecdoche, New York*, who, despite his success in regional theater and his insightful ideas about what makes great theater, has never truly put himself at risk. How could he when he only adapts other people's work? When Caden receives a MacArthur Fellowship "genius" grant and announces his next project, his artist wife, Adele (Catherine Keener), abandons him and takes off to Berlin with their daughter. Only after he is left alone, with Adele heralded as a brilliant painter and his relationship with box-office girl Hazel (Samantha Morton) burned out, does Caden push himself into uncharted artistic territory.

With the MacArthur grant money given "to create something unflinchingly true, profoundly beautiful," Caden purchases a mammoth blimp hangar where he intends to stage his latest production, a play without a script and with no discernible plot focus other than to explore everyday life.[18] Although energized by Caden's lofty ambition to do "something big and true and tough," the actors eventually realize that the "play" is far more immersive and demanding than any of them—including Caden—had previously imagined.[19] Sets intended to resemble city streets, apartment buildings, houses, and alleyways become just as massive and intricate as the "real" structures, blurring the lines between reality and simulacra. As the "play" progresses over decades, inner and outer realities clash, and Caden becomes the wizard at the center of his hyperreal kingdom.

The characters of Charlie Kaufman and Susan Orlean from *Adaptation* and Caden from *Synecdoche, New York* are clearly surrogates for Charlie Kaufman the filmmaker, allowing him to visibly work through the problems of writing and creating that are normally kept from public eyes. Auteur cinema by its very definition is about seeing patterns in a director's work, themes or stylistic choices that reflect the director's personality regardless of the genre he or she is working in. Whether the film is a studio project or an independent feature, whether the film is a work for hire or a personal project, some evidence of a director's personal preoccupations will surface at some point. But it is rare that a commercial director like Kaufman has chosen to work through the process of filmmaking, writing, and art creation in such a transparent manner. *Synecdoche, New York* may be one of the most rigorously trenchant examinations ever filmed of what it means to make art. The film dares to suggest that the process of creating is actually dangerous, fulfilling the hope of Artaud's essays about the stage in his work *The Theater and Its Double*.[20] The film's ultimate message—though hidden beneath layers of artifice and serpentine structure—may simply be that the creation of art is meaningless unless it can be shared with others; the power of the message is in no way diluted because it is difficult to discern. All of Kaufman's narratives are essentially "simple" plotwise. It is the *telling*—through visualization and inventive narrative structure—that gives Kaufman's films their uniqueness and sets them apart.

But for all its structural complexity and brilliance, *Synecdoche, New York* is not an "enjoyable" film. It feels unhealthy, plunging us into its magnified solipsism, constricted in Kaufman's fidelity to crafting a pathologically subjective film experience akin to David Lynch's *Eraserhead* (1977) and much of the work of David Cronenberg—*Videodrome* (1982) and *Dead Ringers* (1988) being two of the director's more suffocating, disturbing, and brilliant films. *Synecdoche, New York* is something of a malformed masterpiece, yet it always feels connected to its conceptual origins, unlike *Adaptation*, which loses itself in farce. One cannot help wondering how Kaufman's previous directors, Spike Jonze or Michel Gondry, would have interpreted the material; based on their earlier collaborations, one may presume they would have balanced Kaufman's mordant outlook with their apparently more positive energy and less jaundiced worldviews.

Synecdoche, New York comes off like a film in crisis, made by a filmmaker at odds with his own vocation. Only time and another production will tell if Kaufman has succeeded in working through his own ambivalence toward the creation of art—especially the creation of true, beautiful, and authentic art.

Notes

1. *Being John Malkovich* rates 92 percent on the Rotten Tomatoes "Tomatometer," making it "Certified Fresh." The rating is an "accolade to theater releases reviewed by 40 or more Tomatometer Critics (including 5 Top Critics) that score at least 75% or higher on the Tomatometer" (rottentomatoes.com). The film also ranks 90 on the Metacritic website, meaning that it has "universal acclaim." The Metacritic rating is a "weighted average in that we assign more importance, or weight, to some critics than others, based on their quality and overall stature" (metacritic.com).

2. The film's domestic box office, according to the website Box Office Mojo, was $22,863,596 (boxofficemojo.com).

3. John Macquarrie, *Existentialism* (New York: Penguin, 1980), 74–75.

4. Film theoreticians, academics, cinephiles, and filmmakers have long debated this issue. From André Bazin's early writings to Andrey Tarkovsky's book *Sculpting in Time* to Noël Burch's *Theory of Film Practice* to countless other works, the issue of how film—the camera—captures real life is a fascinating and problematic concern. And as technology advances, allowing filmmakers to convincingly replicate the most astounding, fantastical "unreal" images on the screen with CGI as well as replicating the most "realistic" settings with a few keystrokes, the debate will no doubt continue.

5. Richard Schickel, "Potholes," *Time*, February 16, 1976 (time.com).

6. "Realities of War," *The NewsHour with Jim Lehrer*, PBS, August 3, 1998 (pbs .org/newshour).

7. Along with other high profile noncommercial projects like Steven Soderbergh's two-part biopic *Che* (2008).

8. *Synecdoche, New York*'s budget was estimated at $20 million; it earned only $3,083,538 domestically (boxofficemojo.com).

9. The film ostensibly began as a horror film when director Spike Jonze was still attached to direct. Liz Ohanesian, "Interview: Charlie Kaufman on *Synecdoche, New York*," *LAWeekly*, October 22, 2008 (blogs.laweekly.com).

10. The ending is foreshadowed earlier in the film when Charlie and Donald discuss

Brian De Palma's 1980 *Dressed to Kill*, a stylish, absurd, postmodern mix of Hitchcockian suspense and the violent misogyny of the Italian *giallo* genre of the 1970s, a precursor to the American slasher genre of the 1980s. De Palma's film is resolved with a preposterous deus ex machina that Donald argues does not work. Later, Robert McKee listens to Charlie's frustrations concerning his screenplay and gives him advice, most importantly that he better not "dare bring in a deus ex machina." Of course, Kaufman delivers just that.

11. *Adaptation* (Spike Jonze, 2002), 00:16:57.

12. The scene is important for a number of reasons in that it foreshadows and immediately establishes the bewildering time displacements that occur throughout the film. Manohla Dargis, film critic for the *New York Times* and one of the most vocal supporters of the film in the United States, perceptively deconstructs the opening moments in "Mirror Reflections on Time's Dualities," *New York Times*, December 31, 2008 (nytimes.com).

13. The character (played by Dierdre O'Connell) tells Caden that she is the mother from Ellen's dream (Ellen is played by Dianne Wiest). O'Connell appears earlier in the film during a television infomercial, which features Caden as well.

14. From Robert Flaherty, who restaged events for his "documentaries" *Nanook of the North* and *Man of Aran* to the French poetic realists (Jean Renoir, Jean Vigo, Marcel Carné); from the Italian neorealists (Roberto Rossellini, Vittorio De Sica, and Luchino Visconti), who wanted to capture objective reality in their socially conscious fictions, to the metaphysical realism of Robert Bresson, Ingmar Bergman, and Michelangelo Antonioni; from the French creators of *nouvelle vague*, who acknowledged that it was impossible to maintain fidelity to objective reality and utilized artifice and experimentation to force a collision of inner and outer worlds, to the films of American independent maverick John Cassavetes, who heightened his gritty, low-budget films with dramatic, emotional truths far removed from the slickness of Hollywood, to Cassavetes's spiritual children of the so-called mumblecore directors (Andrew Bujalski, Joe Swanberg, Aaron Katz)—all of these filmmakers, in their disparate ways, have made the search for authenticity a major focus of their work.

15. *Synecdoche, New York* (Charlie Kaufman, 2008), 00:42:41.

16. Ibid., 00:44:50.

17. Tom Huddleston, "Interview: Charlie Kaufman," *Time Out: London*, April 29, 2009 (timeout.com/film).

18. *Synecdoche, New York*, 00:36:51.

19. Ibid., 00:37:04.

20. Antonin Artaud, *The Theater and Its Double* (New York: Grove Press, 1994).

HUMAN NATURE AND FREEDOM IN *ADAPTATION*

GREGORY E. GANSSLE

Charlie Kaufman's film *Adaptation* is the story of the struggle of Charlie Kaufman (Nicholas Cage) to adapt Susan Orlean's book *The Orchid Thief* into a screenplay.[1] Susan Orlean's book weaves accounts of the history of Florida and of the orchid trade with the story of the arrest and trial of John Laroche (Chris Cooper) for illegally harvesting orchids from a state preserve. Charlie is anxious to preserve the original texture of the book, and he strongly resists the pull to turn the script into a typical Hollywood action film.

As Charlie struggles with his project, his brother, Donald (Nicholas Cage), decides somewhat spontaneously that he will become a screenwriter too. The brothers, despite being twins, are fundamentally opposite. Charlie is self-conscious, awkward, and riddled with anxieties. Donald is optimistic, enthusiastic, and seems to be oblivious to his own foibles. Everything comes easily to Donald. Writing and, for that matter, living is a struggle for Charlie. Despite Charlie's efforts to dissuade him, Donald quickly produces a screenplay that stirs significant interest with Charlie's agent.

Charlie's difficulties with beginning to write his own script deepen, and he reluctantly asks Donald to help him. Donald insists that they need to know more about Orlean. He suspects that there is more to the story than she admits. They travel to New York and begin to investigate. Donald is convinced that Orlean is lying about her relationship with Laroche. She has been making up excuses to travel to Florida to see him. Laroche's casual way of navigating through the difficulties of life and his single-minded focus on orchids attract her. She sees her own life as shallow in comparison. Laroche eventually introduces Orlean to a drug that he can extract from the Ghost Orchid. She becomes addicted and sexually involved with Laroche—to the point of posing on his Internet porn site. Upon discovering Orlean's picture on the porn site, the brothers follow her to Florida.

Charlie is caught while spying on Laroche and Orlean. Realizing that her double life is about to be revealed, she decides that Charlie must be killed. Donald hides in the car while Orlean and Laroche drive Charlie out into the state preserve. The brothers flee into the swamp but are eventually caught. Donald and Laroche are killed, and Orlean breaks down as she finds herself caught between the old life she cannot return to and the new life that is crumbling around her.

Adaptation explores the nature and limits of adaptation on several levels. The first concerns the nature of media and its adaptability. Charlie is trying to adapt a work produced in a text-based medium (Susan Orlean's book) to a work in an image-and-sound-based medium (film). The difficulty of doing so creates one of the deep ironies of the film. The book turns out to be perhaps the least adaptable item in the film. "Why can't there be a movie about flowers?" Charlie asks.[2] The pace of a film must hold the attention of the viewer. Orlean's book is slower, more suggestive and contemplative. Charlie's attempts to preserve the atmosphere of the book fall apart as he and Donald discover that the real story behind the book is exactly the kind of Hollywood plot he did not want to write: fast moving, obvious, and direct.

The second level concerns the portrayal of real people in a highly fictionalized manner. It is difficult to discern where fact ends and fiction begins. The most extreme treatment is reserved for Kaufman himself. He heaps layer upon layer of insecurity on the character that shares his name, then exploits a method he repudiates within the story: the split personality. Charlie's brother, Donald, is what Charlie would like to be but cannot be: confident, uncomplicated, easygoing. And at the same time, Donald clearly admires Charlie and wants to emulate him—for example, to be "smart." Yet Charlie feels deep ambivalence about Donald. He envies Donald's carefree way of living, yet he tries to occupy a superior position both as the more responsible sibling ("A job is a plan. Is your plan a job?"[3]), and as the professional screenwriter ("Don't say 'pitch'"[4]). The blurring of fiction and reality can lead the first-time viewer to be unaware that Donald is wholly fictitious. While there is a Charlie Kaufman in the world, and he has written the screenplay *Adaptation*, there is no such person as Donald Kaufman. The screenwriter Charlie Kaufman doesn't have a brother. The credits indicate that the film is dedicated to the memory of Donald, and Donald's biography is included with the biographies of the other actors in the extra features of the DVD. Most perplexingly, though, is the fact that Donald Kaufman is credited as cowriter of the screenplay *Adaptation,* along with Charlie Kaufman.

Third, throughout the story, we learn about the nearly infinite adaptability of orchids. There is no end to the varieties that can be found or produced in the wild or in the greenhouse. Any environment, even the most remote and difficult, is fertile ground for this flower.

On yet another level, the fourth so far, we see that the flower is the central metaphor for human nature and bears significant symbolic meaning for our understanding of the human ability to change. The film, which is presumably about flowers, is in fact about the human person. The metaphor suggests questions about the degree to which human nature is adaptable. Is it as malleable as orchids? Are there intrinsic boundaries that limit attempts at human adaptation? Can human beings change by virtue of will, or must some other force be at work to effect transformation?

Two thinkers of the twentieth century who explored the implications of theories of human nature are Jean-Paul Sartre (1905–1980) and Walker Percy (1916–1990). Their differing analyses provide insight into the dynamics of the characters in *Adaptation* and also into the philosophical questions the film raises. Although both of these thinkers were primarily motivated by questions of what constitutes a viable life, in this essay I engage Sartre's concern over whether there is such a thing as human nature. This concern, metaphysical as it is, directly shapes his ethical view of how people should live. Percy, by contrast, explores the varying strategies that people adopt to navigate the world. Percy's observations about these strategies, which I discuss below, help reveal the metaphysical views people hold about the nature of human beings.

Jean-Paul Sartre

SARTRE ON HUMAN NATURE

Jean-Paul Sartre was one of the leaders of French existentialism. In the immediate aftermath of World War II, he delivered a lecture entitled *L'existentialisme est un humanisme (Existentialism Is a Humanism).*[5] His aim was to defend existentialism against common criticisms such as the claim that existentialism focuses on human degradation and that it encourages a passiveness in the face of reality rather than a conscious engagement with the world. He describes the starting point of existentialism as Dostoevsky's dictum "If God does not exist, everything is permitted."[6] While Dostoevsky announced this vision with dread, Sartre thought it was the foundation of true freedom. Dostoevsky's claim gives credence to the core insight of Sartre's existential vision: *Existence precedes essence.*

What Sartre meant by this characterization is best seen in contrast with St. Augustine and the Christian Platonists. Plato and his followers believed that eternal universals explain the nature of the particular things in the world. For Plato, these universals, which he called *Forms,* are independent of the physical world, do not exist in space and time, and are more real than any particulars. For example, each beautiful thing in the world is beautiful in virtue of its participating in Form *Beauty* itself, which is eternal, unchanging, and able to be grasped only by the highest thought. In the same way, each horse is a horse in virtue of participating in the Form *Horseness,* or, as Plato would say, "The Horse."

Augustine and other Christians agreed that Plato's Forms are eternal and unchanging. These thinkers argued that they do not exist independently from God, however. The Forms are ideas in God's mind.[7] Being ideas in the divine mind, they are as eternal and as unchangeable as God himself. When God created the world, he did so in accordance with his ideas. The idea of what it means to be a human being, and the nature of human beings, was in God's mind before he created any actual human beings. He then created individual people in accordance with this idea. The idea in God's mind constitutes the *essence* or nature of the human. What it is to be a human being, then, is fixed and eternal.

Sartre rejects this picture of human nature. Because Sartre thought that there is no God, he also thought that there is no prior idea of what a human being must be that constitutes a common human nature. There are existing persons, but they do not come into the world already bearing an essence. Each person creates her own nature; she exists, like all people, before she has any essence. In this way, her nature is up to her. Sartre called this fact a radical freedom. There are no moral or divinely ordained boundaries limiting how someone creates herself. Her only obligation is to choose. Not to choose—that is, to allow the culture around her to mold her into its own image, whether consciously or unconsciously—is to live in "bad faith." Whatever life she lives, she must choose it, and in doing so, she creates her own nature.

Not every choice an individual makes is a choosing of one's nature. A small choice, however, *can* turn out to be one that is nature-creating if it marks a new direction in the person's commitments. For example, if someone chooses to tell a lie, it may be a passing event in his life. If, however, he begins to orient his life around a new identity as a person who *is* a liar, this first choice to lie has nature-shaping implications. The difference between a fundamental choice and a trivial one is not a matter of how important the choice seems at the time. Rather, it is a matter of where the choice leads.

For Sartre, the freedom to create one's nature is part of what gives human life its dignity. Human beings are responsible for what they are and what they become. Externally imposed values that might define the limits of what a person can be have disappeared, along with God. Human beings are free. We are, in Sartre's bracing words, "condemned to be free."[8] We *must* create our own values as we create ourselves.

Sartre holds that there is no meaning to human life except the meaning individuals create for themselves. An individual person can create real meaning. Each person is responsible for the meaning of his life. To evade this responsibility, either by seeking to find meaning in something external, such as God or an external morality, or by rejecting the possibility of meaning altogether is to live in bad faith. Meaning is created and shapes the individual's life deeply; yet it has no reference point beyond the original choice of the individual.

HUMAN NATURE IN ADAPTATION

Four of the main characters in *Adaptation* represent distinct notions of the adaptability of human nature. John Laroche moves from obsession to obsession without a trace of regret. He is the supremely adaptable human being. As he is driving Orlean around Florida, Laroche confesses: "You know why I like plants? Because they are so mutable. Adaptation is a profound process. You figure out how to thrive in the world." Orlean responds, "Yeah, but it's easier for plants. I mean, they have no memory. They just move on to whatever's next. For a person, you know, adapting is almost shameful. Running away."[9] Then she looks out the window. She longs to adapt, but she is afraid to do so. Laroche, by contrast, shows no signs of being encumbered by his commitments or interests: when the latter fade, so do the former. This disposition helps him thrive. It is almost as if he, too, has no memory. Laroche, in this sense, is more like a plant than a person.

Laroche does have a memory, however, and his memories haunt him. He lost his mother in a car accident that was his fault. His wife left him. No one has been loyal to him. His ability to move from obsession to obsession has more in common with an inability to live a stable life than with the freedom associated with the highly adaptable orchid. He is, in the end, not unlike Orlean. Her fragility is on the surface. His is deeper.

Laroche can be seen as an embodiment of Sartre's view of human existence. There are no moral or metaphysical constraints on individual persons. Laroche simply must choose who he will be, from moment to moment. Laroche is living how he ought. Yet he is not living according to a real and objective moral standard. There is no standard. He is choosing his own standard and taking responsibility for his choices. Each new interest becomes for him a fundamental choice—that is, a choice that shapes his direction and desires for an extended period of time. What Laroche illustrates particularly strongly is the fact that one's original choice does not hold any kind of authority over the individual. He is free simply to move on and make another original choice. In Laroche's words, "Done with fish."[10]

Orlean, in contrast, feels trapped by who she thinks she is or ought to be. Consider the irony that emerges when she tells her dinner party about Laroche. On the one hand, she mocks his crudities, but on the other, she is anxious to escape from her tepid, superficial, and judgmental New York world.[11] Orlean began investigating Laroche from the safe vantage point of her authority as an accomplished writer. She was totally unprepared for what her encounter with him would stir up in her. Her assumed superiority over Laroche evaporates as she becomes increasingly mesmerized by his brilliance. As Orlean feels humbled, and vulnerable to Laroche, she is revealed in her aimlessness and shallowness. She admits, but only to herself, "I suppose I do have one unembarrassed passion. I want to know what it feels like to care about something passionately."[12]

When discussing the fact that Laroche's wife left him after the car accident, she admits, "I think if I almost died I would leave my marriage too." In response to his question "Why?" she replies, "Because I could. Because it's like a free pass; nobody can judge you if you almost died."[13] She sees that it would take a dramatic, tragic ordeal to give her the permission to act freely.

Donald seems to be nearly as adaptable as Laroche. He moves through life without care. He randomly chooses to become a screenwriter, yet he is able to succeed. He becomes friends with famous actresses with ease. His ability to navigate his life stands in sharp contrast to the emotional paralysis that marks Charlie. As he and Charlie hide in the swamp from Laroche and Orlean, they discuss a scene from their personal history: Donald talking to two girls in high school while Charlie stood nearby. Charlie told him that the two girls had laughed at him when he walked away. Donald knew they had laughed at him. Rather than allowing their opinion of him to shape who he was, he decided that his love for one of the girls was his own, and she could not spoil it. He tells Charlie, "I loved Sarah, Charles. It was mine, that love. I owned it. Even Sarah didn't have the right to take it away. You are what you love, not what loves you. That's what I decided a long time ago."[14] This decision on Donald's part is revealed to be the key to Donald's understanding of his self. It underscores the nature of his original choice. Rather than becoming distraught by what others thought of him, he took responsibility for who he was. He rejected the temptation to live in bad faith. The revelation in the swamp illustrates Donald's centeredness, showing that of the four characters, Donald is most at home in the world.

Orlean and Charlie are examples of persons living in bad faith. They do not and, it seems, cannot take responsibility for what they have become. Neither Orlean nor Charlie can do the one thing required of them. They cannot choose. They feel trapped in who they are and long to break out. Orlean's bad faith is evident by her reaction to finally seeing the Ghost Orchid. After the long ordeal of trudging through the swamp, getting lost, and having the shallowness of her life revealed by Laroche's biting insults, they stumble upon a Ghost. Her letdown is dramatic. As they drive away in the van, Laroche tries to cheer her up by talking about the drug that can be extracted. She turns to the window and mumbles, "I am done with orchids, Laroche."[15] She had decided she was done, but she wasn't. That very night she takes the drugs Laroche had sent her. Eventually, she destroys her life with drugs and pornography and becomes an accomplice to murder.

Charlie's character is most closely paralleled to Orlean's. While their personalities are very different, each struggles to find his or her way in the world. Each is paralyzed by ideas about what he or she ought to be. While Orlean moves in her New York world with confidence and success, Charlie thinks his one success (writing *Being John Malkovich*) is a fluke. When the agent comments, "Boy, I'd love to find a portal into your brain," he responds, "Trust me, it's not fun."[16] He is riddled with the sense that he does not belong. Even on the set of *Being John Malkovich* he seems unknown and in the way. "What am I doing here? Nobody even seems to know my name. Why am I here?"[17] Charlie's deep discomfort with himself infects his writing process. He cannot begin to frame the story because he is captured by relentless self-doubt.

Walker Percy

PERCY ON TRANSCENDENCE AND IMMANENCE

In his fictional works, novelist Walker Percy explored what happens to people who try to find meaning in the world as they navigate it. The overarching themes of his fiction were captured in *Lost in the Cosmos: The Last Self-Help Book.*[18] Percy frames this work around twenty multiple-choice questions that lead the reader to recognize his own lostness. Despite the progress and power of science, or perhaps because of this progress and power, average people feel lost in a world about which they know more and more while knowing less and less about themselves.

Percy argues that the flourishing of a self depends upon its relation to itself and its relation to the world. "A self must be *placed* in a world. It cannot *not* be placed. If it chooses by default not to be placed, then its placement is that of not choosing to be placed."[19] The self aims to place itself in the world through its understanding of itself in relation to that world. How a self navigates the world can reveal what sort of strategy it embodies in placing itself in the world. Traditionally, the common modes of self-placement were the Totemistic, the Pantheistic, and the Theistic. The Totemistic self is identified with particular things outside of oneself; this strategy is seen in certain nature religions in which the person identifies with, for example, an eagle in light of its strength or a badger in terms of its courage. The Pantheistic self is taken to be identical with God, which in turn is identical with everything that exists. The Theistic self sees itself as a being in relation to another self who has bestowed being upon it. Percy thinks these strategies will not seem viable to most people in the contemporary world.

In the postreligious world, there are two postures from which the self attempts to understand itself. The first is through *immanence*. The self is identified as a consumer of the goods of life. These goods are not limited to food and drink; they include the goods of the self, such as the many strategies to improve the self that are open to a discriminating consumer. The immanent self aims to get the most out of life, whatever it is to which "getting the most" amounts. While the strategies of immanence can be seen in stereotypical middle-class American life—trying to accumulate wealth, improve one's prestige, and acquire and manage myriad consumer goods (homes, cars, and so on)—they also can include less materialist pursuits, such as becoming involved in social causes or taking up meaningful hobbies. In either case, the immanent self is the consumer self. The second mode of identifying the self is through *transcendence*. According to Percy, "In a post-religious age, the only transcendence open to the self is self-transcendence, that is, the transcending of the world by the self."[20] Transcendence is achieved by the ability to step outside of the world, so to speak, and to view it from a privileged position. In our culture, science and art are two domains of transcendence. The scientist, Percy thinks, occupies a Godlike position because she stands outside the world and masters it through knowledge. She pronounces on all of reality. So the scientist, or the scientifically informed layperson, can achieve transcendence through *understanding*. Transcendence of this sort, either for the professional scientist or for the scientifically informed individual, is a kind of orbit. The scientific self orbits the world, and it is from this orbit that he observes, labels, and knows it. With the scientifically informed public, such understanding often comes from talk shows, magazines, and the Internet. The realm of pop psychology is powerful in its ability to give millions of people the sense that they can analyze the emotional and psychological difficulties of their friends and relatives. Readers of pop psychology presume that they are in a position to attain an experience of transcendence, at least in a superficial sense. Professional scientists can be in a more difficult position. They discover great generalizing truths that categorize many of the particularities of our experience. They understand the world through abstraction. However, they risk having the particular things within the world disappear altogether. There are no individual orchids. In their experience, there are only facts about orchids: orchid classifications and orchid biochemistry, for example. For the scientist, the world in all its immediacy, in a sense, vanishes.

The artist's transcendence is achieved through success at diagnosing and naming the maladies of the age. Artists tell a different sort of truth than scientists do. The truth of the scientist is a generalizing truth, while the artist or writer's is a particular truth. It is the truth about particular persons in particular situations. The poet or the novelist reveals truths about human lives by embodying these truths in concrete characters, in specific situations. Readers recognize their own reality in the work. We find ourselves saying, as we read, "Yes! This is how it is for me." Both those who enjoy the work of artists and the artists themselves achieve transcendence through this identification of the particular truths about selves in the world.

Each of these strategies encounters difficulties. The immanent self is always something of a problem to itself. Each particular consumer strategy becomes exhausted and must be replaced by a new one. Each new appeal seems to hold the promise of real peace or freedom, but no strategy can work for long. This fact, Percy argues, explains various features of contemporary life, such as the continuous desire for what is new in fashion and in entertainment. A person's life will fall apart if she runs out of activities to do and things to acquire before running out of time. Another possibility is that she will come to realize that the strategy of the discriminating consumer is doomed to fail. She may lose hope or try to achieve some kind of transcendence.

The difficulty with transcendence is reentry into the world that has been transcended; neither the scientist nor the artist can escape the fact that she is a human person herself. The scientist renders the world tolerable through discovery of generalities. When the scientist finally develops a theory that explains everything about persons, how does she then live, as it were, with them—or with herself? She has also been explained away, but she is still a self in the world and not simply an object. If a psychologist, for example, develops a comprehensive theory of love, he faces the challenge, when he goes home, of loving his own wife. The individual person can be lost in the midst of the theory. A theory is confirmed and rendered plausible only if it treats an individual self as merely an example of a general kind. Such generalization is suitable to explain impersonal things and natural processes, such as photosynthesis and salmon migration; a person, however, is more than simply a particular example of a general truth or natural fact. To aim to explain persons completely in a theory, then, is to attempt to reduce them to mere objects—or at least to ignore the fact that they are thinking and feeling subjects. No matter how impressive the explanation is, the self always remains to be contended with. And it is the particular self that must navigate life in the concrete, immanent world.

When the artist grasps and articulates the ills of the age, she experiences a sense of knowing the world and, thus, achieves transcendence. She has gained real insight. Yet this experience lasts only a short while. The efficacy of art as a strategy for transcendence and for identifying the self is, in the long run, minimal. The orbit of the artist tends to be less stable than that of the scientist. What does the artist do next? How does she then live in the normal, everyday world? Reentering this world for the artist is not often a smooth thing. The self can crash in that it simply cannot adjust itself to the confines of normal life. Percy observes that the transient effect of art explains why so many writers drink and wind up as suicides.[21] He comments, "If poets often commit suicide, it is not because their poems are bad but because they are good. Whoever heard of a bad poet committing suicide?"[22]

TRANSCENDENCE AND IMMANENCE IN ADAPTATION

Adaptation tells a story of how individual people place themselves in the world in which they find themselves. Among the characters, Laroche is almost totally immanent: he is much like the plants he seeks—an organism in a world. Although he attains a level of expertise in his knowledge of orchids, this knowledge barely affects him. The tragedy of Laroche's immanence is that the orchids, with all of their natural history, beauty, and delicacy, get used up and forgotten. The world is forgotten. It is lost. Orchids become mere preludes to Internet pornography. Where it once was an object that captivated Laroche's and Orlean's imagination, solicited them to experience some kind of transcendence, at the end the Ghost Orchid is radically materialized, becoming merely a source of drugs and nothing more.

Orlean is a failure at placing herself in the world. She begins as transcendent, but her transcendence has more in common with that of the scientist than that of the artist. When she takes up her assignment, she thinks of Laroche almost as a specimen to be studied and displayed. As she approaches Laroche from the transcendent posture of the writer, her own life comes to seem pale and insignificant in comparison. The brief experience of transcendence that articulating Laroche's life gives her soon dissipates, and she is left in her New York life—passionless and alone. She fails to reenter the world with any sense of the transcendence she experienced.

Orlean switches strategies and pursues immanence. She longs to become the sort of discriminating consumer that Laroche is, so she begins by becoming a vicarious consumer; she joins Laroche's project. Her great desire is not for flowers at all. "I don't even especially like orchids," she admits.[23] Nor is her passion for Laroche. Her great desire is for passion itself. As indicated earlier, her heart's cry throughout the film is, "I wanted to want something as much as people wanted these plants."[24]

When she finally sees the Ghost Orchid, she suffers tremendous disappointment. The experience she had anticipated did not deliver. Given Orlean's great despair, it is no surprise that she so easily follows Laroche into the world of drugs and pornography. Drugs and promiscuous sex represent, for Percy, the last feeble attempt to salvage a decayed life of immanence. Laroche is correct when he hurls the accusation, "You are just like a leech. You attach yourself to me and you suck me dry. Why don't you get your own life, your own interest?"[25]

Charlie struggles for transcendence. He desperately wants to write a film about flowers. His desire, however, is not to reduce them to general truths or to make them metaphors for life. He simply wants to display their beauty, but as an artist would, rather than as a scientist. He cannot achieve the kind of transcendence in which he is lost in his creative process because he is continually distracted by an impinging immanent reality. At each step, even between each sentence he writes, his difficulties in navigating everyday life disrupt his work. The concrete world, as it were, blocks his efforts to transcend it.

Donald is as successfully immanent as a person can be. He moves from project to project as a discriminating consumer. Yet, unlike most consumers, the things he consumes do not seem to lose their value to him. He is able to maintain genuine delight in the world. His secret lies in his decision that he owns his passions and interests. Rather than adopting his various projects to strive for some kind of transcendence or to fill an empty self, he adopts them as a conscious choice based on real interest.

Films do not articulate or defend philosophical claims. They can, however, help the viewer see how certain assumptions or positions might be worked out in the lives of real people. The characters in the film, though fictional, portray the choices to adopt and embody a worldview, as well as the consequences of those choices. In *Adaptation*, the development of the story suggests that there are significant limitations to human adaptability. Persons are found to be quite unlike orchids. There is a wall of sorts surrounding human nature. Those who attempt to break through it are destroyed in the process. These limits are not the limits of the human *condition*; the limits of the human condition include the particular place and time in which one is born and all of the features that stem from these facts that are outside a person's control.[26] These limits to the malleability of human nature reveal themselves in the failures of the film's characters to navigate the world fruitfully.

Adaptation, then, can be seen as providing a case for the rejection of the notion that there is no human nature. This case is not presented in the form of an argument that the notion is false. Rather, it is based on the observation that the view that there is no human nature is unlivable. While it may seem that whether a view is livable or not is irrelevant to its truth, thinkers such as Sartre and Percy locate the metaphysical question within the context of the human question. The question of how one should live is in some sense as fundamental as the question of what is true about the human person. Both Percy and Sartre explored these questions through the use of concrete characters in fictional settings. These thinkers diverge when it comes to the malleability of human nature. Sartre, of course, thinks there is no fixed nature. Percy thinks there is and it is our failure to grasp it that leads to our inability to navigate the world successfully.

For Sartre, the claim that there is no human nature is grounded in the rejection of the existence of a God who created persons. If Sartre turns out to be wrong about human nature, it does not automatically follow that God does exist. It does suggest, however, that we ought to look again at those metaphysical worldviews that recognize and provide the resources to ground a fixed essence to human persons. Historically, there have been at least three broad categories of theories that provide essentialist views of human nature.

Aristotelian views argue that there is a human nature and that it is found in the function of the person. By identifying how a well-functioning human being lives, we can begin to sketch the contours of human nature. Theistic views also ground a fixed human nature, as Sartre recognized. Some theistic views are also broadly Aristotelian, while others are not. In each theistic view, it is the intention of a God who creates that fixes what it means to be a person. A third kind of view that is hospitable to essentialism about human nature is substance dualism. Thinkers who defend the claim that there is a nonphysical substance also have the resources to provide the grounding for a fixed human nature.

These three essentialist views are often connected. Theists tend to be more amenable to substance dualism than non-theists, and Aristotle's view has been incorporated into the philosophy of those influenced by Thomas Aquinas. While these views are often connected, they are conceptually distinct. Each provides the metaphysical grounding for an essentialist view of human nature. Furthermore, while these positions are not the mainstream positions in philosophy, each has a significant number of defenders.

Adopting an essentialist view of human persons may turn out to provide one with the resources to relate to the world, to other selves, as well as to oneself. A belief in the ultimate mutability of human nature, in contrast, has its liabilities: the characters in *Adaptation* embody Percy's observation that, despite an abundance of sophisticated strategies and highly developed knowledge, the postreligious, antiessentialist human being is still lost in the cosmos.

Adaptation sides with Percy and supplies grounds to reject Sartre's claim that existence precedes essence. Human nature is not completely malleable. Of all the characters, it is Charlie who has the best chance of grasping this message. He does not come to embrace a particular philosophical system. Rather, he arrives at the point where he knows who he is and how he stands in relation to other selves. Perhaps the first indication of this insight is at the end of the ordeal in the swamp when Orlean screams at him, "You fat loser!" He interrupts her, standing against her hatred. "Shut up!" he says. "You're just a lonely old desperate pathetic drug addict!"[27] Later, he tells Amelia that he loves her regardless of her response, showing that he has learned something from Donald's swamp confession. And Charlie discovers how to finish the screenplay. Even though he knows that his idea violates the canons of good writing, it feels right to him. He has chosen. He acts. He has survived threats to his existence. He is now at home in the world.

Notes

In this chapter I significantly expand the ideas in one section of my earlier essay "Consciousness, Memory, and Identity: The Nature of Persons in Three Films by Charlie Kaufman," in *Faith, Film, and Philosophy: Christian Reflections on Contemporary Film*, ed. James S. Spiegel and R. Douglas Geivett (Downers Grove, IL: InterVarsity Press, 2007), 106–21. I want to thank Jim and Doug for help with that chapter. Thanks are due also to David LaRocca for his detailed comments and encouragement. An anonymous reviewer also provided helpful comments. Special thanks to my son, Nicholas B. Ganssle, for penetrating comments on a draft of this essay as well as for many conversations about the issues raised. His insight into *Adaptation* is deep. Everything I have learned about film, I have learned from my children, David, Nick, and Lizzy. Without their insistence, I would never have begun to think about film at all, and I certainly would not have begun to write about it.

1. *Adaptation* was adapted from the book *The Orchid Thief: A True Story of Beauty and Obsession* (New York: Ballantine Books, 2000) by Susan Orlean. The screenplay credits are listed as Charlie Kaufman and Donald Kaufman. It was directed by Spike Jonze. In this essay, I will refer to the *character* Charlie Kaufman as "Charlie." When I refer to the author of the screenplay, I will use "Kaufman." When referring to Orlean the character, I will use "Orlean." I will refer to Orlean the writer by using "Susan Orlean." All references to John Laroche except the first, and all references to Donald Kaufman are to the characters.

2. *Adaptation* (Spike Jonze, 2002), 00:05:30.

3. Ibid., 00:10:23.

4. Ibid., 00:20:58.

5. Jean-Paul Sartre, *Existentialism and Humanism*, trans. Philip Mairet (London: Methuen and Co., 1948). This lecture has been published with various titles, including the most literal: *Existentialism Is a Humanism*, trans. Carol Macomber (New Haven: Yale University Press, 2007). It also has been published as *Existentialism*, trans. Bernard Frechtman (New York: Philosophical Library, 1947). My references are to *Existentialism and Humanism*.

6. Sartre, *Existentialism and Humanism*, 33–34. Dostoevsky does not state this notion in these exact words, but the thought is found in several conversations of Ivan Karamazov in Dostoevsky's *The Brothers Karamazov*.

7. See Augustine, "On the Ideas," in *Eighty-Three Different Questions*, trans. David L. Mosher, vol. 70 of the Fathers of the Church series (Washington, D.C.: Catholic University Press, 1982): 79–81.

8. Sartre, *Existentialism and Humanism*, 34.

9. *Adaptation*, 00:35:22.

10. Ibid., 00:29:06.

11. Ibid., 00:24:52.

12. Ibid., 00:26:20.

13. Ibid., 00:44:28.

14. Ibid., 01:36:04.

15. Ibid., 01:22:11.

16. Ibid., 00:04:32.

17. Ibid., 00:02:58.

18. Walker Percy, *Lost in the Cosmos: The Last Self-Help Book* (New York: Farrar, Straus, and Giroux, 1983).

19. Ibid., 110. Percy's analysis of the person who chooses not to be placed has resonance with Sartre's description of those living in bad faith.

20. Ibid., 114.

21. Ibid., 147–48.

22. Ibid., 121.

23. *Adaptation*, 00:27:14.

24. Ibid., 00:26:15.

25. Ibid., 01:02:42.

26. Sartre acknowledges that one's condition, such as the place and century of one's birth, thrusts one into a particular concrete situation outside of one's control. It is within one's condition that one chooses one's nature. See Sartre, *Existentialism and Humanism*, 45–47.

27. *Adaptation*, 01:44:12.

Synecdoche, in Part

David L. Smith

It is strange that while we are alive, we so often feel that we are not really living. Although we are born into a world—by most accounts, an endless web of interrelation—something seems to separate us from things, from others, and from ourselves. Nature is elusive; relationships are hard; it is even a struggle to be who we are. And so we set to work, devising schemes to overcome the gap, whatever it is. Maybe we think we need more of something, or less; to get closer, or farther away; to find ourselves, or to forget ourselves. But there is always something to be done. And the rub—the final ironic twist in these plots of redemption—is that our attempts to change typically end by reproducing the conditions we sought to escape. Efforts to bring the world closer only push it away. Schemes to change ourselves usually fail because they are devised by the same clueless mind we want to overcome. The supposed cures all turn out to be symptoms of the disease. And so life is lost in the very attempt to realize it. It would all be funny if it were not so sad.

That, in effect, is the ur-plot of a Charlie Kaufman movie. Kaufman is a poet of disappointment, and each of his screenplays is an essay, played out as farce, on the ways people struggle and inevitably fail to realize their own lives, to make themselves whole by overcoming a gap that separates them from the fullness of life as they imagine it. *Being John Malkovich* examines the desire to become whole through a romantic or metaphysical merger with another person—the fantasy that life from the other's perspective, if only we could get inside it, would be more fulfilling than our own. *Human Nature* is a set of variations on the attempt to become ourselves by becoming either more or less cultivated, following nature or rising above it. *Adaptation* traces a writer's struggle to achieve an authentic connection to the world by resisting the narrative conventions embedded in language itself, as if stories were the thing that separates us from the truth of our own lives. *Eternal*

Sunshine of the Spotless Mind examines the desire to perfect life by erasing its errors, the dream of a fresh start. And *Synecdoche, New York* examines what happens when an artist, in the face of death, tries to build something true and satisfying out of time's inadequate fragments, to conjure the whole from the parts.

In every case, according to Kaufman, these quests are self-defeating. Every inside turns out to be just another outside. Nature and culture are no more separable than the north and south poles of a magnet. One cannot talk one's way out of language; one cannot be other than who one is; no one gets out of life alive. On some level, the story is always the same. You thought real life could be sought elsewhere, but there is really nowhere else to go. This, or nothing, is it.

If this is a fair description of the overall mood and message of Kaufman's work, then *Synecdoche, New York* is an exemplary statement and even a kind of culmination of his vision. *Synecdoche, New York* is a remarkably ambitious film whose subject is nothing less than the fundamental human predicament, the paradox inherent in the attempt to become who you are, the riddle of life in time. Critics have either loved it for its aspiration or condemned it for its pretension.[1] My own approach to the film—rather like Kaufman's authorial approach to life—will be neither to praise nor to blame it on balance, but to try to do justice to its complexities. Perhaps Kaufman's project (like life itself) is all beyond redemption, but as we learn from the mysterious Ellen Bascomb (Dianne Wiest) in the film, a certain dignity may be found in the very attempt to sort out the mess.

Before we get to *Synecdoche, New York,* though, two terms already used to characterize Kaufman's project require closer attention: farce and essay. Someone unfamiliar with Kaufman's movies might reasonably assume, based on the above description, that they were pretty gloomy affairs. The fact that they are not bears reflection. Fatal entrapment is Kaufman's subject—entrapment by fate and its finality. There are, however, at least two ways to play out such a story: as tragedy or as farce. In the tragic mode, the audience identifies with the protagonist's frustrated desire and responds with pity. In a farce there may be a similar identification, but we in the audience also stand apart from and hold an advantage over the characters. The premise of the story is that we know something that the characters don't. We see that the characters labor under a misapprehension, a failure to grasp their true situation that renders their struggles absurd. If only John had realized that Mary already loved him, or if only they knew that George was hiding in the closet, they could easily have avoided all the heartache and embarrassment. Meanwhile, though, we enjoy watching the drama unfold. Some would say we enjoy it because we are naturally cruel and like to feel superior, but I would prefer to say that it is because we feel sympathy for the characters, knowing how liable we are to be similarly blind. We are all such fools that certain kinds of mistakes are nearly inevitable.

A Charlie Kaufman film, then, is a peculiar sort of farce in which the characters suffer from what we might call an existential misapprehension— a misunderstanding of the human condition so common and so deep that we are barely even aware of it as a misunderstanding. The error remains virtually invisible because the alternative perspective that reveals it to be a misunderstanding—the knowledge that allows us to see the spectacle as a farce—is itself a hidden or highly elusive commodity, a knowledge we certainly have but never quite possess. Knowing better than we know—dazzled by the blindingly obvious—we simultaneously observe and participate in the play of our lives, vaguely aware that the joke, whatever it is, is also on us.

As an example of what I mean, consider the note struck at the beginning of this chapter. There is a familiar mood in which we feel that we are not really living—that to be fully oneself or fully in the world would be an achievement. The yearning for change or wholeness we feel at such times goes deep; we may even take it for a touchstone of what it is, at base, to be human. And yet there is a structural peculiarity here that may strike us at odd moments. "Become what you are?" we may well wonder. "But what else could I possibly be? Where am I, if not in the world? How am I not myself?"[2] A sense of lack may be built into our nature, but there is also a tautological givenness to our condition that makes this sort of yearning look uncomfortably like the plight of someone casting around for the hat he is already wearing. The urge to "become who you are" is like trying to use a hand to grasp itself or an eye to see itself. The goal cannot be attained because you are already *there*. From this point of view—a common premise of nondualist spiritualities around the world—the sense of lack we so urgently feel is a mystery.[3] The mystery, however, is not so much that we are not whole as that we should ever have imagined that we were otherwise. Wholeness is given in our circumstances; it is not the sort of thing that we could possibly lose. To strive for it or imagine it as a thing to be achieved is to labor under a misapprehension. I submit, then, that it is an unarticulated background knowledge of this sort—a lurking sense of our immanent completeness—that allows us to see the desperate quests for meaning and wholeness undertaken by Kaufman's characters as farce.

To say, secondly, that Kaufman's films are essays is to say something important about the kind of thinking they involve. A modern essay, of the type exemplified by Michel de Montaigne or Ralph Waldo Emerson, is crafted to be a revelation of the mind or self of the author. Whatever its ostensible subject, the space it really describes is subjective, and its topic is what it is like to be a human being thinking about these things. As Montaigne put it, "I myself am the subject of my book."[4] In like manner, Kaufman frequently says that the main goal of his art is to give people himself. "I don't know what else there is to write about other than being human, or specifically, being this human. I have no alternative."[5]

Moreover, these modern essayists share an understanding of the self as a site of contradictions and irreducible complexity.[6] To quote Montaigne again: "My aim is to reveal my own self, which may well be different tomorrow if I am initiated into some new business which changes me." "I must adapt this account of myself to the passing hour. I shall perhaps change soon, not accidentally but intentionally. This is a register of varied and changing occurrences, of ideas which are unresolved and, when needs be, contradictory, either because I myself have become different or because I grasp hold of different attributes or aspects of my subjects."[7] Emerson likewise warns the reader that because his goal as an essayist is subjective verisimilitude, the product of his writing will be as unresolved as a mind in motion. Because the life of the mind is so mixed, he writes, the attempt to portray it will "introduce wild absurdities into our thinking and speech. No sentence will hold the whole truth and the only way in which we can be just is by giving ourselves the lie." We are finite creatures who deal only with aspects and fragments, so the essay must embrace its own fragmentary character. "I know better than to claim any completeness for my picture. I am a fragment, and this is a fragment of me."[8]

Thus, essayists like Montaigne and Emerson are concerned less with providing definitive answers to questions than with representing what it is like to live with them. They are less like philosophers mounting an argument than like playwrights or screenwriters portraying multiple characters and multiple points of view.[9] *Synecdoche, New York*, as an essay in film, has similar qualities of fragmentariness, multiplicity, and irresolution. If it succeeds in making us feel what it is to be human, it is because it falls short—by necessity and by design—in so many of the same ways we do.

Synecdoche, New York, then, is an essay on the simultaneous futility and inevitability of our attempts to become ourselves, to live before we die, to transcend our own shortcomings. The principal limits to the human condition it considers are death and language. Death is a given—an unbreachable wall—but language generally strikes us as an opening rather than a limit. Language, in fact, or representation in general, is the principal stage on which we act out our various attempts to fulfill ourselves, to give life shape and meaning. The film presents such attempts to give life symbolic form as the particular business of artists. Kaufman is clear, however, that it is not only artists who try to organize the world into more satisfying wholes through representation. *Synecdoche, New York*, he says, "is about the creative act of being a human being, not just about what an artist does." Because we are all creatures of language, building representations of reality "is what we do in our daily lives when we tell stories about what's happening to us. We try to organize the world, which isn't organized the way our brains want to organize it. We tell stories about the people in our lives . . . , we make our lives into stories. I don't think we can avoid doing that."[10]

And why would we want to avoid it? Because language, according to Kaufman, is also largely responsible for creating our sense of separation from the actual world. We use language and other forms of representation to organize experience and render our worlds habitable—in effect, to build ourselves models of a world we can live in. But insofar as we inhabit these models, we live at one remove from reality. Language, Kaufman notes, "can't really in most cases get close to the *thing*."[11] In this connection, he tells the story of a depression he suffered some years earlier: "When I was going through it, I couldn't talk about it. The very act of talking about it has made it obvious that I'm not going through it anymore. There is this preverbal or nonverbal kind of thing that is the really-felt thing and once you start to translate it into words, it loses its immediacy or its power."[12] Language is useful for labeling things and putting them into perspective. However, "the thing that you're putting in perspective is always over, you know? And the truth is that it's very hard to live where we really are, but that's the only place we get to live."[13] The representations by which we try to comprehend and lay claim to life, in other words, are the very things that alienate us from it. Language always puts us on the scene too late. "To live where we really are" would seem to be a given—the easiest thing in the world—and in a sense it is. Because we are creatures of language, however, nothing is more difficult. "I struggle with that a lot when I'm writing," Kaufman concludes, "because my things tend to be very wordy. I *like* words."[14]

Much of what *Synecdoche, New York* has to say about the displacing power of language is actually foreshadowed by its title. A synecdoche is a metaphor in which a part stands for the whole (referring to my car as my wheels, for example), and *Synecdoche, New York* is a fantasia on parts and wholes. It studies the ways in which artists and others use words and images to grasp or convey a sense of life as a whole. "Every work of art is a synecdoche," says Kaufman, "there's no way around it."[15] Or again, "There is no way to convey the totality of something, so every artistic creation is at most a representation of an aspect of the thing being explored."[16]

Kaufman's emphasis is on the way these projects fall short. We already know (or are) the thing we want to represent, but the only means we have at hand are too limited to do ourselves justice. Every work of art, then, like every philosophy and every life story, is bound to be incomplete and therefore disappointing. Emerson, an essayist who approached the problem of life in terms strikingly similar to Kaufman's, has a passage in "Experience" that could easily serve as *Synecdoche, New York*'s epigraph: "The child asks, 'Mamma, why don't I like the story as well as when you told it me yesterday?' Alas, child, it is even so with the oldest cherubim of knowledge. But will it answer thy question to say, Because thou wert born to a whole, and this story is a particular? The reason of the pain this discovery causes us (and we make it late in respect to works of art and intellect), is the plaint of tragedy which murmurs from it in regard to persons, to friendship and love."[17] Every love, every friend, every dream we cherish is a synecdoche, a mere part of life in which we seek some echo of the whole we were "born to." The parts may have a charm of their own, but none gives what we ultimately seek. Everything falls short.

Synecdoche, New York, then, explores the paradoxes we create for ourselves by using language and other symbolic forms to overcome the sense of falling short that our reliance on language, in large part, creates. As such, the film is a study in self-defeat; it envisions no way out of this bind short of death, and death is hardly a solution. And yet, like the best in Kaufman's other films, *Synecdoche, New York* also evokes an alternate perspective—a hidden but universally available knowledge—that allows us to see this defeat in a comic and almost tender light. In effect, what this perspective provides, or at least suggests, is a naturalistic mode of transcendence. There is no other world from which help can be expected, and every "elsewhere" we build for ourselves out of words turns out to be fatally flawed—a fool's paradise. Nevertheless, there is a way of seeing our current circumstances that may deserve the name transcendence, if only because this view allows us to live on terms surprisingly adequate to our desire. Nietzsche, for example—to whom Kaufman refers in virtually every script—found a way to transform a sense of entrapment in life's limitations into a kind of transcendence through *amor fati,* the ecstatic affirmation of everything that is so disappointing in our contingencies. Kaufman's *Eternal Sunshine of the Spotless Mind* comes to something quite similar when, in the end, its protagonists say "Okay" to what will probably be recurring heartbreak.[18] *Synecdoche, New York* likewise evokes transcendence by oblique means and inspires reflection on the strategies by which transcendence is pursued.

It begins, though, in disappointment. More specifically, as in every Charlie Kaufman film, it begins in the midst of dire relationship problems. Caden Cotard (Philip Seymour Hoffman) is an artist—a theater director for a regional company in Schenectady, New York—who feels his life to be at a dead end. His wife, Adele (Catherine Keener), also an artist, has become indifferent to him and has lost faith in his work. "Do you really believe that tripe?" she says in response to his elaborate new production of *Death of a Salesman.* "It's not you. It's not anyone. It's not real." Her attacks also play on his fear of mortality. "What are you leaving behind?" she asks. "You act as if you have forever to figure it out."[19] On the whole, Caden seems less concerned with leaving something behind than with finding what might suffice for the present. Nevertheless, death is very much on his mind. His middle-aged body is letting him down in increasingly bizarre ways. His struggles with disease—or apparent disease—epitomize both his sense of life's shortcomings and the urgency of his desire to overcome them.

The peculiar progress of Caden's diseases—their odd habit of coming and going—is a good example of the ways *Synecdoche, New York,* as an essay in film, portrays subjective space. A kind of dream logic is frequently employed in the film to put us inside a character's feel for life. Thus, for example, time passes by leaps within single scenes or at uneven rates among characters. Caden himself appears in cartoons and ads that he sees on television and the Internet—once even on a poster at a bus stop. Hazel (Samantha Morton), Caden's elusive flame, buys a burning house which continues to burn for thirty years until her eventual death of smoke inhalation.[20] Caden's hypochondria likewise becomes a dreamlike caricature of itself. From ordinary worries about arthritis and bowel movements, he soon graduates to the loss of some of his autonomic bodily functions. His pupils won't dilate; to swallow, at one point in the film, he has to consciously perform peristalsis;

to cry, he has to apply eye drops. His life, instead of unfolding naturally, becomes a deliberate reconstruction, as artificial as a piece of theater. This anxious and deliberate approach to life, in fact, is neatly epitomized by his name. "Cotard's syndrome" or "Cotard delusion" is a neurological condition wherein one believes oneself to be already dead. Caden may not be nearly as dead as he thinks he is, but his fears effectively parody what it is to feel that one is not really living.

Despite his marital, romantic, and bodily issues, Caden is not defeated. He is even fairly heroic in his determination to pursue what Kaufman called the "creative project of being a human being," employing language and art to make sense out of his life. Many other characters in the film are involved in a similar enterprise. In the opening scenes, for example, we see Caden's four-year-old daughter Olive (Sadie Goldstein) testing out words as schema for organizing experience. ("Is poop alive?" she asks after producing a green bowel movement.) Often her questions get unreliable answers. ("Am I going to die?" Olive asks, to which Caden replies, "Of course not." And when Olive becomes horrified at the thought of blood running under her own skin, Adele reassures her, "You don't have to worry, baby. You don't have blood.")[21] Adele likewise uses art to give shape to her own tough-minded acceptance of the distances between people, or to the condition described by her surname: Lack. "Everyone is disappointing," she says, adding that it only gets worse the closer people become. Accordingly, in her art of microscopic portraiture, she makes the people in her life indecipherably small, as if seen through the wrong end of a telescope.[22] The point in each of these cases seems to be that art and language are unreliable tools for creating a comprehensive account of life. Words and images give us parts—the self-serving props that we need to get along. They may also be used to obscure or distort the truth when it suits our purposes, as when Olive's interlocutors shy away from blood, death, and excrement—all the facts with which we adults typically conspire not to deal. Caden, however, has set his heart on honesty, or at least on the kind of honesty that can be achieved in theater.[23] His ultimate mission is to use his art to bring excluded knowledge to light. In response to Adele's criticism of the value of his work, for example, he resolves "to do something important. While I'm still here," to "finally put my real self into something." For Caden, "something" means a play, and a play that represents his real self will also have to tell the whole truth about the world he knows. Telling the truth, he believes, means hiding nothing. His emerging artistic ideal, accordingly, is a theater that forces "all of us, players and audience alike, to soak in the communal bath of it, the mikvah. We're all in the same water, after all, soaking in our very menstrual blood and nocturnal emissions. This is what I want to try to give people." Every obscenity must be brought back on stage, every secret revealed. And death above all, the dirtiest and best kept of secrets, is the thing that must be exposed. "We are all hurtling toward death. Yet here we are, for the moment, alive. Each of us knowing we will die; each of us secretly believing we won't."[24] Ultimately, the MacArthur "genius grant" that Caden wins for his work in the theater gives him the means to try to realize this vision of completeness. Like the portal in *Being John Malkovich* or the Lacuna apparatus in *Eternal Sunshine of the Spotless Mind*, the grant in *Synecdoche, New York* functions as a magical enabler or fairy-tale device. By giving Caden what he thinks he wants, allowing him to pursue his dream to the end, it reveals the folly of his desire.

Synecdoche, New York considers several ways of trying to achieve wholeness. Most obviously, it examines Caden's literal-minded ambition to include everything in his play. In effect, Caden is out to break the rule that every work of art is no more than a synecdoche. Empowered by his grant, he sets out to represent life itself, unfiltered and unfragmented. He acquires a vast, abandoned building in Manhattan—a cross between a warehouse, an indoor stadium, and a railroad terminal—that the realtor rather implausibly claims was used in the past to stage Shakespeare. This, in any case, becomes Caden's Globe, the stage on which he will try to reproduce the world.

Caden's attempt, however, leads to an infinite regress. Logically speaking, a representation of everything would have to include itself in the representation. Thus, infernal complications set in as Caden's play becomes part of the world represented by the play. Early on, actors are chosen to represent the people in Caden's life, since the only world he thinks he can represent honestly is his own. Subsequently he finds it necessary to choose more actors to represent the original cast as they too become significant figures in his life. Eventually, he must find someone to represent himself as the director of a play about his life within the play; he must construct a replica of the warehouse within the warehouse, and so on . . . the point being that Caden's project is endless and impossible. Each expression, however refined, falls short of the whole truth about life. As creatures of language, we live only with parts and can produce only synecdoches.

Another approach to the truth of life taken up in *Synecdoche, New York* is the attempt to get *behind* the process of representation, or to realize the immediacy of the moment before it is reflected upon. We see this, for example, in Caden's conception of theater as a place of showing as well as telling. "Here's what I think theater is," he tells Hazel: "It's the beginning of thought. The truth not yet spoken. It's what a man feels after he's been clocked on the jaw."[25] He wants to use expression to get at what is there before discursive thought arises, before narrative imposes its structure and distance. A similar ideal is also very much on Kaufman's mind: "I wanted to try to find the place, even though language is used, where the language is not. I wanted to find that truth. Which is very hard to do I guess because we communicate in language."[26] The ideal shared by Caden and Kaufman is thus to represent life itself, simple and unbroken by self-conscious reflection. Their desire is to occupy the point from which we begin in every instant, but which we lose sight of as soon as we begin to use language. They seek to rediscover, or perhaps experience for the first time, that intimacy with the world we were "born to."

But of course (as Kaufman knows, and as Caden is either too determined or too self-absorbed to realize), the attempt to get behind reflection also puts us in a double bind. That is, there is a structural paradox built into this strategy, much like the paradox involved in "becoming oneself." The desire to do without conscious schemes is already a conscious scheme. The struggle to act effortlessly is already an effort, and therefore self-defeating.[27] While the truth may be as close to you as your jugular vein, it is impossible to *achieve* it because, as Alan Watts used to say, "There is no way to where we are."[28] Kaufman is acutely aware of the problem: "There's always for me contradictions and complications. It's like if you're meditating and if you're desirous of anything, even enlightenment—especially enlightenment—then you're not achieving it."[29] Meditation, that is, aims at a state beyond desire, but as an undertaking born of our desire for such a state, it undermines its own aims. A similar paradox lies at the heart of the attempt to "achieve" our own lives. We alienate ourselves from the world and from ourselves by striving to become what we already are. The yearning separates us from the goal—this is precisely Kaufman's point about the defining, delimiting irony of life. "You have to acknowledge that that striving, that hellish confusion, is the truth of being a person—is inescapable. You're trying to get there, but you're also wanting to get there, and what's the confusion of that, what's the complexity of that? And all I can do, all that I can expect of myself, is to honestly express that tension in my work. If I hope to express myself with honesty, then I have to include all the impurities."[30] To desire a state beyond desire, to strive for a place beyond striving, is to set oneself up for failure. Striving, however, is simply what we do. It comes to us as naturally as telling stories.

The very inevitability of this "hellish confusion," however, suggests a third approach to the problem of conveying life whole. If the simple truth of our lives is inaccessible to reflection, and if the attempt to reach it inevitably ends in a hopeless tangle, then perhaps the failure to possess ourselves is, in a sense, the simple truth about us. Or better, perhaps the failed attempt to discover or create ourselves is the most reliable pointer we are likely to find toward the thing we fail to grasp. Our life, as a collection of fractured particulars, reminds us of something we are but cannot possess or clearly perceive. It reminds us, that is, of our own latent wholeness. And in the light of this wholeness, glimpsed in every failed attempt to achieve it, the parts are transmuted. The sordid or inadequate details of life become transparent to the hidden knowledge we were "born to," to the thing of which everything else falls short. And so the ordinary confusion of life itself becomes a scene of transcendence, as when fate is transformed through *amor fati*. Nothing changes, and yet everything changes its aspect, as when tragedy modulates into farce. Some significant mystery is revealed, and one is left with the sense, if not that all manner of things shall be well, then at least that life deserves our grudging but genuine fondness.

In the long second half of *Synecdoche, New York*, there are several episodes that employ irony to pull the audience toward such a transformative shift in perspective. There is Caden's attempt to include everything in his play; there is the yearning of the adult Olive (Robin Weigert) for narrative closure in her relations with her father; there is Caden's ultimate reunion with Hazel; and there is the plan of the young Ellen Bascomb (Kat Peters) to find happiness through repetition. The ostensible subject in each of these stories is the failure of a character's quest for meaning. The attempt to grasp life in each case is shown to be born of delusion and to end in disappointment. Nevertheless, the mood of the film is not finally tragic. There is something else that plays around the edges, something that transmutes the vision of life presented here into something more welcome—into a reminder of what the characters themselves fail to see. I suggest that the thing that makes the difference—the secret that transmutes tragedy into farce—is the hidden knowledge, shared by author and audience alike, that wholeness, the goal of the characters' quests, is something they already have, or are. Wholeness, said Emerson, is what we are born to. Life in time, meanwhile, commits us to the strange misapprehension that we are somehow not ourselves, or that we do not fully occupy our world. It is in the belief that life is remote and in our consequent struggles to achieve it, however, that life is truly lost. Emerson, again, provides the apt allegory: "The fate of the poor shepherd, who, blinded and lost in the snowstorm, perishes in a drift within a few feet of his cottage door, is an emblem of the state of man. On the brink of the waters of life and truth, we are miserably dying."[31]

And so, in typical Kaufmanesque fashion, the characters in *Synecdoche, New York* pursue the promise inherent in life and, in the process, push it farther away. They want to express something infinitely precious, something that can never really be lost. But in trying to express it, they shatter it into parts, and so they assign themselves the endless project of making it whole again, of making amends. There is something funny, farcical really, in watching them struggle through the process. And what makes it funny? Simply the secret we all share, the thing so obvious that it has to go without saying. If we were not alive, in any case, we would not get the joke.

Notes

1. Strong positive reviews came early from Roger Ebert and Manohla Dargis. See Roger Ebert, "Synecdoche, New York," *Chicago Sun-Times*, November 5, 2008 (suntimes .com); and Manohla Dargis, "Dreamer, Live in the Here and Now," *New York Times*, October 24, 2008 (nytimes.com). A notable dismissal came from Anthony Lane, "Let's Put on a Show!" *The New Yorker*, November 3, 2008, 122.

2. The phrase "How am I not myself?" plays a central role in *I Heart Huckabees* by Kaufman's friend David O. Russell, even appearing on screen following the end credits. See David O. Russell and Jeff Baena, *I Heart Huckabees: The Shooting Script* (New York: Newmarket Press, 2004), 102–3, 120.

3. I have in mind especially the practical or soteriological side of nondualism that identifies path and goal, the ordinary world and the ultimate—or, in Buddhist terms, samsara and nirvana. While this problematic is most thoroughly explored in—and is usually identified exclusively with—advaita vedanta, mahayana Buddhism, and philosophical Taoism, it also arises in western romanticism and its aftermath. The best general account of nondualism in comparative philosophical terms is David Loy, *Nonduality: A Study in Comparative Philosophy* (Amherst, NY: Humanity Books, 1998).

4. Michel de Montaigne, *The Essays of Michel de Montaigne*, trans. and ed. M. A. Screech (London: Allen Lane, Penguin Press, 1991), 1.

5. Kaufman quoted in Rob Feld, "Q & A with Charlie Kaufman and Spike Jonze," in Charlie Kaufman, *Adaptation: The Shooting Script* (New York: Newmarket Press, 2002), 130.

6. For an account of the side of the modern intellectual tradition that positively promotes this sort of ambivalence, see Stephen Toulmin, *Cosmopolis: The Hidden Agenda of Modernity* (Chicago: University of Chicago Press, 1992).

7. Montaigne, *Essays*, 167, 908.

8. Ralph Waldo Emerson, *The Collected Works of Ralph Waldo Emerson*, ed. Robert E. Spiller et al., 6 vols. to date (Cambridge, MA: Harvard University Press, 1971–), 3:143–44, 3:47. There is a close connection between the essay, in this regard, and the theory and practice of the fragment in early German romanticism. For a discussion of the fragment in philosophy that makes specific reference to Emerson, see Simon Critchley, *Very Little . . . Almost Nothing: Death, Philosophy, Literature*, 2nd ed. (New York: Routledge, 2004), 99–162.

9. Kaufman seems to have had something like this in mind when he named his film production company Projective Testing Services. His films, he notes, are like Rorschach blots, designed less to impose a given view of any particular subject than to present a complex whole and allow viewers to draw their own conclusions. See Kaufman's statements in Rob Feld, "Q & A with Charlie Kaufman," in Charlie Kaufman, *Synecdoche, New York: The Shooting Script* (New York: Newmarket Press, 2008), 146.

10. Kaufman quoted in Andrew O'Hehir, "Who Names a Film 'Synecdoche'?" *Salon*, October 24, 2008 (salon.com). Kaufman's point here echoes a widespread view in contemporary cognitive science, according to which the self is constructed by means of a narrative, a kind of continuous interior monologue. See, for example, Daniel Dennett, *Consciousness Explained* (Boston: Little, Brown, and Co., 1991), 416–30.

11. Kaufman quoted in Walter Chaw, "State of Mind," *Film Freak Central*, October 26, 2008 (filmfreakcentral.net).

12. Kaufman, *Synecdoche: Shooting Script*, 138. A similar, even more extreme, contrast between language and lived experience is found in the script for *Human Nature*. See Charlie Kaufman, *Human Nature: The Shooting Script* (New York: Newmarket Press, 2002), 90. In general, the tension between language and lived experience is a persistent theme in Kaufman's work.

13. Kaufman quoted in Laura Barton, "It's Just a Big Mess inside My Head," *The Guardian*, April 18, 2009 (guardian.co.uk).

14. Kaufman, *Synecdoche: Shooting Script*, 138.

15. Kaufman quoted in O'Hehir, "Who Names a Film 'Synecdoche'?"

16. Kaufman quoted in David Carr, "The Universe According to Kaufman," *New York Times*, October 19, 2008 (nytimes.com).

17. Emerson, *Collected Works*, 3:33.

18. See David L. Smith, "*Eternal Sunshine of the Spotless Mind* and the Question of Transcendence," *Journal of Religion and Film* 9, no. 1 (April 2005) (unomaha.edu/jrf).

19. Kaufman, *Synecdoche: Shooting Script*, 31–32.

20. There is a parable, well known in the Buddhist world, in which a burning house represents samsara—cyclic existence and all the suffering it entails—from which the

Buddha proposes to save us. The parable appears in the third chapter of the Lotus Sutra. See, for example, *Scripture of the Lotus Blossom of the Fine Dharma*, trans. Leon Hurvitz (New York: Columbia University Press, 1976), 58–64. The house in *Synecdoche, New York* also seems to represent the imminence of mortality. "It's a big decision," says Hazel's realtor a propos of house buying, "how one prefers to die" (Kaufman, *Synecdoche: Shooting Script*, 26). The significant twist here, however, is that Hazel is not interested in escape or salvation. On the contrary, she is ready to settle down amid the flames. Her striking equanimity as a character goes hand in hand with her easy relation to mortality.

21. Kaufman, *Synecdoche: Shooting Script*, 3, 11.

22. Ibid., 34. A further key to Adele's character is given in the pseudonym she adopts to hide from her public after her return to America from Germany: Capgras. "Capgras syndrome" is another neurological condition, believed to be physiologically related to Cotard delusion, wherein victims become unable to correlate their present experience of faces and persons with their memories. Consequently, they become convinced that all the people they were formerly closest to are now being played by imposters. Adele's way of being in the world thus involves not a failure to believe in her own life, but a refusal to believe in other people. Capgras syndrome also plays a central role in a recent novel by Richard Powers, *The Echo Maker* (New York: Farrar, Straus and Giroux, 2006).

23. The foil, or opposite number, to Caden's quest for honesty is Madeline (Hope Davis), the nightmare therapist, who, like Robert McKee (Brian Cox) in *Adaptation*, gives Kaufman a target on whom to vent his contempt for the self-help industry. Her glib response to life's disappointments is to sell you a means to salvation, a promise reduced to a formula: "Do that and you'll be fine" (see Kaufman, *Adaptation: Shooting Script*, 70). In response to Caden's desire to express his "real self," for example, her pre-packaged advice to him is to focus on the Now, "Nowness" being a major fetish on the contemporary consciousness circuit. This idea of turning to the present, living in one's moment, is a seductively plausible response to something like Kaufman's concern with the way discursive thought removes us from the immediacy of life. As a formula, though, it is simply another objectification, a substitute story in which "the Now" becomes our "elsewhere," the thing to be achieved. Caden, like Kaufman himself it appears, is initially intrigued by the idea, but in the end he is having none of it. "*Is* there a moment?" wonders Kaufman in a recent interview. "I don't think there is. I've heard and tried a lot to do this 'present moment' thing, in meditation and stuff, but there is no present moment. That's my new conclusion" (Kaufman, *Synecdoche: Shooting Script*, 144).

24. Kaufman, *Synecdoche: Shooting Script*, 36, 46, 49, 51.

25. Ibid., 49.

26. Kaufman quoted in Chaw, "State of Mind." In the same interview, Kaufman notes his attraction to the artistic goal that Isadora Duncan set for herself: to perform just "one authentic gesture." It is hard for us to evade the complexity of reflection, to allow something to be simply and completely what it is. But this is what Kaufman takes as the goal of his own art. "I'm trying to see what it takes to stand up and walk to

the door and then express that, to suggest the thing of it economically. It's a beautiful, profound, simple thing."

27. There is a moment in the film when Caden directs an actor on how to walk more naturally (1:28:20). Of course, the actor becomes all the more self-conscious as a result.

28. Alan Watts, *Nature, Man and Woman* (New York: Vintage Books, 1991), 116.

29. Kaufman quote in Chaw, "State of Mind."

30. Ibid.

31. Emerson, *Collected Works*, 3:19.

Nietzschean Themes in the Films of Charlie Kaufman

Daniel Shaw

There are a number of filmmakers whose work has obviously been influenced by one or more philosophers. Some make explicit reference to such figures (as Woody Allen does in several of his films, for example, in *Another Woman* to Martin Heidegger); others reflect their director's familiarity with philosophical ideas without referring to them directly; and still others parallel philosophical theories without intending to do so. The half-dozen major films written (and, in the most recent case, directed) by Charlie Kaufman are some of the most inventive and thought provoking in the history of Hollywood, but his intellectual influences are somewhat murky (especially given his reluctance to discuss them in interviews). This essay will provide clear evidence of the influence of Friedrich Nietzsche on several of his films; and where evidence of explicit influence is not immediately forthcoming, I contend that Kaufman's films often embody Nietzschean ideas, even if they were not consciously intended to do so.

I begin with an overview of the more prominent facets of the philosophy of Friedrich Nietzsche, with quotations from his published works that express them. I then proceed with a brief summary of my Nietzschean interpretation of *Being John Malkovich*,[1] and I then offer similar analyses of several of Kaufman's other major works. Readings of these films will foreground parallels to the key concepts highlighted in the summary of Nietzsche's worldview. My goal is to show that Nietzsche and Kaufman share a perspective on life that might best be described as Dionysian pessimism.

What Nietzsche Stands For

Any attempt to boil down the philosophy of a major intellectual figure into a handful of assertions is risky at best, especially of a protean individualist like

Friedrich Nietzsche. But respected commentators, such as R. G. Hollingdale and Walter Kaufmann, have identified several themes that are characteristic of Nietzsche's corpus. Drawing on their expertise, I will focus on four major philosophical concepts that will define and clarify what I mean by contending that Charlie Kaufman's films are Nietzschean.

Most Nietzsche scholars agree that his most significant philosophical achievements were his critique of Christianity and his affirmation of the *Übermensch,* as well as the concepts of the eternal recurrence and the will to power. To these I would add his revolutionary perspectivism, as well as his view of the self as a concatenation of power drives that continually struggle for dominance within each individual human organism. It must be admitted at the outset that there are few, if any, supermanlike characters in the Kaufman corpus, nor do his films spend much time explicitly critiquing Christianity. This may in part be explained by Kaufman's Jewish heritage. But his films nonetheless embody a distinctively Nietzschean worldview that sounds the other four themes clearly and often. Kaufman makes several direct references to Nietzsche in his screenplays that indicate at least a passing familiarity with the will to power theory, and *Eternal Sunshine of the Spotless Mind* explicitly examines the notion of the eternal recurrence. Kaufman's writing also seems to reflect Nietzsche's perspectivism, as well as suggesting a fractured concept of self that is distinctly Nietzschean.

The central explanatory hypothesis of Nietzsche's worldview is the idea of the will to power, which functions as a theory of value, a depth psychology that reveals the true source of all human motivation and a cosmological theory of the nature of existence itself.[2] As a theory of value, it proposes three measures of progress for the human species: (1) power over self—the idea that the human race will be better off as it becomes more autonomous and self-defining, overcoming the conventional slave morality that has rendered most individuals powerless and other-directed; (2) power over the environment—that is, harnessing nature to better fulfill human desires by bending it to our will; and (3) power of superior individuals over inferiors—that is, there is a natural aristocracy from the progressive and powerful to the regressively weak and powerless, and powerful individuals should rule and direct the herd toward a new and creative future. Nietzsche states this theory of value most succinctly in *The Antichrist*: "What is good? All that heightens the feeling of power, the will to power, power itself in man. What is bad? All that proceeds from weakness. What is happiness? The feeling that power *increases*—that a resistance is overcome."[3]

Eternal recurrence functions for Nietzsche as a crucial measure of *übermenschlichkeit* (that is, what it is to be the overman). The test turns on our reaction to the prospect of repeating this life over and over again without alteration: "If this thought gained possession of you, it would change you as you are or perhaps crush you. The question in each and every thing, 'Do you desire this once more and innumerable times more?' would lie upon your actions as the greatest weight. Or how well disposed would you have to become to yourself and to life *to crave nothing more fervently* than this ultimate eternal confirmation and seal?"[4] We can attain overman status only when we embrace that prospect as a consummation devoutly to be wished.

This transformation of attitude is nothing less than redemptive, as Nietzsche highlights by calling the section in *Thus Spoke Zarathustra* where he discusses it "Of Redemption." Only individuals can redeem themselves: "All 'It was' is a fragment, a riddle, a dreadful chance—until the creative will says to it 'But I willed it thus!'"[5] This betokens an attitude of acceptance of all that occurs and, as he put it in *The Gay Science*, a willingness to live one's life over again exactly as one has before.

Those who achieve an attitude of total self-acceptance have overcome the counterproductive feelings of guilt and regret that have been inculcated to immoderate extremes by our outmoded Christian heritage. These "free spirits" have thrown off the shackles of Christian slavery and accomplished a revaluation of its anachronistic and life-denying priorities. Nietzsche thought of himself as a harbinger of that transformation: "I am a bringer of good tidings such as there never has been."[6] The crisis of nihilism that he diagnosed was brought about by the death of God and the need to find a convincing alternative to immortality that can make an inherently finite life seem to be worth living.

That crisis is not all negative. The collapse of the Christian worldview is brought about by what Nietzsche calls "active nihilism": "Nihilism, it is ambiguous: nihilism as a sign of increased power of the spirit: as *active* nihilism. Nihilism as decline and recession of the power of the spirit: as *passive* nihilism."[7] Active nihilism clears away the obsolete "Idols of the Marketplace" in order to prepare the ground for new, contemporary values. Passive nihilism shrinks from the chaos of existence and joins Schopenhauer in the search for resignation and acceptance. While ever an iconoclast, Nietzsche meets the crisis head on by creating a new interpretation of the meaning of human existence cast in terms of a vision of the future of the human race embodied in his Zarathustra, who speaks of the eternal recurrence, the will to power, and the overman.

Nietzsche was one of the first thinkers to posit a depth psychology that reduced all human action to a single drive (Freud was to follow his lead rather quickly).[8] As he himself immodestly put it, "Out of my writings speaks a *psychologist* that has not his equal."[9] Nietzsche's psychological acumen recognized that apparently opposed motives could stem from a single drive: "By doing good or doing ill one exercises one's power over others [and] the condition in which we do ill is seldom as pleasant . . . as that in which we do good—it is a sign that we still lack power."[10] We cannot admit to ourselves that we help others for the feeling it gives us because of the psychological repression that has resulted from the Christian assault on selfishness, pleasure, and distinction. Most strikingly, Nietzsche attributes a great deal more of the harm that we do to each other to Christian resentment than to selfish striving.

In Nietzsche's view, our faculty of reason acts in service to these drives, and not (as a prominent prejudice of philosophers would have us believe) vice versa. Our interpretations of events are subject to these contradictory drives as well; this explains the gestalt shifts we undergo: "The explanation of this is that today's prompter of the reasoning faculty was different from yesterday's—a different drive wanted to gratify itself, to be active, to exercise itself, to refresh itself, to discharge itself."[11] We are a bundle of such drives, each with its own perspective and each seeking to dominate the entire organism. To become who we are we must put order to this chaos, set a hierarchy of drives, and follow that hierarchy resolutely over time. Nietzsche characterizes this as "nature's moral imperative": "Thou shalt obey, obey somebody, and for a long time, or else you will perish and lose your last remnant of self respect."[12]

A key element in Nietzsche's vision is his so-called perspectivism. The locus classicus for this aspect of Nietzsche's theory can be found in *The Gay Science*: "*Our new 'infinite'*—How far the perspectival character of existence extends or indeed whether existence has any other character than this; whether existence without interpretation, without 'sense' does not become 'nonsense'; whether on the other hand, all existence is not actively engaged in *interpretation*—that cannot be decided. . . . We cannot look around our own corner. . . . Rather has the world become 'infinite' for us, all over again, inasmuch as we cannot reject the possibility that *it may include infinite interpretations*."[13] This multivalence at the heart of human existence is what makes life so interesting and so perplexing. Despite our best efforts, we cannot transcend our limited perspectives, nor can we avoid interpreting the world in our own terms: "There is *only* a perspectival seeing, *only* a perspectival 'knowing.'"[14] The best that we can do is recognize this and try to incorporate other perspectives into our judgments about the world and other people. No one can be truly objective, nor is such objectivity desirable: "But to eliminate the will completely and turn off all emotions without exception, assuming that we could: well? would that not mean to *castrate* the intellect?"[15]

In an article on the therapeutic implications of Nietzsche's perspectivism, Steven Hales and Rex Welshon have aptly observed: "Nietzsche's view of the self is a member of a venerable tradition in philosophy according to which the self is a complex or bundle of desires, thoughts, emotions, moods, etc. The constituents of the Nietzschean bundle self are not properties, however, but drives (*triebe*)."[16] The will to power expresses itself in a multiplicity of ways, in everything from debates about abstract philosophy to waging war. Individuals must exert control over the drives without trying to repress them totally. Most importantly, to be an individual is to have a set of priorities, a hierarchy of such drives that more or less determines how one acts in the world. This is especially challenging because each drive has its own interpretive perspective on the world and seeks to impose that interpretation on the organism as a whole. Part of becoming who we are is choosing to look at the world from one such perspective rather than another. Both perspectivism and this bundle theory of the self are germane to understanding Kaufman's first major screenplay. Like Nietzsche, Kaufman also seems to reject the notion of normalcy that defines our psychoanalytic culture.

Unlike the romantic pessimists who dominated the latter half of the nineteenth century, Nietzsche characterized his own *weltanschauung* (worldview) as a type of Dionysian pessimism, a notion he had toyed with since *The Birth of Tragedy*. As J. F. Dienstag put it in his abstract for an article on the subject: "Nietzsche's Dionysian pessimism is a perspective on life that can draw sustenance, rather than recoil, from the disordered, disenchanted world left to us after the demise of metaphysics. Whereas Schopenhauer advocated resignation, Nietzsche maintained that a new ground for activity could be found apart from the narratives of reason and progress."[17] Dionysian pessimists embrace the chaos that is life, expect no inherent order in the universe, and seek to impose what order they can fashion by the strength of their unbending will. Life may not be rational, and progress is far from inevitable, but seeking to impose one's own sense of rational order and progress is still a quest that can make life worth living.

Crucial to attaining such a worldview is an acute sense of humor. As Walter Kaufmann observed in a footnote to his anthology *The Basic Writings of Nietzsche*: "For Nietzsche laughter became less a physical phenomenon than a symbol of joyous affirmation of life, and a refusal to bow to the spirit of gravity."[18] The most joyous life possible is one based on a realistically pessimistic set of expectations, one that takes great risks despite the odds, where the emotional highs more than outweigh the inevitable lows, and where we never lose our ability to laugh at both ourselves and the many ironies that pervade our world.

Kaufman's unique sense of humor is what first attracted me to his films. It is the manic screwball charm of Kaufman's films that led Roger Ebert to describe him as "one madcap kinda guy."[19] While that is not a phrase often applied to Nietzsche, it is the last of the affinities between the two writers that I will be exploring.

Being John Malkovich

Kaufman's first film,[20] *Being John Malkovich*, is full of humorous notions, from offices with five-foot ceilings to a secretary who claims to be hard of hearing (but isn't) to the central conceit: a portal that allows one to become John Malkovich for fifteen minutes. The film poses a number of questions that are directly related to philosophical theories of personal identity. When people are able to see the world through his eyes and ears, do they *become* John Malkovich? When others are able to bend him to their will, who is he? When he is totally controlled for what is likely to be the rest of his life, does he cease to *be* John Malkovich?

The entire film can best be described as a power struggle, both in its romantic relationships and in its central conceit. Malkovich is hijacked against his will, his consciousness made a repository of observers and eventually manipulators. In the end, he is reduced to being a vehicle of virtual immortality for Captain Mertin/Lester and his cohorts. Throughout, little concern is shown for the extent to which Malkovich has been victimized. Talk about identity theft! But what is so interesting philosophically about the film is that it poses questions about our sense of self that most traditional theories of personal identity completely fail to answer.

My reading of *Being John Malkovich* resolves the major issues here by claiming that it is the will controlling the Malkovich vessel that constitutes that vessel's personal identity (Schwartz for a while, Lester for the duration of Malkovich's life). The rest of the "consciousnesses" that merely observe the world through the vessel's five senses (including eventually the original Malkovich himself) have no impact on his actions (or on the external world in general) after they enter him. Thus, Kaufman's screenplay has an affinity for Nietzsche's bundle theory of the self (as constituted by a number of conflicting "drives" that each seek to control the entire organism). In the end, the drives that most consistently win the battle and are expressed in action define who we are.

Only by defining personal identity in terms of the will that takes action (that is, the dominant drive in the bundle) can one plausibly answer the question of who John Malkovich is at the end of the film: he has become Captain Mertin/Lester. The Malkovich vessel is controlled by Captain Mertin and pursues the same hierarchy of values that Mertin did when he was in the Lester vessel (and apparently will continue to do until Malkovich's body dies). Malkovich has, at best, been reduced to a mere observer (just as Craig Schwartz is within Maxine's young daughter). Both have, to all intents and purposes, ceased to exist. In short, Kaufman's scenario clearly explodes traditional notions of personal identity and begs for a Nietzschean reading to do justice to its innovative approach.

Human Nature

Kaufman followed up the instant success of *Being John Malkovich* with a much lighter but no less entertaining piece, *Human Nature*. One of the least profound of all of Kaufman's efforts (and one of his films with the least success at the box office), *Human Nature* parallels Nietzsche's thought in a few interesting ways. One of the keystones of Nietzsche's attack on Christian slave morality was how it makes us ashamed of our sexual nature. To get us to relinquish all earthly desires for the sake of an imaginary afterlife, Christianity had to attack the three major sources of human happiness in this life: sexuality, selfishness, and power.

In *Human Nature*, Dr. Nathan Bronfman (Tim Robbins) is a deeply repressed researcher who is trying to teach table manners to mice. His girlfriend, Lila (Patricia Arquette), is a hirsute nature-loving woman who hooked up with Nathan for sex (much to her ultimate dissatisfaction). Puff (Rhys Ifans) is a man raised by apes in the wild until adulthood, whom Nathan wants to civilize. The romantic triangle that develops is hilarious.

In regard to his sexuality, Puff is the "more healthy beast," which Nietzsche thought we could once again become after liberating ourselves from the yoke of Christian guilt. As Nathan tells Puff, society requires us to cover up our true desires: "When in doubt, don't ever do what you really want to do." Puff is as direct about sex as any primate, and his effect on others is unsettling. With Puff's help, Lila frees herself from Nathan's traditional expectations and embraces her sexuality (and her hairy body). But, as Mick LaSalle observed in his review for the San Francisco Chronicle, "the movie has a more subtle point—that civilization itself, far from being an instrument of civility, is the most efficient tool through which people are able to implement and get away with their most monumental acts of selfishness and sensual gratification."[21] This is very Nietzschean as well, in that civilized individuals are still seen to be driven by the will to power; they simply exert it by tracing more circuitous routes and utilizing more indirect means.

In an earlier draft of the final screenplay, Lila even makes reference to Nietzsche himself when a tree struck by lightning falls on her and she escapes without serious injury: "As Nietzsche said, whatever doesn't kill you makes you stronger, and that goes double if you're a woman."[22] Kaufman's reasons for omitting this direct reference from the final cut of the film are open to speculation.[23] But its existence in an earlier draft proves that Nietzsche was on Kaufman's mind while he was composing the work.

Adaptation

Adaptation, like Synecdoche, New York, is strikingly postmodern. It is characteristic of Kaufman's inventive genius to do a film about his (fictionalized) self writing a film adaptation of an unadaptable book. Author Susan Orlean (Meryl Streep) comes alive by embracing her instincts (with a little help from an orchid drug), and John Laroche (Chris Cooper) is the natural man of action. Kaufman creates a doppelgänger in his (imaginary?) twin brother Donald, who is everything Charlie isn't. It is an indicator of Donald's artificial nature that the audience cares little when he is killed off.

The relationship between Orlean and Laroche is unlikely. But Roger Ebert identified why it is plausible nonetheless: "Chris Cooper plays a con man of extraordinary intelligence, who is attractive to a sophisticated New Yorker because he is so intensely himself in a world where few people are anybody."[24] Laroche helps Orlean break out of her shell and become who she is, a far more adventurous and lustful individual than she at first seems.

Ebert praises Streep for being "able to begin as a studious *New Yorker* author and end as, more or less, Katharine Hepburn in *The African Queen*."[25] Like that timeless classic, *Adaptation* celebrates both her awakening and the man who wakes her up. One of the central themes of the film is that natural adaptation demands a great deal of flexibility. This too is highly Nietzschean, as the following parallel passages make evident:

> LAROCHE: You know why I love plants? Because they're so mutable. Adaptation is a profound process. It means you figure out how to thrive in the world. People can't sometimes.
> ORLEAN: Well, it's easier for plants; they have no memory. They just move on to what's next. For a person, it's almost shameful to adapt. It's like running away.[26]

He who cannot alight on the threshold of the moment and forget all the past, who cannot bestride this point like a goddess of victory without becoming dizzy and afraid, will never know what happiness is—worse, he will never do anything to make others happy. Acting needs forgetting, just as all organisms need not just light but also darkness to live. As Nietzsche writes: "To determine . . . the boundary at which the past has to be forgotten if it is not to become the gravedigger of the present, one would have to know exactly how great the *plastic power* of a man, a people, a culture is: I mean by plastic power the capacity to develop out of oneself in one's own way, to transform and incorporate into oneself what is past and foreign."[27]

Both Susan Orlean and the fictional Charlie Kaufman become more flexible in the course of their parallel narratives, making progressively more dangerous choices in order to get the most out of their lives.

Eternal Sunshine of the Spotless Mind

The connection between *Eternal Sunshine of the Spotless Mind* and the Nietzschean notion of the eternal recurrence has already been ably pointed out and explicated by David L. Smith and Carole Lyn Piechota, to whom the following summary is deeply indebted.[28] The central conceit of *Eternal Sunshine*, based on the notion that unpleasant memories can be erased from our minds, runs counter to Nietzsche's call for us to embrace "every pain and every joy and every thought and sigh" as constituting who we are as human beings. If there is a single moment at which we feel truly satisfied with ourselves and our world, then we must affirm everything that has happened to us in the past. Change anything and we no longer can become who we are and overcome the guilt, regret, and obsession with the past that are the legacies of Christianity.

Both Joel (Jim Carrey) and Clementine (Kate Winslet) resort to the aid of a company called Lacuna, which operates on the utilitarian notion that lessening the displeasure of painful memories by erasing them will lead to a happier individual. Mary (Kirsten Dunst) provides a Nietzschean rationalization for doing so, in an attempt to impress Dr. Howard Mierzwiak (Tom Wilkinson):

MARY: Do you like quotes, Howard?
HOWARD: What do you mean?
MARY: Oh, you know, like famous quotes? I find reading them inspirational, and in my reading, I've come across some I thought you might like too.
HOWARD: Oh, well, I . . . I'd love to hear some.
MARY: There's one that goes, "Blessed are the forgetful, for they get the better even of their blunders."
HOWARD: That's Nietzsche, right?[29]

This quotation from Nietzsche may seem to contradict the notion of the eternal recurrence, but in fact he is attempting here to refocus our minds on the future rather than the past. The context of this brief quotation makes it clear that what we are to forget are the critical voices of the moralists around us.[30] We must not be limited by the judgments of our contemporaries or the accomplishments of our predecessors. Dwelling on the past gives rise to (and stems from) the spirit of revenge, and we must transform our attitude from a regretful "It was" to an ecstatic "Thus I will it so!"

In this light, Joel Barish's change of heart (resulting in his attempt to resist the mind-erasing process) demonstrates how much he cares for Clementine and has grown as a person. Both Joel and Clementine show remarkable courage in resuming their relationship, knowing (from the tapes sent to them by a repentant Mary)[31] that they are likely to repeat many of the same mistakes that made being together so difficult in the first place. Much of what is unhealthy about the Western romantic ideal has to do with two of its characteristically irrational expectations: that the other will change to suit me better (and that *I* will change the other), and that we will learn from our mistakes and hence avoid them in the future.

Eternal Sunshine is one of my favorite films, precisely because it shatters these unrealistic expectations and still affirms the value of romantic love. It debunks the romantic ideal, yet celebrates one's ability to care for another nonetheless. As such, it represents the epitome of Kaufman's writing to this point in his career. Not only do Joel and Clementine love each other, they have attained the *amor fati* that Nietzsche believed to be a precondition of human greatness.[32] The ability to lovingly embrace our fate can only stem from a profound sense of gratitude for what this life has to offer us. This virtue is surprisingly lacking in Kaufman's latest effort.

Synecdoche, New York

Caden Cotard (Philip Seymour Hoffman), playwright with a MacArthur grant, is the most self-loathing character in the series of such depressive types (Craig Schwartz, the character Charlie Kaufman, Joel Barish, and others) that inhabit Kaufman's worlds. Cotard paints himself into a corner by trying to reproduce his life in miniature, a decades-long project that never sees the light of day. *Synecdoche, New York* is Kaufman's most enervating work, leaving audiences and critics scratching their heads and longing for his earlier, more life-affirming films (a complaint previously leveled at Woody Allen).

David L. Smith insightfully points out that Kaufman is "the lyricist of a sense of entrapment in life, and his screenplays are explorations of various means by which people try to break out."[33] For Smith, the way out for Joel and Clementine is found by embracing something like the Nietzschean eternal recurrence. After trying to escape themselves by erasing their memories of each other, they do an about-face and are willing to chance a relationship they know to be fraught with risk. By contrast, Caden Cotard is a fly who never gets out of his fly bottle. The results are deeply unsatisfying: as Mick LaSalle quipped: "I've had entire months go by faster than the second hour of this movie."[34] At age forty, Cotard resolves to do a play that will reflect his life in its totality. He spends the next forty years (and the second half of the movie) trying to do so, and fails miserably. According to critical consensus, Kaufman's film also becomes a failure in the process.

Caden's "art" ends up being at too many removes from reality to speak to anyone but himself. Stephanie Zacharek correctly identifies the central theme here: "He's been living for the arts so long he doesn't even know what real living is anymore." She goes on to remark that the fictional counterparts in the play overwhelm the originals that they represent: "Bulldozed by the actors who've stepped in to re-create their lives, Caden and Hazel wonder if they're actually real anymore." What Kaufman didn't realize was that "by reinventing the already bulging universe of the movie midway through, [he had turned it] into an uninteresting mess."[35] As art imitates life imitating art, the film generates a chain of simulacra (the warehouse in which the play is staged has a warehouse on the set that has a warehouse on *its* set, and so on) that recedes into infinity. Nietzsche's warning about such extreme self-consciousness is apropos: "He who fights with monsters might take care lest he thereby become a monster. Is not life a hundred times too short for us to bore ourselves?"[36]

The impact of this film is like what Nietzsche condemns in artistic expressions of romantic pessimism: rather than invigorating us to act in the face of the deplorable superficiality of the world, *Synecdoche, New York* is profoundly deadening. Characters such as Cotard embody the deer-caught-in-headlights powerlessness that is symptomatic of what Nietzsche called passive nihilism (and which implies the Buddhistic resignation of Schopenhauer). Worst of all, the film is not very funny.

But this doesn't alter the fact that the rest of the films of Charlie Kaufman are far from boring and that the overall worldview that emerges from his movies champions the unparalleled value of imagination and the crucial role it can play in becoming who we are, while heaping scorn upon the social conventions and *untermenschen* (inferior men) that stand in our way.

In assessing the significance of the parallels between Nietzsche and Kaufman that I've highlighted here, let me quote from the screenwriter himself. In a rare recent interview with Alex Fitch, Kaufman observed: "It's fine with me if you want to attribute or see connections between my work and other people's work, but I am not setting out to do that. There's no question in my mind that I've been influenced by stuff that I've read or the movies I've seen in ways that I can't even articulate. But it's not intentional homage that I am ever doing."[37] I am willing to take Kaufman at his word. I doubt very much that he is consciously trying to depict a Nietzschean worldview in his films. But they embody many facets of Nietzsche's *weltanschauung* nonetheless.

Kaufman may turn out to be another one of Zarathustra's apes (who end up secretly harboring nihilism in their hearts), but I doubt it. Kaufman's body of work (if not his latest effort) exhibits the complexity and lightness, the brilliance of insight and refusal to take himself too seriously, the bold laughter and exuberant sense of play that, for Nietzsche, are necessary conditions for the achievement of *übermenschlichkeit* (what it is to be the overman).

Notes

1. For a fuller treatment of my analysis of *Being John Malkovich* and Nietzsche, see my article "On Being Philosophical and *Being John Malkovich*," *Journal of Aesthetics and Art Criticism* 64, no. 1 (Winter 2006): 111–18.

2. See Walter Kaufmann, *Nietzsche: Philosopher, Psychologist, Antichrist* (Princeton: Princeton University Press, 1975), 209–54, for an excellent treatment of these three aspects of Nietzsche's theory.

3. Friedrich Nietzsche, *The Antichrist*, in *A Nietzsche Reader*, ed., R. J. Hollingdale (New York: Penguin, 1977), section 2, 231.

4. Friedrich Nietzsche, *The Gay Science*, trans. Walter Kaufmann (New York: Vintage Press, 1974), section 341, 273–74.

5. Friedrich Nietzsche, *Thus Spoke Zarathustra*, in *The Nietzsche Reader*, ed. Keith Ansell Pearson and Duncan Large (Oxford: Blackwell, 2006), Part II, "Of Redemption," 276.

6. Ibid., 514.

7. Friedrich Nietzsche, *The Will to Power* (a compilation of unpublished notes), ed. Walter Kaufmann (New York: Vintage, 1968), Part One, "European Nihilism," section 28, 19–20.

8. For an extended discussion of their parallels, see Paul-Laurent Assoun's *Freud and Nietzsche* (New York: Continuum Press, 2002). He quotes from Freud's *Selbstdarstellung*: "Nietzsche is the other philosopher (Schopenhauer was the first) whose intuitions and apperceptions often coincide in the most astonishing ways with the painfully acquired results of psychoanalysis" (37).

9. Ibid., 513.

10. Nietzsche, *The Gay Science*, section 13.

11. Friedrich Nietzsche, *Daybreak*, section 119, in *The Nietzsche Reader*, ed. Pearson and Large, 199.

12. Friedrich Nietzsche, *Beyond Good and Evil*, section 188, in ibid., 342.

13. Nietzsche, *The Gay Science*, 336.

14. Friedrich Nietzsche, *On the Genealogy of Morality*, Third Essay, section 12, in *The Nietzsche Reader*, ed. Pearson and Large, 427.

15. Ibid.

16. Steven Hales and Rex Welshon, "Nietzsche, Perspectivism, and Mental Health," *Philosophy, Psychiatry and Psychology* 6, no. 3 (1999): 176.

17. J. F. Dienstag, "Nietzsche's Dionysian Pessimism," *American Political Science Review* 95, no. 4 (December 2001): 923.

18. Walter Kaufmann, *The Basic Writings of Nietzsche* (New York: Vintage Press, 1960), 421–23n41.

19. Roger Ebert, review of *Human Nature*, *Chicago Sun-Times*, April 12, 2002 (suntimes.com).

20. I will be discussing the films Kaufman has written as if he is the sole author;

this is, of course, patently artificial. Films are collaborative endeavors, and the input of Spike Jonze and Michel Gondry, who each directed two of Kaufman's films, was crucial to their quality and their success. (Jonze directed *Being John Malkovich* and *Adaptation*; Gondry, *Human Nature* and *Eternal Sunshine of the Spotless Mind*.) Despite many differences, I take the four films they helmed to embody a consistent worldview (perhaps the bleakness of *Synecdoche, New York* can be explained by their absence), with many recurrent themes. I have attributed that view to Kaufman, who I believe is primarily responsible for the consistency of that vision.

21. Mick LaSalle, review of *Human Nature*, *San Francisco Chronicle*, April 12, 2002 (sfgate.com).

22. *Human Nature* script on the Internet Movie Script Database (IMSDb.com).

23. It is interesting to note in this connection that Kaufman shows no such qualms in his next venture, *Confessions of a Dangerous Mind*. *Confessions* is the least intellectually challenging of Kaufman's major screenplays, but there the quote from Nietzsche's writings makes it into the final cut. Patricia (a CIA operative played by Julia Roberts) offers the following words of wisdom to Chuck Barris: "The man who despises himself still respects himself as he who despises."

24. Roger Ebert, review of *Adaptation*, *Chicago Sun-Times*, December 20, 2002 (suntimes.com).

25. Ibid.

26. *Adaptation* (Spike Jonze, 2002).

27. Friedrich Nietzsche, "Of the Uses and Disadvantages of History for Life," in *Untimely Meditations*, ed. Daniel Breazeale, trans. R. J. Hollingdale (Cambridge: Cambridge University Press, 1997), 62.

28. David L. Smith, "*Eternal Sunshine of the Spotless Mind* and the Question of Transcendence," *Journal of Religion and Film* 9, no. 1 (April 2005) (unomaha.edu/jrf). Carole Lyn Piechota, "Once More and Innumerable Times More: Nietzsche's Eternal Return in *Eternal Sunshine of the Spotless Mind*," *Film and Philosophy* 11 (2007).

29. *Eternal Sunshine of the Spotless Mind* (Michel Gondry, 2004).

30. Nietzsche, *Beyond Good and Evil*, section 217, in *The Nietzsche Reader*, ed. Pearson and Large.

31. For an enlightening discussion of how Mary unknowingly repeats her mistake and resumes an affair with Dr. Mierzwiak, see Thomas Wartenberg, *Thinking on Screen: Film as Philosophy* (New York: Routledge, 2007), 76–93. See also Christopher Grau's book in the Philosophers on Film series, *Eternal Sunshine of the Spotless Mind* (New York: Routledge, 2009).

32. *Amor fati* (literally "to love fate") is best characterized by Nietzsche in a passage from *Ecce Homo*: "My formula for greatness in a human being is *amor fati*: that one wants nothing to be other than it is, not in the future, not in the past, not for all eternity. Not merely to endure what happens of necessity . . . but to *love* it." "Why I Am So Clever," section 10, in *The Nietzsche Reader*, ed. Pearson and Large, 509.

33. Smith, "*Eternal Sunshine of the Spotless Mind* and the Question of Transcendence."

34. Mick LaSalle, "Long Day's Journey to *Synecdoche*," *San Francisco Chronicle*, November 7, 2008 (sfgate.com).

35. Stephanie Zacharek, review of *Synecdoche, New York*, *Salon*, October 24, 2008 (salon.com).

36. Nietzsche, *Beyond Good and Evil*, section 146, in *The Nietzsche Reader*, ed. Pearson and Large.

37. Charlie Kaufman, interview with Alex Fitch, 2009, scifilondontv.com/audio/ realitycheck_genre_summer09.mp3.

INCONCLUSIVE UNSCIENTIFIC POSTSCRIPT

Late Remarks on Kierkegaard and Kaufman

DAVID LAROCCA

Charlie Kaufman is said to be an anxious man.[1] Or perhaps that is a confused judgment based on speculation over the characters he creates—characters who appear to suffer from anxiety. Or perhaps it is the viewers themselves who experience anxiety in watching Kaufman's films. Still, the anxiety that Kaufman has, reflects, or engenders is not the kind of anxiety we think it is. Kaufman's characters embody a kind of anxiety that bears a closer resemblance to the anxiety Søren Kierkegaard theorized in the 1840s. In what follows, I articulate some points of relation between their work, in particular how Kaufman shares with Kierkegaard a radical deployment of pseudonymity as a way of responding to anxiety. Both writers rely on pseudonymity to transform autobiographical experience from something merely personal to something at a remove from its author—a distancing that enables the work to become relevant to a wider audience, indeed to the human community afflicted by the very anxiety they theorize and dramatize. Pseudonymity, in turn, animates a number of philosophically significant features of their work, which I will address: the possibility of learning truth from lies; metaphysical varieties of acting; the presence of doubles and proxies; and the puzzling effects of work that repeats and reflects back on itself.

Anxiety as a Condition of Experience

Based on a reading of the behavior of his characters, Kaufman has been hailed as "a champion of the freak within. His heroes are not dashing or charming or even heroic. They are, instead, self-loathing, painfully observant, and often profoundly unattractive."[2] Yet this notion of the inner freak manifesting itself in unpleasant ways is tied to a conventional, even medical, notion of anxiety—as something akin to worry, nervousness, or social anxiety disorder.[3] His characters seem to exhibit symptoms of some kind of general anxiety: they pace, frown, fidget, and sweat; they are articulate but self-doubting; preoccupied with big questions yet awkward and easily overcome by small decisions and casual intimacies; serious, but sometimes foolish. But there is something deeper, much deeper, that they are struggling to become aware of and come to terms with.

In *The Concept of Anxiety*, Søren Kierkegaard both inaugurates the existentialist tradition of taking anxiety as a pervasive, underlying condition of human experience and makes it undeniably clear that anxiety is not worry, fear, nervousness, melancholy, or depression—much less fidgetiness and fussiness. Unlike fear and worry, which have definite objects, anxiety is generated by an encounter that lacks definition, or that makes one feel in the presence of formlessness or void. Anxiety, in this sense, is nothing like regular nervousness; it is the dawning awareness of a radical sense of genuine possibility. That is why anxiety may be compared with dizziness.[4] Anxiety emerges when what has been glimpsed is the moment preceding knowledge, a state of infinite possibility when everything can be changed. One feels anxiety not because one has learned an ability to choose good or evil, but because one has fathomed one's connection to the unconditional source of being and value and has discovered the reality of freedom. One is certain something is amiss, but unsure how to articulate what it is. For Kierkegaard, or rather the pseudonymous author of *The Concept of Anxiety*, Vigilius Haufniensis, anxiety is a symptom of one's awareness of possibility. Haufniensis, like Charlie Kaufman, characterizes the difficulty of choosing—and the anxiety that comes from feeling the genuine pressure of this reality.

But it's hard to become aware of that reality if one labors under an impoverished picture of philosophy—what it is and can do. Kierkegaard was mortified by the distortions promulgated by Hegel's philosophical outlook—absolute idealism—because it "radically misrepresented human existence."[5] Interpreting Kierkegaard's disgust in his massive yet incisive *A History of Philosophy*, Frederick Copleston notes: "The really important problems, that is, the problems which are of real importance for man as the existing individual, are not solved by thought, by adopting the absolute standpoint of the speculative philosopher, but by the act of choice, on the level of existence rather than on that of detached, objective reflection."[6] Kaufman has registered his frustration with narrative traditions in cinema that maintain distorting stereotypes of human relationships.[7] Partly because of the nature of cinema itself, viewers are encouraged to believe that film reality tells us something about our predicament beyond the screen. But it can't—or, rather, very seldom does. Kaufman, therefore, has set about to create work that does not simply offer another narrative, but in many ways questions the experience of narrative altogether. Why should a romantic relationship have a telos? Why should a story have an arc, or occur in three acts? From here, we begin to find other questions that appear in the wake of skepticism about narrative's hold on our sense of reality: Why do we believe in the idea of a soul mate? What grounds our faith in causation and linearity? In *Eternal Sunshine of the Spotless Mind*, the characters must choose, not merely think things over interminably. The act of choosing is predicated on a kind of Kierkegaardian "leap" from one worldview to another, and the anticipation of the leap will always intensify one's anxiety. Kaufman suggests that love is a kind of faith that requires decisive action; it is, as Kierkegaard intimates and Copleston characterizes, "an adventure, a risk, a self-commitment to an objective uncertainty."[8] And it has to be constantly repeated, not done once and for all. "Belief," like love, states Copleston, "is not a matter of accepting the conclusion of a demonstrative argument but rather a matter of will."[9] Kaufman's characters keep agonizing over their decisions, which is just as it should be. "Dread recurs as the emotive tonality of the repeated leap."[10]

What exactly can we *do*, if anything, to mitigate or alleviate being anxious? If anxiety is fundamentally existential—a constitutive attribute of simply being human—than nothing can be done. Kierkegaard and Kaufman, though, show us why we ought not suppress our deep-seated anxiety, but instead come to terms with it. They encourage us to understand why anxiety is important to the development of human identity and essential to the promotion of human flourishing. Yet an education in anxiety's importance can't, it seems, be achieved conventionally—for example, by being taught the meaning of one's anxiety in a direct or literal way. One needs to employ devices, to move at oblique angles, to become literary (Kaufman's case) or religious (in Kierkegaard's). Thus Kierkegaard and Kaufman dismiss a scientific approach to human understanding; they are not verificationists seeking to compare or find correspondence between one realm of experience and another. Using Kierkegaard's morphology, we address "inwardness," which entails understanding that who I am is fundamentally a matter of relation—how I position or orient myself to others and the world. This mood is contrasted with outwardness: theorizing, thesis-building, empirically driven, scientific endeavors to control the world. Science, regardless of its sophistication, cannot help us out of our anxiety because anxiety is neither responsive to its methods nor compatible with its objectives (such as elimination or purification, systematizing or uniformity, laws or rules). Reidar Thomte ably articulates a way of understanding this aspect of Kierkegaard's thought: "Thus every human being possesses, or is within himself, a complete expression of humanness, whose essential meaning cannot be gained from scientific studies. That is, neither rational speculation nor natural science will disclose to the existing individual his essential nature and purpose. Self-knowledge is attained by man in existing; that is, self-knowledge is coordinate with the actualizing of one's potentiality to become oneself."[11]

In Kaufman's *Human Nature*, we see a satirical depiction of how science can neither form the self nor account for it. While the body may succumb (or thrive) under the control of scientific knowledge, the self eludes scientific investigation with its invasive, taxonomical methodology. Kierkegaard approached knowledge of the self as Socrates did and lauded the ancient dictum "Know thyself." Kierkegaard finds a related sentiment in the Latin saying *unum noris omnes* ("if you know one, you know all").[12] Kierkegaard's variant of the Socratic notion extends the range of self-knowledge: if you truly know yourself, then you can better understand others.[13] With Kaufman, however, the idea is inverted: you need others in order to know yourself. From Kaufman's vantage, the credo would be rendered "If you know others, you have a chance to know yourself."

In the past century, anxiety has increasingly come to signify both the cause and the symptom of various psychotic and somatic maladies. With each new version of *The Diagnostic and Statistical Manual of Mental Disorders* (*DSM*), the definitions and types of anxiety become more expansive and take on frightfully more intensive negative implications. New labels are given to identify varieties of anxiety-related "disorders" and "syndromes." For Kierkegaard, however, "anxiety is by no means a sign of imperfection." Indeed, "the greatness of anxiety is a prophecy of the greatness of perfection."[14] Likewise for Kaufman, anxiety is not a sign of deficiency or disorder, but a mark of sheer humanness. Why shouldn't it be difficult to talk to the person you find attractive? Why should it be easy to understand another's heart or mind? Why should accounting for one's life—its shape, its meaning—be anything less than one's entire task?

The challenge is not to be, as it were, panicked by anxiety but inspired by it, able to seize its potential for increasing one's self-awareness. "Whoever has learned to be anxious in the right way has learned the ultimate," writes Kierkegaard; "the more profoundly he is in anxiety, the greater is the man."[15] As one matures in relation to one's anxiety, one "becomes more and more reflective."[16]

Pseudonymity and Truth

For Kierkegaard, pseudonymity was a method for divorcing the specificity of his own existential struggle with anxiety, thereby enabling him to reflect less personally on this general human condition—not so much to protect his identity as to liberate his reader to consider her own. He used it for what he called his "aesthetic" works (as opposed to his religious writings, which were published under his own name). It was important that the two kinds of authorship be kept distinct and that readers honor their separation, because they were written for very different purposes. Kierkegaard's aesthetic, or pseudonymous, works were experiments in philosophy and psychology, whereas the religious works were not experimental at all, but rather devotional in nature. Some of the works with pseudonymous authors include *Fear and Trembling* (Johannes de Silentio), *Repetition* (Constantin Constantius, author of the first half), *The Concept of Anxiety* (Vigilius Haufniensis), *Stages on Life's Way* (Hilarius Bookbinder), *Concluding Unscientific Postscript* (Johannes Climacus), and *The Sickness unto Death* (Anti-Climacus). In *Either/Or*, Victor Eremita is said to be the "editor" of articles he found written by an author, "A," with rebuttals to "A" penned by "Judge William."

As it does for many artists, anxiety may be said to motivate the work of Kaufman and Kierkegaard. Yet few artists manage to make anxiety at once a topic of concern and at the same time usefully convey a clearer sense of its nature and implications. One might honestly and profitably read Kaufman and Kierkegaard's work as innovative expressions of anxiety—responses to a deep-seated "sickness unto death," the gravest imaginable existential crisis—that also prevail in aiding the common viewer or reader to see better what is at stake. At the core of their work, we recognize brave replies to the most daunting existential and ethical questions: Why am I here? How should I act? What kind of meaning is possible given that I will die?

Kierkegaard believed that by means of pseudonymity—adopting a "fake" name—he could achieve "indirect communication," a kind of communication that would make people aware of their lives lost in illusion. It may at first glance seem counterintuitive, but Kierkegaard used the deception, fabulation, lies, and fakery of pseudonymous authorship to refract truth. "My work as an author," Kierkegaard writes, "was the prompting of an irresistible inner need, the only possibility for a depressed person, an honest indemnifying attempt by one deeply humbled, a penitent, to make up, if possible, for something by means of every sacrifice and effort in the service of the truth."[17] Similarly, Kaufman uses pseudonymity as a device for accessing deeper truths about human relationships, personal identity, and self-knowledge.

Sometimes Kaufman uses a pseudonym to name a character who seems to resemble him, or stand in for him—Caden Cotard (Philip Seymour Hoffman) in *Synecdoche, New York*, for example—and on at least one occasion he gave a character his own name, in *Adaptation* (giving rise to the question: in what way can one's own name become a pseudonym?). Other times, he will use a pseudonym for the author of the work, as with the play *Anomalisa*. Such pseudonymous works, as they do with Kierkegaard, solicit in us a genuine question about authorship—about the relationship between an author and his work. We find, then, a distinction between a "stage name" and a given, or "real" name; but what relevance, if any, does this have on our sense of the meaning of the work, much less the significance of the artist who created it? One acts "under" a stage name as oneself yet also, at the same time, as another (namely, the character). Pseudonymity is a way of estranging oneself from one's work; and one of the things that Kaufman's recurring use of pseudonymity suggests is an apparent wish to distance himself as author or bring so much attention to the trick that the name—or author—is no longer the focus. We cannot see what is directly in front of us, and for that reason we may be in a better—more receptive—position to see what he wants us to see: not Kaufman, but what Kaufman sees.

Kierkegaard used pseudonyms to achieve the realization of truth through what he called "indirect communication," a variant of the Socratic method. He felt truth could never be revealed, nor illusion vanquished, by direct means: "No, an illusion can never be removed directly, and basically only indirectly. . . . One who is under an illusion must be approached from behind. . . . By a direct attack he only strengthens a person in the illusion and infuriates him."[18] Adopting a pseudonym gives license to the notion that one is taking on a different point of view, inhabiting a perspective that is not one's own; but for Kierkegaard the "deeper significance of pseudonymity" comes from the way the deception brings truth to light. "Do not be deceived by the word *deception*," he says. "One can deceive a person out of what is true, and—to recall old Socrates—one can deceive a person into what is true. Yes, in only this way can a deluded person actually be brought into what is true—by deceiving him."[19] It has become commonplace to speak of mounting an "intervention" for someone who is afflicted, perhaps lost in an addiction or beholden to errors and superstition. Kierkegaard notes the flaw in this approach: "Direct communication presupposes that the recipient's ability to receive is entirely in order, but here that is simply not the case—indeed, here a delusion is an obstacle."[20] As a result, if one really wants to be of help "It means that one does not begin *directly* with what one wishes to communicate but begins by taking the other's delusion at face value."[21] Thus, it is crucial to Kierkegaard's project that Haufniensis—the author of *The Concept of Anxiety*—is understood as entirely distinct from Kierkegaard and also different from all of Kierkegaard's other pseudonymous authors (Constantius, Silentio, Climacus, et al.). "Anyone with just a fragment of common sense will perceive that it would be ludicrously confusing to attribute to me everything the poetized personalities say"[22]—or, indeed, *anything*: "I have expressly urged once and for all that anyone who wants to quote something from the pseudonyms will not attribute the quotation to me (see my postscript to *Concluding Postscript*)."[23]

Kierkegaard's insistent separation of the pseudonymous authors allows for innovations and explorations in the nature of indirect communication, as when his pseudonymous authors write about one another. For example, when Haufniensis comments in *The Concept of Anxiety* on Constantius's *Repetition*: "This is no doubt a witty book, as the author also intended it to be."[24] Fictional authors are thus aware of one another's works, in turn intensifying the remove from Kierkegaard and improving the quality and effect of indirect communication. Kaufman, similarly, does not present a direct analysis of anxiety, but rather lets the wider existential crisis work itself out through the radical specificity of one character in relation to others. We see how anxiety manifests itself in a character's life, and thereby come to recognize it indirectly. When Kaufman is successful, a viewer comes away from the film either better able to understand how another might be suffering in her relation to the world, or perhaps more aware of her own existential condition. What more could be expected of art than by its very lies it reveals truths?[25] Of his own work, Kierkegaard said: "I am convinced that rarely has any author used as much cunning, intrigue, and ingenuity to win honor and esteem in the world in order to deceive it as I have done for the opposite reason—to deceive it into an understanding of the truth."[26]

Kierkegaard's use of pseudonymity illustrates and enacts the theory be-hind indirect communication because it is an act dedicated expressly to the development of reflection.[27] Direct communication is, then, fundamentally about creating a "witness."[28] One who reflects must become more "inward"—not solipsistic, but instead more "aware" of one's radical specificity and one's relationship to others.[29] Witnessing, as the method of science, always points outward to the world; the witness pursues reasons, causes, and general ex-planations. Indirect communication, by contrast, continually reminds each person of his or her own individuality, reinforcing the necessarily fraught relationship between the self and the world that causes anxiety in the first place. Direct communication, with its theories, disrupts this "making aware" by creating schematics that comfort, distract, and otherwise obscure the development of one's particularity.

Along with Kierkegaard's adoption of the Socratic focus on self-knowledge and indirect communication (sometimes referred to as Socratic irony) we find his interest in the notion of the maieutic. Socrates was de-scribed as a "midwife" to philosophy, someone who helped facilitate indi-vidual efforts at philosophical understanding. Importantly, then, Socrates did not give birth to ideas, but helped draw them out of his interlocutors. Kierkegaard claims that "all the pseudonymous writings are *maieutic* in nature."[30] The pseudonym essentially places a divide between the author and his work, allowing the latter to be experienced on its own terms without reference or recourse to the author: "Within an illusion, the maieutic is the maximum, and it also leaves the reader alone with the work, free from ex-traneous interest in the author's personality and personal life."[31] Kierkegaard said: "anyone who wants to quote something from the pseudonyms will not attribute the quotation to me." He concludes, "I regard myself rather as a *reader* of the books, not as the *author*."[32] Kierkegaard is an audience for "his" work and for that reason can be receptive to it, able to let it work on *him* maieutically. Any standard of efficacy in the pseudonymous works lies in the texts themselves, not in the author's claims about it: "If in the capacity of a third party, as a reader," Kierkegaard says, "I cannot substantiate from the writings that what I am saying is the case, that it cannot be otherwise, it could never occur to me to want to win what I thus consider as lost."[33] The "point," or argument, must be evident in the work. The author has no special access to its meaning; the author's intention is moot: "*qua* author it does not help very much that I *qua* human being declare that I have intended this and that."[34] Kierkegaard and Kaufman's rather elaborate employment of pseudonymity, and its attendant power to distance the author from the work, reflects a faith in the importance of individuals. "Oh, to what degree human beings would become—human and lovable things," exclaims Kierkegaard, "if they would become single individuals before God!"[35] By contrast, "the crowd has no ideality and therefore no power to hold on to an idea despite appearances; the crowd always falls into the trap of appearances."[36] Kierkegaard and Kaufman are dedicated to appearances, just not to being immobilized by them. By creating characters—either in the form of pseudonymous authors or actors playing a role—Kierkegaard and Kaufman register their abiding faith in the importance of human specificity. As Kierkegaard intones: "If the crowd is the evil, if it is chaos that threatens, there is rescue in one thing only, in becoming the single individual, in the rescuing thought: that single individual."[37] The reader or viewer who comes face to face with reality in the guise of appearances has a chance to recognize truth in illusions. Being aware of existence in this way sustains the creative potential of one's anxiety: developing and defining one's discrete, individual existence.

Acting as Inhabitation or Impersonation

Pseudonymity allows an author to play a role or engage in role playing. The author is, then, *acting* as an author behind, or as it were under, a stage name. As an actor is said to "disappear" into a part, so the author hides behind a nom de plume. Though Kierkegaard was clear about his reasons for creating pseudonymous authors, he nevertheless was tormented by what to say about his *relationship* to these authors: "I suffer indescribably every time I have begun to want to publish something about myself and the authorship."[38] One outcome of Kierkegaard's struggle is *The Point of View*, an autobiographical register of his insights about what he created. Likewise, Kaufman turns the tormenting task of coming to terms with authorship into the very subject of his work. For instance, by bringing the theater "into film," as he does in the puppet shows of *Being John Malkovich*, the congressional testimony of *Human Nature*, and the Arthur Miller play in *Synecdoche, New York*, Kaufman creates a discomfiting frisson between our judgment of the difference between real and the fake, the "acted" and the genuine. What if we all are always just acting? Or what if in acting—faking it—we get nearer to the reality of our lives? "I think Adele's right when she says I'm not doing anything real," Caden Cotard confesses, only to hear his therapist Madeline (Hope Davis) ask in reply: "What would be real?"[39]

With theater—and the attendant reflections on the nature of acting inherent in any explicit engagement with theatrical forms—Kaufman finds another way to illustrate how others can return us to ourselves. In *Being John Malkovich*, Maxine (Catherine Keener) intuits this fundamental human desire and fantasy when developing an advertisement for the portal: "Ever want to be someone else? Now you can."[40] A version of Maxine's question becomes the tagline of the film, and usefully reminds us of the interrelation between "being someone else" and acting. And Malkovich is, of course, an actor—indeed, an "actor's actor"—but also, as he admits to his friend John Cusack, "an asshole."[41] The bold claims offset one another: he may be one of the "greatest actors of his generation," but he is also vain. Yet his awareness of the esteem doesn't make him incapable of genuine self-mockery; that must also be counted as part of his greatness. With *Being John Malkovich*, we are not asked to be *anybody* else, but Malkovich in particular, which is to say this particular actor. However, once you decide to become Malkovich, that is, Malkovich-as-himself—ordering things from catalogs by phone, eating toast, talking into a tape recorder (even if it is Chekhov's *The Cherry Orchard*), taking a cab, and so on—you get the most boring and familiar aspects of your own life. Desiring to be someone else, even if he is an actor, even a great actor, is foolish, since you are merely desiring to become yourself.

We find this desire to be or become oneself—as another, as other—iterated in different ways in Kaufman's films. In *Being John Malkovich*, for instance, we see Craig Schwartz's (John Cusack) desire for greatness exist in tension with his despair over its possibility. His self-perception and his perception of others are distorted by manifestations of his despair (such as self-alienation and self-disgust), and Kaufman illustrates how these two kinds of perception inform his judgment. Very early in the film Craig watches a biographical profile on television of Derek Mantini, a puppeteer who dangles a sixty-foot Emily Dickinson marionette over Amherst, Massachusetts, while reciting her poetry, a scene that can be taken as a hyperrealized version of Craig's more modest street puppetry, *The Tragedy of Abelard and Heloise*. Craig's persistent acrimony is exacerbated by Mantini's *The Belle of Amherst*, and he concludes on the proceedings to Elijah, his wife's pet "monkey" sitting nearby: "Gimmicky bastard."[42] Craig is jealous of the artist and resentful of his success, but also, importantly, disgusted with himself—disappointed that he is not, or has not become, Mantini. Later in the film, however, when Craig is "in" Malkovich, living as him, having turned Malkovich-as-puppet into a puppet master, at last experiencing the life of a celebrity puppeteer like Mantini, he watches a biographical documentary film about "himself" (viz., Craig-as-Malkovich) and revels in it, commenting with enthusiasm, pride, and even vulgarity to Maxine: "It's really good! I look really fucking amazing. I'd fuck me!"[43] Kaufman suggests that each of us, in some way, performs a version of *Craig's Dance of Despair and Disillusionment* motivated by anxieties over identity, self-worth, and the meaning of creative work.[44] The "dance" affects our very ability to assess what it is we think we see. As these two moments in Craig's life illustrate, when a biographical account is about someone else's life it may seem fraudulent, a lie, full of false claims—bloated, pretentious, and cheap. Yet when the account is about one's own life—and subject to the distorting effects of one's own vanity and self-interest—the account may appear true, substantive, profound, and worthy of praise. In the contrast between unknown-Craig (seeing Mantini) and famous-Craig-as-Malkovich (seeing "himself" as a legitimate peer of Mantini, or perhaps even better than "the greatest puppeteer in the history of the world"), Kaufman highlights the way despair—as a kind of self-alienation—animates and defines differing points of view, especially as it informs self-perception and perception of others. Moreover, conflicting and distorting viewpoints cause anxiety, heartache, and regret in each stage of life: Craig suffers as himself and he suffers in Malkovich, as Malkovich; and ultimately he suffers a kind of purgatory "in" Emily.[45]

Kaufman finds in writers such as Patricia Highsmith "some sort of queasiness of existence that's so subtle and so terrifying that I find masterful and transcendent."[46] He shares Highsmith's talent for employing devices—such as doubles, self-reflexivity, and repetition—to further the emotional stakes of his work. Anthony Minghella's direction of the film *The Talented Mr. Ripley* (1999), based on Highsmith's novel of the same name, appeared the same year as *Being John Malkovich* and bears a nearly identical tagline: "Have you ever wanted to be somebody else?" Though the idea of "doubles" appeared in the marketing campaign for each film, there is a difference between Kaufman's and Highsmith's understanding of being somebody else: namely, the difference between inhabiting the person (being in Malkovich) versus imitating or impersonating (Tom Ripley as Dickie Greenleaf). The two films coincide, however, on the notion of displacing another person, and whether that transformation can ever be sufficiently realized or convincingly sustained. Here we find the difference between "being" and "disguise." Ripley says in voice-over: "I always thought it'd be better to be a fake somebody than a real nobody." But Kaufman is asking what it would mean to be someone else in a metaphysical sense, and whether we are ever in a position to determine which life is real or fake and, moreover, which life—or identity—is truly one's own.

Autobiography and Alterity

While Nietzsche reported a dawning clarity that "every great philosophy up till now has consisted of . . . the confession of its originator, and a species of involuntary and unconscious auto-biography," Kaufman inverts this standard by making conscious awareness of the self the hallmark of his creative work.[47] Kaufman concurs with Nietzsche—as he once said, "Everything is autobiographical, whether you want it to be or not."[48] Yet Kaufman, perhaps more than any contemporary screenwriter and director, explores, celebrates, and suffers the attempt to become aware of the conditions of his own creations. If, as in *Adaptation*, it seems that "he," as Charlie Kaufman (played by Nicolas Cage), is trying to create something beautiful, then it is perhaps all the more unsettling and disorienting that he finds himself written into "his" screenplay *twice*—first by himself, and then by the actor playing him. How can we possibly create something beautiful if we are always coming up against the fact of our existence—its limitedness, awkwardness, decay, and unknownness?

Kaufman, like Kierkegaard, aims for consciousness not of his own self, we might say, but of selfhood or individuality per se. Kierkegaard transformed his autobiographical experience into work that would elucidate and illuminate human specificity, not his own life or predicament. Reading Kierkegaard is not supposed to bring us closer to him, but to ourselves, individually. Kaufman manifests the autobiographical in related though distinctively different, experimental ways. Sometimes he creates a character who starts out as an autobiographer, as in *Synecdoche, New York*, in which Caden Cotard tries to write a play about his life but ends up becoming his own biographer—with actors playing him, taking lines from him, and thereby alienating him from his own identity. At first it seems that only Caden knows his own life, so only Caden could write this play. Yet as the film progresses, we see that Caden doesn't know his life. In a very palpable way, his life is not his to know. In *Adaptation*, the presence of a character named "Charlie Kaufman" gives the impression that Kaufman the screenwriter is somehow simultaneously autobiographer (of himself as author) and biographer (of himself as character). But who is who? One's sense of the "real"

Charlie Kaufman recedes even as the reality of the fictional Charlie Kaufman becomes more prominent and convincing. The folding and indeterminate quality of his status—as author, as character—goes a long way to show how biographer and autobiographer are interrelated. In Kaufman's hands, we see how the practice and art of "adaptation"—or transformation—of one's personal story to a screenplay or film does not mean that we are any closer to knowing that person. These examples draw a portrait of Emerson's claim that "all biography is autobiography"—the notion that in writing about someone else, one is always already writing about oneself because of the values and judgments one brings to the project.[49] And, conversely, in writing about oneself there is always the sense that one is writing about someone else—someone foreign, or other. The autobiographer, like the biographer, will ask in genuine perplexity: "Who *is* this person I've written about?" I can't be the subject of my own autobiography because the person I write about is necessarily different from the person I am; an autobiography is just another kind of fiction. The autobiographer feels alienated from his autobiography—as if the subject of his work is other than him—even as the biographer feels so close to the subject of his biography that he comes to believe that *he* is the true subject of the work.

If one is simultaneously, or even alternately, a biographer and autobiographer, there is a strange sense of being or having a double—as if the biographer always needs both himself and his subject in order to write, and the autobiographer needs both himself and some idealized (or at least fictionalized) version of himself in order to write. When asked what he thinks about "doubles" in his work, Kaufman replied:

> I really should sort of figure this out because I'm asked this a lot but I don't really know. I don't know if it would be fair or helpful for me to say to you that it speaks to this thing that you talk about regarding the ineffable in art—the inarticulate in art. I'm just really attracted to fake reality. On some level it just appeals to me, and when I put myself into a story situation and I don't know where it's going, these permutations just become part of the story and . . . then they, they kind of, what's the word? They . . . [*long pause*] I mean, they please me.[50]

Clearly doubleness pleased Kierkegaard as well, since it was a pervasive element of his work. But Kierkegaard's pleasure was based in his belief that doubleness—what he called "duplexity"—served a philosophical purpose, as Socratic irony did: it helped others become aware of themselves in their specificity, as single individuals. In the opening chapter of his intellectual and spiritual autobiography, *The Point of View for My Work as an Author: A Direct Communication, Report to History* (published posthumously in 1859), Kierkegaard is at pains to admit the doubleness at the heart of his work and make its import evident. In the chapter entitled "The Equivocalness or Duplexity in the Whole Authorship, Whether the Author is an Esthetic or a Religious Author," he writes: "Accordingly, what is to be shown here is that there *is* such a duplexity from beginning to end. It is not, then, as is ordinarily the case with a supposed duplexity, that others have discovered it and it is the task of the person concerned to show that it *is not*. By no means, just the opposite. Insofar as the reader might not be sufficiently aware of the duplexity, it is the author's task to make it as obvious as possible that it is there. In other words, the duplexity, the equivocalness, is deliberate."[51]

Like Kaufman, Kierkegaard lived with his pseudonymous authors as he would with others. Kierkegaard labored to create a world of "aesthetic" writers—his pseudonymous authors—who inhabited an alternate, independent plane of creative existence. We also find Kaufman experimenting with pseudonymous authors and their worlds. For example, the doubles in the film reality of *Adaptation* spill out into extradiegetical reality when we see that it is Charlie and Donald Kaufman who are credited as screenwriters and who win an Oscar for Best Adapted Screenplay. This may be the first time in motion picture history that an imagined, now deceased, twin sibling was nominated for a posthumous Academy Award. (Donald was also nominated—and won—more than a dozen other film awards, with "brother" Charlie sharing the credit.)

Doubleness and double lives are common in the work of several contemporary filmmakers. The story in David Lynch's *Mulholland Drive* (2001), for example, involves women who are doubles—at times one woman becomes the externalization of the other's inner desire, at other points the women exchange identities. In *The Matrix* (1999), the Wachowski brothers posit separate realms of consciousness: the reality of the matrix, which is simulated; and the reality of the real, of which there is little left but an eviscerated, postapocalyptic landscape. Kaufman's recurrent exploration of doubleness, like Kierkegaard's, is grounded in an interpretation of autobiographical authorship; this authorial inventiveness suggests important differences between the structure of storytelling and the nature of fiction.

The prominent antagonistic role that screenwriting coach Robert McKee (Brian Cox) plays in *Adaptation* brings a heightened degree of self-consciousness to the fact that what we're seeing on film is based on a screenplay, and indeed that Robert McKee is a character based on a real-life screenwriting coach named Robert McKee. But this recognition is a quick pleasure compared with the dialectic Kaufman sets up between the character Charlie Kaufman and his brother, Donald (Nicolas Cage), a devotee of McKee's. At issue is how to best create narrative. Is structure important? What is the difference between plot-driven and character-driven? Is voice-over a cop-out, or even a sin? By drawing the viewer into the questions and torments of a screenwriter, Kaufman creates an overt scene of engagement with two concepts at the core of all writing, and at the heart of philosophy since antiquity: narration and imitation, what Plato and Aristotle knew as diegesis and mimesis.

In the *Republic*, Socrates says: "But if the poet should conceal himself nowhere, then his entire poetizing and narration would have been accomplished without imitation. . . . If Homer . . . had gone on speaking . . . as Homer, you are aware that it would not be imitation but narration. . . . Without imitation simple narration results."[52] Socrates regards the distinction as vitally important, fearing that a person who is convinced by an imitation of something will end up believing it to be the real thing ("lest from the imitation they imbibe the reality").[53] In the *Poetics*, Aristotle agrees with the need to be clear about these terms and their impact on our understanding of reality. The poet, he says, describes "a kind of thing that might be. Hence poetry is something more philosophic and of graver import than history. The poet's function is to describe, not the thing that has happened, but a kind of thing that might happen, i.e., what is possible as being probable or necessary."[54] The poet, then, has to determine the nature of his narrative act and the manner of his imitative creation. In short, the poet constitutes a *literary* experience that may or may not bear philosophical consequence: "poetry demands a man with a special gift for it, or else with a touch of madness in him; the former can easily assume the required mood, and the latter may be actually beside himself with emotion."[55] Kaufman's work is sometimes accused of or praised for its "madness" not merely as a sign of genius or originality, but for its capacity to challenge and enlarge our sense of narrative and imitative possibilities.[56] Because he is fundamentally concerned with "what is possible"—the existential freedom that stimulates anxiety—Kierkegaard is also preoccupied with madness. How can an author create without fathoming the possible? Yet in such experimenting he may go too far. As Kierkegaard puts it: "What is the relation between mental derangement and genius; can one be construed from the other? In what sense and to what extent is the genius master of his mental derangement? It goes without saying that up to a point he is its master; otherwise he would actually be insane."[57]

A film viewer is always negotiating the relationship between narration and imitation, but often a film settles that relationship very quickly and then tries hard to maintain it. For example, a state-of-the-art science fiction film reflects the creators' efforts to manifest convincing new conditions for action; if halfway through the film those conditions are changed, contradicted, or otherwise neglected, the viewer will likely no longer be absorbed. The film's success, then, can hinge on audience savvy. Special effects in films such as *King Kong* (Cooper and Schoedsack, 1933), *The Day the Earth Stood Still* (Wise, 1951), and *Planet of the Apes* (Schaffner, 1968) may have impressed viewers at the time they were made (meaning they were enjoyed as entertainments instead of as cultural history), yet in the light of current standards of computer-generated imagery these works fail to create a convincing alternate world for contemporary audiences. Through radical technological innovations, many creators of science fiction films continually attempt to outpace the perceptual habits and expectations of the audience as a way of intensifying its satisfaction with the action. With Kaufman, however, the relationship between the diegetic and the mimetic is continually called into question. When absorbing dramatic action is, as it were, interrupted by a moment of diegesis, the viewer is placed in a new relation to the film—for example, one in which different aspects of the film come into view (some of them in the film, and some of them out of the film).

What is the most accurate way of understanding the relationship between imitation and narration in Kaufman's work? Writing on *Adaptation*, Barbara Simerka and Christopher B. Weimer note that mimesis is "ultimately swallowed up by diegesis; mimetic representation is made to serve diegetic ends rather than the reverse, as occurs in more conventional narratives."[58] On this view, our attention is drawn to Kaufman's screenplay and film as a kind of *ouroboros*, namely, something that consumes itself, or rather that in turning back on itself makes us aware of its existence in a different way. The apprehension that diegesis may have overtaken Kaufman's concern with the mimetic finds credence in his exhaustive exploration of what might be called the kinds or levels of diegesis: the diegetic, the extradiegetic, and the metadiegetic. Again, using *Adaptation* as a point of illustration, consider that we find characters interacting with one another (diegetic), Nicolas Cage as the character Charlie Kaufman voicing the narration (extradiegetic), and Nicolas Cage playing a character named Charlie Kaufman who shares a name with the co-screenwriter Charlie Kaufman (metadiegetic). To further amplify the illustration, we see that within the film reality, or diegetic space, Charlie Kaufman is a pseudonym and Donald Kaufman is a fictional character; and outside of the film reality, or metadiegetic space, Charlie Kaufman is a screenwriter and Donald Kaufman is a fictitious collaborator.

While it may be that, as Simerka and Weimer claim, "the true subject of a postmodern film is its diegesis rather than its mimesis," Kaufman seems committed—along with his director-collaborators, such as Spike Jonze and Michel Gondry—to asking questions about the nature of imitation and making his responses distinguishing attributes of his core project.[59] On this approach, Kaufman's experimentation with diegesis, then, does not overwhelm or obscure his attention to mimesis, but rather makes it visible or otherwise available to viewers. The mimetic is not so much "swallowed up" as returned to us in a new way, often by means of clever, self-reflexive uses of diegesis.[60]

What is unusual about Kaufman's work, and certainly part of his inventiveness, is what might be described as his development of kinds or levels of mimesis. In a conventional narrative fiction film, an actor portrays a character; this is the standard. However, when an actor portrays two characters, such as Kim Novak's Madeleine/Judy in Alfred Hitchcock's *Vertigo* (1958), or when two actors change names, such as Betty (Naomi Watts) and Rita (Laura Elena Harring) in *Mulholland Drive* (2001), we find the effect disorienting and fascinating, a challenge to our conceptions of identity and, more particularly, to our conceptions of the nature of dramatic imitation. Kaufman regularly creates stories in which the linear relationship between actor and character is bent or otherwise redirected. Here are some examples: Charlie Kaufman, screenwriter, then Charlie Kaufman, character (*Adaptation*); Chuck Barris, game-show host, then Chuck Barris, hit man (*Confessions of a Dangerous Mind*); unnamed feral man, then Puff, then Civilized Puff testifying before Congress—a kind of evolutionary progression (*Human Nature*); Gabrielle as French lab assistant who is revealed as Gabrielle the imposter (*Human Nature*); John Malkovich, actor, then John Malkovich, character, that is, while playing himself (*Being John Malkovich*); Craig, Craig-as-puppet, Craig-as-Malkovich, Craig-as-consciousness stuck inside Emily (his own child, whom he conceived while being in Malkovich!) (*Being John Malkovich*); making it seem that Joel and Clementine are in fact different people—and different to each other—when their memories are altered, creating versions of themselves within the story (*Eternal Sunshine of the Spotless Mind*); and lastly, in *Synecdoche, New York*—Caden, Sammy playing Caden, Jimmy playing Sammy (while Sammy plays Caden), then Millicent Weems playing Ellen Bascomb and later playing Caden (while Caden takes over playing Ellen). When Caden at one point considers calling his play *Simulacrum* we get an internal acknowledgment of the film's exploration of layers of imitation—a project evident in Kaufman's work in general.

As poets of possibility, Kaufman and Kierkegaard are necessarily authors, as Aristotle says, with a "touch of madness." Because Kaufman and Kierkegaard plunge headlong into mimetic experiments, they become poised to show us—indirectly—the difficult realities that are ever present, yet so hard to see perspicuously. The characters they create—either as filmed personalities or the "poetized personalities"[61] of the pseudonymous works—function as registers against which any viewer or reader can come to terms intimately with his or her own anxiety. Kaufman's and Kierkegaard's characters solve nothing for us (and very little for themselves), but they do provide a field in which we can approach the difficult, painful fact of the pervasive, underlying condition of human anxiety.

Repetition, Recursion, Reflexivity

Constantin Constantius, the pseudonymous author of *Repetition: A Venture in Experimenting Psychology*, confides that he was "practically immobilized" by the question of repetition: "whether or not it is possible, what importance it has, whether something gains or loses in being repeated."[62] Just as Vigilius Haufniensis said "The more profoundly he is in anxiety, the greater is the man," so Constantius claims "He who wills repetition is a man, and the more emphatically he is able to realize it, the more profound a human being he is."[63] Becoming aware of one's anxiety and willing repetition are part of Kierkegaard's larger project of aiding and improving self-awareness and reflection through indirect communication.

Where Kierkegaard sees human potentiality in terms of self-relation, Kaufman's use of repetition—which entails recursion or iteration—underwrites his belief that others help us become more aware of ourselves. Kaufman makes available the ways in which the very nature of habit inscribes repetition into our daily lives, in our thoughts and actions. Sometimes one's experience of repetition becomes obsessive, even debilitating (*Synecdoche,*

New York); other times, if understood as the condition for mutual understanding, it may enhance intimacy (*Eternal Sunshine of the Spotless Mind*).
Regardless, one's character is reflected in what one does repeatedly, or especially how one repeats things. Aristotle described happiness (*eudaimonia*)
as activity in accord with virtue, and virtue was understood to follow from
excellence in one's activities—in short, one's habits of action. For Aristotle,
happiness and morality were largely based on the development of habits.
More generally, though, one's sense of individuality comes from distinguishing the mode and method of one's habits from their kind; personal identity
can often be understood precisely in terms of how one conducts oneself
differently from others in matters of the most mundane, habitual sort. The
very notions of style and luxury are founded on attempts to overcome the
homogenizing effects of repetition and recursion. Fashions and trends are
ways of creating versions that deviate from norms, sometimes by reap-
propriating them—reappropriation being a kind of return, or cycling back.
We are, then, continually in a process of creation and destruction, making
ourselves look and act a certain way in order, soon enough, to *go on* from
that way to some further self or version of the self.

Caden Cotard, the protagonist of *Synecdoche, New York*, wants to create
"something big and true and tough."[64] Ostensibly, it appears Charlie Kaufman
wanted to do the same in his directorial debut. The critical appraisals of
Kaufman's film and the descriptions of Caden's "theater piece" often include
comments on the coextensive nature of their ambition: in a more positive
light, some see the work as "toweringly ambitious," while others regard it with
more circumspection as suffused with "crippling ambition."[65] Regardless,
Kaufman and Caden are understood as artists working in parallel, both committed to creating something "massive," "uncompromising," and "honest."[66]
Yet what does this doubling show? Has Kaufman succeeded in mounting a
critique of an artist who believes he can make great art without limits—or
does Kaufman's film become the subject of its own critique? Kaufman, like
Caden, may have "tried to do too much," failed to constrain his desire and
his vision.[67] Critics must ask, though, whether Kaufman's effort to create a
meaningful work of art (his film) and his narrative about a man who is trying to create a meaningful work of art (Caden's play) remain in parallel, or
ultimately collapse together. Caden determines that the only way to account
for life is to duplicate all of it; he literalizes what should be left lyrical, suggestive, incomplete; his project is both exhaustive and exhausting. Caden's
literalistic ambition can be contrasted with Kaufman's literary ambition: to

show us fragments, aspects, and details of the many lives of his characters. Where Caden relentlessly pursues an accounting of every moment, of every inch, resulting in a fifty-year-long play that no one sees, Kaufman brings his project in at just over two hours.

Kaufman reflects on the presence of repetition, recursion, reflexivity, and replication in his work:

> When I start going down a certain road with those kinds of things, those conceptual conceits, I find that there's no end to it and it can go as far as I'm willing to take it. There's something expansive to me about the world seen through this conceit. When I realize that you're building a replica of New York City in a warehouse inside New York City that there inevitably has to contain a replica of the warehouse where it's taking place in and once you come to that realization you can't stop. It'll keep going forever, replica after replica after replica. . . . The replica is as real as the "real" as the replica, isn't it? I think there's something appealing and terrifying about that. I'm not really sure why. Does it speak to you in any way?[68]

Like Kierkegaard, Kaufman couples singularity and repetition: he dramatizes the struggle to become an individual even as he dwells on the aspects of life that we share and do repeatedly, aspects that underline the ways we are all the same; think here of Kierkegaard's invocation of *unum noris omnes* as a gloss on the Socratic pursuit of self-knowledge. For example, Kaufman draws scenes in which one's passions betray one's better judgment (*Human Nature*); one's imagination fails to meet one's expectations (*Being John Malkovich*); one's emotional fatigue suggests that loving another is not an easy enterprise, but still necessary (*Eternal Sunshine of the Spotless Mind*); one is possessed by a self-image at odds with self-interest (*Synecdoche, New York*) or opposed to the image others have of oneself (*Confessions of a Dangerous Mind*); one is overwhelmed by the promise of achieving a new truth only to be returned, decidedly, to conventions and clichés, implicated yet again in the sustaining inventions and attitudes that one wears as so many borrowed clothes (*Adaptation*). Kaufman's films are meditations on radical disappointments, especially as they emerge from an individual's attempt to define, express, find, or create himself beyond the standards that assure those disappointments. Kierkegaard, or more properly Constantius, doubts that maturity is a necessary hedge against error and misery: "The smarter he becomes and the more ways he learns to shift from himself, the bigger the mess he makes of life and the more he suffers! A little child is utterly helpless and always emerges unscathed."[69]

The topics of Kaufman's work—from film to film, and even in theater and television—are organically linked in intense and dramatic ways. As a viewer or reader will find, going any distance with a concept in Kaufman's films invariably reveals another, interdependent topic. Personal identity is linked with memory; memory is shown to be a function of the nature of time or the structure of narrative; one's experience of time and narrative seems tied to one's relationships with other people; and other people appear directly involved in the constitution of one's personal identity. Kaufman engages philosophical topics in a way similar to the *ouroboros*, a figure he mentions in *Adaptation* but is recognizable in the Pyramid of Unas in Egypt, Plato's *Timaeus*, and the Jörmungandr of Norse mythology: a being defined by its self-reflexivity, its capacity for both self-creation and self-destruction—and, thereafter, re-creation. Kaufman clearly and soberly notes: "You have to acknowledge that that striving, that hellish confusion, is the truth of being a person—is inescapable. You're trying to get there, but you're also wanting to get there [i.e., desiring a state beyond desire, striving for a place beyond striving], and what's the confusion of that, what's the complexity of that? And all I can do, all that I can expect of myself, is to honestly express that tension in my work. If I hope to express myself with honesty, then I have to include all the impurities."[70] Thus, the eponymous "spotless" of *Eternal Sunshine of the Spotless Mind* is not desirable. Better, Kaufman suggests, to have the mind as we know it—full of impurities, confusion, and other adulterating human attributes. The eternal sunshine of a spotless mind— where a mind is purged of darkness and debris—is what Joel realizes he doesn't want. (The title *Eternal Sunshine of the Spotless Mind* is drawn from Alexander Pope's "Eloisa to Abelard," a poem based on a true, tragic love story that is dramatized in *Being John Malkovich* in the form of marionette theater. Eloisa and Abelard, as puppets, are understood to be analogues for Craig and Maxine, allowing the puppeteer to express his true desire by means of a surrogate.)[71] What's remarkable about the *ouroboros* structure of *Eternal Sunshine of the Spotless Mind*—the way the couple is returned to each other for another chance to make their relationship work—is that they do not simply risk repeating the same mistakes, but choose to be together again knowing they will repeat the same mistakes. They are not new to each other; they have hurt and offended each other—sullied and darkened their intimacy. And yet they want—perhaps despite their instincts and reason—to be together.

Reading Flannery O'Connor, Kaufman was impressed by the depiction of "the grotesque," and his appreciation is reflected in his tendency to dwell on the somatic or bodily qualities of our lapses and failures and also on the way that we can come to ultimately love the very things that most horrify and offend us.[72] The very prospect of repeating one's errors—perhaps especially romantic mistakes—can seem grotesque, a deviation not just from one's habits but one's hopes as well. What feels intolerably offensive to lovers, though, can in a different mood seem not just endearing but the very condition for one's sense of what is lovable about another person. While Joel and Clementine's relationship becomes the site of some kind of eternal recurrence, where they always begin and endure the same arguments, there is yet some progress because they decide to experience that cycle together—instead of breaking up only to repeat the problems with other people. They don't want a new, "pure" relationship with another, but to find a way to commit themselves to the mirthful ups and miserable downs that define their real relationship.

"I like to live in the confusion," says Kaufman about his preference for chaos over the concrete, the muddled over the simple, the meandering over the linear: "When you complicate things, that's when things are more interesting."[73] For Kaufman, it is not needless complexity that is interesting—that is a pleasure for those who merely like to solve puzzles—but a complexity that reveals something true. Part of Kaufman's working against a tradition of romantic comedies involves a fight against a sentimental understanding of human happiness and love—doubtless a very compelling vision, and one Kaufman feels victim to. A significant part of that sentimentality is linked with false notions of purity, for example as they appear in puerile but nevertheless entrenched romantic mythologies such as the first kiss, first love, saving oneself for the right person, and there being only one person in the world that is the proper object of one's affection. A sentimental faith in purity also contributes to the lover's delusional thinking about another person's goodness, or quality. It's not that love blinds us to another's faults, but that sentimental ideas about love obscure our sense for the truth of human persons. We are, according to Kaufman, in need of a corrective: to learn ways of loving the awkwardness, errors, contradictions, and lapses. We are then properly in love when we see the impurity in ourselves and others—and love it.

Kaufman and Kierkegaard's understanding of repetition, recursion, and reflexivity assures us that "the end is built into the beginning."[74] How did we get to the point where impurities and confusion make love possible, genuine, and real? Because Kaufman and Kierkegaard show indirectly the interrelationship between love and anxiety. Faith, like love, requires decisive action; it is, as Copleston says, "an adventure, a risk, a self-commitment to an objective uncertainty."[75] The reality of love depends on one's willingness to be aware of its possibility and capable of choosing it—as poets, as madmen, as creatures willing to consume ourselves in order to re-create ourselves. The only way to begin is to bring an end to possibility—to make a thing actual by committing to it. Every decision is a leap, so every moment will be suffused with the "emotive tonality" of anxiety.[76] And so, at the end, we must begin again.

Notes

1. David Edelstein says Kaufman "explores the inner lives of anxious neurotic depressive solipsists," *New York*, October 27, 2008 (nymag.com). Taien Ng-Chan put *Adaptation* at number three on a top ten list of films about anxiety, *Art + Culture*, September 3, 2009 (artandculture.com). In Arlin Cuncic's "Top 8 Movie Characters with Social Anxiety" Joel Barish from *Eternal Sunshine of the Spotless Mind* is number two, *About*, April 10, 2010 (about.com).

2. Lynn Hirschberg, "Being Charlie Kaufman," *New York Times*, March 19, 2000 (nytimes.com).

3. Cuncic, "Top 8 Movie Characters."

4. "Anxiety is the dizziness of freedom." Søren Kierkegaard, *The Concept of Anxiety: A Simple Psychologically Orienting Deliberation on the Dogmatic Issue of Hereditary Sin*, ed. Reidar Thomte (Princeton: Princeton University Press, 1980), vol. 8, 61.

5. Frederick J. Copleston, *A History of Philosophy*, vol. 7 (New York: Doubleday, 1965), 336.

6. Ibid., 336–37.

7. See "A Conversation with Screenwriter Charlie Kaufman," interview with Charlie Rose, March 26, 2004 (charlierose.com); and "Charlie Kaufman: Life and Its Discontents," interview with Tania Ketenjian, *The [Un]Observed: A Radio Magazine* (theunobserved.com).

8. Copleston, *History of Philosophy*, 344.

9. Ibid., 345.

10. Ibid., 350.

11. Reidar Thomte, introduction to Kierkegaard, *The Concept of Anxiety*, xv.

12. Kierkegaard, *The Concept of Anxiety*, 79.

13. "Adam and Eve are merely a numerical repetition. In this respect, a thousand Adams signify no more than one. . . . No man is superfluous, because every individual is himself and the race." Ibid., 46.

14. Ibid., 47, 64.

15. Ibid., 155.

16. Ibid., 60.

17. Søren Kierkegaard, *The Point of View*, ed. and trans. Howard V. Hong and Edna H. Hong (Princeton: Princeton University Press, 1998), Vol. XXII, 24.

18. Ibid., 43.

19. Ibid., 53.

20. Ibid., 54.

21. Ibid.

22. Ibid., xii.

23. Ibid.

24. Ibid., 17n.

25. Brad Prager notes how for Werner Herzog "an aesthetic lie is at the basis of the work: that which makes it art and not 'the world' *is* its truth." Consequently "art as a lie . . . is truer than the truth." Brad Prager, *The Cinema of Werner Herzog: Aesthetic Ecstasy and Truth* (London: Wallflower Press, 2007), 8–9.

26. Kierkegaard, *The Point of View*, 60.

27. Ibid., 56.

28. Ibid., xii.

29. Ibid., xi, xxi, 12, 50–51.

30. Ibid., 7.

31. Ibid., xi.

32. Ibid., xii.

33. Ibid., 33.

34. Ibid.

35. Ibid., 11.

36. Ibid., 59.

37. Ibid., 69.

38. Ibid., xviii.

39. Charlie Kaufman, *Synecdoche, New York: The Shooting Script* (New York: Newmarket Press, 2008), 36.

40. Charlie Kaufman, *Being John Malkovich* (New York: Faber and Faber, 1999), 44.

41. John Malkovich's complete sentence is pertinent to having a sense for what it is like to *be* John Malkovich: "I *am* an asshole." Joshua Rothkopf, "John Cusack Looks Back on His Crazy '80s," *Time Out: New York* (March 25–31, 2010), 66.

42. Kaufman, *Being John Malkovich*, 4.

43. Ibid., 95.

44. Ibid., 87.

45. Ibid., 3.

46. Kaufman quoted in Walter Chaw, "State of Mind," *Film Freak Central*, October 26, 2008 (filmfreakcentral.net).

47. Friedrich Nietzsche, *Beyond Good and Evil: A Prelude to a Philosophy of the Future*, trans. Helen Zimmern (New York: Macmillan Co., 1907), 10.

48. Ketenjian, "Charlie Kaufman."

49. Ralph Waldo Emerson, *Complete Works*, Concord ed. (Boston: Houghton, Mifflin and Co., 1904), vol. XI, 285.

50. Kaufman quoted in Chaw, "State of Mind."

51. Kierkegaard, *The Point of View*, 29.

52. Plato, *Republic*, in *The Collected Dialogues*, ed. Edith Hamilton and Huntington Cairns (Princeton: Princeton University Press, 1961), Book III, 393c–394b.

53. Ibid., 395c.

54. Aristotle, *Poetics*, in *The Basic Works of Aristotle*, ed. Richard McKeon (New York: Random House, 1941), chap. 9.

55. Aristotle, *Poetics*, chap. 17.

56. See, for example, David Ansen, "Meta-Movie Madness," *Newsweek*, December 9, 2002 (newsweek.com); Todd Anthony, "Screenwriter Has Life of Revisions," *Sun Sentinel*, December 20, 2002 (sun-sentinel.com); Cole Abaius, "Charlie Kaufman Depresses Us and Talks about *Synecdoche, New York*," October 24, 2008, Filmschoolrejects.com.

57. Søren Kierkegaard, *Fear and Trembling*, ed. and trans. Howard V. Hong and Edna H. Hong (Princeton: Princeton University Press, 1983), Vol. VI, 107.

58. Barbara Simerka and Christopher B. Weimer, "Duplicitous Diegesis: *Don Quijote* and Charlie Kaufman's *Adaptation*," *Hispania* 88, no. 1 (March 2005): 93.

59. Ibid., 92.

60. Simerka and Weimer understand Kaufman's work as privileging diegesis over mimesis and therefore regard it as participating in a larger, "postmodern" project: "This emphasis on diegesis is postmodern precisely because it undermines any sense that a film is offering a 'simple' or 'straightforward' mimetic representation of characters' actions. Someone, the viewer is constantly reminded, is telling the story. Essential to postmodern thought is just such a subversive skepticism about the relationship between narrative structures and the concepts of knowledge and truth; postmodernism regards the latter as discursive constructs and therefore as contingent and provisional at best, arbitrary and hegemonic at worst." Ibid.

61. Kierkegaard, *The Point of View*, xii.

62. Søren Kierkegaard, *Repetition: A Venture in Experimenting Psychology*, ed. and trans. Howard V. Hong and Edna H. Hong (Princeton: Princeton University Press, 1983), Vol. VI, 131.

63. Kierkegaard, *The Concept of Anxiety*, 155; Kierkegaard, *Repetition*, 132.

64. Kaufman, *Synecdoche: Shooting Script*, 46.

65. "Toweringly ambitious," Wendy Ide, *Times* (London), May 14, 2009 (thetimes
.co.uk); "crippling ambition," Jonathan Schumann, *Arts and Leisure*, December 4, 2008
(acorn-online.com).

66. Kaufman, *Synecdoche: Shooting Script*, 49.

67. David Stratton, "The State of Semantics," *The Australian*, May 9, 2009 (theaustralian
.com.au).

68. Kaufman quoted in Chaw, "State of Mind."

69. Kierkegaard, *Repetition*, 172.

70. Kaufman quoted in Chaw, "State of Mind."

71. In *Synecdoche, New York*, Kaufman depicts another variation of surrogacy: Caden's daughter Olive (Sadie Goldstein) is "replaced," one might say, by Claire's daughter,
Ariel. At one point, Caden says how much he misses Olive and "the other one," whose
name he can't remember; at another time, he says in a panic: "I have to go find my
daughter. . . . My real daughter. My first daughter" (Kaufman, *Synecdoche: Shooting Script*,
63). The notion that the original is the real and that proxies are lesser forms is reflected
in the cascading, iterated versions of actors playing actors in the film. Each actor can
ask himself: am I necessary if there is another me? Who is playing the better version? If
I can play Caden, who can play me (playing Caden)? Can I be replaced?

72. Michael Sragow, "Being Charlie Kaufman," *Salon*, November 11, 1999 (salon
.com).

73. Kaufman quoted in Michael Spadaro, BeingCharlieKaufman.com.

74. Kaufman, *Synecdoche: Shooting Script*, 114.

75. Copleston, *History of Philosophy*, 344.

76. Ibid., 350.

FILMOGRAPHY

Television

Get a Life
"Prisoner of Love" (1991, episode 28 [season 2, episode 6]), screenwriter
"1977 2000" (1992, episode 34 [season 2, episode 12]), screenwriter

Ned and Stacey
"Computer Dating" (1996, episode 28 [season 2, episode 4]), screenwriter
"Loganberry's Run" (1996, episode 30 [season 2, episode 6]), screenwriter
"Where My Third Nepal Is Sheriff" (1997, episode 35 [season 2, episode 11]), screenwriter

Film

Being John Malkovich (1999): screenwriter, executive producer (Spike Jonze, director)
Human Nature (2001): screenwriter, producer (Michel Gondry, director)
Adaptation (2002): screenwriter, executive producer (Spike Jonze, director)
Confessions of a Dangerous Mind (2002): screenwriter (George Clooney, director)
Eternal Sunshine of the Spotless Mind (2004): screenwriter, screen story, executive producer (Michel Gondry, director)
Synecdoche, New York (2008): screenwriter, producer, director

CONTRIBUTORS

SAMUEL A. CHAMBERS is associate professor of political science at Johns Hopkins University, where he teaches political theory. He is also coeditor of the journal *Contemporary Political Theory*. He writes broadly in political theory, including work on language, culture, and the politics of gender and sexuality. He has most recently published *The Queer Politics of Television* (Palgrave, 2009), a book that explores the intersection of television studies and political theory through the lens of queer theory. The book examines a number of U.S. television dramas, reading them with the tools of queer theory and using them to make substantive contributions to that field, while simultaneously arguing for the broad relevance of the cultural politics of television. His earlier works include *Judith Butler and Political Theory* (with Terrell Carver, Routledge, 2008) and *Untimely Politics* (NYU Press, 2003). With Terrell Carver, he has also edited two volumes, *Judith Butler's Precarious Politics* (Routledge, 2008) and *Democracy, Pluralism, and Political Theory* (Routledge, 2007). In addition to teaching a variety of political theory courses across all levels, he also teaches a course called "The Cultural Politics of Television." He has given numerous lectures and conference presentations on political theory and television and has been a member of a large group of scholars who have worked to develop and advance the nascent field of critical television studies.

WILLIAM DAY is associate professor of philosophy at Le Moyne College, where he teaches courses in aesthetics, film, American philosophy, and Wittgenstein. He is contributing coeditor, with Victor J. Krebs, of *Seeing Wittgenstein Anew* (Cambridge University Press, 2010). Other publications include "*Moonstruck,* or How to Ruin Everything," in *Ordinary Language Criticism*, ed. Kenneth Dauber and Walter Jost (Northwestern University Press, 2003); "The Ends of Improvisation," in *The Journal of Aesthetics and Art Criticism* (2010); and "A Soteriology of Reading: Cavell's *Excerpts from Memory*," in *Stanley Cavell, Literature, and Criticism*, ed. James Loxley and Andrew Taylor (Manchester University Press, forthcoming). At present he is writing a book on what there is to care about in listening to jazz improvisation, as informed by a reading of Wittgenstein and Emerson.

RICHARD DEMING is lecturer in the Department of English of Yale University. He has published articles and essays on contemporary poetics and poetry, film, and philosophy, and works primarily on the intersections of ethics and works of art (both literary and visual), regularly engaging the thinking of Emerson, Hegel, Nietzsche, Benjamin, Cavell, and Danto. He is a frequent contributor to *Artforum* on cinema. In his book *Listening on All Sides: Toward an Emersonian Ethics of Reading* (Stanford University Press, 2008) he finds an intersection of literature and philosophy in the poetics of Ralph Waldo Emerson, Wallace Stevens, and William Carlos Williams that, when read through the lens of arguments offered by Hegel, Cavell, Rorty, and Austin, offers aesthetic models for the construction of community and subjectivity. His collection of poems, *Let's Not Call It Consequence* (Shearsman, 2008) was awarded the 2009 Norma Farber Award by the Poetry Society of America.

DOUGLAS J. DEN UYL is Vice President for Educational Programs at Liberty Fund Inc. and was formerly professor and chair of the Department of Philosophy at Bellarmine University. He works in the areas of ethics, social and political philosophy, and the history of thought. He has published numerous articles and books on such figures as Aristotle, Spinoza, Shaftesbury, and Adam Smith as well as on such topics as film, autonomy, and self-perfection, and love, marriage, and friendship. He contributed the essay "Civilization and Its Discontents: The Self-Sufficient Western Hero" to *The Philosophy of the Western*, ed. Jennifer L. McMahon and B. Steve Csaki (University Press of Kentucky, 2010). Recent books include *Norms of Liberty: A Perfectionist Basis for Non-Perfectionist Politics* (Penn State Press, 2005) and *God, Man, and Well-Being: Spinoza's Modern Humanism* (Peter Lang, 2008).

K. L. EVANS is associate professor of English at Yeshiva University, where she teaches literature and philosophy, American literature, and film criticism. She is the author of *Whale!* (Minnesota University Press, 2003) and the forthcoming *The Missing Limb*, a Wittgensteinian reading of *Moby-Dick* in which she takes seriously, or takes as a piece of logic, Ahab's disemboweling of the proposition that anything a man knows can be tested. Recent publications include "A Machine for Becoming Decent" (*Denver Quarterly*, 2008),

"A Rest from Reason: Wittgenstein, Drury, and the Difference between Madness and Religion" (*Philosophy*, 2010), and "While Reading Wittgenstein," in *Stanley Cavell, Literature, and Criticism*, ed. James Loxley and Andrew Taylor (Manchester University Press, forthcoming).

CHRISTOPHER FALZON is lecturer in philosophy at the University of Newcastle (Australia). He has a special interest in twentieth-century French philosophy, and philosophy and film. His publications include *Foucault and Social Dialogue* (Routledge, 1998), *Philosophy Goes to the Movies* (Routledge, 2002 and 2007), and *Foucault and Philosophy* (coeditor with Timothy O'Leary; Blackwell, 2010). His recent publications in philosophy and film include "Philosophy and *The Matrix*," in *The Matrix and New Theory*, ed. Stefan Herbrechter and Myriam Diocaretz (Rodopi, 2006), and "Peter Weir's *The Truman Show* and Sartrean Freedom," in *Existentialism and Contemporary World Cinema: A Sartrean Perspective*, ed. Enda McCaffrey and Jean-Pierre Boulé (Oxford, forthcoming 2010). He is also the coeditor (with Timothy O'Leary and Jana Sawicki) of *The Blackwell Companion to Foucault* (Blackwell, forthcoming).

GREGORY E. GANSSLE is senior fellow at the Rivendell Institute at Yale University. He has published widely in philosophy of religion, including *Thinking about God: First Steps in Philosophy* (InterVarsity Press, 2004) and *A Reasonable God: Engaging the New Face of Atheism* (Baylor University Press, 2009). He is the author of more than thirty academic papers, chapters, and reviews, including "Consciousness, Memory, and Identity: The Nature of Persons in Three Films by Charlie Kaufman," in *Faith, Film, and Philosophy: Christian Reflections on Contemporary Film*, ed. James S. Spiegel and R. Douglas Geivett (InterVarsity Press, 2007).

GARRY L. HAGBERG is James H. Ottaway Professor of Aesthetics and Philosophy in the Department of Philosophy at Bard College. He held an endowed Chair in the Department of Philosophy at University of East Anglia, Norwich, England, from 2006 to 2009. Author of *Meaning and Interpretation: Wittgenstein, Henry James and Literary Knowledge* (Cornell University Press, 1994), *Art as Language: Wittgenstein, Meaning, and Aesthetic Theory* (Cornell University Press, 1995), and *Describing Ourselves: Wittgenstein and Autobiographical Consciousness* (Oxford University Press, 2008), he edited *Art and Ethical Criticism* (Blackwell, 2008) and coedited *The Blackwell Companion to* *the Philosophy of Literature* (2009). He is joint editor of the journal *Philosophy and Literature*, is on the editorial board of *The Journal of Aesthetics and Art Criticism*, and serves on the executive committee of the British Society for Aesthetics (Oxford). Recent work includes essays for *Seeing Wittgenstein Anew*, ed. William Day and Victor Krebs (Cambridge University Press, 2010) and *Philosophy as Therapeia* (Royal Institute of Philosophy, 2010). Presently he is at work on the coauthored volume *Wittgenstein on Music* and a new book on the contribution literary experience makes to the formation of self and sensibility, *Living in Words: Literature, Language, and the Constitution of Selfhood.*

DEREK HILL is the author of *Charlie Kaufman and Hollywood's Merry Band of Pranksters, Fabulists and Dreamers* (Kamera Books, 2008), a study of the films of Charlie Kaufman, Richard Linklater, David O. Russell, Wes Anderson, Sofia Coppla, and others. His book on the films of Terry Gilliam from Schaffner Press, as well as *Peter Jackson: Interviews* (in which he served as editor), part of the University of Mississippi's Conversations with Filmmakers series, are forthcoming. He has contributed to the *Directory of World Cinema: Japan* and *Directory of World Cinema: American Independent* (Intellect), *Little White Lies* magazine, and to a number of print and online publications. He is also a contributing editor and film critic for the online arts journal *Sinescope*.

DAVID LaROCCA is coordinating producer and consulting editor for the ongoing documentary film project *The Intellectual Portrait Series*. Author of *On Emerson* (Wadsworth, 2003) and editor of Stanley Cavell's book *Emerson's Transcendental Etudes* (Stanford University Press, 2003), he studied philosophy, film, rhetoric, and religion at SUNY-Buffalo, UC Berkeley, Vanderbilt, and Harvard. He contributed "Rethinking the First Person: Authorship, Autobiography, and the Contested Self in *Malcolm X*" to *The Philosophy of Spike Lee*, ed. Mark T. Conard (University Press of Kentucky, 2011); his "Changing the Subject: The Auto/biographical as the Philosophical in Wittgenstein" appeared in *Epoché* (2007). Journal articles on film include "The Limits of Instruction" on Lars von Trier's *The Five Obstructions* (2009) and "A Desperate Education: Reading *Walden* in *All That Heaven Allows*" (2004), both in *Film and Philosophy*; an article on the ontology of Cindy Sherman's photograph *Untitled 153* is forthcoming from *The Journal of Aesthetics and Art Criticism*. His essays have been published in volumes such as *Nietzsche* e *L'America* (Recensioni Filosofiche, Pisa, 2005) and *New Morning: Emerson in the Twenty-First Century* (SUNY Press, 2008). LaRocca, who lives in New York, has made documentary films with Academy Award–nominated director William Jersey and master cinematographer Robert Elfstrom, and attended Werner Herzog's Rogue Film School. For more information, please contact DavidLaRocca@Post.Harvard.Edu or visit DavidLaRocca.org.

DANIEL SHAW is professor of philosophy and film at Lock Haven University and the managing editor of the print journal *Film and Philosophy*. Previous work on Charlie Kaufman includes "On Being Philosophical and *Being John Malkovich*," in *The Journal of Aesthetics and Art Criticism* (2006). He has coedited *Dark Thoughts: Philosophical Reflections on Cinematic Horror* (Scarecrow Press, 2003) and published the volume *Film and Philosophy: Taking Movies Seriously* (Wallflower Press, 2008). His articles have appeared in *Film and History*, the *Journal of Value Inquiry*, and on the websites *Senses of Cinema* and *Film-Philosophy Salon*.

DAVID L. SMITH is professor in the Department of Philosophy and Religion at Central Michigan University. His interest in the religious thought of Ralph Waldo Emerson paved the way for studies of contemporary writers and filmmakers whose intellectual projects seem strikingly similar to Emerson's, Charlie Kaufman chief among them. Smith has previously published two articles on Kaufman: "The Implicit Soul of Charlie Kaufman's *Adaptation*," *Philosophy and Literature* (2006); and "*Eternal Sunshine of the Spotless Mind* and the Question of Transcendence," *Journal of Religion and Film* (2005). Other publications include "'Who Shall Define to Me an Individual?' Emerson on Self, World, and God," *American Journal of Theology and Philosophy* (2009); "'The Sphinx Must Solve Her Own Riddle': Emerson, Secrecy, and the Self-Reflexive Method," *Journal of the American Academy of Religion* (2003); and "'Beautiful Necessities': *American Beauty* and the Idea of Freedom," *Journal of Religion and Film* (2002).

MARIO VON DER RUHR is lecturer in the Department of Political and Cultural Studies at Swansea University (United Kingdom). Author of *Simone Weil, An Apprenticeship in Attention* (Continuum, 2007), he is associate editor of the journal *Philosophical Investigations* and coeditor, with D. Z. Phillips, of many works in the philosophy of religion, including *Religion and the End of Metaphysics* (Mohr Siebeck, 2008), *Religion and Wittgenstein's*

Legacy (Ashgate, 2005), *Biblical Concepts and Our World* (Palgrave, 2004), and *Language and Spirit* (Palgrave, 2004).

INDEX

CPSIA information can be obtained at www.ICGtesting.com
Printed in the USA
LVOW121439311012

305272LV00002B/4/P